Bound with Them in Chains

A Biographical History of the Antislavery Movement

Jane H. Pease

and

William H. Pease

Contributions in American History
Number 18

Greenwood Press, Inc.
Westport, Connecticut

Library of Congress Cataloging in Publication Data

Pease, Jane H
    Bound with them in chains.

    (Contributions in American history, no. 18)
    Bibliography: p.
    1. Slavery in the United States--Anti-slavery
movements--Biography. 2. Abolitionists--Biography.
I. Pease, William Henry, 1924-   joint author.
II. Title.
E449.P37   322.4'4'0973   74-175612
ISBN 0-8371-6265-3

Library of Congress Catalog Card Number: 74-175612
ISBN: 0-8371-6265-3

First published in 1972

Greenwood Press, Inc., Publishing Division
51 Riverside Avenue, Westport, Connecticut 06880

Printed in the United States of America

For
Laura Bornholdt
and Merle Curti

Teachers who made a difference

Remember them that are in bonds, as bound with them; and them which suffer adversity, as being yourselves also in the body.

The Epistle of Paul
to the Hebrews, 13:3

Contents

	Preface	ix
	Key to Manuscript Collections	xiii
1	Prologue	3
2	The Setting	8
3	The Boston Bluestocking: Maria Weston Chapman	28
4	The Kentucky Squire: Cassius Marcellus Clay	60
5	The Quaker Colonizer: Benjamin Lundy	90
6	The Clerical Do-Gooder: Hiram Wilson	115
7	The Negro Conservative: Samuel Eli Cornish	140
8	The Black Militant: Henry Highland Garnet	162
9	The Perfectionist Radical: Stephen Symonds Foster	191

Contents

10 The Political Gadfly:
    Elizur Wright   218
11 The Political Regular:
    Joshua Reed Giddings   245
12 The Gentle Humanitarian:
    Samuel Joseph May   276
13 Some Reflections   308
    Bibliography   319
    Index   327

Preface

The preparation of any book manuscript involves numerous details not directly evident in the text itself and puts its author(s) under obligation to more individuals and institutions than can easily be recounted. We should therefore like to forewarn the reader about those details which have a direct bearing upon his understanding of the text and to acknowledge our obligation to those who have given us assistance in our work.

For what we consider greater readability, we have made several adjustments in material that we have quoted directly. Whenever it was necessary to fit the text of the manuscript we have, without note, adjusted initial capitalization, lowering the case or raising it where the context in which it occurred required it. We have also modified the tense of verbs, noting such change simply by the use of brackets [ ], wherever our text required such modification for smooth reading and wherever it could be accomplished without doing violence to the original. In like fashion we have occasionally changed the person, usually from the first to the third, in indirect discourse, again indicating such change by the simple use of brackets [ ]. Finally, citations to manuscript collections in the footnotes are all keyed to the master listing which appears at the beginning of the book.

Over the past decade, we have undoubtedly taxed the patience of many of our colleagues with our incessant conversations and questions about the nature and content of the antislavery movement. That they still listen is a tribute to their forebearance and kindness. In particular, however, we wish to extend more than the usual thanks to several of our friends and colleagues who have, either by their generous advice and encouragement or by their willingness to read various chapters of the book and give us the benefit of their criticisms and insights, made of our work something more meaningful than it might otherwise have been. By her constant willingness to answer questions, offer assistance, and lend her encouragement, Grace Shaw has given us invaluable editorial insights and advice. Merton Dillon, Benjamin Quarles, and David Smiley have all generously read those portions of the manuscript that deal with their own special areas of interest. Robert Zenowich read the manuscript in its entirety and first set us to rethinking it as a totality. Finally, Bertram Wyatt-Brown has given us the benefit of a searching and minute reading of the entire manuscript, parts of it more than once. To each of these people we give very real thanks and the customary absolution from responsibility.

Along the way, too, we have been fortunate to receive financial assistance, which has greatly relieved the burdens of gathering material. For their kindness and confidence, we thank the American Council of Learned Societies for a grant-in-aid (1965), the American Philosophical Society for a similar grant (1966), and the Coe Research Fund Committee of the University of Maine for a summer research grant in 1967.

Like hundreds of other writers, we have used the resources of scores of libraries and incurred in the process debts beyond recall. To certain individuals and to certain libraries we wish to give special recognition. Three persons and institutions merit very special citation here. John Alden, Keeper of the Rare Books of the Boston Public Library, has over the years been generous beyond the call of duty, for we have been constant visitors to and users of the incomparable antislavery materials over which he presides. In like fashion, we feel a special warmth for George Healey, Curator of the Rare Book Department of the Cornell University Library, where the Samuel J. May collection of antislavery material is housed. During several summers of work on the Cornell campus, Mr. Healey always made us feel that we would like to stay beyond our allotted time. Finally, we wish to acknowledge the day-by-day assistance and kindnesses of James MacCampbell and his staff at the Fogler Library of the University of Maine, Orono. Not only have we enjoyed special access to the university's O'Brien Collection of antislavery and black material and the very good services of the library's interlibrary loan department, but we have appreciated particularly Mr. MacCampbell's continuing interest in our work.

To many other libraries we are also indebted, among them those of Syracuse University, the Ohio Historical Society, Smith College, the Worcester Historical Society, the Massachusetts Historical Society, the American Antiquarian Society, Fisk University, Howard University, Oberlin College, Columbia University, and Harvard University (Houghton, Widener, and Schlesinger). In addition, we owe thanks to the Library of Congress and the New York Public Library. Many libraries, in addition to those major ones just mentioned, also provided a wide array of aid and assistance. To list them all would be impractical, but they range from the Clements Library of the University of Michigan to the town library of Cortland, New York. To each of them, here mentioned or not, we are most grateful.

One other person we wish to thank explicitly: Betsey Miller Shaffer, who not only typed the original manuscript with accuracy and speed, but, what is more appreciated and much more rare, with intelligence and imagination.

Finally we wish to acknowledge with our thanks to the following organizations permissions to use various of the materials incorporated in the text: The American Antiquarian Society, the Amistad Research Center, the Boston Public Library, Butler Library of Columbia University, Cornell University Library, the George Arents Research Library at Syracuse University, the Historical Society of Pennsylvania, the Massachusetts Historical Society, the Maine Historical Society, the Sophia Smith Collection of Smith College, the Vermont Historical Society, the Western Reserve Historical Society, and the Worcester Historical Society.

J.H.P.
W.H.P.

Cape Rosier, Maine
September 27, 1971

Key to Manuscript
Collections

A-ME   Adams Papers, Massachusetts Historical Society, Boston, Massachusetts, Microfilm edition.

A-MHS   Edward A. Atkinson Papers, Massachusetts Historical Society, Boston, Massachusetts.

AL-SL   Alma Lutz Collection, Schlesinger Library, Radcliffe College, Cambridge, Massachusetts.

AMA-FU   American Missionary Association Archives, Amistad Research Center, New Orleans, Louisiana.

AS-MeHS   Antislavery Correspondence, Maine Historical Society, Portland, Maine.

ASP-HSP   Abolition Society Papers, Historical Society of Pennsylvania, Philadelphia, Pennsylvania.

B-CUM   James G. Birney Papers, Clements Library, University of Michigan, Ann Arbor, Michigan.

B-MHS   Henry Bellows Papers, Massachusetts Historical Society, Boston, Massachusetts.

B-WRHS   Briggs Collection, Western Reserve Historical Society, Cleveland, Ohio.

BS-SL	Beecher-Stowe Collection, Schlesinger Library, Radcliffe College, Cambridge, Massachusetts.
C-BPL	Child Papers, Antislavery Collection, Boston Public Library, Boston, Massachusetts.
C-CoU	Lydia M. Child Papers, Cornell University, Ithaca, New York.
C-DC	Frederick Chase Collection, Dartmouth College, Hanover, New Hampshire.
C-FC	Cassius M. Clay Papers, Filson Club, Louisville, Kentucky.
C-HSP	Salmon P. Chase Papers, Historical Society of Pennsylvania, Philadelphia, Pennsylvania.
C-LC	Salmon P. Chase Papers, Library of Congress, Washington, D.C.
C-LMU	Cassius M. Clay Collection, Lincoln Memorial University, Harrogate, Tennessee.
C-NYPL	Lydia Maria Child Letters, New York Public Library, New York, New York. Microfilm edition.
C-OC	Henry Cowles Papers, Oberlin College, Oberlin, Ohio.
Ch-BPL	Chapman Papers, Antislavery Collection, Boston Public Library, Boston, Massachusetts.
Ch-CoU	Henry G. Chapman Papers, Cornell University, Ithaca, New York.
CP-LC	Clay Family Papers, Library of Congress, Washington, D.C.
D-LC	Frederick Douglass Papers, Library of Congress, Washington, D.C. Microfilm edition.
E-BPL	Estlin Papers, Antislavery Collection, Boston Public Library, Boston, Massachusetts.
E-HLH	Emerson Collection, Houghton Library, Harvard University, Cambridge, Massachusetts.
E-MHS	George E. Ellis Papers, Massachusetts Historical Society, Boston, Massachusetts.

F-AAS	Foster Papers, American Antiquarian Society, Worcester, Massachusetts.
F-NYPL	Ford Collection, New York Public Library, New York, New York.
F-WHS	Foster Papers, Worcester Historical Society, Worcester, Massachusetts.
G-BPL	Garrison Papers, Antislavery Collection, Boston Public Library, Boston, Massachusetts.
G-CU	Sydney Howard Gay Papers, Columbia University, New York, New York.
G-HSP	Simon Gratz Collection, Historical Society of Pennsylvania, Philadelphia, Pennsylvania.
G-OHS	Giddings Papers, Ohio Historical Society, Columbus, Ohio.
G-SC	Garrison Family Papers, Smith College, Northampton, Massachusetts.
GJ-LC	Giddings-Julian Papers, Library of Congress, Washington, D.C.
H-HLH	Houghton Collection, Houghton Library, Harvard University, Cambridge, Massachusetts.
H-OC	Hamilton Hill Papers, Oberlin College, Oberlin, Ohio.
J-MHS	Francis Jackson Papers, Massachusetts Historical Society, Boston, Massachusetts.
J-VHS	Oliver Johnson Papers, Vermont Historical Society, Montpelier, Vermont.
K-PAC	King Papers, Public Archives of Canada, Ottawa, Ontario.
L-HLH	Loring Letterpress Book, Houghton Library, Harvard University, Cambridge, Massachusetts.
L-LC	Benjamin Lundy Collection, Library of Congress, Washington, D.C.
L-LS	Loring Papers, Schlesinger Library, Radcliffe College, Cambridge, Massachusetts.

Ln-LC	Lincoln Papers, Library of Congress, Washington, D.C.
M-BPL	Samuel May, Jr., Papers, Antislavery Collection, Boston Public Library, Boston, Massachusetts.
M-CoU	Samuel J. May Papers, Cornell University, Ithaca, New York.
M-MHS	Samuel May, Jr., Papers, Massachusetts Historical Society, Boston, Massachusetts.
Ma-MHS	Horace Mann Papers, Massachusetts Historical Society, Boston, Massachusetts.
McK-NYPL	McKim Papers, New York Public Library, New York, New York.
MS-BCL	Manuscript Collection, Berea College Library, Berea, Kentucky.
MS-CUM	Miscellaneous Collection, Clements Library, University of Michigan, Ann Arbor, Michigan.
MS-FHS	Manuscript Collection, Friends Historical Society, Swarthmore College, Swarthmore, Pennsylvania.
MS-LC	Miscellaneous Personal Papers, Library of Congress, Washington, D.C.
MS-MHS	Miscellaneous Letters, Massachusetts Historical Society, Boston, Massachusetts.
MS-UR	Manuscript Collection, University of Rochester, Rochester, New York.
MS-WRHS	Manuscript Collections, Western Reserve Historical Society, Cleveland, Ohio.
MS-YU	Manuscript Collections, Yale University, New Haven, Connecticut.
N-LC	Negro Papers, Library of Congress, Washington, D.C.
P-BPL	Phelps Papers, Antislavery Collection, Boston Public Library, Boston, Massachusetts.
P-MHS	John Elliot Parkman Papers, Massachusetts Historical Society, Boston, Massachusetts.

Q-MHS   Edmund Quincy Papers, Massachusetts Historical Society, Boston, Massachusetts.

RFG-BPL   R. F. Griswold Papers, Boston Public Library, Boston, Massachusetts.

RS-MHS   Robie-Sewall Papers, Massachusetts Historical Society, Boston, Massachusetts.

S-BPL   Spooner Papers, Boston Public Library, Boston, Massachusetts.

S-LC   Elizabeth Cady Stanton Papers, Library of Congress, Washington, D.C.

S-SU   Gerrit Smith Miller Papers, George Arents Research Library at Syracuse University, Syracuse, New York.

S-UR   Seward Papers, University of Rochester, Rochester, New York.

SS-SC   Sophia Smith Collection, Smith College, Northampton, Massachusetts.

T-LC   Lewis Tappan Papers, Library of Congress, Washington, D.C.

T-RU   Lewis Tappan Papers, Rutgers University, New Brunswick, New Jersey.

U-LC   John C. Underwood Papers, Library of Congress, Washington, D.C.

W-BPL   Weston Papers, Antislavery Collection, Boston Public Library, Boston, Massachusetts.

W-LC   Elizur Wright Papers, Library of Congress, Washington, D.C.

W-MHS   Washburn Papers, Massachusetts Historical Society, Boston, Massachusetts.

W-UR   Weed Papers, University of Rochester, Rochester, New York.

WG-CUM   Weld-Grimké Papers, Clements Library, University of Michigan, Ann Arbor, Michigan.

Wn-MHS   Winthrop Papers, Massachusetts Historical Society, Boston, Massachusetts.

Bound with
Them in Chains

1

Prologue

Although categories and classifications are requisites of formal knowledge, they are inherently limiting, for there is always the danger that significant differences among individual components will be lost. This is especially true in history. People do not comprise a uniform whole and, at least in modern times, have made considerable efforts to individuate themselves. At the same time, history written since the nineteenth-century vogue of the Carlylean "Great Man" has deemphasized individual differences in its search for useful synthesis. So, too, with the history of the antislavery movement.

Russel Nye, for example, based abolitionists' motivation on whites' concern for their own civil liberties; Hazel Wolf found their compulsion in a quest for martyrdom; and David Donald argued that their zeal came from the dynamics of a waning social class. Each interpretation is suggestive but none applies uniformly to the entire movement. Attempts to explore the differences among abolitionists have encountered similar difficulties. They have divided the movement into coherent and competing factions: East against West, radical against conservative, Garrisonian against Tappanite. Yet some crusaders touched base in many societies and factions; others had contact with virtually none. Furthermore, no group remained static. Garrisonianism, for example, was a very different phenomenon in 1840 from what it was in 1833, and in 1860 from what it was in 1854. Even within a given society or faction at a given time, there frequently raged bitter ideological and practical disputes. The antislavery movement was, in fact, as much an everchanging and often contradictory process of diverse means and attitudes as it was a model of cooperation among similarly minded people.

To view abolitionism broadly, therefore, is to comprehend a wide spectrum of differing motives, goals, and methods undistorted by hypothetical categorical uniformity. The ten activists in the struggle to end slavery which this book treats were deliberately chosen for their diversity. That they are only ten instead of the twenty-five originally planned or the fifty or sixty that might be statistically meaningful is a compromise between the ideal and the possible. The original list from which the present ten studies were selected included European revolutionary Charles T. C. Follen, New York merchant Lewis Tappan, second-generation businessman Edward L. Philbrick, author Lydia Maria Child, lecturer Abby Kelley Foster, black nationalist Martin R. Delany, newspaperman and emigrationist Samuel R. Ward, vigilante-activist David Ruggles, schoolmaster and Kansas free-stater Augustus Wattles, Illinois and New York politicians Owen Lovejoy and William H. Seward, reform journalist William Goodell, Garrisonian and later Tappanite cleric Amos A. Phelps, Philadelphia Quakers James and Lucretia Mott, and businessman James Forten. Yet even this list does not encompass all possible types and varieties of antislavery worker. One might as well have included, for example, the prurient pamphleteer George Bourne, the Gideonites at Port Royal like Laura Towne, Mansfield French, or William C. Gannett, the revolutionary John Brown, lawyers David L. Child or William

Jay, and marginal antislavery clerics like Henry Ward Beecher or William Ellery Channing.

The ten subjects finally chosen most closely approached representative diversity. The selection, however, was also conditioned by the availability of material with which to construct a meaningful portrait and by an attempt to avoid duplication. Some subjects were omitted even after chapters for them had been written because it became clear that they overlapped unnecessarily; and some were dropped simply out of personal preference to investigate fully the careers of the final ten. In short, the attempt has been to provide a representative and instructive, rather than an exhaustive, sample.

To construct a social-science model is no more the purpose of the authors than to present a new version of antislavery organization or factionalism. A history of antislavery societies and their internal divisions would, indeed, permit more uniform and institutional treatment but it would exclude those men and women who operated alone and were linked only loosely, if at all, to formal associations. Similarly, a more encompassing statistical study would sacrifice individual differences and internal contradictions to the construction of new categories. Concern for the mavericks is no aimless lark, for they were extremely important in shaping the abolitionist message and often reached an audience different from and as large as those reached by organized groups.

The concern, then, is with individual men and women who, for significant periods in their lives, were bound to the antislavery crusade as a central or controlling goal. Necessarily many who opposed slavery were not so entirely engaged in abolitionist activity and are excluded, as are those who came to the movement so late as to have only short careers in it. The reformers here studied perceived themselves, in widely varying ways, as bound to slavery not with the physical chains that marked the bondsman's plight but by conscience, economic interest, political condition, or a similarity of social status. To free themselves and to free the slaves, they gave significant energy, time, talent, and funds to the cause, which was often the only thing that tied them together.

Much of the antislavery movement consisted of men talking to men, appealing directly to their idealism, their self-interest, their fears, their hopes and ambitions. Much of its impact lay in their varying styles of presentation. William Lloyd Garrison stirred up the apathetic as the mild Benjamin Lundy never could, yet he also aroused a vitriolic antagonism that Lundy seldom encountered. Some of their audience reacted less to the written words of editors and authors than to the varying techniques of platform lecturers like the smooth Wendell Phillips, the fiery Stephen Foster, or the mild Sallie Holley. Some took umbrage at the shocking imagery that Abby Kelley used but responded sympathetically to the same message from the benign and gentle Samuel J. May. Free Negroes, rejecting the paternalism of the American Colonization Society and impatient with white abolitionists, looked favorably upon the efforts of Henry Garnet and Frederick Douglass to organize the black community.

That many of these diverse styles found sustenance or shelter within the same society at one time or another does not make them individually or collectively a function of that society—or even the shapers of its course. The formal leadership of the American and Foreign Anti-Slavery Society and of the Liberty party remained nearly static from their inception until their collapse. Control of the American Anti-Slavery Society shifted only twice in its thirty-seven years, and for twenty-five years, from 1840 to 1865, it never left the hands of a small group in Boston. The excitement and the action was not in antislavery headquarters but in the campaigns of its agents and editors, who most often followed their own consciences rather than institutional policy.

The drive for abolition is better examined, therefore, in the lives of its participants than in the history of its institutions. Viewed by almost all its supporters as primarily a campaign to change public opinion, it gave to individuals embracing it a scope for their talents, ambitions, and theories, which ultimately shaped events. There were, to be sure, impersonal forces at work in the economics of cotton and slavery, the politics of sectionalism, and the social forces of large groups. Yet a small group of willful men and women made an imprint on nonslaveholding America in the antebellum years not to be underestimated.

The most famous of them have been studied as individuals. Garrison and Phillips have numerous biographies; Birney, Tappan, and Weld have very good modern studies. But the less visible or second-rank leaders have until recently enjoyed considerably less attention. Through their lives, this book assesses the antislavery movement, less to chronicle its narrative than to probe its complexity. Neither a return to Carlylean heroics nor an attempt at psycho-history, which tells more about the individual than his impact on society, it is a venture in collective biography to illuminate a social movement.

The study of individuals is no substitute for institutional history or social-science analysis but rather a supplement and complement to them. It allows an explicit study of microcosms and a representation of the relationships that shape the macrocosm. In large part, contemporaries of the movement saw it as a manifestation of individual maniacs who in their frenzy, fanaticism, and delusions would wreak havoc on the country politically, economically, and socially. Southerners put a price on Arthur Tappan's head; Boston Yankees tried to lynch Garrison; New Yorkers burned Lewis Tappan's house; radicals were known as "Abby Kelley men" and women. They responded to individuals rather than to the associations with which those individuals were affiliated. In this respect, at least, the critics were probably right.

2

The Setting

Jamestown was still a young settlement and Plymouth was not yet a reality when the first Negro servants were introduced into Virginia. Although in the first years after 1619 they occupied a position not dissimilar to that of white indentured servants, they came, by the latter part of the seventeenth century, to constitute a separate class of inhabitants, not only in Virginia, but throughout the American colonies. In the beginning, the need for labor, always pressing in a new settlement, had impelled the settlers to experiment with a variety of labor systems; they imported white indentured servants, they pressed Indians into servile labor, and finally they found in captured Africans the cheapest, most efficient, and most stable labor force. That chattel slavery became a peculiar feature of the South was the result of climate, economics, and agricultural structure. Its more limited and restricted existence in the North stemmed from the prevalence there of economies in which slave labor did not pay.

Embedded though slavery was in the colonial social and economic fabric, it invited criticism not only in the North but in the South as well. By the middle of the eighteenth century, men made uneasy by slavery moved to ameliorate its worst evils and, in some cases, to abolish it. The humanitarianism of the Enlightenment and the idealism of the Revolution combined in the North to restrict the abuses of slavery and to institute laws that ultimately led to its extinction. In New York, for example, restrictive legislation passed as early as 1785 led by 1827 to total abolition.

Even in the South, where legislatures refused to stem slavery, an antislavery current disturbed calm acceptance of the institution. There, after the Revolution, the first antislavery societies were established. In Virginia, where Thomas Jefferson and James Madison eloquently encouraged manumission, their neighbor and friend Edward Coles emancipated his slaves and removed them to Illinois, where he became a major force in excluding slavery under the state's first constitution. Sectarian groups also raised the antislavery banner. Most notable of all were the Quakers, whose Anthony Benezet and John Woolman stood as luminaries among eighteenth-century American humanitarians. So, too, Methodists and Baptists bore testimony against slavery and, in the nineteenth century, formed their own antislavery societies.

From these colonial and early national beginnings, the antislavery crusade emerged. The American Colonization Society, founded in 1817, drew to its ranks such distinguished Southerners as Bushrod Washington, James Madison, and Robert G. Harper, as well as many Northerners who, in a later decade, became abolitionists. Concerned primarily with the issue of the free Negro in the white community, the society drew strength from humanitarianism and fear alike. In the South, the free Negro posed a threat to the entire social fabric; and in the North, he was similarly feared as a threat to community stability. Thus the society's program to export free Negroes to Africa—regarded by most whites as the black man's home—reflected a change from earlier Northern attitudes. While it may, therefore, have been misleading to call the

American Colonization Society a Southern-dominated organization (as Northern abolitionists were soon to do), and while it was equally fallacious to call it an abolitionist front organization (as many Southerners came to designate it) it seemed clear that its orientation was essentially Southern. Nonetheless the society, in its early years, attracted many whose first concern was to end slavery and who only later considered colonization antithetical to their aim. Indeed many antislavery crusaders continued to accept colonization—though not in Africa—as a way of providing succor and haven, freedom and training, education and self-reliance for fugitive slaves, as well as for free Negroes. Quaker Benjamin Lundy attempted, unsuccessfully, to establish a colony for Negroes in Mexico. Frances Wright founded Nashoba in Tennessee to which Southern slaveowners might send the slaves they wished to manumit. And occasionally free Negroes in the North, though generally opposed to colonization, thought separate communities in North America were preferable to living within predominantly white society.

The American Colonization Society, however, seemed increasingly to beg the issue of slavery. Not only did it slight the heart of the problem, but, Northern antislavery folk contended, by removing free Negroes whose very lives argued against its necessity, it entrenched slavery. Disillusioned with repatriation to Africa, disenchanted by the society's failure even to transport a significant number to their ancestral domains, and thoroughly disheartened by the society's avoidance of the central problem, Northern antislavery men turned their attention elsewhere.

Disillusionment with colonization was not, however, the only impetus toward founding the American Anti-Slavery Society. Antislavery enthusiasts from Boston to Baltimore and westward to the Mississippi were caught up with the British campaign against slavery during the 1820s and with its dramatic success in ending the institution throughout the empire in 1833. But perhaps the greatest stimulus to American abolition came from William Lloyd Garrison, a Boston newspaperman of humble origin who early caught the spark of antislavery zeal. Editor for a season of a reform paper in Vermont, a veteran of Benjamin Lundy's *Genius of Universal Emancipation,* Garrison launched, with the first issue of the *Liberator,* in 1831, an attack on slavery whose force, militancy, and direction were new to American antislavery. Cumulatively made uneasy by colonization, inspired by British example, goaded by Garrison, abolitionists, in 1833, founded the American Anti-Slavery Society.

When the delegates assembled in Philadelphia that December, they were concerned almost exclusively with freeing slaves and gave little attention to the ultimate condition of free blacks. The critical issue, to use their term, was immediate emancipation. The term was precise; the meaning was not. Whether they meant the immediate accomplishment of the task implied, or, more realistically, gradual achievement of a goal immediately defined, they were in fact agreed on the fundamentals. Immediate emancipation gradually achieved, as some put it, or gradual emancipation immediately begun, as others phrased it, really meant the same thing: ending slavery as quickly as possible—without compensation to slaveholders, and without qualification.

This was the heart of their belief and the definition of their program. It was also an exercise in purgation for, they said, all Americans, slaveholders or not, were stigmatized by the sin of slavery when they acquiesced in its existence. Slavery, therefore, was not confined to the individuals nor even to the section immediately involved. It was, in the last analysis, a national institution. For its sins all society was responsible. By thus defining slavery as a sin requiring both individual and social catharsis, the abolitionists consolidated Christian and Enlightened views, which emphasized men's natural goodness, stressed their obligations to their fellows, and insisted on equal rights for all.

The scope of their commitment, however, did not prevent dissension within the ranks of the American Anti-Slavery Society. The society was part of that age of reform when hope for a more perfect future, belief in an improvable present, and an urge to eliminate the blemishes of American society gave meaning to socially conscious Americans. Though it came to overshadow all other reforms and to absorb the energies of most reformers, antislavery reform was, in the beginning, only a small part of this larger reforming movement. Thus the loyalties of many were divided. Some abolitionists embraced women's rights and nonresistance. Others accused them of using antislavery societies to further other reforms and of subverting antislavery work thereby. Let all reforms reenforce one another, said the former. Let us not vitiate the antislavery crusade, said the latter.

Multiple reform was not the only divisive issue. To those who felt that antislavery was purely a moral crusade, political action seemed to compromise, if not to negate, their principles. Others, claiming greater realism, insisted that political action was the surest road to abolition. During the late 1830s, the latter urged formation of an antislavery political party; the former argued vigorously against it. In the end, the conflict made of politics a principal focus for maneuver and debate.

Religious affiliation proved as controversial as politics. Like so many reform groups of this Middle Period, the American Anti-Slavery Society was composed largely of church members and clergymen. Those who unequivocally put abolition first, waging holy war against the sin of slavery, were appalled to see clergy and church condoning slavery in the South, refusing to deny the bond of fellowship with slaveholding co-religionists. But the issue was not quite so simple. Clerics, and the conservatives among them in particular, could and did agree that preaching against slavery was essential. But they could not accept the radical abolitionist argument that the institution of the church might, in the process, be shattered. To do so would be to attack the very house of God, whose strength and vitality it was the churchman's duty to uphold. Thus clerics stood aghast at the vehemence with which antislavery zealots attacked them, and the zealots, in turn, fought back. So hard did they sometimes drive their arguments that they invaded divine worship, incited mob violence, and cast odium upon religious societies. Small wonder then that in Massachusetts, at the very heart of antislavery activity, most churches were closed to antislavery speakers by the late 1830s. Small wonder that in reply antislavery's arch-agitators, Stephen Foster and Parker Pillsbury, cheerfully disrupted church services. Small wonder that those who were primarily church-oriented felt ill at ease in many antislavery societies.

As 1840 approached, the opposing forces more and more divided into two major camps. On the one hand, there were those who gathered around the person and influence of Garrison in Boston; they excoriated the churches and "came out" from them in accordance with the biblical injunction to abandon any corrupt society. It was they, their opponents charged, who weakened antislavery by mixing it with other reforms; by inviting women to participate in antislavery conventions and to serve on the boards of the national, state, and local societies; and by incorporating nonresistance into antislavery doctrine. In turn, their opponents gathered around the Tappans in New York, emphasized their clerical and religious convictions, and thoroughly disapproved any multiple reform admixture.

The fundamental difference between the two groups was that the Garrisonians were more interested in radical social change; the Tappanites, in conservative social evolution. The former were more venturesome; the latter, more staid. Symbolic was the primacy those New York businessmen, Arthur and Lewis Tappan, attributed to fiscal responsibility, a primacy which the radicals denied, arguing that the work must take precedence though debt followed in its train. So they fought over fund-raising, over launching new projects or continuing old ones, and over whether the Tappanite-controlled national society or Garrison-controlled state societies should administer available funds.

In May 1840, the two groups clashed head-on. At the American Anti-Slavery Society's annual meeting, held in New York, Garrisonians turned out en masse, dominated the convention, and, in the end, took control of the society. In so doing, they became known as the "old organization." The Tappan forces, in turn, walked out of the convention and formed their own "new organization," the American and Foreign Anti-Slavery Society.

The dispute was both disruptive and dysfunctional; after 1840, even though the essential principles and goals remained intact, the presence of two organizations did nothing to clarify the issues but only multiplied the time and energy spent on continuing dissensions between the two societies, as well as within them. Although the American Society limped on until the Civil War; the American and Foreign, which, as Louis Filler has remarked, was never much more than a paper organization, died out in the 1850s, its members dispersing into other organizations. But by the mid-forties even the American Anti-Slavery Society was little more than a name, its officers Massachusetts men whose principal vehicle was their state society.

The rupture of 1840 did not, however, destroy antislavery associational activity. Particularly after 1843 important antislavery work was carried out by various state groups—the Pennsylvania, Ohio, and Massachusetts antislavery societies were perhaps the most important—and by local and sectarian groups, notably the Methodist and Baptist antislavery societies. After 1840 too, the moral uplift, personal purging, and private salvation, which had characterized antislavery activity, were increasingly replaced by political action.

By 1838, abolitionists had begun systematic questioning of political candidates about their commitment on specific antislavery issues. Customarily the candidate was sent a questionnaire, asked to state his position, and politely informed that his response was important because his answers would be published. Thus political pressure was brought to bear by abolitionists who otherwise eschewed direct political involvement. In the long run, however, the technique was so unsuccessful that political activists espoused formation of an antislavery political party.

Largely through the labors of Myron Holley of Rochester, New York, the Liberty party was organized in 1839. Concerned with the single idea of abolishing slavery, it would not be diverted and weakened by ancillary issues. It was a party based on principle, not expediency, and dedicated to extirpating a major national sin, not to winning office and power. Its purpose was to offer an alternative to the major political parties. Was it not true that the Democracy in the North was dough-faced; that the party as a whole was Southern-dominated? Was it not true that Democrats and Whigs alike refused to act on behalf of the slave? Where had they stood in 1836 on the issue of the Gag Rule; what had they done to eliminate slavery and the slave trade in the District of Columbia; how many party men dared risk their political careers in the cause of the slave?

Nor did the major parties bypass antislavery only at the national level; they avoided it also at the state level. In New York, for example, where antislavery feeling was strong and politics lively, the state legislature refused to repeal the law that allowed slaveholders to bring and keep slaves in the state for as long as nine months, as it refused to guarantee jury trials to those claimed as fugitives from slavery. In Massachusetts, a legislative committee gave short shrift in 1836 to the antislavery delegation which appeared before it to protest the governor's appeal for new laws to restrict their activity. And in Ohio, the infamous Black Code, a series of laws dating back to 1804 which restricted Negroes' freedom to enter or to settle in the state, remained on the books until the 1840s, although it was seldom enforced after 1829. Surely these seemed reason enough for the formation of a third party—an antislavery party.

Neither on the state nor on the national scene, however, did the Liberty party achieve much following or success. Few nonabolitionists participated in it, while many antislavery crusaders argued that it would be no less subject to expediency and opportunism than the major parties should it ever approach power. In New York, where the party was strongest, it was caught in the acrimonious feud between old and new organization. Even more critical was the inherent weakness of its single-planked platform. American politics demand that a political party, to be viable, must embrace a variety of issues and cut across the principal political, economic, and social questions of the day. This fact the more astute antislavery politicians soon recognized. Staunchly opposed to slavery, they nevertheless sought the broader support requisite to put a political party in power by constructing a platform that abandoned immediate emancipation in favor of nonextension of slavery.

Why they should have thus shifted their position was not hard to understand. By 1848, the war with Mexico won and the Mexican Cession acquired, the nation debated the disposition of the new territory. Whether the land won from Mexico should be slave or free soon overshadowed all other questions and opened the door for the formation of the Free Soil party. Antislavery men joined with dissidents from the old parties to construct the multiplatform of FREE SOIL, FREE SPEECH, FREE LABOR, AND FREE MEN, and offered the former Democratic president, Martin Van Buren, as their candidate. The voting tallies vindicated the new departure.

In hindsight, it is clear that the Free Soil party stood midway between the Liberty party and the Republican party. The passage of the Fugitive Slave Bill in 1850, the passage of the Kansas–Nebraska Bill four years later, the collapse of the Whig party after the election of 1852, the clear domination of the Democratic party by its Southern wing, and the growing uneasiness of many in the major parties—antislavery Democrats and Conscience Whigs alike—cleared the way for a new political alignment. Not a few dedicated abolitionists but political leaders drawn from both major parties, building on the ruins of the old system and inspired by an issue which was clearly of crisis proportions, erected a new political organization of the first rank. At last the antislavery forces could look to a major political party whose orientation was, in the larger sense, antislavery, but whose platform embraced a multiplicity of issues to draw wide support. Through its agency, slavery was to be abolished within the decade.

Yet the 1850s did not witness a smooth transition to Republican politics or a satisfaction with the wider popular acceptance of general antislavery principles. On two counts the decade was little more satisfactory than that which had preceded it. Republican politics was beset with compromise even as it spoke an antislavery language; and the imperatives of the Fugitive Slave Law generated a wholly new response of obedience to a higher moral law alone among rank-and-file abolitionists. Thus, not only did the politics of third-party abolitionism continue, but the radicals within the ranks more and more espoused the politics of disunion and the techniques of violence. If most Americans still clung to the hope of peaceful change by moderate means, the voices of direct confrontation with ideas, with institutions, and with evil became stronger and more insistent. That the war which came did not always match their vision in no way diminished the relevance of their disaffection.

❊❊❊

While much of antislavery activity was directed to moral exhortation and political action, there was also activity on behalf of fugitive slaves and free Negroes. Friends of the free blacks

founded schools, established special communities, and prof-
fered a variety of educational assistance. The Oneida Institute
in upstate New York provided both academic and manual
training. In Ohio, Oberlin College made education in liberal
arts and theology available to blacks as well as whites.
Organized Negro communities in Upper Canada offered
refuge from persecution, safety for the fugitive, and an opportunity to farm the land, learn trades, attend grade schools,
and develop the arts of self-government and political participation.

The assistance to free and fugitive Negroes was not confined
to such limited institutions. In Massachusetts, Garrison and
his colleagues agitated successfully to legalize interracial marriage. In Pennsylvania and New York especially, during the
1840s and 1850s, free Negroes organized and participated
in conventions to achieve full suffrage and equal rights. In
various cities they formed vigilance committees, whose task
was to watch for "kidnappers" seeking to seize fugitives and
return them to the South. And after 1850 they confronted
authority directly. In 1851, in Syracuse, they snatched the
fugitive Jerry McHenry from the law and spirited him safely
away to Canada; in Boston, in 1854, they tried, at the cost
of life but unsuccessfully, to prevent the slave Anthony Burns
from being returned South. And, when open warfare broke
out in Kansas between Northern and Southern factions,
abolitionists were not averse to sending arms, as well as
prayers, to those fighting, as they saw it, the antislavery battle.

Echoing the moral convictions of the 1830s, the pleas for
political action of the 1840s, and the resort to direct action
in the 1850s, the majority of antislavery men in 1861 accepted
civil war as the last resort. Many who had been pacifists and
nonresistance enthusiasts a decade earlier now supported the
party of Lincoln. If they were dubious of Lincoln's intentions,
and if they feared his political expediency, they nonetheless
accepted war, not because it would suppress rebellion but
because it was a way to free the slave.

Their faith was not misplaced. The Emancipation Proclamation marked the climax of the antislavery movement; the Thirteenth Amendment was its apparent fulfillment. The extinction of slavery had been achieved through political power and its ultimate extension, war. Yet it is fair to say that, without the work of the antislavery societies for the thirty years prior to the war, without their propaganda and action in the cause, the favorable public opinion requisite to successful political action would not have developed. And the war power alone would have been insufficient to end a social system that a century of agitation had failed to weaken.

Yet there was a denouement. Neither the Emancipation Proclamation, Appomattox, nor even the Thirteenth Amendment quite fulfilled the imperatives of antislavery's broadest obligations. The slave was no longer bound, but the freedman was not yet wholly free. Whether it was the purview of the old antislavery organizations to pursue this second goal became the focus for a great debate. Just as most Americans considered the merits or demerits of various Reconstruction measures, so too abolitionists argued over freedmen's aid, black suffrage, land distribution, and related issues. The American Anti-Slavery Society itself was unable to decide where duty lay, and in 1865 it was rent again when some insisted its work was done, while others fought hard enough to keep it alive until 1870. But however one viewed the renewed factionalism within antislavery ranks, it remained clear that the broader potential of the antislavery vision remained stillborn.

❦❦❦

Who then were the abolitionists who played such varied roles in this national drama? The roster of individuals is imposingly long. The names of their leaders are still familiar, but the diversity of their views and the variety of their methods make generalization about them difficult indeed. Yet from the very

beginning of the movement distinctions were made—extremist and moderate, orthodox and perfectionist, Garrisonian
and Tappanite, Bostonian and New Yorker, old organization
and new, Eastern and Western. In the wake of contemporary
divisions, historians have followed.

The defense of Garrisonian primacy, which marked participant Oliver Johnson's 1879 history of the movement and
the Garrison children's 1880s biography of their father, was
reflected in biographies of Garrison and Phillips well into
the twentieth century. The Tappans, Birney, and Weld, on
the other hand, despite William Goodell's advocacy of their
positions in his early antislavery history of 1853, received considerably less attention until the 1933 publication of Gilbert
Barnes' *Antislavery Impulse,* which made Theodore Weld the
hero of an evangelical movement that Yankees, led by Garrison, had largely distorted and disserved. For the next thirty
years, until 1961, when Dwight Dumond published his com-
prehensive history of the crusade, he and his many students
broadened the trail which Barnes had blazed, focusing on
the primacy of evangelical and political antislavery applied
largely outside of New England. Their critical treatment of
perfectionist extremists has more recently been reinforced
by biographies of Garrison by Walter Merrill and John L.
Thomas, the latter of whom probed the editor's psyche in
depth.[1]

[1]For a more general survey and listing of antislavery history, see the bibliography; for an assessment of recent writing, see Merton Dillon, "The Abolitionists: A Decade of Historiography, 1959–1969," *Journal of Southern History*
35 (November 1969): 500–522; Oliver Johnson, *William Lloyd Garrison and
His Times*... (Boston: Houghton, Mifflin, 1881); Wendell Phillips Garrison
and Francis Jackson Garrison, *William Lloyd Garrison, 1805–1879*... (New
York: The Century Co., 1885–1889), 4 vols.; William Goodell, *Slavery and
Anti-Slavery; A History of the Great Struggle*... (New York: William Goodell,
1853); Gilbert H. Barnes, *The Antislavery Impulse, 1830–1844* (New York:
D. Appleton-Century Co., 1933); Dwight L. Dumond, *Antislavery: The Crusade
for Freedom in America* (Ann Arbor: University of Michigan Press, 1961);
Walter M. Merrill, *Against Wind and Tide: A Biography of Wm. Lloyd Garrison*
(Cambridge: Harvard University Press, 1963); John L. Thomas, *The Liberator:
William Lloyd Garrison, A Biography* (Boston: Little, Brown, 1963).

In response to such psychological dissection of reformers' motives and to David Donald's attribution of a reform commitment emerging from declining social status, both Martin Duberman and Betty Fladeland, in articles published in the early 1960s, recalled historians to rational analysis of individual abolitionists. But their summons, with few exceptions, has done little to remold the rigid dualism of earlier antislavery history. Anne C. Loveland and Bertram Wyatt-Brown, reexploring orthodox evangelicalism in greater intellectual depth and with greater subtlety than their predecessors, still define it as one of two central themes in abolitionist history. Aileen Kraditor's analysis of abolitionist ends and means relabeled the duality as one between radicals (Garrisonians), who would make fundamental, indeed revolutionary, change in many American institutions, and reformers (the evangelically and politically oriented), who would save the prevailing social structure by ameliorating specific ills. But to the new terms Kraditor brought a Garrisonian partisanship, which marked a return less to earlier historical portrayals than to antebellum infighting. Indeed, the fervency of some recent writing, like that of civil-rights supporter James McPherson and New Left enthusiast Howard Zinn, has not only revived the debate over antislavery organization but has added a new vibrancy with the discussion of the movement's reform or radical nature.[2]

[2]David Donald, "Toward a Reconsideration of Abolitionists," in his *Lincoln Reconsidered: Essays in the Civil War Era* (New York: Alfred Knopf, 1956), 19–36; Martin Duberman, "The Abolitionists and Psychology," *Journal of Negro History* 47 (July 1962): 183–191; Betty Fladeland, "Who Were the Abolitionists?" *Journal of Negro History* 49 (April 1964): 99–115; Anne C. Loveland, "Evangelicalism and 'Immediate Emancipation' in American Antislavery Thought," *Journal of Southern History* 32 (May 1966): 172–188; Bertram Wyatt-Brown, *Lewis Tappan and the Evangelical War Against Slavery* (Cleveland: Case Western Reserve University Press, 1969); Aileen S. Kraditor, *Means and Ends in American Abolitionism: Garrison and His Critics on Strategy and Tactics, 1834–1850* (New York: Pantheon Books, 1969); James M. McPherson, *The Struggle for Equality: Abolitionists and the Negro in the Civil War and Reconstruction* (Princeton: Princeton University Press, 1964); Howard Zinn, "Abolitionists, Freedom-Riders, and the Tactics of Agitation," in *The Antislavery Vanguard:*

The collective impact of these extensive historical writings on antislavery, of which only a few major works are mentioned here, has largely overshadowed efforts to escape a rigid dualism and to suggest more complex patterns. Yet those efforts have been made in such diverse studies as Howard Bell's, Larry Gara's, and Benjamin Quarles' explorations of the unique black role in abolition, Wyatt-Brown's assessment of Garrisonian tactical conservatism, James Stewart's examination of Garrisonian practical political activity outside the ineffectual, conscience-soothing Liberty party, and Fladeland's insistence that there is no unitary or dualistic answer to who were the abolitionists.[3]

Any attempt to see the antislavery movement as a unified whole or to understand it as a series of neat cleavages along geographic, economic, or religious lines, is, in fact, to overlook the variety and interplay within a remarkably complex movement. Its participants did largely agree that slavery was a sin to be repented and purged. But the ways in which they defined sin and prescribed the manner of repentance and purgation explain the wide appeal of this originally esoteric reform movement and demonstrate, as well, the dangers it ran of internal paralysis.

There were those in the crusade who brought to the slaves' cause an American version of the aristocratic tradition of noblesse oblige. Who, however, could be further apart than the London-educated Boston bluestocking Maria Weston

---

New Essays on the Abolitionists, ed. Martin Duberman (Princeton: Princeton University Press, 1965).

[3]Howard H. Bell, *A Survey of the Negro Convention Movement, 1830–1861* (New York: Arno Press, 1969); Larry Gara, *The Liberty Line: The Legend of the Underground Railroad* (Lexington: University of Kentucky Press, 1961); Benjamin Quarles, *Black Abolitionists* (New York: Oxford University Press, 1969); Bertram Wyatt-Brown, "William Lloyd Garrison and Antislavery Unity: A Reappraisal," *Civil War History* 13 (March 1967): 5–24; James B. Stewart, "The Aims and Impact of Garrisonian Abolitionism, 1840–1860," *Civil War History* 15 (September 1969): 197–209; Fladeland, "Who Were the Abolitionists?"

Chapman, and the Kentucky planter Cassius Marcellus Clay, renowned for his fierce application of the bowie knife and pistol? Yet Chapman, dedicated to physical nonviolence, was verbally violent in the cause of Garrisonian immediatism, while Clay, physically direct and violent, could compromise politically and support gradual emancipation as readily as immediate abolition.

Many were motivated by firm religious conviction, but their application of similar principles varied widely. Benjamin Lundy, a quiet Quaker, whose generosity was guided by an inner voice, tried to further universal emancipation through newspapers and colonization. Hiram Wilson, a Finney-oriented evangelist, made of his life a deliberate martyrdom to give secular and Christian guidance to Negro refugees in Canada. Samuel Cornish, a free Negro from Maryland, after a struggle for a modest education, became a Presbyterian minister. Despite his efforts on behalf of his fellow blacks, he never surrendered his conservatism, which restrained him from challenging economic, political, or social institutions other than slavery. By contrast, Henry Highland Garnet of New York exhorted early Negro conventions to demand full civil equality for freemen and, on occasion, came close to counseling slaves to revolution. Nor were black abolitionists the only extreme radicals; Stephen Foster, New Hampshire farmer and preacher, wrote that revolution was the only remedy.

Such direct challenges to the entire status quo seemed extremely dubious procedure to those who preferred to work through established institutions and political channels. Two Ohioans of Connecticut extraction were among this number. Elizur Wright, Jr., worked for a new antislavery party, while Joshua R. Giddings struggled valiantly within the Whig fold to effect change. Both men sought orderly action within constitutional limits to expunge the blight of slavery.

Less institutionally oriented, there were those whose humanitarianism led them to a variety of actions in their con-

stant attempts to better the lot of all their fellow citizens.
To some of their colleagues they seemed gadflies; to others,
earnest but insufficiently vigorous. But they won support from
those who admired their liberal goals and their nonabrasive
methods. In this manner, Samuel Joseph May, a Unitarian
minister, served the enslaved and deprived as a perennial,
persistent, and professional reformer.

The way in which antislavery reformers reacted intellectually to slavery shaped their methods. Consequently method
was one of the most hotly debated issues among them. At
one angle of vision stood William Ellery Channing, who
rejected abolitionists at the same time that he rejected slavery.
Upset by the extremism and socially abrasive language of
Garrison in the *Liberator* and of Garrison's followers on the
lecture platform, sure that association with these men whose
every word stirred mobs to throw bricks and rotten eggs was
ineffective, Channing argued that men of conscience could
best serve the antislavery cause by individual testimony. To
join with others in societies, he contended, was to run the
risk of violating one's conscience by association with actions
and words one disapproved. Yet there were those much
influenced by Channing to undertake reform who could not
accept his dictum on association. Henry and Maria Chapman
were moved to resign from his church; and Samuel J. May,
whose childhood was one of close familiarity with Channing
and who, after he became a Unitarian minister, preached
for a while in Channing's church, became not only a member
of various antislavery societies but the agent of one. And
others, men as diverse as Benjamin Lundy and Cassius Clay,
while they did not oppose associations, did the bulk of their
antislavery work independently.

More central to actual debate was the manner of organization that would best serve the cause. Should one, for instance,
stay in one's church and try to bring it to antislavery as did
Amos Phelps in his work with the Congregational churches
of Massachusetts; or should one "come out" from the church

because it was a corrupt and unclean body, which tolerated the sin of slavery? Samuel Cornish, Presbyterian minister, stayed in and decried his church's discrimination against Negroes. On the other hand, James G. Birney called the church the "Bulwark of Slavery"; and Stephen Foster, after unsuccessful attempts to win the Congregational churches to the antislavery crusade, decided that all American churches were one immense "brotherhood of thieves."

"Come-outerism" was not confined, however, to ecclesiastical institutions. Liberty party men came out from the old parties, especially the Whig party, because they found them controlled by the slave interests. Free Democrats and Free Soilers came out from the old parties because they despaired of antislavery action in them. Not all, however, who found the existing political system wanting or corrupt could, like Elizur Wright, find solace in third parties. When Garrison burned a copy of the American Constitution at a Fourth of July celebration, he acted out the conviction of his immediate colleagues that the very heart of American government was so undermined by the proslavery provisions of the Constitution that political action under its authority was intolerable. Thus Garrisonians like Wendell Phillips and Maria Chapman damned all political action—through major parties and third parties alike—and urged antislavery men to surrender their public offices. Late in the 1850s, Stephen Foster proposed organized anarchist action in the formation of a disunionist, antipolitical party. And at dead center in the maelstrom of antislavery political debate were a few like Samuel J. May who were simply apolitical, who generally refused to vote because it meant compromise with evil, but who, in the 1850s, turned sporadically to political action which promised movement toward the abolition or the restriction of slavery.

If abolitionists differed over their appropriate relationship with state and church, so also did they differ over the relation of their movement to other reforms. Maria Chapman, Abby Kelley Foster, and Lydia Maria Child were united in this at least; antislavery societies, they believed, must accept and demonstrate equal rights for women. Some, like Elizur Wright, said that although they believed in both crusades, to link them would seriously reduce antislavery support. Others quoted St. Paul's strictures against women's speaking in public and were incensed at linking the godly cause of antislavery with the unscriptural advocacy of women's rights. So it was with other reforms—peace, sabbath reform, and communitarianism among them.

The greatest significance of the debate about abolition's relation to other reforms, however, lay in its reflecting one of the deepest and most decisive of the divisions which split the movement. Some were reluctant reformers. Slavery, they knew, was a gross sin, which marred the conscience of individual Americans and violated the spirit of republican government. Eliminate slavery, they said, but leave intact an otherwise sound and desirable system. They looked with scorn and dismay at their fellows who were not content to challenge one major institution, but who sought massive and multitudinous reforms in the social and economic structure. These, the positive, the dedicated reformers offended society in a variety of ways. Abby Foster wore bloomers. Charles C. Burleigh refused to cut his hair and beard. Stephen Foster not only bathed daily in cold water but advocated the practice publicly. Maria Chapman, whose children were brattish, argued that parents had no right to use force to discipline their offspring. Samuel J. May carried his opposition to violence to a condemnation of the American Revolution. Conservatives like Lewis Tappan, Amos Phelps, and Samuel Cornish saw their associates' idealism as ridiculous fanaticism in the service of a secular millennialism. Not only did such coworkers hinder the antislavery cause, but, should they succeed, they would create a world totally unacceptable to orthodox Calvinists.

From still another vantage point, further cleavage emerged. Some found in or created from their reform activity a new orthodoxy, a set of beliefs mandatory for true believers in antislavery. William Lloyd Garrison, Abby Foster, and most especially Maria Chapman argued that adherence to properly defined antislavery principles was far more important than specific actions undertaken in the cause At the opposite pole stood those pragmatists or activists who, although they shared many of the same ideological commitments, searched for and seized upon a variety of feasible steps to implement their beliefs. Henry Garnet went from antislavery lecturing to political action to exclusively black action and back. Hiram Wilson and Benjamin Lundy experimented with colonization and organized Negro communities, as well as with preaching and writing. It was not a line between thinkers and doers but between those who put meticulous adherence to ideology first and those who put effective achievement of given goals first.

The antislavery host was thus a variegated group. Its adherents differed widely about method, ideology, and nuance. Those who were united on one position often found themselves in opposite camps on another. Yet it is important not to let the differences blur the common dedication they shared—to end slavery. They sought not to meliorate the institution, but to end it as soon as possible. Their means, their timing, and their specific arguments diverged. Abolitionists who could and did cooperate in their common crusade also could and did give themselves over to sharp and bitter infighting. The story of their effective action and the story of their differences, difficulties, and feuding are alike parts of the history of the antislavery movement.

3

The Boston Bluestocking:
Maria Weston Chapman

Into the ranks of substantial Boston in the mid-1830s strode the commanding figure of Maria Weston Chapman. Both forceful and able, she exuded the Brahmin essence, though Brahmin in fact she was not. Her impact was well attested by James Russell Lowell: an "expansive force, without a sound, / That whirls a hundred wheels around," she was the Joan of Arc of the antislavery movement.[1] Lowell saw her as she saw herself.

Maria Weston came from a family modest in wealth but rich in the assurance of its Pilgrim ancestry. Born in Weymouth, just south of Boston, in 1806, she was sent to England as a young girl where she lived with the family of her uncle, Joshua Bates of Baring Brothers, and was educated in the best English fashion. As a young woman, however, she rejected a life abroad, returning to Boston in 1828 to become principal of the newly founded Boston High School for Young Ladies. Married in 1830 to Henry Chapman, a

[1]Quoted in "G," "In Memoriam, Maria Weston Chapman," *Woman's Journal,* July 18, 1885.

young Boston businessman of established family, she was soon free to live the patrician life.[2] Every inch the image of a princess in her youth, she had, wrote her friend, the English observer, Harriet Martineau, a "slender, graceful form" and a "noble profile"; her long "golden hair" set off, said Edmund Quincy, a "dazzling complexion" and the "swift eyes of clear steel-blue" which Lowell admired. Even in her old age she radiated a "kind of victorious beauty" and "entered a room like a public person." She stood, observed Quincy, thoroughly fascinated, "at the head of the human race—men or women." The admiring Irish Garrisonian Richard Webb described her as unselfish, sweet-tempered, full of moral courage and hearty sympathy. Her opponent Lewis Tappan, leader of the anti-Garrisonians in New York, found her considerably less than sweet. She was, he was sure, "a talented woman with the disposition of a fiend," who, he added admiringly, "manag[e]s W. L. G[arrison,] W[endell] Phillips, [Edmund] Quincy[,] &c. as easily as she could 'untie a garter.' " Chapman was self-assured, aristocratic, arrogant, and talented.[3]

The dedication and determination which provoked both eulogy and damnation were displayed early in the Chapmans' married life. Both Henry and Maria became leaders in reform in the 1830s, and, after Henry's death in 1842, Maria persisted for another twenty years. As a Harvard student, Henry, in

[2] For biographical data on the early years of Chapman, see Maria A. Kasten, "Maria Weston Chapman," *Dictionary of American Biography,* ed. Allen Johnson and Dumas Malone (New York: Scribners, 1928*ff*), IV, 19; "M. W. Chapman," *Englishwoman's Review* 149 (September 15, 1885): 399–402; Wendell Phillips Garrison and Francis Jackson Garrison, *William Lloyd Garrison, 1805–1879: The Story of His Life, Told by His Children* (New York: The Century Co., 1885*ff*), II, 49.

[3] The descriptions of Maria Chapman are drawn from a variety of sources, noted in the order of their appearance in the text. Harriet Martineau, *Autobiography, with Memorials by Maria Weston Chapman* (London: Smith, Elder & Co., 1877), II, 28; Edmund Quincy to Richard D. Webb, January 29, 1843, Q-MHS; John Jay Chapman, *Memories and Milestones* (New York: Moffat, Yard & Co., 1915), 209–212; Richard D. Webb to Edmund Quincy, October 27, 1848, W-BPL; Lewis Tappan to Gamaliel Bailey, letterpress, October 26, 1843, T-LC.

the interest of reform, had become a teetotaler; as an antislavery businessman, he foreswore numerous profitable undertakings. Both Chapmans sacrificed social position and pleasant connections in the same cause. These decisions marked an unflinching dedication to principle and displayed the kind of courage which Maria Chapman had in abundance—to stand against the community and her own social circle, undaunted by public disapprobation, serene in the face of crisis.

Noting that the role of reformer was "necessarily a marked one," Chapman took consolation in a sense of martyrdom. Voluntary abasement in the cause was her fulfillment. Not a "companion of princes" but a "servant of slaves," she welcomed service in any form, " 'The first in shame & agony / The meanest in the *lowest* Task.' " Yet, if the meaning of martyrdom was epitomized by Christ, Maria Chapman was no martyr, but rather one who gloried in the feeling of martyrdom. Abby and Stephen Foster, Nathaniel P. Rogers, and William Lloyd Garrison could well be called martyrs in the antislavery cause, for their suffering was personal, physical, deep, searing. Hardly so much can be said for Maria Chapman, whose understanding of the martyr's condition was belied by her all too clear understanding of where she herself stood in the whole picture. Abolitionists, she complained wearily, "are laden with ignominy merely from the circumstance that they were a little better than the generality of their neighbours."[4]

From her exalted moral pedestal, Chapman reached out to her European peers for support and assistance. Leaving the American scene just when the Mexican War had thrust the slavery issue into the center of politics, Chapman spent the years from 1848 to 1855 in England and on the continent, giving her daughters the same educational and social exposure which had marked her own youth. Like most other abolition

[4]The first and third quotations are from Chapman to John B. Estlin, February 28, 1846, E-BPL; the middle one is from Chapman to Mary Estlin, March 8, 1858, E-BPL.

ists who ventured abroad, she battened on the attentions of the great and near great who at home largely ostracized radical reformers. At the same time, she systematically tapped British and French society for the American cause. Lady Byron, Harriet Martineau, de Tocqueville, Beaumont, Lamartine all lent their names, through her, to it. And even her relative isolation at home had never subverted the absolute assurance of her own position. Moreover the eminence of her station translated itself effortlessly into her conviction of the absolute rightness of her views. Little wonder that Thomas Wentworth Higginson observed that she "had the bearing that might befit a line of duchesses." He was right, and Maria Chapman knew it. Ironically she thought herself immune at the same time from its consequences, able to excoriate her antislavery enemies for their nonrepublican qualities, able to insist that it was she who was the "real republican."[5]

Without question Chapman was a Garrisonian, yet her attitudes and assumptions were far indeed from those of the persistent agitators whose egalitarian vision Aileen Kraditor portrays in her radical–conservative analysis of the abolition movement. Nor was there anything in Maria Chapman's background to have impelled her irresistibly into antislavery. Most Bostonians, early in the century, shunned the issue of slavery and worked for more respectable charities if they sought to "do good." Neither ancestry, education, nor social position necessarily marked Maria for reform in general or antislavery in particular. Her decision to abandon London society to become principal of the Boston High School for Young Ladies

[5]The quotations, in order, are found in Chapman to the Editor of the *National Anti-Slavery Standard,* n.d., in the *Liberator,* July 18, 1851; Thomas Wentworth Higginson, "Anti-Slavery Days," *Outlook* 60 (September 1898): 47–57; Chapman to John A. Collins, February 23, 1841, G-BPL. For her efforts to tap the resources of well-known Frenchmen, see Chapman to John B. Estlin, January 4, 1850, E-BPL; Chapman to Elizabeth Pease, May 4, 1851, G-BPL.

suggests a quest for independence or, at least, a devotion to genteel uplift, but not a commitment to unpopularity.

It is difficult to isolate the precise impetus that drew Maria Chapman into the antislavery crusade. Certainly both she and her husband were influenced by their close friend and pastor, William Ellery Channing: his religious liberalism, his optimism, his commitment to reform. Yet Channing never became an abolitionist and questioned the utility of associations in achieving reform. If his preaching led the Chapmans to oppose slavery, it was the fiery speeches of George Thompson, the English abolitionist, and the mob violence roused by his appearances that made them antislavery activists. The year of the most active antiabolition riots, 1835, saw Henry elected treasurer of the Massachusetts Anti-Slavery Society and Maria, corresponding secretary of the Boston Female Anti-Slavery Society. It was she who rallied the ladies when on October 21 their meeting was threatened by an angry mob out to lynch Thompson. When Boston's Mayor Theodore Lyman begged them to disband their meeting, it was she who protested the lack of police protection, who insisted that formal parliamentary adjournment precede dissolution of the meeting, who organized the frightened women to walk calmly, two by two, through the mob. Not surprisingly, the crowd decided to move on to the Chapman house, and changed their plans only when, discovering Garrison in his office, they went after him.[6]

Drawn, like so many, to abolition by concern for civil liberties, Maria Chapman soon became a tireless crusader. Although her introduction to the movement coincided with Henry's tuberculosis and the pressures of a growing family, her commitment was no revolt from the Doll's House or escape from family strains. It was built on the conviction she shared

[6]Chapman to Elizabeth P. Nichol, January 8, 1854, SS-SC; *Liberator,* August 1, 1851; Deborah Weston, diary, October 20, 1835, W-BPL. On the general question of women's entering and working in the antislavery movement, see Jane H. Pease and William H. Pease, "The Role of Women in the Antislavery Movement," Canadian Historical Association, *Historical Papers Presented at the Annual Meeting. . . . 1967,* 167–183.

with many abolitionists, male and female alike, that slavery violated the natural rights of both blacks and whites.

Unlike many of her colleagues, however, Chapman preferred to avoid the popular limelight. Seldom during her career did she address a public meeting. She did, it is true, speak for ten minutes to the convention of antislavery women in Philadelphia's Pennsylvania Hall in 1838 where, if the reports are accurate, she was a dramatic success. Her crimson cape standing out against the Philadelphia audience's Quaker gray, "she acquitted herself nobly" while a mob surrounded the building.[7] Significantly, she never repeated the performance, which proved to be a prelude to a severe physical and mental collapse.

That she shunned the public in no way suggested that Chapman was one of those scions of the old upper class, stripped of power and engaging in reform in frustrated despair. Quite the contrary. Her avoidance of public platforms indicated neither a grudging activity nor inactivity. She used her reform position to double advantage, exerting a leverage customarily denied women of her class while prosecuting her antislavery activities with vigor. "I am not willing," she wrote pointedly to the Essex County Women's Convention in 1842, "to give those much credit for loving the cause, who had rather sit still, than work for it. . . ."[8] Work she did. She sat on numerous committees, councils, boards, and groups year after year. Between 1835 and 1862, she served at least fourteen years on the business committee of the Massachusetts Anti-Slavery Society, and a like number as member of its executive committee. During the 1830s and 1840s, she served at least once on the central committee of the Boston Female Anti-Slavery Society, headed its petition campaign in the late 1830s, acted as its foreign corresponding secretary for eight years, and wrote its annual reports. In addition, she served on the business

[7]William Lloyd Garrison to Sarah Benson, May 19, 1838, G-BPL.
[8]Chapman to the Essex County Women's Convention, n.d., in the *National Anti-Slavery Standard*, October 6, 1842.

committee of the New England Anti-Slavery Convention at
least ten times between 1839 and 1860. At the national level,
she was a member of the executive committee of the American
Anti-Slavery Society for at least thirteen years, its corresponding secretary for one, and a member of the business committee
for two.

Chapman did not take her obligations lightly. In 1841 and
1842, when she and Henry spent considerable time in Haiti
for Henry's health, she continued her work there. She collected local articles, which she forwarded to the antislavery
fairs in Boston; she helped to rewrite the constitution of the
Philanthropic Society of Porto Plate, a West Indian auxiliary
of the American Anti-Slavery Society. At home, too, she
assisted local antislavery efforts, as when, in 1835, she helped
to found the antislavery society in Hingham. Also, over the
years, she acted, with Edmund Quincy, as a temporary editor
of the *Liberator* when Garrison was absent or ill. From 1844
until she went to Europe, she was a member of the editorial
committee of *National Anti-Slavery Standard,* the organ of the
American Anti-Slavery Society. In the 1830s and early 1840s,
she circulated petitions, mostly for the abolition of slavery
in the District of Columbia, but also for ending discrimination
on the railroads, for repealing the antimiscegenation law of
Massachusetts, and for recognizing Haitian independence.[9]

Equally important, from 1839 until 1858 Chapman edited
a gift book annual, the *Liberty Bell.* Carrying short stories,
poems, essays, and related material by well-known opponents
of slavery, it was designed to popularize the antislavery message. "Opposition to the abolition of slavery is so great here

[9]The record of Chapman's services in various antislavery societies is com-
piled largely from the reports of the societies as they appeared in the *Liberator,*
passim; also Boston Female Anti-Slavery Society, *Annual Reports,* passim. For
her special activity in Haiti, see, for example, Henry G. Chapman to Henry
Chapman, Sr., May 14, 1841, Ch-CoU. Her other various antislavery activities
are noted in widely scattered references in the *Liberator;* the *National Anti-
Slavery Standard;* and in the following collections: C-BPL, BS-SL, W-BPL,
and A-ME.

[in America]," wrote Chapman, that we must treat the public "like children, to whom a medicine is made as pleasant as it[s] nature permits. A childish mind receives a small measure of truth in gilt edges where it would reject it in 'whity-brown.' "[10]

∞∞∞

More than any single contribution, it was what Maria Chapman was and stood for that gave her a commanding position among the Garrisonians. Tenaciously and zealously, she held to—and demanded that others hold to—the simple Garrisonian creed: immediate and uncompensated abolition of slavery, as well as to its corollary insistence on full civil liberty for blacks and whites. The connection between the two was critical in turning her into a committed abolitionist. On the heels of mob violence against abolitionists in Boston and throughout New England and New York in the fall of 1835, she wrote that "the Question now is the right of whites as well as the rights of blacks—Therefore we must *strongly assert our right to plead for the blacks.*" The Garrisonians' rejection of expedient moderation and their refusal to temper their pleas to avoid violence was one way to maintain the purity of their faith; the other was their insistence on severing connections with all who condoned slavery in any way. "I am a believer," said Chapman, "in the duty & the policy of sundering all connection with bodies whose course is mainly wrong; as a practical building up of that wrong." It was this "come-outer" argument that turned the Garrisonians against the churches and underlay their refusal to support "wrong-headed" action even

---

[10] For a general discussion of the *Liberty Bell,* see Ralph Thompson, "Liberty Bell and Other Anti-Slavery Gift Books," *New England Quarterly* 7 (March 1934): 154–168. The quotation is from Chapman to [Mary?] Estlin, January 27, 1846, E-BPL.

though that action might be on the side of the antislavery angels.[11]

Garrisonianism was essentially a millennial faith, argued in absolute terms. The character of the argument conditioned, in turn, the character of action. Distinguished by the dual verbal artillery of the lecture platform and the antislavery press, Garrisonianism was a thirty-year tribute to endless discourse, to interminable exhortation, to limitless verbiage. Garrisonians largely avoided direct action, whether in politics or on behalf of free Negroes. The important work, they argued, was "soul" work—the purging of sin. That done, slavery would die of its own accord, and subsequent problems would take care of themselves. "How Can I Help End Slavery?" asked Chapman after twenty years of experience in the antislavery cause. Not, she answered, by furthering colonization; not by political action; not by purchasing individual slaves and freeing them; not by joining vigilance societies or the underground railroad; not by establishing schools for Negroes; not by boycotting slave produce; for all these were partial measures, treating symptoms and avoiding the hard realities. How then? She replied with Garrisonian directness, setting forth what for twenty-two years had been the only right way: support the American Anti-Slavery Society. "Never, since the world was," she asserted with the bold assuredness of the elect, "has any effort been so clear, so strong, so uncompromising, so ennobling, so holy, and, let me add, so successful." For, she added conclusively, the American Anti-Slavery Society used the "only possible *moral* means,—the means employed with success on every other occasion where important changes are to be made:—the propagation of principle, the spreading of information, the presenting of argument, appeal, entreaty, denunciation, as the case may require, through agents, newspapers, books, tracts and lectures."[12]

[11]Chapman to [?], October 21, [1835], W-BPL; Chapman to Sydney H. Gay and [?] White, September 16, 1843, G-CU.
[12]Maria Weston Chapman, *How Can I Help to Abolish Slavery?* Anti-Slavery

The argument was, of course, rigidly doctrinaire and posed for the Garrisonians a constant dilemma. On the one hand, they touted the breadth of their views and their willingness to entertain differing positions within a wide antislavery spectrum; yet an inner core insisted on complete conformity to a dogma remarkable for its narrowness. "You would probably be amazed at our toleration if you were here," Chapman wrote expansively to her English friend Mary Estlin. "Differences of opinion that I verily believe you in England could call *too* wide to unite, here are made of no account by the might of our principles of freedom & *immediatism*."[13] But her definition of immediatism circumscribed toleration and diversity. Its very rigidity precluded alternatives.

Admitting that Garrisonians shunned most "worldly or political" activity, Chapman denied that their approach was narrow. They simply went "on strong in the Lord," whose ways they knew best.[14] Accordingly she turned hard upon backsliding antislavery Southerner Cassius Clay. "Do not mistake me so much," she assured Clay, commenting on his support of the Mexican War, "as to think that I have judged you by my own moral standards. I have always felt and seen the great difference between the absolute right of the antislavery men of the North, and the relative right that you proposed as your object; between their immoveable adherence to principle, and your changeful obedience to impulse. . . ." Clay did not need to read the rest of the letter to discover that Chapman thought he sought to "serve God and Mam-

---

Tract No. 14 [Boston: American Anti-Slavery Society, 1855], 7; Maria Weston Chapman, [Appeal for the Twenty-second National Anti-Slavery Bazaar], *Liberator,* December 7, 1855. For a sympathetic modern view of the abolitionist as agitator, see Aileen S. Kraditor, *Means and Ends in American Abolitionism: Garrison and His Critics on Strategy and Tactics, 1834–1850* (New York: Pantheon Books, 1969), 11–38.

[13]Chapman to [Mary?] Estlin, January 27, 1846, E-BPL.

[14]Chapman to the Ladies of Scotland, August 12, 1835, SS-SC. This letter was probably never delivered, since it was to have been carried by David and Maria Child, whose English trip in 1835 was canceled.

mon," a service which, she concluded, was "the crowning wickedness of Americans."[15]

"I consider," she had earlier written David Child, "[that]
'platformism' [is] essential to the abolition of slavery." Her
career was a dedication to enforcing the Garrison brand. As
early as 1839, when the Boston Female Anti-Slavery Society,
reflecting the general infighting of the period, was itself split-
ting, Chapman had asserted that she did not know people
but spoke only to principle. Her rival for power, Lucy Ball,
thought differently. "Yes, you do Mrs. Chapman, know persons," she shot back; "you think nobody is an abolitionist who
does not think just as you do. You told us the other evening
you did not consider us abolitionists." Fifteen years later, John
Murray Forbes suggested to her that she should "soar Lower"
and be less dogmatic.[16]

That Chapman did not heed these strictures, was made
abundantly clear in her summary of the place occupied by
the American Anti-Slavery Society: "It alone has, on the subject of slavery, the truth, the whole truth, and nothing but
the truth, and is not afraid nor ashamed to proclaim it, as
of all things most precious, at every risk and cost, as only
able to make free...."[17]

Battened in the righteousness of that position, Maria Chapman and her Boston confreres counted up thirty years of
antislavery work, not only dispensing the truth as they saw
it but riding herd on heretics who kept the movement in
constant agitation and made of Chapman the drill-master,
who thoroughly enjoyed the "cut & thrust spirit of the refor-

[15]Chapman to Cassius M. Clay, July 25, 1846, in the *Liberator,* August
7, 1846.

[16]Chapman to [David L. Child, 1843], fragment, C-BPL; [Maria Weston
Chapman, "Right and Wrong in the Anti-Slavery Society"], printed as a
Liberator Extra, October 1839; John Murray Forbes to Chapman, June 16,
1855, W-BPL.

[17]Maria Weston Chapman, "Report of the Twenty-third National Anti-
Slavery Bazaar," in the *Liberator,* January 30, 1857.

mers."[18] It was her milieu, fighting the dragons of slavocracy, indifference, and divergent factions. To forward her cause, she collected and disbursed large sums of money, drafted innumerable resolutions, and laid the plans for myriad conventions, meetings, and lecture tours. To help her in the fight, there gathered around her a tight cadre, the Boston Clique.

The Boston Clique enjoyed remarkable power. Its members, who had long been a majority on the executive board of the Massachusetts Anti-Slavery Society, after 1843 dominated the American Anti-Slavery Society. By dominating the national society, they swayed Garrisonian groups and instruments throughout the North—the *Pennsylvania Freeman* and its parent society, for example, or the *Anti-Slavery Bugle* and the Ohio brethren. Though the Boston Clique did not hold the reins of power directly, its control was no less real; it set the tone, it established the pace, and it laid down the policy of Garrisonianism.

Eminently respectable, the clique was talented and experienced as well. Paternalism, prestige, and financial and intellectual assets gave it the power to keep the movement pure and uncorrupted by worldly influences. Lawyer Ellis Gray Loring, merchant prince Francis Jackson, preacher Samuel May, Jr., of Leicester, joined with those whose inheritance freed them to be full-time reformers—Wendell Phillips and Edmund Quincy, with the poet James Russell Lowell, and with the eager Weston sisters—teachers, reformers, and, with the exception of Maria, spinsters all. Chapman's coterie was, observed the hostile critic, historian George Bancroft, a "squad of blue-stockings and abolitionists." "I don't know," wrote Chapman to an English friend, describing them, "whether you know it . . . but one of our advantages is, that, if there

---

[18]Samuel E. Coues to Edmund Quincy, January 13, 1841, Q-MHS.

be here properly any such thing as social rank & respectability . . . the Boston abolitionists are that thing;—some by
wealth, as America counts riches,—some by various antecedents,—some by high intellectual gifts. . . ." Chapman was
determined to use this "real advantage."[19]

Leading her fellow abolitionists with single purpose, Chapman was dubbed the "great goddess" by her enemies and
Lady Macbeth by her friends. Her home and the *Liberator*
office were the meeting places for the clique. If her control
was not absolute, her power was substantial. It was she, who,
"when the pro slavery flood rises" delighted to marshal the
Boston Clique and to storm the southern bastion "with hearts
of CONTROVERSY!"[20]

First among the major controversies that pitted abolitionist
against abolitionist was the clerical issue raised in 1837, which
began the battle between conservative abolitionists who would
limit their crusade to slavery alone and radical millennialists
who would embrace antislavery in universal reform. When
orthodox ministers attacked Garrison not only for his perfectionism but for his assertion that the churches sustained slavery, he retorted with further accusations. Chapman, too,
immediately joined the fray. The clergy, she thought, were
standpatters, stuffily orthodox, and antireform. They hindered all good causes. In particular, she complained in the
Fourth Annual Report of the Boston Female Anti-Slavery
Society, women were hindered from acting in the cause by

[19] According to Child, Maria Child to Ellis G. Loring, December 5, 1838,
C-NYPL, she had recently seen a letter written by George Bancroft to Mrs.
Jonathan Dwight in which he made the remark about the Boston Clique;
Chapman to Mary Estlin, March 8, 1858, E-BPL.
[20] Edmund Quincy to Caroline Weston, November 13, 1844, J-MHS;
Edmund Quincy to Richard D. Webb, January 29, 1843, Q-MHS; Chapman
to David L. Child, December 29, 1842, C-BPL.

their ministers.[21] By their actions, the clerical abolitionists caused "doubt & perplexity in the abolition publick mind." They had rent the antislavery ranks asunder. The only solution was to rout the clerics. "My prayer has ever been," she wrote Elizur Wright, though not without second thoughts, "that the ecclesiastical despotism of this land be abolished at the same stroke that freed the slave & I see now, that without the abolition of the former the latter cannot be."[22]

Within the year, although the underlying issue was still the divergence between universal reform and more narrowly defined antislavery, the immediate focus shifted from the clerical issue to the woman question when, at the New England Anti-Slavery Convention, the ladies were excluded from membership. Then Henry Stanton and Amos Phelps, both agents of the American Anti-Slavery Society, joined the earlier leaders of the clerical appeal, Charles Torrey and Alanson St. Clair, who opposed mixing women's rights with antislavery. What had begun in 1837 as a clerical appeal against antislavery radicalism became, by 1839, a major test between conservative and radical factions of the antislavery movement. Peering from the citadel of Boston, Garrisonians were sure that they were the intended victims of concerted clerical orthodoxy. Privately Chapman suspected more tawdry motives in the clerical subversion. "There are now," she wrote to Sarah Grimké and Angelina Weld, "more deadly foes to freedom than the slave-holder in the field—the canting & hypocritical, calling themselves abolitionists, prating of the 'poor slave' to secure a miserable salary."[23]

[21]Boston Female Anti-Slavery Society, *Fourth Annual Report* (Boston: Isaac Knapp, 1837), 71-72.
[22] Chapman to Jane and William Smeal, December 1, 1837, SS-SC; Chapman to Elizur Wright, [September 1837], W-BPL.
[23]Much of this analysis Chapman developed in her *Right and Wrong in Massachusetts* (Boston: Henry L. Devereux, 1840); see particularly 52 and 93-126. See also her letters to Abby Kelley, March 14, 1839, F-AAS; to Gerrit Smith, March 27, 1839, S-SU; and to Deborah Weston, April 4, 1839, W-BPL. The quotation is from her letter to Sarah Grimké and Angelina Grimké Weld, May 15, 1839, W-BPL.

Thus aroused, Chapman and her fellow Garrisonians fought fire with fire; it was sometimes dirty business. By dubious and devious means, she obtained private letters written by Charles Torrey attacking Garrison and published them in *Right and Wrong,* the annual report of the Boston Female Anti-Slavery Society. When the indignant Torrey protested, Chapman wrote him that "such letters have a far other character than that of private correspondence. Taken in connection with their author's course towards the anti-slavery public, they become a public concern. To suppress them is in my estimation wrong:— to make them public, right and duty to the anti-slavery cause."[24]

⛓⛓⛓

Chapman's first base and her training ground in factional controversy was the Boston Female Anti-Slavery Society, whose annual reports she had written since 1836. Entitled *Right and Wrong in Boston, in Massachusetts, in the Anti-Slavery Societies*—wherever Chapman thought that the right needed encouragement and the wrong chastisement—they were more than the annual reports of the society, more than critiques of the current state of the movement; they were partisan Garrisonian propaganda against both slavery and antislavery heresy. All the reports issued between 1836 and 1844, except probably only those for 1839, 1842, and 1843, were such Chapman missives. Here more consistently than anywhere else she displayed the power of her pen.

Not surprisingly, she also occupied a commanding position when the society itself was rent by factionalism. Mirroring the disputes which disrupted the entire antislavery movement, the women argued the clerical issue. The conservative faction was led by Mary Parker; the Garrisonian by Chapman. The storm broke over the 1837 annual report, when Chapman

[24]Chapman to Charles T. Torrey, November 22, 1839, in the *Liberator,* November 29, 1839.

rejected a suggestion that it be edited to reflect the society's conservative position more accurately. Either she would write it as she wished, she asserted, or she would not write it at all. To edit was to tamper; to tamper was to impugn her reputation. Neither side would give in, and backstairs maneuvering became intense. At a special meeting, Chapman hotly defended the report. Pleading ignorance "of the customs of societies," she defended her course: "I only know that, as I respect the freedom of the society I mean also to preserve my own untrammelled." The report was finally accepted by a two to one vote, but, in the process, the lines had been drawn. "Miss Parker & friends," Chapman wrote in clear recognition of what was happening, "thought Mrs Chapman & friends obstinate—Mrs C & friends thought Miss P & friends wanting in their usual integrity."[25]

Matters had not changed much when, in 1839, the society again quarrelled over the proper relationship of the state to national societies, over competing local antislavery publications, and over the use of inflammatory speakers. Chapman once again led the Garrisonians to the attack. The result was more hard feeling. "I learn," Chapman wrote Abby Kelley, "that many of the board say that as 'doubt exists whether or no Mrs Chapman has ever been *converted,* it may be also doubted whether any thing she can possibly do in the Society will be blessed to the cause.' If the slaves condition be the *tragedy* of human life, surely these things are the *farce.*"[26]

The farce continued through the winter and into the spring of 1840. Finally, at an April meeting, Catherine Sullivan moved that the Boston Female Anti-Slavery Society be dissolved. A roll-call vote followed, and President Mary Parker ruled that the society was dissolved.[27]

[25]Maria Weston Chapman, [Summary of Board and Full Meetings of the Boston Female Anti-Slavery Society, 1837], ms., W-BPL.

[26]Chapman to [Abby Kelley], March 14, 1839, F-AAS.

[27]The details of the struggle for control of the Boston Female Anti-Slavery Society are from several sources: the *Liberator,* 1838–1840 passim; the *Massachusetts Abolitionist,* 1839–1840 passim; scattered correspondence in W-BPL

Refusing to recognize the dissolution of so useful a society, Maria Chapman called for a meeting to elect new officers. On April 11, Maria Child presided over a rump session where new officers were elected and action taken to continue the society under the old name. Here Chapman was at her most effective. Working behind the scenes, marshaling her forces around her, she had had the wit to hold her ground, to move into the vacuum created by the opposition, to out-maneuver them simply by asserting that the rump was no rump and by acting on the assertion so forcefully that others believed it. Thus she captured control of the Boston Female Anti-Slavery Society for the Garrisonians by de facto, if not parliamentary, victory and successfully excluded from power the Parker faction. For a few years more, the Boston Female Anti-Slavery Society and its annual reports proved a most useful vehicle for the Chapman, old organization point of view. More important, it shaped the style of Chapman's subsequent career.

Long before this victory Chapman had come to control the society's major source of income and its major contribution to antislavery work, the Anti-Slavery Fair.[28] Launched in 1834 by a small group of Boston ladies under Maria Child's leadership, it was a bazaar where one might buy everything from apples and free-labor sugar to objets d'art and gift books, hear antislavery lectures, and, on occasion, see uplifting dioramas. In its second year, desperate for a salesroom in antiabolitionist Boston, the fair was held in the house of the elder Chapmans and thereafter Maria managed the whole show. She extended its scope by soliciting contributions from antislavery advocates in England and Ireland, sending boxes

---

and G-BPL; and in particular from Chapman's *Right and Wrong in the Anti-Slavery Societies,* which appeared as a *Liberator* Extra [1840] and was published as the *Seventh Annual Report* of the society (1840).

[28]The details of the Anti-Slavery bazaar are derived principally from two sources: the *Liberator,* passim; and letters in W-, Ch-, E-, G-, and M-BPL. See also the "Report of the Twenty-Second National Anti-Slavery Bazaar," the *Liberator,* January 25, 1856.

of French items when she was living abroad, and even then leaving the bazaar's management in the safe hands of her sister Anne Weston.

The fair served the cause well. During the 1840s and 1850s it netted an average of $4,000 per year—money which went principally to support the *National Anti-Slavery Standard.* It was a major money-raiser. Yet despite its organizational connections, Chapman viewed the bazaar as her own, much as she had the Boston Female Anti-Slavery Society and its reports. As long as she thought it useful, she continued it; but when, in 1858, she thought that other means would raise more money, she unhesitatingly abandoned it with little thought for any society's assent. In its place, she substituted the Subscription Anniversary. With a vision worthy of Madison Avenue, she projected the new money-raising venture—a moral uplift soirée, complete with musicale, speeches, tea and cookies, and conversation to draw the wealthy and relieve them of large sums of money for the cause. Men, she noticed, had been of little use in running the fair; a socially chic soirée would utilize their resources. "We will ... bend on a *50-salon-power,* in the largest hall we can find, & receive their subscriptions, & give them a cup of tea, & take the opportunity to interchange information & counsel with them.... It will be a great day & new era...."[29]

Assuming that she had the support of the mainstays of the fair—the women of the fair committee and those from outlying antislavery societies who had participated in it—Chapman set to work. All, so she said, encouraged and supported her plan for a Subscription Anniversary.[30] But few, even among the Boston Clique, remembered being consulted. She "has some great plan," Samuel May, Jr., wrote, "to super-

[29]For Chapman's plans for the Subscription Anniversary, see her letters to Elizabeth P. Nichols, January 2, [1858, misdated 1860], September 20, [1858], G-BPL. The quotation is from her letter to Mary Estlin, March 8, 1858, E-BPL.

[30]Chapman to Mary Estlin, March 8, 1858, E-BPL.

cede, & wholly eclipse, the Bazaar. But what it is she does not tell us,—or, gives such indistinct and uncertain glimpses, as are of little satisfaction." Irish friends reported that Chapman simply presented the anniversary plan as a fait accompli. "She did not *suggest* the matter," wrote Eliza Wigham from Dublin in some pique, "she *announced* it & so widely that we had no other idea left than to make up our minds & at once look about for the best plan of modifying our operations [for supporting the old Fair] to suit the new order of things."[31]

In Boston, Samuel May, Jr., was concerned about Chapman's arbitrary action because the other women involved—his wife included—had little voice in the decision. "I feel that it would be wrong for the rest of us to abandon it," he wrote to Richard Webb in Dublin, "*simply because* Mrs. Chapman can do no more for it...." "She should have remembered," May continued in a stinging rebuke to Chapman and her course, "that there were some 30 other ladies, not one of whom perhaps saw the matter as she did—certainly the vast majority of whom did not—and it was due to them ... to have had the whole case fully & fairly laid before them...."[32]

The episode illustrated Chapman's impatience with customary female roles. The idea of soirées she doubtless had brought back from England where they were frequently tendered antislavery visitors. In them Chapman saw a vehicle better adapted to her ends. In England, however, soirées had been run by the men; in America fairs were run by women. In thus adapting the soirée to the American antislavery movement, Chapman effectively had cut out from participation the more conventional women like Mrs. May and Eliza Wigham. That she should have been unmoved by their protests was natural, for she identified herself with leading women litterateurs like Eliza Follen, Harriet Martineau, and Harriet Beecher Stowe, not with those whose efforts centered in tatting

[31]Samuel May, Jr., to Richard D. Webb, March 30, 1858, M-BPL; Eliza Wigham to Samuel May, Jr., April 16, 1858, M-BPL.
[32]Samuel May, Jr., to Richard D. Webb, March 30, 1858, M-BPL.

for bazaars. Chapman demanded stronger, more spectacular action.

Widespread uneasiness about Chapman's lady-bountiful authoritarianism was countered by her supreme self-assurance, which justified it as necessary.[33] Gaining in April 1858, just three months after she launched her project, the fair committee's reluctant agreement that she try her new plan, she pulled it off with aplomb. "Boston's best people did appear," she wrote, "in great numbers, (as moralists count numbers) & paid their sixty, fifty, 20—10—5 dollars each in the prettiest way in the world." "I must say," she said, looking back on it a year later, "it was nothing less than an inspiration of the most fortunate kind, that put a stop to the *Fair,* & substituted the *Anniversary.* Already we are telling very strongly in a social as well as in a pecuniary capacity."[34]

It was hard to swallow, but even Samuel May had to admit that the net of $5,700 was $1,500 more than he could remember from any of the earlier fairs. Maria Chapman had racked up another "splendid success" as she, herself, put it.[35]

⛓⛓⛓

Sure of what constituted antislavery truth, sure of what was best to maintain antislavery organization, Chapman was no less sure of what constituted abolition's correct relationship to other reform, to politics, and to the world at large. No sooner, in fact, had she become an antislavery crusader than she became a feminist. Rejecting all assumptions that antislavery women should play subordinate roles, she insisted that her own vigorous involvement was perfectly ladylike. When

[33]Chapman and her sisters admitted the authoritarian nature of the move in a conversation with May, which he reported to Webb in his letter of June 6, 1858, M-BPL.

[34]Chapman to J. Miller McKim, January 29, 185[9], M-CoU; Chapman to Mary Estlin, January 4, [1860], E-BPL.

[35]Samuel May, Jr., to Richard D. Webb, February 20, 1859, M-BPL; Chapman to J. Miller McKim, January 29, 185[9], M-CoU.

arguments against equal rights for women were adduced from the Bible, Chapman answered that it had been distorted by "commentators and translators and partial reasoners." "Men," she quipped, "always solve the problem of woman's deficiency by attributing it to natural inferiority."[36] Her dominant role belied both inferiority and deficiency, and she demanded full membership rights for women in the American Anti-Slavery Society.[37] She condemned the traditional female, that victim of "domestic tyranny," incapable of doing the necessary work of reform, unable to exert herself for others. Chapman's argument against the over-refinement of the Victorian parlor was accompanied by denunciation of the women who, in accepting a place in it, became mere toys to "gratify the perverted tastes" of men. Independent women who "would possess the love of good men, or be mothers of a noble race," she argued, must cast aside such "harem notions" and exercise "self-denial and exertion for the good of others."[38]

After Henry's death in 1842, Maria talked less and less about the equality of both sexes standing together against evil and more and more about the superiority of women reformers. Frequently viewing the antislavery cause as her own bailiwick, she never questioned her competence to run it. "When one is perfectly right," she wrote David Child just a year after Henry's death, "one neither asks nor needs sympathy." And, nearly twenty years later, she consoled reformer Caroline Dall, who had been charged with having a superior air, that "there is no one who has been obliged to wrestle & prevail who has not been accused of it, as if it were a crime, instead of being, as it is, a momentary necessity upon

---

[36]Maria Weston Chapman and M. Ammidon, "Address of the Boston Female Anti-Slavery Society to the Women of Massachusetts," *Liberator*, August 13, 1836; this address was part of Boston Female Anti-Slavery Society, *Third Annual Report* (Boston: The Society, 1836), in which see particularly 27–28. Boston Female Anti-Slavery Society, *Fourth Annual Report*, 75–76. Chapman to Mary Estlin, December 12, [1852], E-BPL.

[37]Chapman to [?], draft, [1839], Ch-BPL.

[38]Boston Female Anti-Slavery Society, *Third Annual Report*, 77.

those who are born to set right the time that's out of Joint." Chapman had come, indeed, to assume not the equality but the superiority of women. Convinced that men accepted equal rights for women "whenever, in situations of peril and difficulty, they have looked up for aid to women superior to themselves in ability," observing at the same time that men have generally preferred to marry inferior women, she finally decided that marriage was, for a woman of talent, an unfortunate choice.[39]

Henry's untimely death, Maria's inherent snobbery, and the bitterness engendered by organizational infighting pressed Mrs. Chapman into the manner which grated on many of her colleagues. Ever ready to give pompous, overbearing, and self-assertive instructions, she chastised and advised the Childs, Henry Highland Garnet, Frederick Douglass, Wendell Phillips, and many lesser antislavery luminaries as well. Nor is there evidence—except self-righteous pique that anyone could doubt her infallibility—that Maria recognized the growing resentment which her directives produced.

Yet great as the impact of Henry's death was on Mrs. Chapman, one cannot attribute to it her involvement in antislavery work, for she had become an activist by 1835. And after Henry's death, she did not simply bury despair in frenetic activity, but acted rather to fulfill demands which her own conviction of superiority and her sense of mission had long since placed upon her. As for being a woman, she was inferior to no one—certainly not to men collectively. When the right of women to participate in the American Anti-Slavery Society's activities was raised, Chapman expressed her hope that "the party uttering [such sentiments would] be called to order [,] this being not a question of *Woman's* rights ... but *Members*

---

[39]Chapman to David Lee Child, October 12, 1843, C-BPL; Chapman to Caroline H. Dall, June 9, 1860, C. H. Dall Papers, Massachusetts Historical Society; Chapman to William L. Garrison, April 15, 1849, in *Liberator*, May 18, 1849; Harriet Martineau, *Autobiography with Memorials by Maria Weston Chapman* (London: Smith, Elder & Co., 1877), I, 11-29.

rights–*persons* rights."[40] To have her rights as a human being denied her because she was a woman was, in all cases, intolerable.

Yet even for Chapman, the vehement assaults on the civil liberties of abolitionists and feminists brought anguish and personal crisis. After her one major speaking effort at the 1838 convention of Antislavery Women in Philadelphia's Pennsylvania Hall, the building was mobbed and burned to the ground as its occupants feared for their lives. On her return journey to Boston, Chapman broke down and was hospitalized in Stonington, Connecticut, seemingly hopelessly insane.[41] She had been burdened for months with the exhausting demands of fund-raising and related antislavery labor, and was distraught both over Henry's increasingly debilitating tuberculosis and over the death of his sister, a staunch supporter in their antislavery efforts. Yet such was her character that not only did she quickly recover, but she went on to become rigid and unyielding, lest in bending to pressures and tensions she give way again.

A leader in the formation of the Non-Resistance Society in 1839, which rejected all use of force and, by extension, all human government, Chapman was by 1840 thoroughly committed on those issues that were central to the split that rent the antislavery movement in that year.[42] With vigor, delight, and abandon she hurled herself into the debate. If, she argued, one was expected to take the "highest ground" and come out of proslavery churches, then, surely, one should take the "highest political ground" and disavow political involvement. That meant, she explained in a *Liberator* editorial

[40]Chapman to [?], draft, [1839], W-BPL.

[41]On Chapman's severe illness, see the comments of Garrison and Maria Child in William L. Garrison to George W. Benson, May 25, 1838, G-BPL; Maria Child to Louisa Loring, June 3, 1838, L-SL.

[42]Chapman to Elizabeth Pease, March 13, 1843, G-BPL; the quotation is from Chapman's article explaining the nonparticipation stand which appeared in the *Non-Resistant,* April 20, 1839.

in 1843, annulling the proslavery United States Constitution, refusing to take any part in government with slaveholders, and avoiding all political action. The "snakes"—men like Joshua Leavitt, Amos Phelps, and Lewis and Arthur Tappan—who had formed the new organization, the American and Foreign Anti-Slavery Society, should be ignored when they espoused not only political involvement but also an antislavery third party.[43]

Girded in righteousness and breathing fire, Chapman went to work on the Garrison-hating Liberty party men. James Birney, she felt, was impossible. He had "stabbed at the vitality and integrity of the cause to procure a nomination, [and] offered up the American [Anti-Slavery] Society as a propitiation to public sentiment. . . ." Henry Stanton, an erstwhile fellow-laborer, had turned "impudent as a highwayman's horse"; and Joshua Leavitt, a leader in third-party politics, Chapman dismissed as a "coat shuffling impudent" man.[44]

Not only were third-party men antislavery heretics, they were pawns of the major parties as well. Dupes, fools, and dangerous men, it was not suprising that they were individually corrupt and collectively endangering the entire cause with moral decay. Beriah Green, Gerrit Smith, George Bradburn, Arnold Buffum, and many more had all been good antislavery men. Now they were being led down the primrose path of political dalliance. Political action could destroy "the last hope of a paramount moral movement, for the salvation of both [the slaves and the slaveholders] from the horrors of civil convulsion & the consequent loss of a half a thousand years of happy & uninterrupted improvement. . . ." It meant civil

---

[43]*Liberator*, September 15, 1843. Chapman called the new organization men "snakes" in her letter to David L. Child, April 14, 1843, C-BPL.

[44]Chapman to Elizabeth Pease, March 16, 1840, G-BPL. Chapman's comments about Birney are in the Boston Female Anti-Slavery Society's *Eighth Annual Report* (Boston: The Society, 1841), 15–17; about Stanton in her letter to Deborah Weston, April 22, [1842?], W-BPL; and about Leavitt in her letter to David L. Child, December 29, 1842, C-BPL.

war with the "consequent wickedness & Barbarism that always follows [even] the most righteous war."[45]

Yet Chapman did not keep the nonresistant, "no human government" faith pristine. Admitting in 1843 that she could imagine an uncontaminated Liberty party, in 1848 she argued that the Free Soil party could prove useful if only it did not win an election. It was office holding, not the political campaign, that corrupted; consequently a party kept out of office and pure in principle could exert a useful "moral effect." "Success," she feared, "would be their moral extinction."[46] Voting, too, could be moral if one scattered one's votes in order to weaken the major parties. And in the early 1850s, she found a politician and office holder, Joshua Giddings of Ohio, who, alone among the antislavery congressmen, she adjudged faithful enough to be thoroughly reliable. By 1857, when the crisis in Kansas and the developing strength of the Republican party made slavery the national issue, Chapman endorsed direct political action and urged sending antislavery agents into the "Black Belt" of New Jersey, southern Pennsylvania, Ohio, and Illinois to counteract that sentiment which had lost John Charles Frémont the election in 1856.[47]

Despite her tactical shifts, not unlike the political maneuvers she disdained as corrupt, Chapman upheld the principle of disunion to the very eve of the Civil War. "If I did not *feel* it to be *right*," she had said of the dissolution of the Union in 1843, "I should *see* it to be *expedient*." It was the logical conclusion to coming out from all association with slaveholders—in churches, in parties, and in government. In 1857,

[45]Chapman to J. Miller McKim, October 22, 1843, M-CoU; Chapman to Abby Kelley, [October ?, 1843], F-AAS. The Commentary on Green, Smith, Bradburn, and Buffum, and the quotation are from her letter to William L. Garrison, August 4, 1843, G-BPL.

[46]Chapman to J. Miller McKim, October 22, 1843, M-CoU; Chapman to Elizabeth Pease, November 29, 1848, G-BPL.

[47]Chapman to John W. Estlin, [December ?, 1852], E-BPL; Chapman to Samuel E. Sewall, August 9, 1857, RS-MHS.

the year she appealed for antislavery agents to create Republican sentiment, she defined their larger goals as "abolition or disunion," and added that "we shall not get either in three years,—but *we shall* get an Anti-Slavery administration, as one of the incidents of the war...." By 1860, disunion seemed inevitable. In February 1861, she anticipated it and cheered it on. Here was the last resolution of antislavery and non-resistance principle, identical with that proposed in 1843—disunion.[48]

For twenty-five years, Maria Weston Chapman was active in the antislavery movement. Then, when the Civil War came, she stepped back and gradually withdrew from active participation. She saw that conditions were changing. War, secession, and the movement toward actual emancipation required new approaches. "I dont doubt many who saw me, young, publishing tracts & circulating petitions," she mused, "would smile to see me, old, firing salutes;—but no matter: New occasions make new duties;—'Time makes ancient good uncouth.'" The old antislavery movement had been a prelude, a means of focusing the slavery issue. Now, with victory imminent, it was time to begin the real work of emancipation. "Despotism," she wrote on the eve of Lincoln's election, "is driven into open day. To meet it, requires devotion, industry, and the sacred fire of a true enthusiasm. It requires energy, co-operation, and the discipline of selfcontrol."[49]

She had made that statement as part of her annual plea

[48]Chapman to [David L. Child, 1843], fragment, C-BPL; Chapman to Samuel E. Sewall, August 9, 1857, RS-MHS; Chapman to Elizabeth P. Nichols, December 10, 1860, G-BPL; Chapman to Mary Estlin, February 11, 1861, E-BPL.

[49]Chapman to Edward A. Atkinson, April 15, [1862], A-MHS; Chapman in the call for the annual Subscription Anniversary, in the *Liberator*, August 10, 1860.

for Subscription Anniversary contributions. But even as she said it she was convinced that the festival had outlived its usefulness. By July 1861, it was clear that contributions from England were falling off, and that the festival could provide only part of the necessary funds. Therefore she urged everyone to give directly to the American Anti-Slavery Society. Yet even that was redundant, for she was now of the opinion that the society lacked a meaningful policy, and that it was no longer useful. In 1862, therefore, Chapman dropped out of festival work and soon thereafter abandoned her efforts for the American Anti-Slavery Society. Most Americans, she observed in the summer of 1861, were now supporters of antislavery, so there was no longer any need for the society. The frantic efforts of Garrison, Parker Pillsbury, Wendell Phillips, and others to keep up enthusiasm seemed rather beside the point, an attestation to the moribund state of the antislavery crusade. So she urged dropping the *National Anti-Slavery Standard*. The now old guard, like Oliver Johnson, found Chapman's course "inexplicable." It was inexplicable because Johnson and others like him could not imagine giving up the *Standard* without implying also the abandonment of the American Anti-Slavery Society, which was exactly what Chapman had in mind. "The time has gone by," she wrote to J. Miller McKim, Philadelphia abolitionist, "when it is of importance that our organization should be held together any longer than it like to hang together...." "All hail," she apostrophized, "thou coming generation, that shall take up the work where our unqualified hands must leave it." That was in the fall of 1861. By May 1863, she was even more insistent that the society should be disbanded. With the Emancipation Proclamation now a fact, the "way to do the remaining work," she admonished, "is not to herd apart from the rest of the world, that has the actual burden on its shoulders."[50]

[50]William L. Garrison to Oliver Johnson, July 3, 1861, G-BPL; Chapman to J. Miller McKim, November 2, [1861], G-BPL; Chapman to Elizabeth Laugel, August 6, 1861, W-BPL; Oliver Johnson to [Samuel] May, [Jr.], Au-

In an apparent about-face, therefore, Chapman urged strong support for the government so that it could fulfill the promise of emancipation. Antislavery leaders should go to Washington to advise the administration. When the war had come, Chapman had counseled wholehearted support, abandoning nonresistance and defense of civil liberties. "The land," she wrote to Garrison, "is now virtually under Martial law, &, indeed since last January; & it is now the only law we *can* ask any thing under. Habeas Corpus, & all manner of civil process are nothing but a hindrance;—freedom of speech not possible;—to carry on successful war. All *we* can say *helps* the government now. It is not free speech but admitted service." Reformers, she urged, must join hands and help the nation through its struggle. Abolitionists, she concluded, must renounce disunion. In 1862, when Lincoln proposed gradual, compensated emancipation, Chapman accepted it as a distinctly forward step: "I feel as if the work was virtually done!—is not this message from the very last & highest quarter, a proof of it?"[51]

The Emancipation Proclamation symbolized the end of slavery, and it marked the effective end of Maria Chapman's involvement in the antislavery crusade. Except for an interest retained in the Massachusetts Anti-Slavery Society, she dropped out of sight. Her work had been to shape the nation's mind, not to assist bondsmen in realizing freedom. The task was now for others to complete that which the antislavery hosts had so well begun. "What the gov't sees the people *ready* for it does, & Thus I think it most advisable to show readiness. Our lectures of 30 years standing do not put the case nearly so squarely & effectually as the rising generation.

gust 27, 1861, J-VHS. Chapman to McKim, November 2, [1861], G-BPL; Chapman to Elizabeth Laugel and Anne Chapman, May 15, 1863, W-BPL.
[51]Chapman to William L. Garrison, [August 1861], G-BPL; Chapman to J. Miller McKim, [September 1861], G-BPL. The quotations are, in order, from Chapman to Garrison, [Fall 1851], G-BPL; Chapman to [John B. Estlin], March 10, 1862, E-BPL.

This is very natural. *We* were trained to a preparatory work, & well we have performed it[,] but that work is no longer needed."[52]

⛓⛓⛓

At one point early in Chapman's antislavery career, the clerical abolitionist Nathaniel Colver is reported to have said that, in old organization circles, "Garrison was entirely ruled" by her.[53] Neither a totally accurate nor adequate summation of Chapman's role, the observation contained a remarkable amount of truth. Abby Kelley, feminist and antislavery lecturer, thought that "so far as I have been able to learn the minds of the abolitionists [,] M. W. Chapman is the person to bear up our banner, boldly and gallantly, and at the same time with all due hum'ty to *all* persons, whatever may have been their different degrees of progress, if they are sound at heart." Chapman was, so Kelley thought, "our Moral Napoleon." And Samuel May, Jr., for all his annoyance with Chapman's handling of the bazaar episode, indicated that she had a breadth of vision and a genuine love for the antislavery cause which transcended petty personal views. She may differ, he wrote to Richard Webb in 1859, but "she will never wrangle." [54]

Still, Chapman's leadership of the Garrisonians and of the Boston Clique did not go unchallenged. She was overbearing and overwhelming. Not only was she always sure she was right, she frequently made her pronunciamentos in an almost unintelligible transcendental language (she considered Emerson her spiritual mentor). Her ideas, said Samuel May, Jr., with some exasperation, were "difficult of reception, & even of comprehension, often, to most of us. . . ." Richard Webb,

[52]Chapman to Elizabeth Laugel, January 17, [1864?], W-BPL.
[53]Deborah Weston to Anne W. Weston, April 16, [1839?], W-BPL.
[54]Abby Kelley to Stephen Foster, March 28, 1843, F-AAS; Samuel May, Jr., to Richard D. Webb, August 7, 1859, M-BPL.

across the Atlantic in Dublin, was also baffled by her muddiness. The problem, thought May, was that Chapman went about "on stilts, in her language," a characteristic which, in fact, defined her entire character.[55]

The fact of the matter seems clear: Chapman was not well beloved by her colleagues. Sydney Gay, who knew some of her sisters, thought she was "ye *Capt.*," "highly cultivated, of high breeding & fine conversational powers," but for all that not "a *personal* favorite." "People," he concluded, "are not at ease in her presence." Oliver Johnson, piqued because she wished him to drop the *Standard,* thought she was imperious, narrow, bigoted, and full of self-love. "If she is tired," he wrote bitterly to Samuel May, Jr., "and wants to withdraw, she need not therefore tear the house down. Why not let others keep the Standard going if they will? And why can she not put in *their* hands the threads of influence which she has so long held, and let them do the best they can?"[56] That Johnson was angry is clear, yet he touched accurately upon Chapman's arbitrariness and abrasiveness. Criticism or no, however, Chapman never lost her sense of command. She held her position until her voluntary retirement during the Civil War, and even in her retirement she played the grande dame, the unhumbled leader.

Much of the explanation of her remarkable leadership lies in the fact that it was geared to a single end. Her technique, whether it was in-fighting, money raising, editorializing, or simply marshaling the troops, all postulated one end: propaganda. The idea was the important thing, and nothing could stand in its way. Chapman never moved from that position, nor did she subordinate it to practical action. The clarity of the idea was etched within the framework of *Right and*

[55]Chapman to Margaret [?], [186-?], H-HLH; Samuel May, Jr., to Richard D. Webb, April 12, 1859, April 15–16, 1860, M-BPL.
[56]Sydney H. Gay to Richard D. Webb, July 19, 1848, G-BPL; Oliver Johnson to [Samuel] May, [Jr.], August 29, 1861, J-VHS. See also Johnson's letter to May, February 11, 1862, J-VHS.

Wrong. Chapman thus produced a total polarization. There were no gray areas, no shadings, no tolerable differences of opinion. All variation from Chapman's concept of the right was heresy or treason. Against such treason and heresy Chapman fought. This was the crux of the clerical issue, the 1840 split, and her authoritarian handling of the Boston Female Anti-Slavery Society and the Anti-Slavery Fair crisis.

It may be argued that with the coming of the Civil War, Chapman actually did change her position. When war came, she dropped the pure antislavery societies to support government as the social agency best suited to fulfill the promise of the old antislavery host. "I do *not* think it best," she maintained in 1863 when she was giving up antislavery work, "to keep a machine grinding, after the time has come that the grist is better ground at social or state-hoppers."[57]

Yet she was as inflexible in her new conviction as in her old and saw in those who would continue the societies the sectarianism she had denounced three decades earlier. Nor did she ever suggest that at any one point in time her position had not been correct. Her grandson, John Jay Chapman, recalled the formidable old woman who "really believed that the memory of the wicked should rot, and that the wicked were—almost everyone in the past, and a good many among the survivors."[58]

Chapman had been a mighty Amazon in the war against slavery. Handsome, forceful, intelligent, paternalistic, a born leader, she never lost her self-assurance. At the end of her active career, she wrote a most revealing note to her daughter. "I Bless my Stars daily & hourly, that the stress of life & death for thirty years under the responsibilities of the cause has not left me either denaturée or deterioreé;—It is not so with the abolitionists generally, I am saddened to ob-

[57]Chapman to J. Miller McKim, [November 1868?], M-CoU; Chapman to Mary Estlin, December 29, 1863, E-BPL.
[58]John Chapman, *Memories and Milestones,* 214–215.

serve...."[59] Until her death in 1885 she recounted to her grandchildren the sagas of "the ins and outs of ancient controversy" in near Homeric style. In them lay the record of her own strength and weakness—her tenacity, her rigidity, her egotism. Her cause had triumphed, yet for thirty years more she savored her victories within the crusade equally with its ultimate success. For all her loyalty to Garrison and despite her centrality in his faction's activities, Chapman is far from most conceptions of the Garrisonians. She and the Boston Clique with whom she worked operated from a position not only of moral superiority but also of social superiority. Radicals they appeared, but by the mid-1840s they had become rigid of thought; they were more concerned with imposing a new orthodoxy than with experimenting. Unlike antislavery lecturers and editors, they were only indirectly involved in agitation and were principally concerned with wielding power within and through reform societies. Chapman's constant suspicion of those who took pay for their antislavery service displayed her conviction that reform should come through the noblesse oblige of those wealthy enough to support themselves. Indeed, Maria Weston Chapman, on whose critical role in Garrisonian abolition her contemporaries broadly agreed, was less a radical egalitarian agitator than a Tory democrat.

[59]Chapman to Anne [Chapman], [186-?], W-BPL.

4

The Kentucky Squire: Cassius Marcellus Clay

At the same time that Maria Chapman emerged as the grande dame of Boston abolitionism, an old-stock Southern gentleman was rising to dominate the Kentucky antislavery movement. Cassius Marcellus Clay, like the more famous James G. Birney, was to the Kentucky manor born. Like Birney, he sought to turn state and national political institutions to the work of emancipation. But the contrasts between these men were greater than their similarities. Birney, won to immediatism by the evangelism of Theodore Weld, freed his slaves, established an antislavery paper, and was soon driven from his native state by mobs and forced to reestablish his press across the river in Ohio. When he turned to politics, it was to the highly idealistic Liberty party, whose presidential candidate he was in 1840 and 1844. Clay continued to live at White Hall, his family seat near Lexington, throughout his antislavery career. When his press was mobbed, he had his antislavery paper printed in Ohio but continued to edit it in Kentucky. Passive to the pleas of religious evangelism and moral reform, he came to antislavery by way of economic arguments. Slavery, he thought, stifled Kentucky's agriculture, hampered its industry, and discouraged its white laboring class. His politics were equally removed from idealized abstraction, and, though he tried to build an emancipation party in the state, he was increasingly concerned with building for himself a political base from which to rise in national politics.

If the struggle to end slavery was the central theme of Cassius Clay's career, it was confounded by paradox, inner contradiction, and expediency. Unlike the Garrisonians and their patrician standard-bearer, Maria Chapman, he espoused a program which was flexible and often reflected self-interest and racism. His principles varied with the occasion. Yet his opposition to slavery remained firm. To it he sacrificed social and political popularity and economic security. Never did he flee the actuality of slavery in the slave state which was his home. He stayed and fought.

Clay's background equipped him to play an aristocratic role. His father, Green Clay, whose life set a challenging model Cassius never could quite meet, had left Virginia in his youth and moved to the Kentucky frontier. There he made his fortune mainly in land speculation and built the imposing White Hall. His economic success won him the quick rise in status that Southern frontier culture offered, and accompanying political prestige. Green Clay served in the Virginia legislature and was a member of the ratifying convention for the new federal Constitution. Later, when Kentucky became a separate state, he served in its constitutional convention and in both houses of its legislature. During the War of 1812, he was a general of volunteer troops. When he died in 1828, he left Cassius, born in 1810, the youngest of five children and three brothers, the 2,000-acre White Hall estate, entailed with seventeen slaves, and one-sixth of his total land claims south of the Tennessee River, amounting to some 40,000 acres, also in trust. Cassius remembered his father as "a man of fortune" and "a long head," foresighted and shrewd, and also as a man stern and unbending toward his children.[1]

Whether as part of his shrewdness or his sternness, Green Clay saw that Cassius was educated well beyond the nine months of schooling that had comprised his own formal tutelage. So he was sent first to the common schools, then to a private tutoring school, subsequently to the Jesuit college in Bardstown, on to Transylvania University, and finally to Yale. The trip to New Haven in 1831 taught Cassius the value of his family's social and political connections. He stopped in the capital to greet President Andrew Jackson and dine with Martin Van Buren. His stay in New York was eased by a letter of introduction to the president of Columbia College. Even the Brahmin Edmund Quincy readily conceded in later years that Cassius Clay was indeed a gentleman.[2]

That he was so much the gentleman served to separate him from the reformers with whom he was often associated. He enjoyed wine and never became a temperance advocate. He opposed women's rights and deplored women's suffrage. Frequently involved in duels and brawls, he was no supporter of the Peace Society or the Non-Resistance movement. He never even opposed slavery on absolute moral grounds, though he did, on occasion, damn the institution as *"an evil morally, economically, physically, intellectually, socially, religiously, politically...."* Claiming late in life that he was converted to antislavery by Garrison, he did urge Christians, especially the clergy, to stand strong against the peculiar institution, but he was no moral reformer. Well after his exposure to the

---

[1] Cassius M. Clay, *The Life of Cassius Marcellus Clay. Memoirs, Writings, and Speeches* ... (Cincinnati: J. Fletcher Brennan & Co., 1886), 25–26. A second volume was indicated in the extended title, but never appeared. The standard modern biography of Clay is David L. Smiley, *Lion of White Hall: The Life of Cassius M. Clay* (Madison: University of Wisconsin Press, 1962).

[2] Clay to Brutus J. Clay, March 27, 1831, CP-LC; Edmund Quincy to Clay, May 28, 1860, C-LMU.

Garrisonian argument, he told the Kentucky legislature in 1841, "I am no reformer of governments. I leave slavery where I found it; 'tis not a matter of conscience with me; I press it not upon the consciences of others. . . ."[3]

The truth of the matter was that Clay's principal interest was the economic growth of his native state. Undoubtedly he was impressed by hearing Garrison at Yale, but he was more impressed by the industry and prosperity of the North. Like his cousin Henry Clay, Cassius was a Whig and wanted to build the country with internal improvements and manufacturing establishments. With many other Southerners, he shared a concern about soil exhaustion, which the one-crop plantation system induced. Economic diversification and prosperity, which the Northern union of agriculture and industry, of town and farm embraced, was his goal for Kentucky.[4]

It was to save his state, not to purge his soul of sin or to recognize his common humanity with the slave, that Clay became an antislavery man. Slavery, he preached in 1841, was "the clog which has staid the march of [Virginia's] people, the incubus which has weighed down her enterprize, strangled her commerce, kept sealed her exhaustless fountains of mineral wealth, and paralyzed her arts, manufactures and improvement. . . ." "This," he concluded emphatically, "is the cancer which has corroded her revenues, laid waste her lowlands, banished her citizens, and swallowed up her productions." He was determined that it should not happen to Kentucky. Through the years he hammered unremittingly at the same theme. Slavery, he argued in 1845, had blocked the development of common schools in the state. It had also,

[3]Clay's lack of reform enthusiasm is illustrated in his *Life*, 60, 69, 95–96, and in his *The Writings of Cassius Marcellus Clay: Including Speeches and Addresses*, ed. Horace Greeley (New York: Harper & Brothers, 1848), 32, 256, 266–267. On the value of the conversion by Garrison, see Smiley, *Lion of White Hall*, 238–239. On Christianity and slavery, see the *True American*, December 9, 1845, in Clay, *Writings*, 358–360; *Anti-Slavery Bugle*, December 9, 1854. The quotations are in *Free American*, March 4, 1841, and the *National Anti-Slavery Standard*, August 12, 1841, respectively.
[4]Smiley, *Lion of White Hall*, 21–24, 29–30.

he added in 1856, channeled all resources in the South to cotton growing and foreign trade rather than to "domestic industry, ... home manufactures, home labor, and a home market for ourselves."[5]

All of these things ultimately sapped the well-being of Kentucky's white laborers. Slavery blighted the cooperation between capital and labor requisite to a factory system and in so doing deprived labor of the wages which Whiggish capitalism would presumably ensure. Indeed Clay, in a vision suggesting a paranoid style, saw a collusion between Northern capital and Southern slaveholders to chain his section exclusively to agriculture and slavery while the North flourished amid factories and free labor. The economics of slavery were thus entangled in a class issue. Clay concluded that when Daniel Webster urged maintenance of the status quo, he spoke to and in the interests of slaveholders, rich clerics, and Northern millionaires. Against these, Clay upheld the Jeffersonian dream of a republic of yeoman farmers fortified by small-scale entrepreneurs. The best interests of the country and freedom, he argued, were secured by a large "middle class of small landholders" rather than by the oligarchies of economic domination, North or South. Unless this class was preserved and strengthened, "the great non-slaveholding masses of the whole Union" would become pawns in a game played by the Southern aristocracy and Northern cotton merchants.[6]

[5]*Free American,* March 11, 1841; Clay, "To the People of Kentucky," January 1845, in *Liberator,* February 21, 1845; Clay, *Speech of C. M. Clay Before the Young Men's Republican Central Union of New York ... October 24th, 1856,* quoted in Smiley, *Lion of White Hall,* 161.

[6]For Clay's economic views, see Clay, *Writings,* 268–269, and 368–369, 452, 348–352, and 357, for *True American* citations to issues of December 13, 1845, May 13, 1846, November 18, 1845, and December 2, 1845, respectively. The quotations are from Clay to Daniel Webster, April 3, 1850, in Clay, *Life,* 202; and Clay to J. Maybury et al., n.d., in *Anti-Slavery Bugle,* July 5, 1851.

Clay, simply by his location and lack of tight identification with Northern abolitionists, may well fall outside the sociopsychological interpretation of the slave power conspiracy which David Davis explores in his *The Slave Power*

The implications of this game for Kentucky were clear. As long as the slave system persisted, fastened on the state by economic conspiracy, it would undercut free labor economically and subvert the dignity of labor psychologically. Idleness had become and would remain the most exalted value among white men. Finding no labor to employ in its factories because of this complex, capital would leave the state. And as there was less employment for free labor, more nonslaveholding whites would emigrate until public education collapsed altogether and the tax base disappeared. It was truly a vicious circle which Clay perceived as the 100,000 persons connected with slaveholding increasingly wiped out the interests and rights of the 700,000 whites of Kentucky who were not. The white majority was to be sacrificed for some 200,000 slaves.[7]

Clay's stay in New Haven and his admiration for things Northern, principally economic growth, expanding cities, burgeoning factories, and general prosperity, only made him a more intense Southerner. Whether drawn by sectional loyalty or by his inheritance, he returned to Kentucky as soon as he was graduated from Yale in 1833, read law in a Lexington law office, and married the town belle, Mary Jane Warfield, after a comic-opera near duel with one of her rejected suitors.[8] In 1835, when he was just twenty-five, he was elected to the state legislature.

He immediately undertook to champion the interests of the nonslaveholders, which were neglected by the dominant slavocracy. From 1835 to 1840, he fought for free common schools. He not only sought state-supported internal improvements but challenged out-of-state attempts to control the economic growth of Kentucky. Then, in 1841, he broached

---

Conspiracy and the Paranoid Style (Baton Rouge: Louisiana State University Press, 1969).

[7] Clay, "Speech at Lexington, August 1, 1851," CP-LC.

[8] The story is in Smiley, *Lion of White Hall,* 31–33.

the subject of slavery directly in a vigorous argument against repeal of an 1833 law barring the importation of slaves into the state. The move to repeal, he charged, was a slaveholders' conspiracy to increase their economic power and to control the state.

This argument before the general assembly heralded the formal beginning of Clay's antislavery career as it also signaled the end of his professional political career. In his reelection campaign in 1841, he defended his opposition to reopening the slave import trade in Kentucky by a disingenuous claim that he was actually trying to sustain locally high slave prices from the depreciation that an influx of cheaper slaves would bring. Poor antislavery, it was also feeble politics, and Clay was defeated by a militant proslavery opponent. His personal disappointment spurred him on to new charges. He predicted ominously that importation of slaves would lead to a "flood of southern blacks . . . desolating our State," and, ultimately, to slave insurrection and the end of white supremacy.[9]

The tone of Clay's antislavery message was clearly not egalitarian. He shared Southern fears that blacks in large numbers constituted a real danger to Caucasian racial purity although he differed in considering slaves more dangerous than free Negroes. Observing an increase in the number of mulattoes in the state, he exaggerated it in his defense of the institutions of marriage, the family, and the home and in his appeals to preserve the purity of "Saxon blood." In case his position was still unclear, he explicitly denied that he was an abolitionist "in the sense in which the enemies of all moral progress would have you believe," and added

[9]Clay's fight against repeal of the 1833 law is in ibid., 43–54. See also Lowell H. Harrison, "The Anti-Slavery Career of Cassius M. Clay," *Register of the Kentucky Historical Society* 59 (1961): 295–317, for a good summary of this issue, as well as other facets of his career. For the 1841 speech, see *National Anti-Slavery Standard,* August 12, 1841. Also see Smiley, *Lion of White Hall,* 56, on an 1843 speech on the same issue. The quotation is in Clay's Speech to the Citizens of the 8th Congressional District, December 20, 1843, in *Liberator,* February 2, 1844.

that he certainly would not "sanction insurrection and massacre." For that, he declared, his "wife, children, mother, brothers and sisters, and relations and friends, [were] all hostages of [his] sincerity." He spelled it out clearly in his White Sulphur Springs address in 1843, and reiterated it again and again. In 1855, he still placed race loyalty first as he wrote the antislavery Kentucky evangelist John G. Fee: "With regard to servile insurrection I should certainly not desert my own blood for any other—where the destruction of one or the other race seems necessary."[10] It was not so much his choosing sides in a race war as his sharing Southern fears about such a phenomenon which set him apart from his Northern antislavery counterparts.

His close ties with the culture of his section shaped the entire tenor of his thought and the pattern of his life. He was a Kentuckian and a member of the prominent Clay family who expected social position and political influence. Yet the course he pursued after 1840 brought him neither: he was excluded from polite society, and he never gained the political power he so desperately wanted.

Although Clay had responded sympathetically to the formation of the Liberty party, which, he thought, embraced "a large portion of the virtue, intelligence and legal knowledge, [as well as] the Christianity and patriotism of the North," he remained a Whig. In 1844 he stumped the North for cousin Henry, trying to draw away from Birney a part of the Liberty party vote. But his efforts to make the slaveholding Henry Clay palatable to abolitionists ran the danger of overturning the Whig base elsewhere. Henry chastised Cassius for his overly explicit antislavery appeals to Northern audiences, calling them misleading and harmful. Though the

[10]*True American,* June 17, 1845, in Clay, *Writings,* 238; *Liberator,* May 5, 1843; *National Anti-Slavery Standard,* June 8, 1843. Quotations are in Cassius M. Clay, *Speech . . . Against the Annexation of Texas . . . in a Mass Meeting of Citizens of the Eighth Congressional District, at the White Sulphur Springs . . . December 30, 1843* (Lexington: Printed at the Observer and Reporter Office, 1844), 6; Clay to John G. Fee, December 18, 1855, MS-BCL.

reprimand stung, Cassius remained a Whig until the end of
the decade, on the one hand dandling the Liberty party, on
the other stumping loyally for slaveholding Whig candidates,
including Zachary Taylor in 1848.[11] He was not yet prepared
to yield his Clay political heritage.

ꙮ

If Clay's persistent Whiggery gave him an aura of consistency,
it scarcely veiled the contradictions that marked his public
career. Nowhere were the internal conflicts more evident than
in his much touted manumission of his slaves in 1844. The
action delighted the abolitionists, who praised Clay's dedication and courage, only to be disillusioned when they discovered that he still retained slaves. His original decision to manumit seems to have been triggered less by principle than by
the alleged murder of his infant son and the attempted murder
of another by one of his slaves. Shortly after this event, at
any rate, Clay did free the slaves he personally owned. He
did not, however, free the alleged murderer but sold her,
as well as her brother, mother, and sister. They, it developed,
were among the slaves left him in trust by his father, whom,
he argued, he could not manumit because they actually
belonged to his children. Clay's claim to have been a non-
slaveholder after 1844 was, therefore, open to legitimate question, for the rest of the entailed slaves were never freed until
the Civil War brought emancipation. In later years, when
the antislavery forces were less sanguine about Clay than they
had been in 1844, they never let the matter drop. John Fee

[11]The quotation is from Clay, *Speech Against the Annexation,* in *Liberator,*
February 2, 1844. Smiley, *Lion of White Hall,* 66; Harrison, "Anti-Slavery
Career of Cassius M. Clay," 300–301. See also on Clay's support of Henry
his letter to W. I. McKinney, March 20, 1844, in *National Anti-Slavery Standard,*
April 4, 1844, published also as *A Letter of Cassius M. Clay . . . to the Mayor
of Dayton* ([Utica]: Jackson & Chaplin, [1844]). Also Clay to Horace Greeley,
January 25, 1845, F-NYPL; Clay to [Salmon P. Chase], March 20, 1846.
C-HSP; Clay to [William H. Seward], December 22, 1848, S-UR, for his
Whig loyalty.

referred to the status of those slaves in 1855; and six years later the *Anti-Slavery Bugle* underscored the fact that Clay had enjoyed the use of the entailed slaves over the years.[12]

Before the ugly truth did out and while Clay still basked in the sun of abolitionist praise, he further raised his standing among them by establishing an antislavery newspaper in Kentucky. Its existence rather than its originality thrilled them, since the *True American* was not remarkable for content. Its fame rested on the drama surrounding its publication. Like Birney's *Philanthropist* and Elijah Lovejoy's *Alton Observer,* the *True American* was immortalized by the violent opposition it engendered. The issue of August 12, 1845, carried an article written by a South Carolina slaveholder arguing that free Negroes ought to be granted political equality at once in preparation for the day when slavery, manifestly unprofitable, would be abolished. Clay, in bed with typhoid fever, denied responsibility for the article, claimed that he had not even read it, and said that an assistant had mistakenly set it as the lead article. But Clay could not claim similar innocence for his own editorial, which appeared in the same issue, discoursing on slavery and the American Revolution. It was typically vague, florid, and flamboyant in style, ending with a stirring peroration: "But remember you who dwell in marble palaces, that there are strong arms and fiery hearts and iron spikes in the streets, and panes of glass only between them and the silver plate on the board, and the smooth skinned woman on the ottoman. When you have mocked at virtue, denied the agency of God in the affairs of men, and made rapine your honeyed faith, tremble! for the day of retribution is at hand, and the masses will be avenged."[13]

[12]*Watchman of the Valley,* n.d., in *Liberator,* July 12, 1844; Clay to Cincinnati *Gazette,* May 2, 1845, in *Liberator,* May 23, 1845; Clay to John G. Fee, December 18, 1855, MS-BCL; *Anti-Slavery Bugle,* April 27, 1861. In 1859, Clay explicitly denied owning slaves after 1844; see Clay to Simeon S. Jocelyn, December 17, 1859, AMA-FU.

[13]Smiley, *Lion of White Hall,* 90–99; quotation is in *True American,* August 12, 1845, in Clay, *Writings,* 285.

His neighbors, sure that this was Clay's response to the South Carolinian's article, responded predictably. So inflammatory an editorial, anticipating black insurrection, rape of white women, and devastation of property could scarcely be tolerated, touching as it did the very quick of Southern fear. Clay's explanation that the revolutionaries to which he referred were white gained as little credence as did his denial of responsibility for the lead article. Two days later, therefore, three fellow citizens issued a warning, endorsed the following day by a public meeting, which charged that the *True American* was "dangerous to the peace of our community, and to the safety of our homes and families," and demanded that Clay cease publication at once.[14]

Clay, still feverish but more hot with anger, counterattacked at once. He got a *True American* extra off the presses early on August 15 denouncing the cabal organized against him. He insisted that he had referred to white, not black, revolutionaries. He chided the plotters for attacking a sick man. "Go tell your secret conclave of cowardly assassins," he threw at them with reckless bravery, "that C. M. Clay knows his rights and how to defend them."[15]

No matter what the enthusiasm of Northern abolitionists for Clay's retort, his neighbors were not impressed. Neither extreme was much struck by the third *True American* extra issued just in time for the second public meeting's consideration on August 18. Thinking better of his earlier brashness, Clay now assured the Lexingtonians that had he been in charge, the offensive Carolinian article would not have been printed, that he would be more careful in the future, and that he had no personal or political associations with abolitionists.

Unconvinced by Clay's promises for the future, his

14*True American Extra,* August 15, 1845.
15Ibid. The quotation is from the report in the *American and Foreign Anti-Slavery Reporter* 2 [3] (1845): 66. The *Reporter* carried the whole story, as did the *Liberator.*

townsmen decided to eliminate the press. Clay, foreseeing the danger long since, had prepared for battle. The *True American* offices were a redoubt of strength. Outside doors were lined with sheet iron; two brass four-pound cannons loaded with shot and nails were placed inside, ready to fire when the doors, secured by chains, were opened slightly to give a clear aim at the charging mobs; sundry Mexican lances and guns completed the arsenal in the shop; and a trap door for escape led onto the roof. In the event all else failed, a keg of powder sufficient to demolish the whole establishment was at the ready.

The scenario gave promise of a confrontation worthy of a Western cinema. The action, however, fell ludicrously short; in fact, there was no action. Clay left his office undefended while the "Committee of Sixty" entered the shop, carefully packed the press, and shipped it across the Ohio to Cincinnati. So bizarrely had it happened that some suspected collusion between Clay and the committee. Both denied the allegations, although Clay later asserted that his friends, planted on the committee, had restrained the mob. In any case Clay claimed the last laugh when he refused to redeem his press. Instead he sued for damages. As long as the matter was in litigation, the committee paid storage charges in Cincinnati to avoid being subject to a charge of theft. Meanwhile Clay set the *True American* on other presses. Finally the court awarded Clay damages of $2,500 and gave the committee legal possession of the equipment they had seized and stored.[16]

In the North the antislavery press cheered Clay's victory and carried the story widely. The *Liberator,* the *Standard,* and the *Anti-Slavery Bugle,* Garrisonian all, joined the Liberty party's *New Jersey Freeman* in finding those "who [had] laid violent

[16]In addition to sources already cited, see also Clay, *Writings,* 296–300; Clay, *Life,* 107; the *New Jersey Freeman,* October 1, 1845, which carries Clay's denial of a deal in Clay to Benjamin Urner et al., September 4, 1845; and American and Foreign Anti-Slavery Society, *Annual Report* (New York: American and Foreign Anti-Slavery Society, 1848), 30. Smiley, *Lion of White Hall,* gives extended coverage to the affair and its surroundings in Chapters 6–8.

hands upon Cassius M. Clay's Printing Press, ... guilty of
a crime of the blackest atrocity. ..." Yet they could not back
Clay completely, for, as the *Bugle* put it, he was not "an
abolitionist occupying the true position."[17]

Although Clay had won in the affair of the *True American*,
the paper itself did not long survive. Faced with a declining
circulation and increased printing costs, Clay turned it over
to his associate John C. Vaughan and his brother Brutus.
By the end of 1846, the paper had died, but only after, as
Clay insisted, it had reestablished a free press in Kentucky.[18]

Even had practical problems not intervened, Clay would
probably have surrendered the *True American* to play the true
patriot. Avid as his opposition to Texas annexation had been,
the war with Mexico roused his martial spirit. Although he
had argued that annexation would violate the Constitution,
contravene the "laws of nations, and [be a] just cause of war
on the part of Mexico," bringing to the United States national
disaster, the events of May 1846 changed his stance.[19] He
had, in Boston's Tremont Temple in 1844, thundered forth,
*"When I shall be called upon to rally to the standard of my country,
inscribed with 'ETERNAL SLAVERY,' I am bold in the avowal that
though I profess to be as brave as most men, I have no heart for
such a contest—I AM A COWARD IN SUCH A CAUSE!"*[20] But when
American blood reputedly fell on American soil and troops
marched off to war, Cassius Clay could not resist the lure
of arms.

Although he had condemned Polk's provocative actions and
had urged the United States to withdraw from foreign soil,
he was pure patriot when, on May 20, 1846, he called on
Kentuckians to aid their country. Maria Chapman was revolted

[17]*New Jersey Freeman*, September 9, 1845; *Anti-Slavery Bugle*, August 29,
1845.
[18]Clay to Subscribers, December 18, 1847, in *Weekly Chronotype*, January
15, 1848.
[19]Clay, *Speech Against the Annexation*, in *Liberator*, February 2, 1844.
[20]Speech in Tremont Temple, September 19, 1844, in *New Jersey Freeman*,
August 14, 1846.

by his performance. When she heard that he had accepted a commission in a Kentucky military company, she wrote him off as a traitor to the antislavery cause. Her close friend, Eliza Follen, scorned him for "aiding the perpetrators of robbery and murder." Even the *New Jersey Freeman,* which had so lauded his bravery in the sacking of the *True American,* suggested that Liberty party men had always "doubted the purity of C. M. Clay's intentions."[21]

Captain Clay was unfazed by the reactions. Neither mentioning that his election to rank in the volunteer corps was probably purchased nor alluding to his disappointment at being only a captain when his father had been a general, he proclaimed his call to duty the "greatest honor ever given an American citizen."[22] In this spirit he joined his company, drilled, and went off to war amid ruffles and flourishes but with minimal training. Perhaps it was well that almost as soon as he reached the front he was captured and spent the war in a Mexican prison camp. Here he conducted himself well and earned a reputation for bravery and honor in most unpropitious circumstances. Then he was repatriated, his military career at an end.

With some candor Clay explained that he had gone to war not so much from patriotism as "to *prove* to the *people* of the South that I warred not upon *them,* but upon *Slavery.*"[23] That maintaining his status in Kentucky and his attachment to Southern mores was also personally satisfying does not detract from the honesty of the statement. His whole explanation does, however, shed light on his system of values, for he remained critical of the war itself.

[21]*True American,* May 27, 1846, in Clay, *Writings,* 464–466; sketch of a speech delivered at Lexington, May 20, 1846, in Clay, *Writings,* 475; Clay to Maria W. Chapman, June 30, 1846, in *Liberator,* July 17, 1846; *National Anti-Slavery Standard,* July 2, 1846, an editorial written probably by Eliza Follen; *New Jersey Freeman,* July 18, 1846.

[22]Quoted by Smiley, *Lion of White Hall,* 116.

[23]Clay to [Horace Greeley], December 10, 1846, in *National Anti-Slavery Standard,* January 14, 1847. The *Chronotype,* January 12, 1847, dates the letter December 19, 1847.

At a Richmond, Kentucky, reception in 1848, celebrating his return from the war, he once again condemned annexation. Texas could, he averred, have been annexed constitutionally only by formal treaty. The joint resolution had usurped the Senate's treaty-making powers as the President's seizure of the territory to the Rio Grande had usurped congressional war-making prerogative. The United States, in absorbing Texas, had simply preyed on Mexican weakness, and the North had consented to the Southern dream of slavery's expansion out of material self-interest. "Give her *the price of blood*," Clay said bitingly, and the North "is always contemptibly tame."[24]

Viewed from Richmond, Clay's Mexican War behavior made sense. Here was the Clay Kentuckians knew and loved: the fighter, the patriot, the vindicator of Southern mores. Viewed from Boston, it made no sense at all. Here was the apostate crusader, the renegade reformer, the hypocrite, the cynic. It was little wonder that abolitionists and Cassius Clay viewed each other with mutual perplexity, suspicion, and distrust.

Clay's distaste for abolition extremism was of long standing. When he was first elected to the general assembly in 1835, during the height of national antiabolitionist uproar, he had opposed holding a state constitutional convention that might debate slavery. He believed the time was ill-chosen to consider emancipation because of the "fanatical incendiaries" whose antislavery agitations disturbed Clay and his fellow Kentuckians alike. Five years later he again referred to abolitionists as "fanatics"; and in 1845, after nearly all real opponents of slavery had condemned it, Clay became a life member of the American Colonization Society. It was in that same year, paradoxically, that Clay first gave Garrison and his fol-

[24]*Anti-Slavery Bugle*, March 31, 1848.

lowers grudging credit for their brave, if clumsy, discussion of slavery.[25]

The abolitionists were never sure which side of Clay they should respond to. Lewis Tappan, impressed by a particularly good letter on slavery, which Clay had published in the New York *Tribune* in 1843, called it "admirable," and elsewhere referred to him as a "Noble fellow." But Tappan's close colleagues thought otherwise. Amos Phelps criticized Clay's gradualism, his deceitful dalliance with the Liberty party, and his duplicity in urging black enfranchisement in New York while he was silent at home. He was viewed with the same suspicion in Garrison's circle. The editor himself questioned whether Clay's freeing his slaves was enough to make him a "trust-worthy abolitionist." Maria Chapman's sister questioned the integrity of the *True American*, which promised not to interfere with the "legal rights of slaveholders." In New York, the *National Anti-Slavery Standard* thought Cassius' support of cousin Henry in 1844 raised real questions about his presumed antislavery convictions.[26]

Clay's inconsistencies did little to reassure or convince his critics. The *Anti-Slavery Bugle,* which had chastised his apparent insincerity in supporting the Mexican War after his total rejection of Texan annexation, was thoroughly perplexed by his damnation of the war after he had volunteered to fight it. Frederick Douglass found Clay a craft which sailed "pretty well in calm weather" but got "dreadfully water-logged in a storm." Henry C. Wright, whose language was as flamboyant as his creed was extreme, called Clay a "queer chap ... ;

[25]Clay, *Writings,* 46; Asa Earl Martin, *The Anti-Slavery Movement in Kentucky Prior to 1850* (Louisville: Standard Printing Co., 1918), 111; Certificate of the American Colonization Society, dated April 25, 1845, C-LMU; Clay, *Writings,* 278.
[26]Lewis Tappan to Gerrit Smith, letterpress, December 9, 1843, T-LC; Tappan to Salmon P. Chase, March 11, 1844, C-HSP; Amos A. Phelps, editorial, *American and Foreign Anti-Slavery Reporter* 2 [3] (February 1846): 101; *Liberator,* April 12, 1844; Caroline Weston to Friend, May 1, 1845, in *Liberator,* May 9, 1845; *National Anti-Slavery Standard,* October 10, 1844.

reckless as a hyena; destitute of moral principle as a shark; absurd and ridiculous as a monkey; a bundle of contradictions."[27]

What made it so difficult for the main body of antislavery folk, of whatever faction, to understand Clay was the fact that their initial assumptions and final goals differed so markedly. Clay never hid the racism that underlay his antislavery. While he insisted that he was not "insensible to the injuries inflicted on the African race," he admitted that he was "actuated by a still higher motive—the greater motive of achieving the complete independence and liberty of [his] own, the white Anglo-Saxon race of America...."[28]

When, then, Clay urged political equality for Negroes, abolitionists questioned his sincerity. He admittedly had little interest in humanitarian uplift; he was convinced that blacks were and probably always would be inferior to whites. How could he reconcile that view with demands for universal liberty and equality? Nor did his advice to Northern blacks to raise themselves by acquiring wealth and competing economically as entrepreneurs tally with his observations that Negroes generally lacked "self-reliance," and were divinely destined "for the sun and the banana."[29]

The point, of course, was that the black man was largely irrelevant to Clay's antislavery. Slavery was an evil because it encroached on the white man's civil liberty and threatened his life and property. He dedicated the *True American* to freeing yeomen and poor whites from slaveholders. They were, as he saw it, "the slaves of slaves," deprived by the slaves'

[27]*Anti-Slavery Bugle,* March 31, 1848; *North Star,* April 27, 1849; Henry C. Wright to William L. Garrison, July 13, 1849, in *Liberator,* July 27, 1849.
[28]*Anti-Slavery Bugle,* January 30, 1846.
[29]See, for example, Clay, *Speech Against the Annexation,* 7; his address in Broadway Tabernacle, January 1846, in Clay, *Writings,* 198–199; and at Belknap Street Church, May 9, 1853, in *Liberator,* May 27, 1853; also one at Frankfort, January 10, 1860, C-FC; Clay to Editor, *New York World,* February 19, 1861, quoted in David Smiley, "Cassius M. Clay and John G. Fee: A Study in Southern Anti-Slavery Thought," *Journal of Negro History* 42 (1957): 204, which contains the quotation.

masters of "the right of petition, trial by jury, liberty of speech, freedom of the press, and the right of habeas corpus." "As much as I abhor slavery," he wrote to Daniel Webster, commenting upon the March 7 speech on the Compromise of 1850, "I abhor the defense more. One strikes down the liberty of the African; the other, mine. One enslaves a people; the other, the human race."[30]

As Clay defined its essence, slavery was "the mother of mob law." Government was, he argued in Lockean terms, designed to protect men and their rights and liberties against the violence of other men. Government's role vis-à-vis slavery automatically followed, for "resistance of law by violence is rebellion and treason, in all cases, and should be punished with the severest infliction; because it is the greatest of crimes by inducing *all others*."[31]

Clay's experience during the *True American* crisis with government that did not enforce the law to "prevent one individual from trampling upon the rights of another" reinforced his belief that "without *law* there is no *liberty*." But what if government proved derelict and refused to enforce the law? Then and only then the individual was better outside it, for by acceding to it he effectively stripped himself "of the natural rights of self-defence." This conclusion only led Clay to further apparent inconsistency. If he was to live in Kentucky, he must, as he wrote to Gerrit Smith in 1855, depend "upon an appeal to the sacredness of law." Yet in 1845 it had not been so clear. "A government," he wrote shortly after his press had been attacked, "which leaves us not as much protection against the trespass of another as

---

[30]Clay to Anti-Slavery Convention at Cincinnati, May 15, 1845, in *National Anti-Slavery Standard,* July 10, 1845; Clay to Daniel Webster, May 25, 1850, in Clay, *Life,* 198. Here Clay follows a pattern analyzed in Russel B. Nye, *Fettered Freedom: Civil Liberties and the Slavery Controversy, 1830–1860* (East Lansing: Michigan State College Press, 1949).

[31]Clay, Speech at the Republican State Convention, [ca. April 1860], (Cincinnati, Ohio) *Daily Gazette,* April 28, 1860, clipping in C-FC; *True American,* July 22, 1845, in Clay, *Writings,* 282.

we had in a state of anarchy or nature, is an usurpation, and ought to perish. *Slavery is that government!*"[32]

If Clay's course was marked by inconstancy and inconsistency, he had at least seemed faithful to the goal of complete emancipation in Kentucky. During the late 1840s, he had suggested various plans for ending slavery in the state, and, in 1851, he made an unsuccessful bid for the governorship on an emancipationist ticket. Yet even these efforts failed to satisfy abolitionists, for each plan he proposed projected a gradualism so extended that no immediatist could accept it. Nor were his plans any more acceptable in Kentucky. His gubernatorial defeat after the failure of his effort in 1849 to incorporate compensated emancipation in the revised state constitution ended the struggle.[33]

Perhaps Clay's defeats soured him. Certainly they frustrated him and drove him to a course in the 1850s yet more fraught with tergiversation. After 1851 his motives became as mixed as his policy was confusing. His search for new political vehicles designed to achieve antislavery goals was muddied by his increasing eagerness to hold major public office; his political ambition was distorted by a nearly pathological overestimation of his national importance.

Holding political office traditionally marked the Southern gentleman. Green Clay's long service to his state had shaped a model for Cassius that the son's opposition to slavery had

[32]*True American*, May 20, 1846, in Clay, *Writings*, 462; *True American*, July 22, 1845, in Clay, *Writings*, 282; *American and Foreign Anti-Slavery Reporter* 2 [3] (December 1845): 88; Clay to Gerrit Smith, April 24, 1855, S-SU; *True American*, May 20, 1846, in Clay, *Writings*, 462.
[33]For Clay's emancipation plans, see, for example, *Liberator*, August 29, 1845, reporting his speech of August 16, 1845; *True American*, November 4, 1845, in Clay, *Writings*, 337–340; and for a later plan his "Speech... at Lexington, Ky., Delivered August 1, 1851," 11–12, CP-LC. On the gubernatorial race, see Smiley, *Lion of White Hall*, 143–147; Clay to William H. Seward, April 24, August 8, 1851, S-UR.

cut short. Now, if he was not to fail altogether in having
a political career, Clay must seek national office. The turning
point may have come before 1851 in his quarrel with Henry
Clay. Cassius had been embittered when his cousin had publicly charged him with misrepresentation. In turn, Cassius
had blamed the older man for endangering the Whig party
and aiding the assault on the *True American;* he called his
cousin a liar and a slanderer, unfit to carry on the family
authority which Cassius's father had held. It was Cassius who
deserved Henry's position and following.[34]

Whatever his motives, Cassius Clay pursued national office
while he denied, in traditional manner, that he was seeking
it. In 1852, he declined, before they were even offered, both
presidential and vice-presidential positions on the Free Soil
ticket. Shortly thereafter, at a party testimonial dinner for
John P. Hale, he announced publicly that he was above personal ambition. The Republican party, as it became a major
party, was another matter, and in 1860 he offered himself
as a compromise presidential candidate in case the Seward
and Chase forces reached a stalemate. He had, he modestly
admitted to both men, been one of the principal founders
of the party and had rendered it great service.[35]

Clay had indeed hoped and worked for a new party with
some enthusiasm since 1844. He had hoped, both in 1848
and 1852, to merge Whigs, antislavery Democrats, Liberty
party men, and Garrisonians under one banner. Even his
support of Taylor in 1848 he justified on the grounds that
Taylor would most likely destroy the old parties. In the same

[34]For Clay's bitterness against Henry, see Clay, *Life,* 103; Clay to Horace
Greeley, September 9, 1845, F-NYPL; Cassius Clay to Henry Clay, April
13, 1848, in Albany *Patriot,* April 26, 1848; Clay to J. B. Thorpe, May 19,
1848, F-NYPL.

[35]Clay to William H. Seward, December 22, 1848, S-UR; Clay to Gamaliel
Bailey, July 5, 1852, in *Anti-Slavery Bugle,* July 31, 1852; Speech in Mas-
sachusetts in Honor of John P. Hale [1853], C-FC; Clay to Thurlow Weed,
March 8, 1860, W-UR; Clay to William H. Seward, May 21, 1860, S-UR;
Clay to Salmon P. Chase, May 26, 1860, C-LC.

way, his race for the governorship in 1851 was meant to launch a statewide emancipationist political organization. In 1852 with the Whig party greatly enfeebled and the Liberty party only a rump, and radical at that, he had joined the Free Soilers.[36]

He was comfortable with the Free Soil party's attenuated antislavery, its complement of experienced politicians, and its advocacy of free soil and free men. His speeches of the period appealed to working-class whites against aristocratic domination and played down emancipationist arguments. The government, he told a Free Soil convention in Cleveland in 1851, should "make every man a land-holder." He was careful to point out that Northern urban labor was bowed down under the weight of slavery's "oppressive tyranny." To this problem, Northern Whigs would give no heed for they were the "landed property holders," "the conservatives of the country," who, "in the final struggle, [would] join the slave interests of the South." Time and again he repeated to Northern audiences as he had earlier to Kentucky ones that the laboring classes were exploited and oppressed by Southern slaveholders. He had not deserted his old themes, but had nationalized them. In 1860, he defended the Republican party against charges that it was the black man's party by countering that the Democracy was "the party disposed to sacrifice all the rights of the white man for the nigger."[37]

If his economic attack on slavery remained clear and central

[36]Clay to Horace Greeley, September 9, 1845, F-NYPL; *True American,* April 29, 1846, in Clay, *Writings,* 450–451; Clay to Salmon P. Chase, July 14, 1848, C-HSP; Clay to William H. Seward, October 4, 1850, August 8, 1851, August 24, 1852, S-UR; Clay to Joshua R. Giddings, September 3, 1851, G-OHS.

[37]For the quotations, see *National Anti-Slavery Standard,* October 9, 1851, quoting from the Cleveland *True Democrat,* n.d.; and "Speech . . . at Covington, Ky., to Laboring Men. 'Ossawatomie Brown's' Cause Considered," [ca. December 1860], C-FC. On poor white labor, see, for example, Clay's speech to the New York Anti-Slavery Society Lecture Course, December 28, 1854, in *National Anti-Slavery Standard,* December 30, 1854.

to his position throughout the 1850s, the rest of his argument grew as fuzzy as his purposes in making it. Whether his party work—he did campaign ardently in numerous elections—served public ends rather than private ambition is moot. Whether his increasingly murky style was designed to cope with complexity or to enlarge his appeal by fitting the message to the audience is equally unsure.

❦❦❦

The relationship of the Constitution to slavery was a topic no political abolitionist could ignore. Clay never retracted his argument that the Constitution already recognized slaves as persons, but he did befog his early contention that Congress and the federal government lacked jurisdiction over slavery in the states. Slavery, he had long argued, was a municipal institution, which to exist must be legalized by state constitutions since it was not guaranteed by the federal Constitution. On this contention, which implied that slavery could be eliminated by state action or, more simply, by the failure of states to legalize it, he had based his campaign for Kentucky emancipation.[38]

His own failure to effect any change in his native state and his increasing embroilment in national politics made some opening for federal action necessary. He found it in his own version of popular sovereignty, embodied in a public statement he issued from White Hall in 1853. Slavery was a civil institution made by "the people"; therefore, the people by majority vote could unmake it. He specified no mechanics by which the people would make their voice heard, whether it should be by constitutional amendment or a simple statute. Nor did he carry the concept further. He did, however, suggest

[38] For Clay's early constitutional views, see his arguments in a variety of speeches in Clay, *Writings,* 65–66, 162–163, 352; see also Clay to T. B. Stevenson, January 8, 1845, in *National Anti-Slavery Standard,* January 30, 1845.

to the Young Men's Association of Chicago the next year
that a servile insurrection would free men to choose sides
and decide the issue by force of arms.[39]

The existence of federal authority over the territories and
the District of Columbia had enabled Clay, from the 1840s,
to agree with the abolitionist assertion that Congress had no
right to establish slavery within these jurisdictions and had
the undoubted right to abolish it in the District of Columbia.
To this position Clay adhered during the 1850s' disputes on
the territories. He scorned Webster's assumption that the laws
of nature excluded slavery from New Mexico and California
and warned that slavery would establish itself wherever it
was profitable. Four years later, he opposed opening Kansas-
Nebraska to the institution on these same grounds.[40]

Clear enough in his opposition to extension, Clay willingly
tempered his position to the immediate demands of Republican politics. Hoping to carry Kentucky for the young party
in 1860, he assured his Frankfort neighbors that Congress
did have the power to establish slavery in the territories and
that he would oppose prohibiting the admission of a new
slave state.[41]

The accommodation of Republican Party politics and anti-
slavery to the attitudes he shared with Kentuckians and
Southerners generally applied even to the Fugitive Slave Law
of 1850. When it was first passed, he denied that Congress
could force free states to return fugitives. Their obligation
ended, he asserted, if they simply refrained from obstructing
federal agents. Yet the law did oblige all citizens, as well as
state officials, to aid in apprehending and returning runaways.

[39]*Liberator,* September 30, 1853; Sketch of Address to the Young Men's
Association of Chicago, July 4, 1854, C-FC.
[40]Speech to the Citizens of the 8th Congressional District, December 20,
1843, in *Liberator,* February 2, 1844; Clay to Daniel Webster, March 26,
1850, in Clay, *Life,* 201; Sketch of Address to the Young Men's Association
of Chicago.
[41]Speech at Frankfort . . . , January 10, 1860, C-FC.

At this Clay rebelled, determined to violate the law himself and to aid others who joined him. He was not, however, moved by the humanitarian and religious scruples which made the radical Stephen Foster and the idealist Samuel J. May defy the same law. For Clay, the issue was once again white freedom. The law, he wrote in 1859, violated "all the safeguards of freedom—jeoparded the life, liberty and happiness, not only of the humble and hated African, but of every proud Saxon in the land, and made justice a mockery in all its forms"; and, he added, it *"humiliated and degraded our manhood,* and fitted us to be ourselves slaves, which our masters long since designed."[42]

Emasculated by the law, frustrated by the failure to halt extension, threatened by the increasing dominance of the "slave power," Clay flailed about for remedies. Having asserted after the Compromise of 1850 that no compromise could bind the future, he reversed himself in 1852, and in 1860 claimed that the Missouri Compromise was as binding and so much a "part of the Constitution itself" that the Kansas-Nebraska Act could not repeal it. Likewise, although he deplored the dissolution threatened by some Southerners and the disunion Northern abolitionists sought, he toyed with their ideas. In 1850 he wrote Webster that rather than return fugitive slaves and sacrifice free men's liberties, he would support disunion.[43]

Where he drew the line was unclear. "For my part, regarding slavery, as it exists in America, as the most atrocious of all despotisms," Clay wrote in the same letter to Webster, "I yet prefer it—greatly prefer it—to anarchy. Any Government on

[42]Speech at National Mass Convention of the Friends of Freedom, Cleveland, September 24, 1851, Clay to Wendell Phillips, April 5, 1852, both in *Anti-Slavery Bugle,* October 4, 1851, May 8, 1852. Clay to S. O. Griswold et al., n.d., in *Liberator,* June 17, 1859.

[43]*National Anti-Slavery Standard,* April 10, 1851; Smiley, *Lion of White Hall,* 152; Speech at Frankfort; Clay to Daniel Webster, March 20, 1850, in Clay, *Life,* 189.

earth is better than none." To Seward a couple of weeks later he said, "If justice and the cause of liberty . . . are to be given up for union I say let it perish!" And three years later to his antislavery colleagues in the North he wrote, "You fight outside of the Union; I within it. So long as we agree in purpose, we will agree to disagree in the means."[44]

The key to his ambiguity he gave Garrison in 1857. "I am for the Union, or any other government," he explained, "just so long as it protects my rights, and no longer. . . . I am still for the Union, because I hope for more safety in it than out of it. When, if ever," he concluded, "I shall change this my opinion, then I would war as heartily upon the Union as I would upon a highway robber."[45] The issue in disunion, in constitutional interpretation, in emancipation was the freedom and rights of white men. Though Clay addressed his arguments to labor and the poor, he was at least as much concerned with his own survival and success as a farmer, politician, and gentleman in his father's tradition. An enlightened conservative, he would bend down to help the oppressed—be they white or black—and in so doing save himself.

A sorry incident involving the Kentucky evangelist John G. Fee illustrates the degree to which even Clay's concern with white civil rights gave way to his own self-interest. Clay had given Fee land on which to build a church and establish a school. When, in 1855, Fee had been threatened for his antislavery activities, Clay had come to his defense, calling for volunteers with rifles, shotguns, revolvers, and kitchen knives to attend a joint Fee–Clay public meeting and fight off attackers. Yet when Fee espoused the politics of the Radical

[44]Clay to Webster, March 20, 1850; Clay to William H. Seward, April 6, 1850, S-UR; Clay to William L. Garrison et al., November 21, 1853, in *Liberator*, December 9, 1853.

[45]Clay to William L. Garrison et al., March 5, 1857, in *Liberator*, March 20, 1857.

Abolitionists, a remnant of the Liberty party, and fell away from the Republican party, Clay was no longer so ardent in defending his rights. The cleric had become revolutionary, insurrectionary, and dangerous. Two years later Fee was run out of Kentucky for his abolitionism, and Clay raised not a hand to protect him, putting his own position and regional mores ahead of principle.[46] A duelist in his youth, Clay was also well known for his recourse, in political brawls, to gouging, shooting, and, once, even disembowelling. "Thanks to bowie knives and pistols, a man may speak some truth in Kentucky, if he has friends enough, and they well enough armed, and resolute enough to intimidate the slaveholders." That the relationship with Fee was quite otherwise, Clay made clear at a Berea meeting at which he defended his desertion of Fee. They had been "political comrade[s] up to such time as he, in his wisdom and what he conceived it to be his duty to his God and his country, felt in conscience bound to separate himself from the Republican party." In so doing, Fee had exceeded Kentucky tolerance, and Clay had warned him that his radical abolitionism would do so. He concluded his speech by asking whether Fee had "any more right to my physical and personal sacrifice of limb or of life in his defense, than the Democratic party or the Union party in this commonwealth? I say he has not." The Radical Abolitionists, of course, thought otherwise and resolved at their 1860 convention that Clay's actions were "in perfect keeping with his baseness." It would have been hard for even the most latitudinarian abolitionist to have viewed him otherwise in 1860.[47]

[46]For the background to and defense of Fee, see John G. Fee to Clay, October 17, 1854, MS-BCL; W. H. Kirtley to Col. Johnson, July 2, 1855, in Cincinnati *Gazette,* July 23, 1855, as copied by *Anti-Slavery Bugle,* July 28, 1855; Clay to Salmon P. Chase, July 5, 1855, C-HSP; *Frederick Douglass' Paper,* August 3, 1855, from the Cincinnati *Gazette,* n.d.; Clay to James S. Davis, October 8, 1857, from a clipping of *The World We Live In,* Cincinnati, April 14, 1860, MS-BCL; John G. Fee to Clay, August 27, September 17, 1857, MS-BCL; Clay to Gerrit Smith, November 20, 1857, S-SU.

[47]On Clay's brawling and duelling see, for example, Smiley, *Lion of White Hall,* 52, 139–141; E. J. to Marius [Robinson], July 15, 1854, in *Anti-Slavery*

By then Clay had greatly modified or given up the principles on which his antislavery reputation rested. Both personal ambition and the frustrations inherent in being an antislavery Southerner contributed to his constantly diminishing sense of reality. He had sacrificed his property and devoted his life to opposing slavery. He had won thereby neither the support of his neighbors nor the approval of abolitionists.

The beginning of the Civil War clearly marked the degree to which Clay's antislavery efforts had given way to political ambition. The bleak winter of 1860–1861 he devoted almost exclusively to efforts to obtain the high political office to which he thought himself entitled. He demanded that Lincoln appoint him either Secretary of War or minister to Britain or France. He informed the President-elect that by virtue of his past services to the Republican party he was entitled "to a portion of the controling interest in the administration of its destiny." Sure that some demonic force was impeding his recognition, he blamed his fate on Secretary of State William Seward, who, he claimed, cut him out from party and public rewards because Clay had "refused to go for him in the Convention of 1860." His fantasies, as they were reflected in the nostalgia of his later years, even led Clay to claim that he had been the principal defender of Washington in April 1861, had been offered the command of the Union armies by Lincoln, and had turned it down in patriotic self-denial. In any event, Clay was forced to console himself with exile in St. Petersburg as minister to Russia.[48]

Bugle, July 29, 1854, reporting Clay's address to the Democrats of Iowa, July 14, 1854; Speech at the Republican State Convention of Kentucky, clipping from Cincinnati *Daily Gazette*, April 28, 1860, C-FC; Resolution of the Radical Abolitionist Convention at Syracuse, August 29–30, 1860, in *Douglass Monthly*, October 1860.

[48]Clay to Abraham Lincoln, January 10, 1861, Ln-LC; Clay to Horace Greeley, November 12, 1868, F-NYPL; Clay to George P. Putnam, June 14, 1864, F-NYPL.

Still the old antislavery flame flickered. Clay praised Frémont's abortive attempt to emancipate the slaves of his Western command late in 1861. In the summer of the next year, recalled to make room for Simon Cameron as his successor in Russia, he campaigned in the North for emancipation and even tested out Lincoln's plan for emancipation on the Kentucky legislature. So effective was he in this guise that Wendell Phillips praised him more earnestly than had any abolitionist since the middle 1840s.[49] But Clay was eyeing Washington, not Boston, for approval and reward. Once again he was shunted off to Russia when Cameron refused the appointment.

With the end of the Johnson administration, his exile in St. Petersburg gave way to exile at White Hall. Bitter at being denied further political office, he fretted and fumed over Reconstruction. He suggested a peonage system for the South under which freedmen would work for wages and be granted political equality as soon as they proved "worthy of the boon." There must, he said, be genuine civil, political, and economic rights for all, but under home rule by those who in 1861 had remained Unionists. A supporter of Andrew Johnson, his views were similar to those of that other border state loyalist on the manner in which Reconstruction should be accomplished. He approved of the Tennessean's veto of the Freedmen's Bureau Bill; he opposed granting freedmen the governmental role which Radical Republican congressional leaders would give them. In 1871 he wrote Frederick Douglass that to continue Radical Reconstruction policy was sheer foolishness. The Radicals, he contended, only widened the gulf between black and white in the South which Liberal Republicans would close. "The whites," he explained, who were "superior in numbers and at present in intelligence & wealth in the South," should govern there. While unenlightened men

[49]Clay to Abraham Lincoln, September 27, 1861, Ln-LC; Smiley, *Lion of White Hall,* 191; Wendell Phillips to Clay, August 19, 1862, C-LMU.

in the North pointed to the Ku Klux Klan as the measure of Southern evil, Clay contended that "it was the disfranchisement of the leading minds of the South, and the fatal attempt to subject the Saxon race ... to the minority of the African freedmen, which bred the foulest excrescence of slavery—the Ku-Klux clans."[50] In fighting the aftereffects of slavery as in fighting slavery itself, Clay remained constant in his concern for white men's rights and liberty.

❦❦❦

Clay lived into the twentieth century, dying in 1903. During his last thirty years, he lived in a world of memory, reconstructing in fantasy a career that more nearly accorded with his hopes and ambition. The Clay who emerged had led a Southern antislavery force, engineered the Republican party, shaped Lincoln's emancipation policy, and struggled to rebuild the South. His political defeats had all come at the hands of vicious and unprincipled enemies.

Neither his autobiographical writings nor his reputation explain the nature of his war against slavery. Far from the idealism that characterized the antislavery movement, it looked to abolition as the expedient solution to a practical problem at a given place and time. Clay preached gradualism, immediatism, and colonization as each seemed feasible. All his arguments, however, rested on the same economic and political premise: slavery oppressed the nonslaveholding white as much as the enslaved black. Never did the plight of the black American, slave or free, engage his interest.

Yet his course denied him a political base in his home state, so necessary to the life style he sought as a Kentucky gentle-

---

[50]Cassius M. Clay, *Speech ... Before the Law Department of the University of Albany, N.Y., February 3, 1863,* 2nd ed. (New York: Wynkoop, Hallenbeck, & Thomas, 1863), 19–20, C-FC; Clay to George D. Prentice, March 13, 1866, in Clay, *Life,* 317–318; Clay to Frederick Douglass, July 15, 18 [28], 1871, D-LC, Reel 10. Final quotation in Smiley, *Lion of White Hall,* 223.

man. Unwilling to accept his fate, Clay, in his pursuit of personal popularity and political power, destroyed the very principles which had led him to it and further weakened the base from which he argued the very real economic and class issues which shaped his crusade. Because he was constantly shifting his position and beclouding the premises upon which he stood in order to achieve more immediate goals, he never welded an antislavery based on white supremacy and defeat of an economic and political slave power conspiracy into a coherent whole. Because he sought to use politics to free Kentucky of slave power domination, he was denied political office. Because he sought to use antislavery to gain political strength, he lost credibility.

One may argue that Cassius Clay was a sheer opportunist; that he was psychologically disturbed; or that there was a shrewdness in him which few fathomed. A product of the South and its Jeffersonianism, as well as its frontier tradition, Clay can better be understood in its context than in a setting among acknowledged antislavery leaders. That he stayed in Kentucky, that he continued to work there against slavery in itself demonstrates a major variant in a movement primarily Northern in orientation and outlook. His economic arguments, his political course, and his personal style still further demonstrated the diversity inherent in the antislavery crusade. A self-proclaimed aristocrat like Chapman, he could not have differed more from the style and outlook of the Boston Clique.

5

The Quaker Colonizer:
Benjamin Lundy

Maria Chapman turned her talents largely to organizational activity and to furthering the Garrisonian doctrine, while Cassius Clay struggled with the issues of white civil rights and the economic well-being of his native Kentucky. Unlike either of these, Benjamin Lundy was less concerned with the institution of slavery or with its social ramifications than he was with the slave as an individual suffering human being. A New Jersey Quaker, Lundy, as a young man, had gone to Wheeling, in western Virginia, in 1809. There he learned the saddler's trade, and there he discovered the peculiar institution. Brought face to face with coffles of slaves, bound together and destined for the deep South, he was so appalled that he determined to "break at least one link of that ponderous chain of oppression. . . ."[1]

Thus aroused, Lundy devoted the rest of his life to ameliorating, as directly as he could, the condition of the

[1]Merton L. Dillon, *Benjamin Lundy and the Struggle for Negro Freedom* (Urbana: University of Illinois Press, 1966), 6–7, quoting Lundy in the *Genius of Universal Emancipation*, November 1832.

90

bondsman. An editor, he early turned journalism to the service of abolition, but for the most important part of his career he tried, amid constant obstacles, to establish colonies where blacks might achieve or realize their freedom. His work exacted a heavy physical toll and demanded a toughness which his slender build, diffident manner, and retiring personality belied. Garrison thought him unable to "sustain a temporary conflict with the winds of heaven," but Lundy proved his early friend and later critic wholly wrong.[2]

Not only iron-willed and persistent, Lundy was also an intensely practical worker. He thought himself unlike most other reformers and philanthropists, who, he said, "think forty times before they act." He seemed not to fit into the developing mainstream of abolitionist activity; while his fellows became increasingly concerned with the sin of slavery, Lundy always put primary emphasis on directly ameliorating the sufferings of the slave. He set about his task zealously. "I shall not hesitate to call things by their proper names," he wrote early in his career, "nor yet refrain from speaking the truth whenever I think it may subserve the cause of liberty and justice.... I shall fearlessly and resolutely pursue the straight forward course that duty points out, equally regardless of the petit cavilling of hypercritics, and the imperious dictum of self-created censors."[3] Lundy marked his course a full decade before Garrison made a similar promise in the opening issue of the *Liberator*.

There was little in Lundy's background that foreshadowed his role as a major antislavery colonizationist. Born in 1789 in Greenville, New Jersey, to Quaker parents, he was doubt-

[2]*Journal of the Times*, n.d., quoted in *The Rights of All*, May 29, 1829.
[3]Benjamin Lundy, "Journal," September 6, 1828, quoted in William C. Armstrong, "Benjamin Lundy; The Founder of American Abolitionism," in his *The Lundy Family and Their Descendants... With a Sketch of Benjamin Lundy* (New Brunswick, N.J.: Heidingsfeld, Printer, 1902), 364; *Genius of Universal Emancipation*, August 1821.

lessly exposed to the Friends' tradition of humanitarianism
and perhaps even to John Woolman's castigations of slavery.
Yet as a youth Lundy had little direct knowledge of slavery,
for, although it still existed in the state, it was fast disappearing.
Certainly he was little exposed to the Federalist strongholds
in New Jersey from which American Colonization Society support came, nor did his experiences link him with the planters
and lawyers who were turning to African colonization. His
ties with the Quaker community remained strong. After his
Virginia sojourn, he settled in the Quaker-dominated village
of Mount Pleasant, Ohio, and in 1815 married a Friend, Esther
Lewis. Shortly thereafter he began his antislavery work in
nearby St. Clairsville, to which he had moved. He acted as
agent for the Mount Pleasant *Philanthropist,* a general reform
newspaper, and, in 1816, he founded the Union Humane
Society, devoted to ending racial prejudice, fighting for universal civil rights, assisting free Negroes in the state, and
opposing the notorious Ohio Black Code.

His work for the *Philanthropist* whetted his interest in journalism, and he planned to take over the Mount Pleasant paper,
but first he had to dispose of his saddlery business, which
he took to St. Louis to sell. While the business disruption
of the panic of 1819 and then the politics of the Missouri
Compromise detained him, the *Philanthropist* was otherwise
disposed of. Undaunted he established his own paper, the
Genius of Universal Emancipation, in Mount Pleasant in 1821;
and, when the Tennessee Manumission Society offered to
print it, he moved it to Greenville. Soon convinced that a
more central location in an eastern city and the better mail
service available there would increase circulation, Lundy
moved the *Genius* to Baltimore in 1824.

While the various moves suggested growth, the *Genius*
seemed always on the brink of disaster. Despite its nearly
seventy agents, North and South, the paper never prospered
financially. Neither the organ of a society nor the recipient
of official support, it was frequently saved from collapse only

by sporadic last-minute assistance. Luckily, even before he moved to Baltimore, Lundy had active contact with the American Convention for Promoting the Abolition of Slavery and its affiliate, the Pennsylvania Society for Promoting the Abolition of Slavery. Both groups provided periodic assistance by subscribing to multiple issues of the paper. Nonetheless, the venture remained precarious, though Lundy never lost faith. Emancipation, he wrote cheerfully to Isaac Barton of the American Convention in 1825, is "progressing, as fast as we can expect"; and he thereupon changed the *Genius* from a monthly to a weekly. He justified the change by a rapid growth in subscribers from 50 in 1824 to 250 in 1825. He boasted in 1826 of further increases with 350 weekly and 700 monthly subscribers.[4] Whether elated by success or discouraged by frequent reverses, he kept the *Genius* going as a most irregular monthly and with long hiatuses until his death in 1839.

Journalism was Lundy's most consistent antislavery work, and the *Genius* was a significant contribution to the cause. In the first issue in 1821, he wrote: "Happy will it be for our country, happy will it be for the countless thousands that are to succeed us, and to inhabit the vast and fertile regions of America, if this hydra of iniquity can be vanished, ere the arm of vengeance is raised, and the destroying angel, the gory fiend of *Intestine War*, is permitted to lay waste our cities, our villages, and our fields, and to consign their possessors to the sword."[5] To this end Lundy labored at his press.

Journalism, however, was only part of his work. He was also active in a variety of societies. From his first efforts, with the Union Humane Society, he believed as did his successors in the 1830s in the efficacy of organizations. Groups of committed men could, he thought, effect practical change and convert ideas and dogmas into positive action. Therefore,

[4]Lundy to Isaac Barton, March 8, 1825, January 10, 23, 1826, in ASP-HSP; *Genius of Universal Emancipation*, March–April 1825. The quotation is from the March 8, 1825, letter.
[5]*Genius of Universal Emancipation*, July 1821.

when he lived in Tennessee, he participated in the Greenville branch of the Tennessee Manumission Society, and in 1823 served as its first president. Throughout the 1820s he served on the acting committee of the Quaker-dominated American Convention for Promoting the Abolition of Slavery. He was a member of the gradualist Pennsylvania Society for the Abolition of Slavery and, after 1825, was active in the Maryland Anti-Slavery Society. In 1827, he helped found the National Anti-Slavery Tract Society of Maryland. His trip through the Northern states in 1828 to raise funds for the *Genius* was also designed to organize antislavery societies. Garrison, soon to be Lundy's editorial partner and later his most vigorous critic, reported that the Quaker editor had toured nineteen states, established numerous societies, circulated petitions against slavery in the District of Columbia, and showed himself in all ways to have a "heart . . . of gigantic size." "No reformer," he continued, "was ever more devoted, zealous, persevering, or sanguine."[6] In later recognition of this service, he was elected in 1837 a manager of the American Anti-Slavery Society.

As he sought action through voluntary societies, so too Lundy looked to government and undertook political action. "In my view," he said, "the subject of Universal Emancipation is a political one, in the most emphatical sense of the word. . . ." In 1824, he argued persuasively that emancipation could be achieved only by political action. Moreover, since slavery was a national, not a sectional, evil, only national action could eliminate it. Nonetheless Lundy urged political participation at all levels of government. First and foremost, he believed, one must vote for candidates sympathetic to antislavery goals. Once officials were elected, they must be pressured to help abolish slavery. While he was in Missouri in 1819–1820, Lundy campaigned for an antislavery constitution for the new state.

[6]*Journal of the Times*, December 12, 1828, quoted in George A. Lawrence, "Benjamin Lundy, Pioneer of Freedom," *Journal of the Illinois State Historical Society* 6 (July 1913): 201–202.

He wrote letters to the press and organized political action groups. Here, according to his most recent biographer, he first became aware of the importance of political action. Here also he discovered that the unity of the South in the Missouri debates was attributable to *"Power, Patronage, Political influence, &c."*[7]

As soon as he had his own press, he used it to expose the misuse of government. When he returned to Ohio and established the *Genius,* he lashed out against a proposed Massachusetts law to bar the immigration of free blacks into the Bay State and compared the attempt to the similar Ohio Black Code under which he lived. Several years later, in 1824, he castigated Henry Clay's presidential candidacy because the Kentuckian's "sentiments on the subject of slavery, [were] of the most obnoxious character." In the same year, he pressed forward the petition of the Tennessee Manumission Society for abolishing slavery in the District of Columbia and tried to influence neighboring Illinois while that state considered a proposed change in its constitution to permit slavery. The amendment showed, he scolded, "evidence of political and moral depravity."[8] Then, having settled in Baltimore, Lundy actively campaigned in 1825 for his friend and sympathizer Daniel Raymond, who was a candidate for the Maryland General Assembly. From the very beginning of his publishing career, therefore, Lundy supported political action as a necessary and legitimate weapon in the antislavery crusade.

As he became increasingly involved in organizational work, politics, and journalism, Lundy developed his antislavery views. In general, he accepted the antislavery ideas current

[7]*Genius of Universal Emancipation,* March 1824; Dillon, *Lundy,* 42; *Genius of Universal Emancipation,* January 1824.
[8]*Genius of Universal Emancipation,* February, April 1823 respectively for the quotations.

in the 1820s and contributed little new in the way of theory or doctrine. Apart from his assertion of racial equality, his condemnation of slaveholders for black degradation, and his attack on color prejudice in the North, Lundy enunciated the customary arguments. Like most other opponents of the institution, he denounced the domestic slave trade with its encouragement of slave breeding and kidnapping of freemen. Tailoring action to principle, he served in 1828 on the Committee on the Internal Slave Trade of the American Convention "to enquire into the expediency of petitioning Congress to pass a law, prohibiting the transportation of slaves for sale from and to the several States and Territories of the United States, by sea."[9] Its report reiterated the arguments Lundy had already made.

He shared also the aversion of many Northerners to slavery in the District of Columbia. He lashed out in the *Genius* at the hypocritical inconsistency of Congressmen from free states who did not press the issue of abolition in the District. "How can you return to your constituents," he taunted them, "unconscious of shame, or guilt, after you have been revelling in voluptuous ease upon the labour of slaves, when at the same time, you yourselves profess to be opposed to the vile practice, and are aware that no such privilege would be allowed you at home?" His ire aroused, he drafted for the American Convention in 1828 "an address to the citizens of the United States relative to the Abolition of slavery in the District of Columbia." The District, he said, was national territory; consequently all citizens had a right to speak about conditions there. Furthermore, since Congress governed the District, the entire nation was responsible for its institutions. The demands

[9]Lundy's antislavery views are set forth in the *Genius of Universal Emancipation* during the 1820s, passim. See also his *Life, Travels and Opinions . . . Including his Journey to Texas and Mexico . . .* (Thomas Earle, Compiler, Philadelphia: William D. Parrish, 1847), 214–215. American Convention for Promoting the Abolition of Slavery and Improving the Condition of the African Race, *Minutes of the Adjourned Session of the Twentieth Biennial American Convention . . . Nov. 1828* (Philadelphia: Samuel Parker, 1828), 14.

of justice, mercy, and American free institutions, Lundy concluded, made abolition in the District imperative.[10]

These specific concerns were merely ancillary to the major one of emancipation. Although the Northern states had largely adopted policies either of immediate or gradual emancipation by 1800, antislavery proposals for the South for the most part had focused on individual manumission or sporadic public efforts to end the slave trade. Lundy reconciled these positions and melded from them a plan for the gradual but universal termination of slavery. In several 1821–1822 issues of the *Genius,* he suggested a group of actions to achieve his goal. The federal government should end interstate commerce in slaves, abolish slavery both in federal territories and in the District of Columbia, and admit no new slave states into the Union. States should provide for gradual emancipation by encouraging cooperative action between slaveholders and state governments, by sponsoring annual emancipation conventions to collate means and ways of implementing the program, by declaring the offspring of slaves free, and by providing, if there were a great many slaves, for a "system of *tenantry,* to continue a certain length of time, at the expiration of which, all should be entitled to their liberty."[11]

Such a diverse and largely voluntary plan seemed to Lundy to create no constitutional issue. Power to protect the public peace and tranquility lay with Congress, and slavery clearly threatened them. Gradual emancipation, varying in specifics to suit the requirements of the several states, would serve national tranquility and prevent the dislocation, disorder, and insurrection, which, some thought, an immediate and uniform abolition might precipitate. Thus Lundy asserted that "nobody urge[d] on *'immediate'* liberation of the slaves." Yet even he was skeptical of pleas of disorder. Insurrection was more likely

[10]*Genius of Universal Emancipation,* January 1824; American Convention for Promoting the Abolition of Slavery, *Minutes, 1828,* 16–20.
[11]*Genius of Universal Emancipation,* September 1821, March 1822; the quotation in February 1822.

to occur, it seemed to him, if the slaves were not freed or
if the owners were not prepared to accept the process. No
emancipation in history, Lundy claimed, had ever led to revolt.[12]

Stimulated by these doubts and suspicious that fears of servile war were being used to delay emancipation, Lundy in
1824 began to shift from gradualism to immediatism. He
warned Americans that they were "treading upon an awful
magazine of combustible materials, the explosion of which
is seemingly not far distant... ," and that inaction was far
more dangerous than quick action. Impressed by the English
abolitionist Elizabeth Heyrick's *Immediate, Not Gradual
Abolition,* Lundy commented pithily on its "nervous language
and strong reasoning." On the other hand, neither Lundy
nor the English immediatists called for full political rights
and civil liberties for the freedmen. They assumed that the
newly liberated slaves would be "placed under a benevolent
and disinterested supervision, which [should] secure to them
the right to obtain secular and religious knowledge, to worship
God according to the dictates of their conscience, to
accumulate wealth, &c., &c."[13] Lundy's immediatism, in consequence, was a quickened form of gradualism. It differed
from the later Garrisonian version because it remained a concrete plan, not an ideological abstraction.

In focusing on service to blacks rather than on individual
repentance of sin, Lundy was obliged, as Cassius Clay did
later, to examine the economics of slavery and emancipation.
Lacking in sophistication, his analysis nevertheless added
another dimension to his thinking. Appalled by the sloth and
greed of men who stole the labor of others, he asked rather
poignantly in an editorial of 1822 whether "this great
nation... [must] be held back in the race of moral improvement by the minions of Ambition and cold hearted

[12]Ibid., April 1824, January 1824, November 1822; the quotation is in
October 1822.
[13]Ibid., October, December, 1824; Lundy, *Life, Travels and Opinions,* 260.

Avarice ... ?"And two years later he linked exploitation with vain display: "Had Industry and good management taken the place of idle pomp; & a spirit of virtuous enterprise supplanted the prevailing fondness for dissipating sports & amusements," slavery might long since have ended.[14]

To overcome the fruits of personal sin and economic waste, Lundy proposed to demonstrate the economic superiority of free labor and to challenge the slave economy with a boycott of its products. In 1823, he had prophesied that free labor could and would break the Southern slaveholders' monopoly on the cotton and sugar market. On the one hand, it encouraged production of cotton and sugar by free labor. On the other, because of better quality, lower price, or buyer preference, these goods would drive out Southern produce until free labor replaced slave in its growth and manufacture. In 1826 Lundy put the idea to the test, opening a store in Baltimore that offered only free-labor products. The next year, he praised the establishing of the Free Produce Society of Pennsylvania and, in October, proposed that a committee be appointed by the American Convention for Promoting the Abolition of Slavery to "make enquiry... [about] what experiments have been heretofore made, and are now making, on the American Continent and Islands, in relation to the cultivation of the products of cotton, rice, sugar, tobacco, &c. by free labor, or by slaves whose condition has been so meliorated as to approach the condition of freemen, shewing what is [sic] the relative advantages between free and slave labor." The following year the new committee, of which Lundy was a member, reported that there was "good quality free-labor sugar" grown in the West Indies, that there were some free-labor experiments with sugar in Florida and Louisiana, that the same was true for coffee in Haiti and South America, and for tobacco in Ohio, which currently undersold slave-produced tobacco from Virginia. It concluded that the rapid

[14]*Genius of Universal Emancipation,* July 1822, January 1824.

extension of manumission and free labor in Mexico was the
best argument in favor of the system.[15]

The free-produce idea, though it was by no means the exclusive motivation, gave impetus to Lundy's most ambitious project to cut into the slave power: his attempt to establish a
settlement of American blacks in Mexico. Seeing free produce
ever as a handmaiden of emancipation, rather than the
reverse, Lundy linked it to colonization, yet another effort
aimed at portraying slavery's economic inadequacy and its
necessary doom. Once again, Lundy's program was innovative
neither in its conception nor its application. In the decade
during which his antislavery ideas matured, colonization was
the major focus of antislavery activity; and the American
Colonization Society, founded in 1817, was popular until the
late 1820s with bona fide opponents of slavery. What set Lundy
apart from his fellow colonizationists was the locale he chose
and the drive and imagination he applied toward realizing
his plan.

From the outset he avoided much of the stigma which
quickly attached to the Liberian venture because of its presumed Southern bias. He insisted that colonization be a voluntary choice for American blacks. They had, he observed, every
right to remain in the United States, for "the country in which
a man is born, is his rightful home, if he makes it his choice. . . .
No matter what adventitious circumstances may have placed
his ancestors there; no matter what may be his appearance,
occupation or pursuit; so long as he conducts himself with
honest propriety, he cannot be compelled to quit his native
land, by human authority, without a violation of the principle
of justice, as well as the clearest provisions of the law of
nature."[16]

The right of blacks to reject expatriation once established,

[15] Ibid., September and November 1823; American Convention for Promoting the Abolition of Slavery, *Minutes . . . 1827* (Baltimore: B. Lundy, Printer,
[1827]), for resolution adopted October 4, 1827; and also its *Minutes, 1828*,
25–27.
[16] *Genius of Universal Emancipation*, October 1824.

Lundy then pointed to the practical advantages it offered. In part a sop to the Southern fear of a large and dissident free Negro population, which Lundy himself never quite relinquished, colonization would also free blacks from white American prejudice. Settled in their own colonies, they could enjoy real equality and make real progress. Then white Americans, their fears of racial stress diminished and their estimate of black potential raised, would be the more speedily won to antislavery sentiment and would expedite complete emancipation.[17]

Africa, however, never appealed to Lundy as the best place to effect colonization. Settlement there was tainted by the American Colonization Society's use of the continent as a dumping ground for troublesome blacks, a goal that became ever more evident as its leaders displayed their very limited desire to end slavery. Of its officers and members, Bushrod Washington had sold his slaves, Charles Mercer opposed restricting slavery in Missouri, and Henry Clay approved extending slavery into new federal territory. Even had the society's program been less suspect, it was still impractical, for Africa was far distant, expensive to travel to, and its climate was difficult for blacks accustomed to North America to adjust to.[18]

Both the practical and the organizational difficulties led Lundy to develop his own schemes. His first choice for colonization was Haiti. Close to the United States, it would cost little to get there; its climate was superior to that of Africa; and the government offered to welcome black Americans and help them establish new homes.[19] Early in 1826, therefore, Lundy went to investigate Haitian conditions and to explore colonization possibilities. He hoped to arrange with the government or the local philanthropic society for concrete assistance to emancipated slaves who might choose to come

[17]Ibid., February 1822, October, November 1824.
[18]Ibid., October 1821, September 1823.
[19]Ibid., December 1823; Dillon, *Lundy,* 88–89.

to the Caribbean country from the United States. Lundy was pleased with the reception of his plan in both countries. Some American Negroes considered it the best opportunity for "the emigration of their class for the purpose of ameliorating their condition." One Haitian observed the "noble opportunity" it provided the Haitian government.[20]

Thus encouraged, Lundy sought the support his venture required. The American Convention for Promoting the Abolition of Slavery petitioned the national government to support emigration wherever blacks wished to settle. Various individuals and groups, at Lundy's urging, did go to the island republic. Virginia sent 88 blacks and North Carolina sent 119. On his second trip to the Caribbean in 1829, Lundy took with him twelve ex-slaves from Maryland.[21] But the failure of the Haitian government to keep its promises of aid and land distribution killed the scheme. The trickle of emigration to Haiti was inconsequential.

This failure did not discourage Lundy, for he was involved as well in colonization plans for the American West and Canada. In 1822, he had responded favorably to a North Carolinian's plan for the former and had printed it in the *Genius,* calling it "something of a practical nature." Likewise, he was sympathetic to the Tennessee Manumission Society's proposal the following year that blacks be colonized in American territory—though just where remained vague. Lundy undertook to make it more specific. His original choice of site was either Alabama or Mississippi. There, he suggested, about one hundred slaves, purchased for the purpose, should be placed on the land in a cooperative community. The fruits of their labor would repay the cost of their settling and train-

[20]Lundy to Isaac Barton, January 23, 30, 1826, ASP-HSP; "Extract of the Journal of Humphrey Wainwright, a Man of Color, 30 Years Resident in the Republic of Hayti, and Member of the Haytian Abolition Society," March 13, 1826, W-LC.

[21]American Convention for Promoting the Abolition of Slavery, *Minutes . . . 1826* (Baltimore: B. Lundy, Printer, [1826]), 42; Lundy, *Life, Travels, and Opinions,* 29; Lundy to Thomas Ridgeway, June 27, 1829, ASP-HSP.

ing. After five years, they would be discharged from the community free to establish permanent homes wherever they wished. The plan was similar to that which Frances Wright undertook at Nashoba in Tennessee in the mid-1820s. Her community was, in fact, based largely on Lundy's ideas and won his approval until he was repelled by its social radicalism and wavering interest in the blacks whom Wright had settled there.[22]

Soon afterward the Wilberforce community replaced Nashoba in Lundy's conception of an ideal settlement. There, just north of the town of London in Canada West, in 1830, several hundred Negroes fleeing the Ohio Black Code and Cincinnati race riots, established a cooperative community. Under black leadership, they planned schools and economic development. The American Convention of the Free People of Color and various antislavery philanthropists hoped that the Wilberforce colony would prove successful. Lundy was no less enthusiastic. In 1832, following a trip he had made to study the settlement's progress, he wrote, it "will be, by far, the most important [of all the various Canadian settlements], as there are men of known intelligence and public spirit there, who will give it a consequence, that probably will not, at least very soon, be attached to the others."[23] Again, his high hopes were dashed. By 1836, Wilberforce had collapsed, a victim of poor management, chicanery, and poor organization.

A final scheme for colonization—this time in Mexico—began to mature in Lundy's mind around 1830. It was almost his last major antislavery action and embraced the ideas and attitudes that his career, until then, had generated. It would offer a path for private manumission to become general emancipation. It would demonstrate conclusively the superiority

[22]*Genius of Universal Emancipation*, January 1822, March, 1824; Dillon, *Lundy*, 96–97; *Genius of Universal Emancipation and Baltimore Courier*, October 15, 1825, the title of a weekly edition published simultaneously with the monthly edition at this time; *Genius of Universal Emancipation*, April 26, 1828. The quotation is in the January 1822 issue.

[23]*Genius of Universal Emancipation*, March 1832.

of free labor and sustain the free-produce movement. It would be intensely practical with little concern for ideological rigor and would accept, for instance, compensated emancipation, provided it was not made in a way which sanctioned the right of one man to own another.

∞∞∞

When Lundy first went to St. Louis in 1819, he had heard of Moses Austin, projector of extensive American settlement in Mexico, and even then had encouraged at least one Negro to scrutinize the province of Texas for "suitable situations for free people of color." In 1822, he noted approvingly Mexico's plan to abolish slavery. In 1829, he expressed alarm at American designs to buy Texas and return it to slavery. Mexico, legally purged of slavery, seemed an excellent spot to colonize ex-slaves and prove that free labor could grow the crops customarily associated with involuntary service. That Garrison called the notion "visionary and unprofitable" did not in the least deter Lundy.[24]

On his return from Canada in the spring of 1832, he sounded out his antislavery friends' response to a Mexican venture. Encouraged, he decided to make a quick trip to Texas, to check the possibilities there as he had earlier done in Haiti. With a $100 loan from the American Convention to help defray his expenses, he reached Texas, contacted the proper officials, and, in July 1832, petitioned the governor of the states of Coahuila and Texas for a land grant. He related his own antislavery background, described his recent trip to Canada, and explained his earlier Haitian venture to

[24]Merton Dillon, "Benjamin Lundy in Texas," *Southwestern Historical Quarterly* 63 (July 1959): 48. Report of J. C. Brown, in Benjamin Drew, ed., *A North-side View of Slavery: The Refugee: or, The Narrative of Fugitive Slaves in Canada. Related by Themselves* . . . (Boston: J. P. Jewett & Co., 1856), 241. *Genius of Universal Emancipation,* August 1822. Lundy to Vicente Guerrero, November 20, 1829, A-ME, Reel 504, enclosed in Lundy to John Quincy Adams, July 13, 1836. *Liberator,* January 22, 1831.

convince the governor of his sincerity and competence. Then, appealing to the governor's idealism, he asserted that black emigration to Mexico would help reduce prejudice in the United States and hasten complete emancipation. He wished, therefore, to settle on the Trinity River some four hundred families, most of whom would be black and emancipated expressly for that purpose.[25]

After an interview with the governor, Lundy came away sanguine. He returned quickly to the United States, organized a second trip, and returned to Mexico in the spring of 1833 to initiate the project. All went well at his first meetings with Santiago del Valle, secretary of state for Coahuila and Texas, and with the governor. The latter promised to grant Lundy the requisite land. As soon as the Mexican Law of 1830 barring American entry into the country was repealed, he promised, Lundy would receive the land he sought. After some delay, the law was repealed to become effective in May 1834.

The way now seemed clear, although the preliminaries had taken longer than Lundy had anticipated, so he again returned to the United States to raise money and make detailed arrangements. He arranged for his new friend and Monclova landlord J. Blackaller, a British subject, to look after his interests during his absence, and especially to procure two grants of land for Lundy when the time was appropriate. Meanwhile, Lundy arrived exhausted and sick in Nashville in May 1834. He had traveled most of the way on foot, burdened by a heavy knapsack, and had suffered intermittently from cholera and other debilities. While he recuperated there at the home of a friend, he wrote a long letter to Gerrit Smith reviewing the accomplishments of his trip. On the land Blackaller was to procure for him, he told the philanthropist, he could settle up to seven hundred families. The venture promised success. The Mexi-

[25] American Convention for Promoting the Abolition of Slavery, Acting Committee, "Minutes," ms. (2 vols., 1804–1837), Minutes for April 13, 1832, ASP-HSP; Benjamin Lundy, Petition to the Governor of the State of Coahuila and Texas, July 5, 1832, L-LC.

can climate was salubrious. The land was productive. Here
a colony would prosper. Here free labor could be tested in
the most favorable circumstances. "Not a shadow of a doubt
now exists in my mind," he wrote, "of the practicability of
making such experiments, upon as extensive a scale as we
please; and the *irresistible* influence which they must necessarily
have upon the system of slavery in America, will be transcen-
dantly important." All it would take, Lundy believed, was "a
little more toil, and *patient, unflinching perseverance.*" Then,
he said, "I shall be enabled to show further what may be
done in the *practical operation* of the great principles which
I have publicly (though feebly) advocated more than fifteen
years."[26]

His rosy anticipations were undermined one by one. Dubious of all colonization after Garrison had published his exposé
of it in *Thoughts on African Colonization,* antislavery sentiment
and antislavery money (by 1834) flowed elsewhere. Lundy
could gather little support, financial or otherwise. Moreover,
free Negroes showed no interest in distant settlement. Rejecting African colonization altogether, they viewed moving
elsewhere in North America as an extreme measure to be
undertaken only under great pressure. As Pittsburgh Negroes
had commented in 1831, "Here [in America] we were born,
here will we live by the help of the Almighty—and here we
will die, and let our bones lie with our fathers." Thus stymied,
Lundy was forced to emphasize the expediency and temporary
character of his plan, to tone down his enthusiasm, and press
it forward as a limited and partial remedy.[27]

Undaunted by the obstacles he met at home, he returned

[26]The complete narrative of Lundy's trips to and from Texas and Mexico
may be followed in Lundy, *Life, Travels, and Opinions,* 63*ff,* and in Dillon,
Lundy, 175–220; the quotation is in Lundy to [Gerrit Smith], a printed letter
with a note enclosed, May 5, 1834, S-SU.
[27]Quoted in William Lloyd Garrison, *Thoughts on African Colonization ...*
(Boston: Garrison & Knapp, 1832), part II, 35; see also Dillon, "Benjamin
Lundy in Texas," 55–56.

to Texas in the summer of 1834. There the news was even worse. His presumed friend Blackaller not only had failed to secure his land, ostensibly because the governor refused to award any more grants, but refused to make Lundy the loan he had promised him and for which he already held the collateral. Lundy sadly decided that the Englishman was personally dishonest and a traitor to the antislavery cause. He also had to admit that he had been "completely baffled in [his] attempts to establish colonies in Texas."[28]

Resilient in the face of apparent disaster, Lundy determined to try to procure land in the province of Tamaulipas. So, in the fall of 1834, he journeyed to Matamoros to negotiate with Tamaulipas officials. Given some encouragement by the Minister of Colonization, Colonel Juan N. Almonte, he kept his spirits high while he turned again to his saddler's trade for financial support. As the weeks dragged by, his optimism lagged. His new associate, a former Mexican army officer, the mulatto Nicholas Drouet, whose reputation was that of an unsuccessful speculator, disappointed him as had Blackaller. Meanwhile, all around him Lundy saw European speculators snatching the land he so wanted while his poverty, honesty, and naiveté left him landless.

After months of dreary existence in Matamoros, his luck seemed to change. On March 10, 1835, he and the provincial governor signed an agreement by which Lundy was granted a maximum of about 172,000 acres, the exact amount to depend upon the number of settlers over the minimum of 250 families, which he would bring to Mexico. He would be free to administer the land as he saw fit, acting either as landlord, speculator, or donor. For its part, the state of Tamaulipas contracted to survey the land, establish towns, and provide one town lot and 120 acres for each family. It would exempt the settlers from all but municipal taxes for

[28]Lundy, *Life, Travels, and Opinions,* 128.

the first five years of their residence. It guaranteed the colony religious and political liberty and freedom from racial discrimination.[29]

So good an agreement seemed ample reward to Lundy for his time and suffering. The Negro citizens of Matamoros gave him a vote of confidence and approved his plan. Even the local white citizens adopted resolutions welcoming new black settlers, hoping that they might "by a proper exercise of their faculties, according to their various talents and capacities soon acquire wealth, respectability and honor, however humble may have been the stations they have previously occupied when prejudice reigned triumphant over them and tyranny had shrouded them in darkness and obscurity." His efforts, Lundy wrote happily to his aged father, were "crowned with success."[30]

Although the agreement required actual settlement before the land grant was formalized, Lundy was not concerned. He began at once to draw up a list of prospective settlers. There was R. R. Graham of Nashville, who promised to provide some Negroes; Andrew Donelson's estate, which promised twenty-one blacks; and an unidentified Southern philanthropist who said he would provide one hundred settlers. Lundy even could begin to count on some funds to launch the venture. He found on his return home in May 1835, "sick, exhausted, and destitute of money," that William Turpin had left him a $1,500 bequest. More important, he concluded in January 1836 a partnership agreement with Lyman Spaulding whereby Spaulding would underwrite the cost of the experiment in return for a division of any profits that might accrue from it.[31]

[29]Benjamin Lundy, *A Circular Addressed to Agriculturists, Manufacturers, Mechanics, &c. on the Subject of Mexican Colonization* ... (Philadelphia: J. Richards, 1835), 3–6.

[30]Lundy, *Life, Travels and Opinions*, 174; quotations are in Armstrong, "Benjamin Lundy," 386; Lundy to Joseph Lundy, April 15, 1835, L-LC.

[31]Lundy, *Life, Travels and Opinions*, 182; Armstrong, "Benjamin Lundy," 375–376; the quotation and Turpin bequest as reported from the *Western*

He even received some support from prominent abolitionists. Lydia Maria Child, widely known author of *An Appeal on Behalf of that Class of Americans Called Africans,* and her husband David Lee Child, an enthusiastic promoter of free produce, decided to join Lundy in Mexico. The support was a real boost for Lundy, because these were leading antislavery people, and their endorsement lent prestige. So pleased was he that he wrote David at length regretting that because he already had a partner he could not place Child in that position. But he did offer him the lure of personal economic advancement, which he himself had only begun to anticipate as a side effect of the venture. Lundy wrote, "A wide door is open . . . for a man of enterprise; and my project will present him with a large field for its exercise"—a field of some 11,800 acres for Child.[32]

Then as rapidly as they had taken shape, the Tamaulipas plans collapsed as the Texas Revolution destroyed forever Lundy's plans. Maria Child had earlier predicted the war and urged him to abandon the project. Neither abolitionists nor free blacks would be safe in traversing this area settled by American slaveholders eager to attach their land to the United States. The war only made the situation more impossible, for the Lone Star Republic embraced that part of Tamaulipas where Lundy's grant lay. "Depend on it, we *are* upon the eve of an important Crisis," he had written to John Quincy Adams in June, 1836. "I fear it is 'all up' with *my enterprise* in Tamaulipas." He was right. As he predicted to Adams, he would soon place himself "in an attitude to do *something else.*"[33]

Methodist, n.d., in *Liberator,* May 23, 1835; Armstrong, "Benjamin Lundy," 388–390.

[32]Lundy to David L. Child, January 25, 1835 [1836], C-BPL.

[33]Lundy to John Quincy Adams, June 9, 1836, A-ME, Reel 504.

The "something else," it was soon evident, was the campaign against Texas annexation. Frustrated in his colonization plans by the revolution, Lundy was doubly opposed to adding Texas to the Union as a slave state. So with others he organized the Pennsylvania Anti-Slavery Society in the fall and winter of 1836–1837 and helped lead its petition campaign against annexation. In February 1837, he drafted a report analyzing the import of allowing Texas to join the Union. The South, he wrote, was pressing to add another slave state, which would thereby so increase slavery's representation as to ensure its control of the national Congress. Furthermore, he asserted, Northern land speculators were poised to make "immense fortunes by the most extensive swindling operations," and were, therefore, aiding the slaveholders in their campaign.[34]

Lundy was not content merely to draft resolutions and write society reports. Once again he felt the journalist's urge to broadcast his message and, bypassing his semicomatose *Genius,* established in 1836 in Philadelphia a new paper, the *National Enquirer.* Generally antislavery, its particular concern was opposing annexation. Furthermore it gained steady support, for within the year the Pennsylvania Anti-Slavery Society made it an official organ.

Both his work on the *National Enquirer* and in the Pennsylvania Society somewhat assuaged Lundy's disappointment over the Mexican disaster, but neither offered the consolation which his contact with John Quincy Adams did in their joint battle against annexation. Between 1836 and 1838, a correspondence of considerable proportions developed between them. Lundy supplied Adams with material on Texas and Mexico to aid the Congressman in his fight in the House. "Perseverence, *perseverence,* my friend!" he urged on the elder statesman. There was, he assured him, a "*wide field* opening" for his "active and valuable labors." As he informed Adams early in their collaboration, "Our publications have opened

[34]*National Enquirer,* February 18, 1837.

many eyes."[35] Undoubtedly Lundy was right. His pamphlet on Texas and Adams' speeches in the House of Representatives publicized the issues widely. Unquestionably Adams made good use of the material supplied to him by Lundy. The arrangement, nonetheless, was far more important and exhilarating to the quiet and often defeated Quaker than to the ex-President, for it restored his ego and gave him a field of effective political action otherwise closed to him.

Whatever his techniques, Lundy developed a new theme in his war against annexation. Central to it was the idea of conspiracy leading to Southern independence. A " 'Southern Confederacy,' " he wrote to Adams in June 1836, "has long been in contemplation." "Unless the Despots of the Slave States," he added significantly, "can establish their authority over the Union, safely and *permanently*, they will, *ere long*, endeavor to 'set up for themselves.' " The strides already made were apparent in the federal government's failure to keep supplies from reaching the Texas insurgents. It became thereby a party to the increase of slave territory, willing perhaps even to involve the whole nation in war to achieve that end. "I fear, indeed," he wrote to Adams, "that we shall be linked in the contest before our *thoughtless* citizens are aware of it."[36] Lundy, who from 1822 until the failure of his Mexican venture had worked in the South and based his hope on the conversion of slaveholders to universal emancipation, now suspected the futility of his whole life's work, defeated by a sinister and power-hungry conspiracy. The Texas Revolution had killed not only his dream of Mexican colonization but was threatening his hopes for voluntary Southern action to end slavery.

Perhaps it was this dismay, as well as his residence in Pennsylvania, that led him to fight for the rights of blacks in the North. He pleaded that alleged fugitive slaves deserved jury

[35]Lundy to John Quincy Adams, May 27, June 14, December 17, 1836, A-ME, Reel 504, except the first, in Reel 503.
[36]Lundy to Adams, June 16, 14, 1836, A-ME, Reel 504.

trials; he sought for Negroes' freedom of movement and opposed incorporating a provision in the new state constitution that would severely limit further black settlement in the state as the Ohio Black Code already did in Ohio. He went still further to urge the justice of full Negro suffrage in the state and attempted also to kindle enthusiasm for antislavery political action there.[37]

So he filled the void which the abortive Mexican venture had left. Then suddenly in the spring of 1838, he resigned as editor of the *National Enquirer* and determined to move West. He planned to revive the *Genius* and continue it there, but his motives were largely personal. He wanted to live near his children whom he had seldom seen since 1830 and to gain a little economic security. Before he left, he wished to attend the grand opening in Philadelphia of the new reform auditorium, Pennsylvania Hall. His wish was gratified, and he was even permitted to store his personal belongings and papers in the building. Within a matter of days, a mob incited to action by its revulsion at the Anti-Slavery Convention of American Women which held its meetings in the new building, undertook to destroy it. First their racket and rocks had forced the dispersal of the meeting. Then, as Lundy sadly wrote Adams the next day, "our splendid 'Pennsylvania Hall' was, last night, *reduced to ashes!*—the work of a *Slavite mob!!!* I am, myself, the greatest *personal* sufferer,—having lost *my all!* —My books, papers, clothes—almost everything—are gone— totally sacrificed upon the altar of Universal Emancipation."[38]

Shortly thereafter, Lundy headed west. He settled in Hennepin, Illinois, built himself a house, and prepared to reestablish the *Genius*. But it was too late for him to start over. His health had been undermined by his travels. He

[37]Lundy to Francis James and [?] Paul, February 13, 1837, MS-FHS; Lundy to James, February 27, March 26, 1837, MS-FHS; all discuss the jury trial issue. See also *National Enquirer,* June 17, October 5, 1837.
[38]Lundy to John Quincy Adams, May 18, 1838, A-ME, Reel 509.

suffered an attack of the bilious fever and died after a short illness on August 22, 1839, at the age of fifty.

🔗🔗🔗

The diversity of Benjamin Lundy's antislavery career complicates any attempt to evaluate his significance. To some, like Wendell Phillips, his agitation against Texas annexation was his principal contribution to the cause, the substructure on which Adams' fight in the Congress was built.[39] On the other hand, Lundy's maintenance of an antislavery press and his attention to encouraging sympathetic organizations did much to keep the movement to end slavery alive through the dull years of the 1820s. Certainly the *Genius of Universal Emancipation* was one of the major antislavery newspapers. Lundy himself, it seems clear, however, thought his principal contribution was his work for colonization. It alone, in however limited a way, made visible inroads on slavery. To Mexican colonization, Lundy sacrificed the *Genius* and all other antislavery work for almost four years. From it came the weapons and inclination to fight Texas annexation. Within its scope, the free-produce argument, conditions for manumission, and, ultimately, general emancipation seemed to merge.

The centrality of colonization in Lundy's work helps place him in the broader movement. His ideas were a little old-fashioned by 1830—or so farsighted as to anticipate the emigration movement popular among blacks in the 1850s. Until his last years, he put his faith in Southern action to end slavery and sustained that faith by convincing slaveholders to manumit when he offered them the promise of practical coloniza-

[39]Wendell Phillips, "Speech at the Melodeon," January 27, 1853, in Massachusetts Anti-Slavery Society, *Twenty-first Annual Report* (Boston: Prentice and Sawyer, 1853), 111–112. Dillon, *Lundy*, vi, 244, bears out the Phillips assessment that Lundy's antiannexationist campaign was his major contribution to antislavery.

tion. He was so little given to theorizing and so ready to accommodate all views that he almost made colonization the last step of any ideology—gradualism or immediatism, compensatory or confiscatory emancipation, mass emigration or mass enfranchisement of freedmen.

Finally, if he was anachronistic, smacking of eighteenth-century rationalism and Quaker piety rather than nineteenth-century romanticism, he was mundanely practical, ready to utilize existing institutions, making of communitarianism not utopianism, with which he had little sympathy, but a sound economic enterprise, which would turn out better goods at less cost. That existing institutions proved unresponsive and communitarianism elusive may only indicate that abolition was not a practical venture suited to old-fashioned, hardheaded approaches. As a result Lundy appears as quixotic as Hiram Wilson, sponsor of the Dawn community in Canada, or David Child, who undertook a disastrous experiment with free-labor sugar in Northampton, Massachusetts, which brought not sweetness but bankruptcy. They were all devoted to a practical resolution of fundamental problems; they were all highly impractical in their methods.

Nonetheless, from the quiet that followed the debates of the Missouri Compromise until Garrison began to raise his angry voice in the *Liberator*, Lundy struggled to rouse opposition to slavery. He once wrote that he knew the time when there was "but a solitary voice" against slavery. By 1837 it was different, and he was pleased at the progress already made. Ironically enough, he had, in all the "marked and visible" change of the 1830s, remained "a solitary voice."[40]

---

[40]*National Enquirer,* January 14, 1837.

6

The Clerical Do-Gooder:
Hiram Wilson

The grim, tedious, day-to-day field work of antislavery, as Benjamin Lundy's career attested, offered little power, prestige, or political allure. Nonetheless it was that activity that brought broadest contact with those whom the abolitionists would convert to their cause, and, in some cases, with those whom the work was intended to benefit. Many earnest and dedicated men and women, varying widely in the talents they brought to the cause, were enlisted to lecture, sell the printed propaganda, and collect funds to provide the following and the means which more prominent leaders would then direct. Hiram Wilson, though his career varied from the most common pattern, was one of these.

A graduate of Oberlin College, Wilson dedicated his ministry to Canadian Negroes, fugitive from both Southern slavery and Northern discrimination. Antislavery to the core, he and his fellow missionaries directed their energies less to ending slavery than to helping refugee Negroes realize and meet the demands and possibilities of freedom—with physical and spiritual aid, with academic education and vocational training.

115

Crossing at the Niagara and Detroit frontiers, American blacks arrived seeking the legal protection and freedom from discrimination which British territory offered. With them came the American missionaries who sought to help them. With them Hiram Wilson spent his adult life.

Born in Acworth, New Hampshire, in 1803 of undistinguished parentage, Wilson inherited the New England dedication to moral uplift which stimulated so much reform during the Middle Period. After early training at Kimball Union Academy, he attended the Oneida Institute in upstate New York. There he was part of a manual labor school, an institution which allowed students to support themselves and learn a trade while they studied—an educational device peculiarly suited to Wilson's later work in Canada. From Oneida, Wilson went, in 1833, to the newly founded Lane Theological Seminary in Cincinnati, seat of evangelical Calvinist ministerial training in the West. Although he played no role in the anti-slavery debates which rocked the school and shocked the Southern-oriented city, Wilson did join with the Lane Rebels, as they were known, in demanding the right to discuss controversial topics, in demanding, actually, the students' right to freedom of speech.[1] And when, rebuffed by the school authorities, the rebels forsook Lane and, as a group, trekked northeastward to the new college at Oberlin, Ohio—so liberal that it welcomed women and Negroes—Hiram Wilson joined them. Thus his New England heritage, his defiance of the status quo at Lane, and his evangelical training with Charles Grandison Finney at Oberlin shaped him to the reform temperament of the Middle Period. Combining evangelical and missionary zeal with humanitarian concern, he was prepared to devote himself to the welfare of the black American.

Although limited in talents, Hiram Wilson was an intensely devoted man and a man of some vision. He gloried in adversity, of which he had more than his share, and created for

[1]For the Lane student statement, see the *Liberator,* January 10, 1835.

himself a kind of martyrdom. Twice married, he expected his wives not only to share the tribulations of his life but to join him in his labors, usually as teachers. Yet for all his intensity, Wilson remains a shadowy figure whose personality, though clearly visible, is overshadowed by the mission that delineated his character and informed his actions. Wilson's importance lies not in himself but in his career. He was a prime example of that evangelical antislavery type: preacher by profession, reformer by vocation.

It was perhaps premonitory of Wilson's career that it began under inauspicious circumstances. Like his fellow Lane Rebels, Wilson was too radical to win financial assistance from the American Board of Commissioners for Foreign Missions. More seriously, he was one of the less talented members of the Lane group. Weighed by the antislavery magnates in the East, he was found wanting. The Young Men's Anti-Slavery Society of New York, wrote Elizur Wright in rejecting Wilson's plea for support, had learned "by rather costly experience . . . to employ none but *first rate* agents." And Wilson "must have grown rapidly since he graduated," observed Wright, "if he can be numbered in that class. In regard to sincerity, knowledge of the subject, and circumspection," he added with the kindness that precedes damnation, "I have no doubts of him—[.] But has he," he continued in the same breath, "the efficiency, the vis vividu, the galvanism that can reanimate the dead as well as the steadfastness that can withstand the onset of the living?"[2]

Confidence in the West, however, overruled skepticism in the East. Theodore Weld, Lane Rebel and antislavery lecturer, thought well of Wilson. Finney found $25 to give him before he set out for his Canadian post. And, shortly after his arrival in Canada in 1836, the American Anti-Slavery Society, con-

[2]Elizur Wright to Theodore Weld, [January 29, 1835], in *Letters of Theodore Dwight Weld, Angelina Grimké Weld, and Sarah Grimké, 1822–1844*, ed. Gilbert H. Barnes and Dwight L. Dumond (Gloucester, Mass.: Peter Smith, 1965), I, 204.

vinced by Weld, sent him a commission as an official agent.[3]
Thus Wilson became one of the select group of antislavery
missionaries known to history as the Seventy.

⛓⛓⛓

As soon as Wilson had established himself in Toronto, his
home and headquarters for the next four years, he began
a systematic investigation of the Negro's condition in Canada.
He traveled about Canada West making direct observations;
he sent out questionnaires to influential people. How honest,
industrious, and temperate, he asked, were the blacks in
Canada West? What was the crime rate among them? Were
they paupers?[4] The questions asked were revealing, for they
provided not only information about the Negro in Canada,
but they told a good deal about Wilson himself. They were
exactly those questions asked by all nineteenth-century Protestant American missionaries about their charges, whether
Negroes in Canada, aborigines in the South Seas, or Indians
on the American frontier. Though the language varied, the
implication did not: salvation—and conversion—would be
after the American fashion.

The answers which Wilson received from his questionnaire
must have been encouraging. They quite uniformly
announced that Canadian blacks were no worse than the Canadian whites among whom they lived. But they were destitute,
these "degraded children of Africa," and badly needed aid.
In turn Wilson informed James G. Birney that they were
relatively "exempt from pauperism, from intemperance and
from the grosser forms of vice." The report marked Canadian

[3]Robert S. Fletcher, *The History of Oberlin College from its Foundation to
the Civil War* (Oberlin: Oberlin College, 1943), I, 246–247; Wilson to
[Charles] Ray, March 9, 1841, in the *Free American,* April 8, 1841.

[4]For the questionnaire and the answers which Wilson received to it, see the
National Enquirer, August 24, 1837.

Negroes for a campaign of mental, moral, and physical improvement.[5]

Goaded by optimism, Wilson knew the fight would be difficult. The refugees had been "excluded from the society of the whites, and from the advantages of the common schools. They [were] truly a degraded people, and why should they not [have been], under such depressing influences? They enter[ed] the province poor, and ignorant, and wretched, [were] protected in their persons and property, but denied those advantages which [were] calculated to refine and elevate human character." Opportunity called to raise the downtrodden, bring them into the white community, and "refine and elevate" them in best reformer fashion.[6] And Wilson's energies, though not directed toward the initial task of freeing the slave, were unmistakably directed toward the equally important task of showing that abolition was no misguided adventure.

The road Wilson trod was rough. Traveling by foot, his pack on his back, seeking food and shelter either outside or at the humble dwellings of scattered settlers, Wilson plied his mission back and forth across the largely uncleared wilderness, westward from the Niagara frontier through London and Chatham to Amherstburgh and Windsor and back along the lake to his Toronto base. Establishing schools for whites and Indians as well as Negroes as he went, he quickly moved on, hoping that others of equal benevolence would keep them staffed and provide their operating expenses. Wherever he went, he gave unstinting counsel and aid to Negro refugees whose welfare was his principal concern. He attended a variety

[5] From the answer of Captain R. G. Dunlop, MP for Huron County, January 27, 1837, in ibid. Birney was reporting what he had learned from Wilson during a recent trip to Toronto; see James G. Birney to Lewis Tappan, July 14, 1837, T-LC.

[6] Wilson to Elizur Wright, November 19, 1836, in the *Emancipator*, December 22, 1836.

of conventions—antislavery society annual conventions at home, more specifically refugee-oriented ones in Canada. In 1838, he was part of a Toronto meeting which opposed extradition of Negro lawbreakers to the United States for trial. In June 1841, he walked sixty-five miles to London to attend a convention on Negro education. On his visits and in his letters to the United States, he constantly consulted with his antislavery colleagues, solicited funds, asked for food and clothing, and searched for teachers to instruct the children in the schools which he had started.[7]

In the early years, his efforts brought returns. By 1839, Wilson had established at least ten schools and had recruited fourteen teachers (mostly from Oberlin) to conduct them.[8] Into his house in Toronto came a constant stream of refugees eager to find new homes in Canada. "His table," wrote a visitor from Auburn, New York, "is surrounded by numbers of fugitives, who are sick and unable to labor, or are waiting until they can procure places of employment." This "ocular demonstration" of his "working abolition" and personal privation aroused in the observer "a more determined spirit of devotion and perserverance in the good cause." Through it all, Wilson's zeal did not flag. "Our cause, brother," he wrote cheerfully as he faced on one occasion five newly arrived fugitives with nearly exhausted supplies "is right onward."[9]

Wilson's work, however, was plagued by shortage of funds and shortage of help, and his family teetered often on the edge of real poverty. Shortly after he went to Canada, he

[7]Material on the activities of Wilson must be pieced together from scattered sources; see, for example, William Raymond to William L. Garrison, January 1, 1840, in the *Liberator,* January 24, 1840; Wilson to Elizur Wright, September 28, 1837, in the *National Enquirer,* October 12, 1837; the *Western Herald and Farmers Magazine* (Sandwich, Upper Canada), August 14, 1838; Wilson to John W. Alden, June 18, 1841, in the *Free American,* July 1, 1841.

[8]Wilson to Charles T. Torrey, February 21, 1839, in the *Colored American,* June 1, 1839.

[9]W. O. Duvall to Editor, September 13, 1840, in the *National Anti-Slavery Standard,* September 24, 1840; Wilson to John W. Alden, May 31, 1841, in the *Free American,* June 10, 1841.

and his Ohio–Oberlin friends organized the Canada Mission, which, after 1840, drew most of its support from upstate New York clerically oriented abolitionists. Among the mission's board of directors were the wealthy philanthropist and Liberty party supporter, Gerrit Smith; William Goodell, onetime editor of the anti-Garrisonian *Emancipator;* Samuel Porter, Rochester businessman; and James C. Fuller, well-to-do British Quaker philanthropist of Skaneateles. Though largely a paper organization, the Canada Mission actively assisted Wilson and his teachers and fellow missionaries and published an annual report of their work in Canada West. Between 1836 and 1841, it sponsored at least forty different missionaries on the Canadian frontier and channeled funds and supplies from the United States to Wilson and his fellow workers.[10]

Still, Wilson met constant obstacles. Always short of funds, always needing more missionaries and teachers, he wrote a steady stream of begging letters. From Goodell, he sought more people to help him; from Gerrit Smith, more money. The costs of maintaining his family, the expenses he incurred for his teachers, the costs of the aid that he constantly gave refugees, he explained, outstripped the contributions he received. Yet, as his needs expanded, his ability to solicit funds was subverted by a distinct diminution in the moral support given him. After two years as one of the Seventy, Wilson was abruptly dropped from the ranks of paid agents in June 1838. The ostensible reason was the American Anti-Slavery Society's lack of funds in the midst of a severe depression and the society's belief that he could "accomplish as much without any connection with the Society" as he could with it. Although he was assured that the decision did not reflect

[10]For the work of the Canada Mission, see, for example, its annual report in the *Liberator,* March 17, 1843. Other material is found in scattered places; for example, Wilson to Editor, June 24, 1841, in *National Anti-Slavery Standard,* July 8, 1841; the *Massachusetts Abolitionist,* February 11, 1841; the *Free American,* July 1, 1841; the *American and Foreign Anti-Slavery Reporter* 2 (September 1, 1842): 80.

on his capacities as a missionary and agent, the assurance was unconvincing.[11] Forced to prune its payroll, the society eliminated Wilson, who lacked personal dynamism and pursued a peripheral task in a distant place.

Not surprisingly Wilson was piqued at the turn of events. "As the Ex. Com. have thought best to dispense with my services hereafter as their agent," he wrote Lewis Tappan, controller of the society's purse strings, "I shall consider myself discharged from the responsibility of an agent of the Society, but not from the responsibility of raising up an outraged and wickedly-neglected people." He was determined to continue his missionary labors, "relying alone upon the God of the oppressed, who is able, and I doubt not will abundantly provide. . . ."[12]

Instead of giving up in anger and despair, Wilson turned to an idea with which he had long toyed. Together with Josiah Henson, an escaped slave soon to be a leader among Canadian Negroes, he planned a black settlement organized around a manual labor school. An organized ethnic community was not a new idea, and Wilson was familiar with the Wilberforce settlement established by Cincinnati blacks in Western Ontario. Although it had failed by 1836, it had left the residue of its experience and potential. To it Wilson now turned.[13]

As he later remembered it, the idea of a Negro settlement had first come to him while he was a student at Oberlin.

[11]Wilson to William Goodell, August 24, 1839, in the *Liberator*, October 11, 1839; Wilson to Gerrit Smith, December 18, 1839, S-SU. The quotation from the "Resolution of the Executive Committee of the American Anti-Slavery Society" was reported by Wilson in his letter to Charles Ray, March 9, 1841, in the *Free American*, April 8, 1841.

[12]Wilson's remarks to the executive committee of the American Anti-Slavery Society are from an unidentified and undated clipping in Lewis Tappan's journal for February 23, 1836–August 30, 1838, attached prior to the July 16, 1838, entry, T-LC. Tappan supplied the identification of Wilson for the clipping.

[13]The Wilberforce settlement and its history, with which Wilson was familiar, are described in William H. Pease and Jane H. Pease, *Black Utopia: Negro Communal Experiments in America* (Madison: The State Historical Society of Wisconsin, 1963), 46–62.

If he could buy land near Amherstburgh, close to American markets and projected railroad lines in Michigan, as well as in the heart of the Canadian black population, he could establish a genuine organized community. There refugees would work as farmers, growing tobacco, sugar beets, and mulberries for a silk industry; there he could aid and settle new immigrants who poured in along the Detroit frontier. There too, he would found a manual labor school in "the centre of a numerous settlement . . . equally accessible to white & coloured students. . . ." "In this way," he argued, "prejudice against color will be completely destroyed & a bright example will be given to the world of a community differing in complexion but harmonizing in the great object of human existance."[14]

Thus Wilson hoped to combine the practical program of Oneida with the social goals of Oberlin in an experimental institution. Joined by Henson and backed by James Fuller, Wilson launched the new community of Dawn Mills, near Dresden in Canada West. With $800 which Fuller had raised on a business trip to England, Wilson purchased 200 acres of land for the settlement. Title to the land was vested in a board of trustees, half Negro and half white. Then ceremoniously, in the middle of the Canadian winter, Wilson "called a few persons around [him], white and colored, near the centre [of the lot], upon the banks of the Sydenham [River], and consecrated the ground to the God of heaven. We formed a semi-circle," he wrote, "upon the South side of a majestic oak which spread its branches to the heavens, where we sung praises to the Most High, bowed the knee in four or five inches of snow, and had a refreshing season of prayer, five persons praying in succession before we rose." Then, on November 28, 1841, the Dawn experiment began. Shortly thereafter, Wilson left Toronto and settled his family in the new colony.[15]

Along the banks of the Sydenham, Wilson planned to estab-

[14]Wilson to Henry Cowles, January 2, 1837, C-OC.
[15]Pease and Pease, *Black Utopia*, 64. The quotation is from Wilson to Friend

lish a series of common schools open to all the inhabitants
of the area. In turn, the manual labor school at Dawn would
"raise up competent teachers of color to supply destitute
places" and receive their products for more advanced training.
The school also would "quality young men of talent & piety
to proclaim the 'glorious gospel of the blessed God' with clear-
ness and power"; it would "bring forth upon the Anti Slavery
battle ground colored champions who [would] wage a successful warfare somewhat after the manner of the Washingtonians
in the Temperance cause by narrating their wo[e]ful experience of slavery[.]" Admitting whites and Indians, as well as
blacks, the institute would "tend directly and powerfully to
the destruction of prejudice," a major goal of all his antislavery
activity.[16]

It was a noble dream. During the first year of settlement,
twelve acres of land were cleared, a schoolhouse with a fifty-to-
sixty student capacity was erected, and a school dormitory for
twenty students was put up. By 1845, four years later, there
were seventy acres of land cleared and under cultivation; by
1847, one hundred acres. By then the settlement boasted some
fifteen wooden buildings, two brick ones, a barn, and two
schoolhouses, in addition to the institute. The value of the
settlement with its improvements was listed at that time as
about $11,000, and the industries conducted there included
a sawmill, a gristmill, and a ropewalk.

More important than these developments was, of course,
the manual labor school, the British American Institute of
Science and Industry as it was hopefully, if a little pompously,
called. Opening its doors in December 1842 with nine pupils,
it reached its zenith in 1845 with eighty students and two
teachers; by 1847, its enrollment had already started to

Chaplin, December 29, 1841, in the *Emancipator and Free American,* January
20, 1842; it had been copied from the *American Citizen,* n.d.

[16]Wilson to Hamilton Hill, April 25, 1843, H-OC. The final quotation
is from the *Seventh Annual Report* (1844) of the Canada Mission, 8–9; the
report was signed by Wilson.

decline. At its height, the school had a juvenile department with students ranging in age from five to twelve and an adult department whose students ranged from twelve to twenty-five and over. Their studies embraced the three R's, history, and geography, as well as mechanics and domestic arts. The institute pupils, Wilson reported to the Canada Mission, are "to be trained thoroughly upon a full and practical system of discipline, which aims to cultivate the *entire being,* and elicit the fairest and fullest possible developments of the physical, intellectual and moral powers."[17]

Wilson's letters in 1844 and 1845 glowed with pride in the school and its pupils. It seemed from his own reports and those of others that he had succeeded in his quest for a field of activity in which he could combine his zeal to preach and evangelize, his desire to reform through education, and his urge to contribute to the antislavery cause by aiding the fugitive slave. When he returned from his English fund-raising tour of 1844, the executive committee of the Canada Mission commended his labors, accompanying the report which he submitted "with a certificate implying approbation and confidence in Mr. Wilson, and the work at Dawn Mills. . . ." The next year, approval came from the *Oberlin Evangelist,* which said that the Dawn "enterprise [was] one of the noblest of the age." And from inside the community, Josiah Henson, never one to underestimate his own prowess, wrote expansively to George Ellis in Boston, "Our Institution is in a prosperous condition and bids fare [sic] to do well."[18]

But even as the community prospered, Hiram Wilson's hopes and dreams were being blighted, for the bright words

[17]Canada Mission, "Sixth Annual Report," in the *Liberator,* March 17, 1843; Report of the Dawn Committee, October 4, 1845, in the *Liberator,* November 14, 1845; Wilson to George Whipple, December 14, 1847, AMA-FU. All contain information relating to the description of Dawn and its school. The quotation is from the Canada Mission Report, which was signed by Wilson.

[18]The executive committee's commendation was printed as an extra, 2d edition, in the *American and Foreign Anti-Slavery Reporter* (April 1844); Josiah Henson to George E. Ellis, March 16, 1846, E-MHS.

did not really mask the difficulties under which the settlement and the school labored almost from the beginning. By 1848 Wilson was compelled to confess that the institute was declining, in part, at least, because the community received no formal support from any of the major missionary societies.[19]

The poor leadership that plagued other organized Negro communities in Canada characterized Dawn as well. Although Josiah Henson was the patriarch of the settlement, it was Wilson who was the principal administrator; and he was simply not a good executive. He lacked talent; his leadership was ill-directed and listless. Lewis Tappan, long and extensively connected with the administration and financing of reform and evangelical projects, entertained grave doubts about him. When Wilson sought funds from Tappan for the institute, the latter launched inquiries which showed the standards this businessman–philanthropist expected from projects he backed. Was Wilson "doing well"? Did he use the money entrusted to him faithfully and beneficially? Was he an able administrator? Were his plans sound?[20] Assuredly, Tappan remembered the American Anti-Slavery Society's decision to drop Wilson from its agency in 1838. And the answers which Samuel Porter of the Canada Mission returned did not overcome his long-standing doubts about Wilson.

Tappan's doubts were not unjustified. Isaac Rice, observing from his missionary post in Amherstburgh, wrote to Tappan in 1845 that conditions at the institute were "quite critical." Although he admitted to a "perfect confidence" in Wilson, his language reflected the style of the period rather than real trust in Wilson's ability. "The Brethren [at Dawn,]" he continued, "try to do well, but I fear there is not heft & balance of mind & that deep knowledge of Human Nature" necessary to the successful operation of such an experiment. Joshua Leavitt, inherently more friendly to Wilson than Rice,

[19]Wilson to Edmund Quincy, September 27, 1848, in the *Liberator*, October 27, 1848.
[20]Lewis Tappan to Samuel D. Porter, November 9, 1844, T-LC.

indicated that, although "Wilson has done great good as a most laborious pioneer in looking after the poor fugitives from American oppression," he (Leavitt) did "not feel so much confidence in his ability to manage an institution of learning or any other matter involving a large expenditure of money."[21]

Wilson's troubles at Dawn were personal as well as institutional. His private finances were soon in disrepair as a result of severe illness in the family and the death of his first wife. He had to sell much of the land he had bought in Dawn, and he was still deeply in debt.[22] Moreover, it soon became evident that his conduct and style irritated a substantial number of Negroes. In 1847, he was attacked by William Newman, who had been brought to Dawn in 1845, appointed secretary of the executive committee, and charged with straightening out the settlement's financial affairs. Newman immediately conducted an investigation, presented his findings to the executive committee, and made recommendations for improvement. The committee upheld his findings but took no action on the recommendations. He therefore resigned his position and journeyed to Oberlin in January 1847, where he vented his spleen against Dawn and, more specifically, against Wilson. Newman, implying that Wilson was thoroughly disliked in the country, alleged that he was unable to preach in any black church in Canada. The same charges were repeated in July 1847 at the annual convention of the True Wesleyan Connexion of Canada, which, however, discounted them and vindicated Wilson. But the damage had been done. Finally, the Drummondsville Convention of Canadian and American Negroes in 1847 made it clear that all was not well at Dawn. It heard testimony about the affairs of Dawn, listened

[21]Isaac Rice to Lewis Tappan, January 29, 1845, T-RU; Joshua Leavitt to John Scoble, March 9, 1843, in Annie H. Abel and Frank J. Klingberg, eds., *A Side-Light on Anglo-American Relations, 1839–1858* ... ([Washington]: The Association for the Study of Negro Life and History, 1927), 121–125.

[22]See, for example, Wilson to Dear Brother, October 18, 1850, AMA-FU, in which he described his earlier difficulties. The records of Wilson's land sales are in the Kent County, Ontario, Registry Office records.

to charges that it was ill managed, and, although it vindicated the personal honesty of Josiah Henson, moved to oversee the accounts and affairs of the settlement. Hiram Wilson had to recognize that his connection with Dawn was propitious for neither one. Capitulating to that fact, weighed down by financial burdens, and smarting under the attacks inspired by loss of confidence, he severed his official connection with the British-American Institute in the fall of 1847.[23]

Wilson nevertheless remained at the settlement for the next three years, carrying on his missionary work independently. But labors as teacher, missionary, and operator of common and Sabbath schools brought in little money. By March 1848, he was threatened with the loss of his house, and faced the prospect of leaving Dawn to seek work elsewhere. Friends in the East, learning of his plight, raised enough money to settle his outstanding debts, but the crisis was symbolic of Wilson's failure.[24] He constantly begged funds; he constantly needed cash to keep himself and his work going. It is clear why men like Lewis Tappan, who were the financial mainsprings of reform, were so dubious about Wilson, a typically fuzzy-headed reformer, grand of vision but short on accomplishment, and totally devoid of the ability to make his projects economically self-sustaining. Certainly the financial backers expected a clear return on their investment in reform, and just as surely Wilson provided scant evidence of any such return.

As his influence declined at Dawn, Wilson was more and more written off by friends and former supporters. Mrs. Brooks, missionary teacher in the Queen's Bush, who lived nearby and knew his work well, thought "but little of Mr Wilson's plans," although she "consider[ed] him a good man." In 1848, his English support waned. Liverpool contributors

---

[23]For the full Newman episode and the story of Wilson's final failure at Dawn, see Pease and Pease, *Black Utopia*, 69–83.

[24]Wilson to William L. Garrison, March 25, 1848, in the *Liberator*, April 7, 1848.

notified him of their last contribution; Joseph Sturge of Birmingham refused any further donations. The cruelest blow of all, however, came from New York City. Most explicit and direct was Lewis Tappan's decision to cut Wilson off entirely. He wrote Wilson in 1848: "I have made up my mind, dear brother, that you are not a suitable man to be at the head of an enterprise—that much money has been wasted at Dawn Mills[,] that the scheme was an injudicious one. You have not," he continued, assessing Wilson's incapacities with brutal directness, "sufficient judgment or financial skill for such an enterprise. Still," he continued, honeying over what he had just said without essentially changing the meaning, "as a teacher you might do good. As a preacher I learn that you are not acceptable to the colored people, lacking animation, vivacity & free utterance. I think you will not be displeased at my telling you my opinion in this friendly way," he added with a characteristic lack of perception about human feelings. Making it quite clear that he did not wish publicly to be thought to have any confidence in Wilson's plans or undertakings, Tappan did conclude that he thought Wilson "a good man & a true friend of the people of color." Then, in a peroration that threw crumbs to the incompetent, he added, "I feel desirous that you should be able to devote yourself to some useful work." Clearly, Tappan wrote to Joseph Sturge, "H. W. is a good man but not fit to be at the head of any enterprise."[25]

That Wilson should have continued his missionary and reform efforts after such a mauling is remarkable. That he stayed for two more years at Dawn Mills is incredible. Yet he did. Though not without complaining, he accepted the fact that he had been unceremoniously dumped by his antislav-

[25]Mrs. Brooks' comment was reported in Lewis Tappan to Joseph Sturge, letterpress, May 1, 1848, T-LC. On the end of English aid, see Lewis Tappan to Wilson, letterpress, April 25, 1848, T-LC; Wilson to George Whipple, May 23, 1848, AMA-FU. Tappan's long comment is in his letter to Wilson just cited; his concluding observation about Wilson is in Tappan to Sturge, letterpress, May 23, 1848, T-LC.

ery colleagues. Much of his time he devoted to farming for his own livelihood. The rest of the time he devoted to his missionary activities and to his work with the common and Sabbath schools at Dawn. There were rewards for his efforts and Wilson was proud of his achievements. "My hands are full," he wrote to Frederick Douglass in 1849. "I am furnishing the best of instruction to rising of 50 scholar[s] during the week, my wife and Mrs. [Lorena] Parker assisting me. We also have a peculiarly interesting Sabbath-school of 70 scholars. Superintending this school in the morning, and preaching in the afternoon, constitutes my regular Sabbath-day labors, and yet I have frequent appointments to fill in Dawn and vicinity besides. We are doing all we can for the benefit of the refugees and children."[26]

But while he expressed joy with his work, he also spoke bitterly of its hazards. His credit was exhausted, he complained, and he desperately needed help. "This is a sad picture," he said, "but the truth must be told." In December 1848, he was about to mortgage his property in order to raise money. A month later he petulantly pointed out that he had no connection with the British-American Institute and that he received neither hindrance nor help from it. Furthermore, he whined to George Whipple, "I have had opposition ever since I have been in the country, & so have all others who have done any good[.] I care not for it," he added, "but when professed friends prove themselves to be enemies in disguise & busy themselves in alienating from me the hearts of those who have formerly been true & faithful there is required the faith of an Abraham & the patience of a Job[.]"[26a] "My days in Canada are numbered," he predicted to Douglass.

But true to his mercurial nature, Wilson constantly shifted ground. There was, he assured George Whipple in 1849, no

[26]Wilson to George Whipple, May 23, December 21, 1848, AMA-FU; Wilson to Editor, January 6, 1849, in the *North Star*, January 19, 1849.

[26a]Wilson to Edmund Quincy, September 27, 1848, in the *Liberator*, October 27, 1848; Wilson to George Whipple, December 21, 1848, AMA-FU; Wilson to

prejudice against him in Canada and he could preach successfully there. Many Negroes, he thought, wanted him for an
itinerant preacher and he must labor on to break down the
barriers erected by prejudice. In 1850, in spite of a drastic
decline in the number of students in his day and Sabbath
schools, he noted cheerfully that he had an "interesting school
through the winter for male scholars." Boasting joyously to
Garrison that he had collected $300 on a recent tour to the
East, he wrote Elizabeth Montfort in Portland, Maine, at the
same time and complained bitterly of lack of support and
need of money to forestall disaster: "We shall doubtless have
to leave soon & spend the balance of our brief pilgrimage
in some other section of the Lord's Vineyard."[27]

When indeed Wilson finally did leave Dawn in 1850, he
left with bitter commentary on its failure. "The Manual Training Institute here," he wrote in February 1850, "ran well for
a season, and accomplished much good; but since my resignation [in 1847] . . . and the decease of James Cannings Fuller,
one of the Trustees, it has run down, and can hardly be
resuscitated again without a miracle." To Garrison he
defended his rapport with Canadian Negroes, explaining that
the failure of some of them to appreciate the help he had
given them stemmed from their division into rival sectarian
camps where they followed the lead of their white mentors.
He did not blame them for their lack of "gratitude towards
their [white] benefactors, who have toiled and suffered on
their behalf"; yet, he admitted, this was largely why he was
leaving Dawn. And, once he had gone to live in St. Catherines,
he rejoiced in his freedom from "the 'strife of tongues' &
the merciless assaults of enemies who in their deception and

Hamilton Hill, January 6, 1849, H-OC; Wilson to Whipple, January 16, 1849,
AMA-FU.

[27]Wilson to George Whipple, January 16, 1849, AMA-FU; Wilson to William
L. Garrison, July 22, 1850, in the *Liberator,* August 2, 1850. The quotations
are both from Wilson to Elizabeth Montfort, March 8, 1850, AS-MeHS.

hypocrasy [sic] palm themselves off upon the Christian public as friends of God...."[28]

Neither bitterness and resentment at the persecution he felt nor his clear failure to reach many of the blacks to whom he wished to minister was sufficient to drive him from his commitment to Negro fugitives in Canada. Indeed he did seriously consider moving to the American Midwest for his wife's health, but passage of the new Fugitive Slave Act in 1850 made him decide to settle in St. Catherines on the Niagara frontier. "I know not how others feel with regard to those *superlatively wicked black laws*," he wrote in great agitation, "but as for myself I owe no respect to them & shall treat them as a nullity & abide the issue. May God blast the nefarious designs of avaricious man thieves."[29] And so, with the needs of the new fugitives from America's most recent injustice clearly in mind, he established his last post in Canada.

⊖⊖⊖

There were already nearly 2,000 Negroes in the St. Catherines area and, between September and December of 1850, another 3,000 arrived from the United States. Thus once again Wilson settled down to the endless task of assisting the refugees from America, of playing his role of preacher and teacher to the destitute and needy. Between 1850 and 1856, he took into his house about 125 refugees, and one can only hazard how many scores more he assisted in their adjustment to their new environment. To them, he gave food and clothing; to the literate, a Bible; to the rest, a spelling book. He offered them advice and counsel, as well as fuel and medicine. He journeyed to neighboring towns to see that they were properly located, and he encouraged them to save their money to buy land upon which to settle.

[28]The quotations are from Wilson to William L. Garrison, February 12, July 22, 1850, appearing in the *Liberator* for March 1, 1850, and August 2, 1850, respectively; Wilson to George Whipple, November 20, 1851, AMA-FU.

[29]Wilson to George Whipple, October 1, 1850, AMA-FU.

In St. Catherines, he continued also his educational work. He organized and conducted schools for refugees and for white children. He established Sabbath schools; and, as was his fate, the auspicious 170 pupils that he counted in 1851 had dwindled to 80 by 1853. His day school was perhaps more successful, for it employed for a time two teachers. In addition, he helped find teachers to staff the government school in St. Catherines.[30]

To his educational and refugee work, Wilson added a ministry to the seamen working boats on the Welland Canal. On Sundays, it was his custom to supervise the Sunday school, "preach once ... to the colored people, and walk about 8 or 10 miles in the course of the day up & down the Welland Canal, distributing Religious, Peace, & Temperance Tracts, to the sailors, & hold one service on board a vessel usually about 5 ocl P.M. & preach to the sailors."[31] Here, one suspects, Hiram Wilson was happiest and most successful.

For a while, it even seemed possible that Wilson might avoid his customary financial problems, for he had convinced the American Missionary Association to appoint him official missionary for the St. Catherines work, and from them he received a $400 annual salary. Yet again Wilson encountered opposition from Lewis Tappan, who controlled the American Missionary Association's purse strings. Wilson had complained that $400 was insufficient to support his family, assist the refugees who constantly were in his home, aid the teachers who staffed his schools, and pay other miscellaneous expenses

---

[30]The record of Wilson's activities is gleaned from a series of his letters to various people. See, for example, in order of their appearance, one to William L. Garrison, December 4, 1850; another to Francis Jackson, October 25, 1854; another to Garrison, January 1, 1856, all in the *Liberator*, December 13, 1850, November 24, 1854, January 11, 1856. Also a letter to George Whipple, April 24, 1851, AMA-FU; one to Henry Bibb, January 1, 1853, in *Frederick Douglass' Paper*, February 4, 1853; and another to Whipple, November 20, 1851, AMA-FU. One to [Hannah Gray], March 22, 1853, in Hiram Wilson, "Letters," *Journal of Negro History* 14 (July 1929): 344–350. And another to Whipple, May 1, 1851, AMA-FU.

[31]Wilson to Hamilton Hill, May 24, 1853, H-OC.

of his work. He argued for $600 a year plus a separate $100
fund to be used in assisting refugees. Tappan disagreed and
asserted that Wilson was supposed to raise one-half of his
salary himself since the AMA was directly responsible for
only $200 of his salary.

Indeed Wilson did raise considerable money. He was, in
the idiom of the day, a beggar of no mean talents, but he
insisted that whatever he collected was his own to use as he
saw fit. Tappan thought otherwise. Whatever Wilson collected
he should report to the AMA, which would then allot him
the entire $400 salary. If, however, he insisted on using his
collections at his own discretion, then the association would
consider them part of his salary.

Although Tappan as usual contended that he had complete
faith in Wilson's Canadian mission, he implied that Wilson
was failing to live up to the bargain he had made in accepting
a contract from the AMA. His failure to do so made Tappan
suggest that Wilson "had best 'fight on his own hook.' "
Ultimately Tappan prevailed when the association's Committee on Canada Missions on January 14, 1853, decided "after
a free interchange of views relative to the efficiency of Mr
Wilsons labors in Canada & elsewhere . . . to recommend to
the Executive Committee to withhold the aid asked for by
Rev Hiram Wilson, so soon as it can be done without injustice
to him." Wilson may have been technically correct when he
insisted that he had thereupon voluntarily resigned his commission and had pursued his work "on a voluntary footing,
dependent, under God upon the labor of my own hands,
and voluntary contributions from the benevolent who know
me. . . ."[32] But the fact was that, once again, Hiram Wilson
had unceremoniously been fired.

[32]The quotations appear in Wilson to Lewis Tappan, December 29, 1852,
AMA-FU; George Whipple, "Minutes of the Committee on Canada Missions,"
January 14, [1853], in AMA-FU; Wilson to Hannah Gray, June 15, 1853,
N-LC. On Wilson's financial contretemps with the American Missionary
Association, see also Wilson to Whipple, August 30, December 17, 1851,
AMA-FU.

Though now fifty years old, Wilson refused to give up. He continued to beg and piece together a precarious living. From Gerrit Smith, he requested $300 to help pay for the construction of his house in St. Catherines, built largely with a legacy left his wife. His income in 1856, he told Smith, came largely from small pledges of $10 each from Boston friends, a $150 a year salary from the Massachusetts Society for the Propagation of the Gospel, and commissions from a part-time agency for the J. P. Jewett publishing firm of Boston. The going was tight and in 1859 he was narrowly saved from having his property seized for debts by the timely contributions from friends in New Haven and Boston.[33]

Whether his monetary difficulties or his view of political reality in the United States forced his decision, Hiram Wilson in 1861 decided to abandon his labors. Since 1859 he had been "strongly inclined to the opinion that the idea of '*under-ground Rail Road*' ought to become obsolete every where north of Mason & Dixons Line so that there will be no more necessity for fugitive slaves running to Canada." And shortly after the outbreak of the Civil War, in October 1861, he claimed that all Negro refugees were well settled in Canada and rejected further aid for them. Then, almost unnoticed, on April 16, 1864, Hiram Wilson died.[34]

⛓⛓⛓

Throughout his career, Hiram Wilson was dogged by misadventure. Dedicated though he was to the welfare of black refugees, he inspired attack from many Negroes. In Toronto, militant Peter Gallego charged that during its early years, the Canada Mission was too paternalistic and that it degraded

[33]Wilson to Gerrit Smith, June 19, 1856, S-SU. Wilson to Hannah Gray, January 14, 1859, in Wilson, "Letters," 344–350.
[34]Wilson to Gerrit Smith, September 17, 1859, S-SU; Wilson to William L. Garrison, October 30, 1861, in the *Liberator,* November 8, 1861. Obituary notice in the *Liberator,* May 13, 1864.

Negroes and kept them depressed. Self-respecting Negroes, he claimed—and he had suffered oppression and discrimination and had reason to know—resented the assistance of the Canada Mission. The way to independence, he implied, was through individual action. In the United States, Charles Ray of the *Colored American* claimed also that Wilson and the Canada Mission encouraged caste by establishing separate schools for blacks—a charge Wilson denied vigorously. Ray further contended that the Canada Mission made Canadians of the refugees. Let them be assisted by the New York City Vigilance Committee, he urged; then they would remain Americans. In nearby Windsor, Mary A. Shadd and the *Provincial Freeman,* the leading black newspaper of the area, lashed out vitriolically against Wilson during the 1850s. The *Freeman* published a long disquisition from a Mrs. Williamson of St. Catherines, which charged that Wilson was scorned by the townspeople as an intermeddling evangelist; that he was servile, hypocritical, and "avaricious"; and that the misguided Negroes of St. Catherines were happy "to have a Missionary to think for them instead of thinking for themselves." To this, Mary Shadd added that Wilson lived off the Negroes in a "brick mansion." Where, she queried caustically, had all the money gone that Wilson had raised for his philanthropy? Then, when Wilson, giving up his work, contended that the Negroes had at last been taken care of, Shadd countered that they were still coming into Canada, that the American Civil War had not diminished their numbers, and that the work of providing for them was by no means finished.[35]

Wilson's difficulties did not lie solely with black antipathy.

[35] Peter Gallego to Editor, January 25, 1841, in *National Anti-Slavery Standard,* January 28, 1841; Charles Ray writing in the *Colored American,* February 20, 1841. The *Provincial Freeman* attacks can be followed in two letters to the editor, signed "Q" (Mrs. Williamson), dated March 13 and April 5, 1856, respectively. The quotations are from these letters. Mary Shadd's remarks are from the *Freeman,* of which she was an editor, for January 19, 1857, which contains the quotation, and from her letter to William L. Garrison, n.d., appearing in the *Liberator,* November 29, 1861.

He was also the victim, after 1840, of the fighting between antislavery factions. To a large extent a pawn in the infighting, he had, from his earliest missionary days, been identified with the anti-Garrisonian faction. Though Wilson never personally took part in the battles that engaged the two groups, his clericalism and the nature of his activity almost automatically identified him with new organization, which centered around Lewis Tappan. Moreover, in 1840, he had supported the Liberty party candidacy of James Birney. He had approved of what he called "ballot box abolitionism" and had admonished New Yorkers to go "TO THE POLLS FOR OUR RESCUE!"[36] From its inception in the late 1830s, Wilson had been defended by the voice of Massachusetts clericalism, the *Abolitionist,* from the attacks which Garrison and Nathaniel P. Rogers, editor of the New Hampshire *Herald of Freedom,* had leveled "against this noble man and his holy enterprise."[37] So, in one of those peculiar twists of history, Hiram Wilson was identified as a Tappanite by the opposition despite the fact that Lewis Tappan had so little faith in him. Regularly, therefore, Wilson was attacked by the Garrisonians while he was denied support from the Tappan faction. Tarred with the support which archclerical Charles Torrey had briefly given him in the *Massachusetts Abolitionist,* he was criticized not only in the columns of the *Liberator* but in the *National Anti-Slavery Standard* as well. Maria Chapman summed up the old organization's view of the "Hiram Wilson Society" as pro-slavery and insufficiently attentive to "the great idea of freedom."[38]

Attacks from rival groups, however, give little understanding of Hiram Wilson's particular place in the antislavery movement. Wilson represented the generalist as antislavery

[36]Hiram Wilson to [?], n.d., letter fragment printed in the *Massachusetts Abolitionist,* September 17, 1840.

[37]From a letter dated January 27, [1841], to the *Massachusetts Abolitionist,* of February 11, 1841, and signed *"A Follower of no Man, But a Friend to All."*

[38]Maria Chapman writing in the *Liberator,* January 12, 1844.

enthusiast. He was a reformer, preacher, missionary, teacher, administrator. When he was preacher, he was an evangelical Methodist trying to save the unconverted. When he was missionary, he ministered to all who needed uplift and the saving word of Christ. When he was teacher, he founded schools and institutes for children of all colors, backgrounds, and ages. When he was antislavery reformer, he combined these other labors in order to aid fugitives from slavery and discrimination and to demonstrate that ex-slaves could prosper in a free society. He was that type of reformer, so common in the Middle Period, who, largely inspired by a religious zeal, applied himself to the solution of secular problems.

The ultimate question remains: what did Hiram Wilson add to the antislavery movement? Constantly distracted from his work by his nearly eternal quest for funds, Wilson was also an incompetent administrator. The Dawn community and manual labor school, the locus of his highest hopes, was not only a dismal failure in itself but also did nothing to end slavery and little to provide the free Negro a place in predominantly white North American society. Despite Wilson's dedication to the idea of integration, which became a major principle of the British-American Institute, few whites or Indians ever took advantage of the school. Nor was that surprising, for Wilson's efforts there were almost totally directed toward blacks. The crux of the matter was that neither Dawn nor any other organized Negro community made much impress on the fundamental issues of antislavery.

It is also to the point to question the relevance of the Canada Mission to American antislavery. The Canadian work affected relatively few Negroes, for in Canada in the three decades before the Civil War there were probably no more than 40,000 blacks, perhaps as few as 20,000. Furthermore, it was largely inconsequential that Wilson in St. Catherines aided scores of Negroes in his own home or otherwise as they passed through the community, for Hiram Wilson was a lone operator, well removed from the American audience whose guilt of slavery he would purge. Nor did he ever have much real contact with the major antislavery organizations. He did, to be sure, attend from time to time the meetings of the American Anti-Slavery Society, the Massachusetts Anti-Slavery Society, the New England Anti-Slavery Convention, and the Canadian Anti-Slavery Society. But he was never at the center of things, and he could never make his weight felt in matters that counted. Finally, though he was sympathetic to the idea of antislavery political action, Wilson did nothing of importance to push it. Partly this was because he lived in Canada. But he apparently saw little connection in Canada between Negro welfare and political action, a connection which William King, a white leader of another black Canadian community, saw clearly and utilized.

Hiram Wilson's reform career was shaped and molded by his evangelical ministry. Unlike most of his antislavery colleagues, he had close physical contact with those he would aid. He was able to realize his humanitarianism in the concrete; he was saved from abstract remoteness, which characterized many abolitionists. At the same time, he had very little concept of the nature of antislavery or of the theory of missionary action. His truly philanthropic heart and genuine antislavery zeal foundered on a naive reliance upon other men's bounty and God's direct aid. At bottom he was ill-equipped, ill-suited to his work. Small in competence, he was a whiner by nature with an essentially unpleasant personality, a man of good intentions marred by self-righteousness unrelieved by compensating ability. When his career was over, he had accomplished little of lasting significance. Partly this was the fault of Wilson himself; partly of the methods he employed. As a loner, as a generalist reformer, he was shut out from the mainstream of antislavery thought and from the mainstream of antislavery activity and influence. Yet, like Benjamin Lundy, he had acted directly to aid American blacks to overcome not only slavery but the deprivations it had brought them individually.

7

The Negro Conservative:
Samuel Eli Cornish

Samuel Eli Cornish was a "gentleman of great worth, universally respected"; an active participant in the antislavery crusade; a staunch opponent of the American Colonization Society and an equally active supporter of the American Anti-Slavery Society; and a supporter of Liberty party candidate James G. Birney for the presidency in the 1844 election. He was "remarkable for his retiring modesty, polish of manners, and propriety of deportment."[1] So wrote William Goodell in his obituary eulogy to Cornish in 1858. As far as it went, it was an accurate assessment. Cornish had been well known in antislavery circles, not only in New York, but throughout the North. His name occurs frequently in the records of the movement. Later historians have consistently singled him out as an important black leader in the fight to end slavery and to elevate the Negro. Yet in many ways, Samuel Cornish, of all the black abolitionists and early civil-rights activists, remains the least known.

[1]*Radical Abolitionist,* December 1858.

Of humble background like Wilson, Cornish was born, probably in 1795, in Sussex County, Delaware, the child of free Negro parents. Of his youth there is no record except that when he was twenty he left home and went to Philadelphia. There, under John Gloucester, pastor of the First African Church, Presbyterian, he was educated and prepared for the ministry. It was a minimal education, two years at best, consisting of little more than English grammar and elementary theology, supplemented by much practical experience. Frequently Cornish preached for the ailing Gloucester, and, after being licensed in 1819, he spent a year as an itinerant preacher and missionary among the slaves of Maryland's Eastern Shore.

When in 1821 Cornish was ready for his own parish, he went to New York City, where he organized a Presbyterian congregation among the black community. Ordained the next year by the New York Presbytery, he became pastor of the group, now formally the New Demeter Street Presbyterian Church. He served this parish until 1828 when he resigned and was succeeded by the young Princeton-trained clergyman Theodore S. Wright. His resignation, however, did not interrupt his missionary work to blacks within and outside the city, which he continued until 1840, but rather increased his itinerant preaching. In addition, but very briefly, in early 1832, he served Gloucester's church in Philadelphia, whose pastorate he had rejected in 1824. A decade later he was, for a short time, minister of the Negro Presbyterian Church in Newark. His last settled parish was with the Emmanuel Church in New York City, which he had also helped to organize.[2] Throughout his life, Cornish's pastoral career, although sporadic, shaped his career as an abolitionist. Never did he part from his clerical vocation, although he practiced it in many guises. His reform outlook, like his theology, was conser-

[2] The general career of Cornish is covered in Howard Nathaniel Christian, "Samuel Cornish: Pioneer Negro Journalist" (Master's thesis, Howard University, 1936), 1–56.

vative, committed but not innovative. He was humble with other men of God and paternally instructive in leading his flock. Within the antislavery movement, he was a clerical conservative, as much at odds with Garrisonian perfectionism as with young black militance.

For black abolitionists more than for white, antislavery work demanded not only a commitment to free the Southern slave but a constant effort to uplift the Northern Negro. Samuel Cornish fit this pattern. Either as a member or an officer, he served a variety of antislavery organizations. A founder of the American Anti-Slavery Society, he sat on its executive committee for at least five years between 1833 and 1840. He was a manager of the Union Evangelical Anti-Slavery Society in 1839; a founder, manager, and member of the executive committee of the Union Missionary Society in 1842; and a founder, in 1833, of the New York Anti-Slavery Society. From 1840 to 1853, he sat for at least nine years on the executive committee of the American and Foreign Anti-Slavery Society and was at least once its recording secretary. In the mid-1840s, he helped organize the American Missionary Association, acted on its executive committee for three years, and was a vice-president from 1848 until his death a decade later.

His committee work, however, comprised the lesser part of Cornish's work, for his mulatto-brown skin linked his fate to the welfare of all free Negroes in the North. Like the black Henry Highland Garnet and the white Hiram Wilson, Cornish found greater satisfaction in the direct human contacts, which aiding free Negroes involved, than in preaching abstract antislavery truth to whites. Nonetheless, he found the two modes of action complementary, for the latter was an integral part of the former. How better, he asked rhetorically in 1829, could white people help the free Negro than by joining antislavery societies.[3] For himself, however, he would first choose to edit an antislavery newspaper directed at the black community. In three separate journals between 1827 and 1839, he considered the Negro's place in the North, as well as in the South, discussed the role of both blacks and whites in achieving racial equality, and exhorted Afro-Americans to rise in society and provide for their own welfare.

Despite the number of papers he undertook, Cornish's total editorial tenure was of short duration. In the spring of 1827, he joined John Russwurm in editing *Freedom's Journal*, the first distinctly black press in America. He stayed in that post only six months. Two years later, he became editor, for a season, of the successor to *Freedom's Journal*, *The Rights of All*. Then a decade intervened before Cornish assumed his final editorial position with the *Colored American* from 1837 until the middle of 1839. Brief and intermittent though his newspaper work was, it showed Samuel Cornish at his reforming best. Here was the test of his antislavery labor.

⛓⛓⛓

Cornish's work on *Freedom's Journal* laid the foundation for his later editorial career. The paper was devoted to the "stimulation of race-pride" and concerned largely for "the rights, & [i]nterests of the coloured population." During its brief life it helped, wrote Cornish, "to remove the many abuses which exist among [my] brethren, to promote habits of industry and economy, and to inculcate the importance of an improved education."[4]

The tenor of the *Journal's* message was clearly that of self-help, a theme which Cornish subsequently emphasized in *The Rights of All*. It essentially preached the American Protestant

[3]*The Rights of All*, September 18, 1829.
[4]Bella Gross, "Freedom's Journal and the Rights of All," *Journal of Negro History* 17 (1932): 257; *The Rights of All*, May 29, 1829.

ethic: hard work, abstemiousness, devotion to the gospel of success. Cornish drove the theme hard and applied it specifically to his black readers. They tended, he wrote, to waste their time and substance. "We grasp after flowers," he challenged them, "and neglect solid and whol[e]some fruits!!! Is there scarcely a family of any respectability among us, who does not spend from ten to fifty dollars annually in unnecessary gratifications. . . ." If they didn't spend their money prodigally, he said, they frittered away their time loitering around courthouses and traipsing after military parades, when instead they should be directing their energies toward useful and productive goals. They should be raising money for the "establishment of libraries, reading rooms, schools, academies and one general college embracing all the mechanical arts, with a thorough classical education. . . ."[5]

Cornish had earlier displayed this trust in the efficacy of education to improve society when in 1827 he had commended Gerrit Smith for supporting ministerial training for Negro youth. Smith's project, he averred, would greatly assist "our unhappy and degraded race"; but it was not the only schooling which blacks needed. All Negroes, he insisted, should receive a general education to prepare them to assume the full responsibilities of citizenship. "The coloured population of our country," he wrote in a May 1829 editorial, "should become more acquainted with men and things, [with] some knowledge of the history of nations, the Geography of countries, and their moral and physical resources. . . ." Thus would their ambition and spirit of enterprise be excited; thus would they be stimulated to effective self-help.[6]

Cornish not only preached the virtues of education, but took positive steps to secure it for his fellows. While editor of *The Rights of All*, he supported New York's African Free

[5]*The Rights of All*, September 18, 1829.
[6]Samuel Cornish and John Russwurm to Gerrit Smith, April 16, 1827, S-SU; *The Rights of All*, May 29, 1829.

Schools, then teaching such future Negro leaders as Henry Garnet and Alexander Crummell. During 1827 and 1828, Cornish was agent and liaison officer for the schools, explaining to parents the program and encouraging them to enroll their children. Beyond this, he was expected "to enjoin a punctual attendance at school, as well as to promote the general objects of the Institution." That he was successful at his work, the schools' historian, a contemporary of Cornish, attested when he noted that his efforts had "been productive of much good to the parents" and of "great benefit" to the schools.[7]

Schools and newspapers were not, however, the only means Cornish used to elevate free blacks. He actively encouraged the first annual convention of blacks, held in Philadelphia in 1831, and was one of its principal agents. Quick to recognize the utility of the conventions as vehicles for Northern Negroes' welfare, Cornish did not retain his initial enthusiasm. By the end of the decade, he feared that convention-going had become an almost pathological syndrome. Suffering from "convention fever," Negroes became travel prone and diverted their energies from more serious undertakings.[8]

If he felt uneasy about conventions, Cornish did not turn his back on their object. He supported wholeheartedly the conventions' persistent calls for Negroes to buy their own land and settle on it. During the 1830s, he worked closely with Gerrit Smith, who distributed thousands of acres of land in upstate New York to the poor and, in particular, to blacks whom he deemed worthy. Like his enthusiasm for education, his trust in the yeoman farmer was a commonplace of his country and his time. Put a man on the land, Cornish wrote,

[7]Charles C. Andrews, *The History of the New-York African Free-Schools, From Their Establishment in 1817, to the Present Time* . . . (New York: Printed by Mahlon Day, 1830), 69.
[8]First Annual Convention of the people of Colour, *Minutes and Proceedings* . . . *1831* (Philadelphia: The Committee, 1831), 7; *Colored American,* December 1, 1838.

and he would become self-reliant, virtuous, physically healthy, and economically independent.[9]

Cornish also served New York's predominantly Negro Phoenix Society, which sponsored day and evening adult schools, operated libraries and reading rooms, encouraged vocational training for city blacks, and strove for general mental and moral uplift. In similar spirit, he served as New York City agent and admissions officer for Gerrit Smith's school for Negroes at Peterboro, the philanthropist's upstate home. Also in the 1830s, he backed Simeon Jocelyn's abortive plans for a Manual Labor College in New Haven. And, when he was not occupied with educational activity, Cornish participated in the New York City Committee of Vigilance, designed by its militant leader David Ruggles to guard blacks from the kidnappers who would return them to Southern bondage.[10]

Of the many agencies with which Cornish was associated during the 1830s, the most inclusive was the American Moral Reform Society. Philadelphia based, the society grew out of the Fourth Convention for the Improvement of the Free People of Colour held in Philadelphia in 1834. Its aim was "to extend the principles of universal peace and good will to all mankind, by promoting sound morality, by the influence of education, temperance, economy, and all those virtues that alone can render man acceptable in the eyes of God or the civilized world"—all this through the dissemination of practi-

[9]Gross, "Freedom's Journal," 270. In the mid-1830s, philanthropist Robert Rose had established a community for Negroes in northeastern Pennsylvania, based not on land-ownership, but on tenancy. Cornish disapproved because it did not seem really to benefit blacks. Cornish et al. to Gerrit Smith, May 3, 1835, S-SU.

[10]Lewis Tappan, *The Life of Arthur Tappan* (New York: Hurd & Houghton, 1870), 158; Cornish to Gerrit Smith, March 24, 1834, S-SU; Cornish et al. to Smith, May 3, 1835, S-SU; First Annual Convention of the People of Colour, Minutes and Proceedings . . . 1831, 7; *National Anti-Slavery Standard*, August 20, 1840; New York Committee of Vigilance, *First Annual Report* (New York: Piercy & Reed, 1837), 83.

cal and uplifting literature. Cornish was not only a society member, but for two years was one of its vice-presidents.[11]

The multitude of causes which Cornish undertook during the 1830s led to a dissipation of his energy and ultimately to a decline in interest. He fell out with Ruggles—the cause may have been that Ruggles' greater radicalism offended Cornish's essential conservatism—and lost his interest in the Committee of Vigilance. By the end of the 1830s, he had apparently ceased his active support for the African Free Schools. Then, with the collapse of the Phoenix Society's girls' school and his own failure to convince the Tappans to channel funds originally earmarked for the New Haven college to its revival, Cornish withdrew from active participation in that society's work. He became discouraged with the American Moral Reform Society, complaining that its aims were too vague, too diffuse, too visionary, and too little directed to the specific needs of the black man.[12]

Whatever the immediate causes of his disaffection, Cornish was clearly restless. Less and less did general reform satisfy him. More and more, he came to put Negro economic, social, and civil rights first. Thus the American Moral Reform Society looked feeble to him because its flabby leadership and diffuse goals made it neither a "BATTERING RAM" nor a "MIGHTY ENGINE" against inequality and slavery. "Our people have

[11]Convention for the Improvement of the Free People of Colour, *Minutes of the Fifth Annual Convention . . . 1835* (Philadelphia: William P. Gibbons, 1835), 31–32; American Moral Reform Society, *Minutes and Proceedings of the First Annual Meeting . . . 1837* (Philadelphia: Printed by Merrihew and Gunn, 1837), 7–12, quotation on 6.

[12]On the Ruggles contretemps, see *Colored American*, November 3, 1838, February 23, July 27, 1839; Dorothy Porter, "David Ruggles, An Apostle of Human Rights," *Journal of Negro History* 28 (1943): 39–40. For Tappan, *Colored American*, July 1, 1837; and for Moral Reform Society, *Colored American*, August 26, 1837.

too long been neglected . . . ," he complained in the *Colored American* in the summer of 1837. "Our white population are annually and monthly increasing their mental facilities and strengthening their moral resources. If we do not bring all our means and energies immediately to bear upon the condition of our people, the distance will widen between them and their pale-faced brethren."[13]

Thus agitated, Cornish, once again an editor, directed the *Colored American* toward the needs and aspirations of free blacks, which Northern white society ignored or denied. The newspaper, established in March 1837 by Philip Bell and subsidized by Arthur Tappan, quickly gained approval and support. The American Anti-Slavery Society applauded its program "to elevate and inform colored Americans, to correct public prejudice, and to advance the sacred cause of immediate emancipation." The American Moral Reform Society, ignoring Cornish's disillusionment, found the paper "a valuable acquisition to our cause." This approbation from white abolitionists and black reformers alike illustrated again the interrelationship of antislavery and Negro rights. Cornish vowed that the *Colored American* would "thunder" out its message until civil rights and equal justice were enjoyed by all Negroes. Furthermore, he pledged the paper both to unite the disparate elements of the black community and to inform the white community of Afro-Americans' aspirations. "The Press," he enjoined his fellow blacks, "must be supported, that by it our people may be reached, their minds cultivated, their habits changed, and their moral and religious character raised and made uniform, or we never can occupy a higher level in Society nor sustain suitable relations to God and to man."[14]

The solutions Cornish had proposed in *The Rights of All*

[13]*Colored American,* August 26, 1837.
[14]Tappan, *Arthur Tappan,* 185; the resolution of the American Anti-Slavery Society appeared in the *Liberator,* June 2, 1837; American Moral Reform Society, *Minutes, 1837,* 22; *Colored American,* March 4, 18, 1837.

he elaborated and refined in the *Colored American*. Focusing most sharply on individual and collective self-help, Cornish's editorials became more insistent that free Negroes exert themselves to complete the progression from slavery to full equality. Thus Cornish linked work to free the slave and to elevate the free man into one integral campaign.

Indeed the latter was as necessary to the former as the former to the latter. "God hath laid on us great responsibility . . . ," Cornish admonished his free black audience. "We have to act an important part, and fill an important place, in the great cause of humanity and religion—and in the work of emancipation. On *our* conduct and exertions much, very much depend." He challenged Northern Negroes to show conclusively that they had thrown off the "useless, vulgar, and sinful habits and practices" of bondage. If they did not do so, he warned, they would furnish their enemies with the "strongest arguments,with which to oppose the emancipation of the slave, and to hinder the elevation of the free."[15] Free men of color, Cornish continued, must show that they practiced the same virtues, ascribed to the same values, and desired the same goals as their white neighbors. "We should cultivate honesty, punctuality, propriety of conduct, and modesty and dignity of deportment." To destroy contrary assertions among whites, free blacks must be "prodigies of unceasing effort, and of undying enterprize." They must be economical and unostentatious. They must refrain from the "madness of money speculation." They must frequent libraries and reading rooms and attend public lectures. They must avoid the moral degradation of theaters, dance halls, bars, and gambling dens.[16]

Nor should they stop with rigorous imitation of the virtuous paragons of the white community but rather they must surpass them. Only when free blacks melded into the majority culture patterns would they be totally assimilated, and only then could they set such a standard for the whole community that they

[15] *Colored American,* March 4, May 6, 1837.
[16] Ibid., May 6, March 25, March 18, 1837.

would lead it to universal emancipation. "On *our* conduct, in a great measure, [the slaves'] salvation depends," he observed. "Should we establish for ourselves a character—should we as a people become more religious and moral, more industrious and prudent, than other classes of [the] community, it would be impossible to keep us down." "This we should do," he continued; "[because] we are more oppressed and proscribed than others, therefore we should be more circumspect and more diligent than others."[17] Black Americans should, in short, become more white than white Americans.

There lay a fundamental contradiction. "Before our colored population can ever be elevated in the scale of being," Cornish explained, "they must be made to respect themselves, [and] to feel as much their relations to God and to men and things, as do any other class of the community. Throw them under responsibilities, and then you will make a people of them."[18] But how could one achieve identity, independence, or self-reliance if one shared the standards of the opposition and insisted that the sharing made assimilation the desired goal? It is doubtful that Cornish ever confronted the dilemma his conflicting assumptions posed. He continued to preach both distinctive identity and total assimilation, hoping thereby to achieve not only an end to slavery but genuine equality for all Americans as well.

It was as a propellant to these ends that Cornish saw education. Restating the arguments which he had first set forth in *The Rights of All*, he said little that was new, but only drew his illustrations from the issues immediately about him. Deeply concerned that only a quarter to a third of the eligible black children in New York City attended school in 1837, he prodded ministers and parents alike, urging especially systematic visits to parents, initiated in Philadelphia by the Association for the Moral and Mental Improvement of the

[17]Ibid., March 4, 1837.
[18]Ibid., April 8, 1837.

People of Color and in New York by Cornish himself as agent for the African Free Schools. To be poorly educated, he knew, was to be crippled. "We have sadly, ourself, experienced the folly and fatality of this course," he pointed out in a December 1837 editorial, "and therefore are prepared to advise and sympathize with others on the subject." Finally, he argued that education should be practically oriented. Young people, he thought, should not waste their opportunities by becoming "classic drones" or "polished flirts."[19]

When the occasion presented itself, therefore, Cornish gladly served on an American and Foreign Anti-Slavery Society committee in 1840 to help in "securing funds from benevolent individuals, to be loaned or expended for the benefit of meritorious persons of color, especially young men of uncommon abilities and moral worth, with a view to aiding them in acquiring a knowledge of mechanical arts, and in obtaining a good education." It was a good program, and, in a generation given to optimism, it was little wonder that Cornish was cheerful over the prospects: "Our infant sons, should we give them suitable advantages, will be as eligible to the Presidency of the United States, as any other portions of the community; and it is our wisdom, if possible, to give them as ample qualifications."[20]

Cornish's optimistic acceptance of the American success story was not surprising, for he lived in the halcyon days of the reformable and perfectible Middle Period, and, even as a black man, he imbibed its hope and excitement. He did not conceive of prejudice as a pervasive element in American attitudes. He was not, of course, unaware of the color line

[19] Ibid., June 24, March 25, August 12, and quotations in December 16, and March 4, all 1837.
[20] *American and Foreign Anti-Slavery Reporter*, September 1840, 35; *Colored American*, June 24, 1837.

in America. He was himself a Negro; he lived in a ghetto
in New York City, and he ministered to a Negro constituency.
Yet so great was his faith in the brotherhood of all men that
he believed black Americans could achieve it almost solely
by their own efforts. As early as 1829 he had blamed Negroes
for chasing after flowers instead of working for solid achievements to improve their lot. He said that anti-Negro prejudice
was not inherent in whites but was largely a reaction to black
slothfulness. In meriting acceptance by whites, blacks would
automatically cause white prejudice to disappear.[21] In a very
real sense, Cornish blamed racism on blacks' lack of self-
respect, self-reliance, and self-help.

Yet these rather naive assumptions about prejudice conflicted with Cornish's actual experiences. With his children
denied that education he preached and himself the butt of
unequal treatment in spite of all his efforts at moral superiority, Cornish was obliged to act and respond. His move from
New York City to Belleville, New Jersey, clearly suggests just
how difficult it was for him to decide where prejudice lay and
why it was directed against his family.

When he became editor of the *Colored American,* he pointedly
admonished blacks to avoid any actions that might stereotype
them in the eyes of whites. Vacations, he argued, cost money
and unnecessarily exposed Negroes to the indignity of Jim
Crowism. So, too, did their willingness to occupy Negro pews
in churches. Turning the tables, Cornish also condemned
abolitionists for demanding less from Negroes in compensation for their presumed inferiority. "We would have our
friends and brethren know," he chastened them, "[that] unless
our moral and intellectual attainments *be measured by the same
rule, and brought, to the same standard* by which our white
brethren are tried and estimated, we cannot occupy the same
place in society, nor be held in the same repute."[22]

Asserting the principle, however, proved easier than attain-

[21]*The Rights of All,* September 18, 1829.
[22]*Colored American,* June 10, August 19, May 27, 1837.

ing the fact. At Pattison's Restaurant, whose clientele was largely clerical and missionary, Cornish could not get even a cup of tea. Worse still, he daily and continually endured the snubs of his fellow clergymen. "Such is the influence of prejudice against color," he admitted in the *Colored American* only a month after he became editor, that even to fill a vacant pulpit ministers "will *pass* [*a colored brother*] by as though he were an infidel,—hated of, and a hater of God." Worst of all, however, was the prejudice displayed in the schools. Cornish was appalled at differential pay scales for black and white teachers. He was infinitely saddened that his own children, because of their color, were unable to enter advanced schools in New York available only to whites. When in 1837 he had tried to enroll his oldest child in a new Presbyterian school, a friend had advised him to "start a school of your own, where your colored children can be taught the higher branches, and not come in contact with the prejudices of the whites."[23]

It was to protect his children from these prejudices that Samuel Cornish decided to leave New York City. The reasons he gave for moving his family to rural New Jersey reflected standard American values. He believed, he said, in the virtue of the rural environment. Cities were crowded and sinful, endangering the very moral fiber of the nation. Living in them was costly, and Cornish had suffered financial strains in New York. The panic of 1837 had made philanthropists less generous, the *Colored American* was in trouble, and Cornish's salary was in arrears. The times seemed propitious for a return to rural simplicity. Yet it is questionable whether Cornish would have made the move had it not been for his children. He had written as early as April 1837, "We are . . . making preparation to leave an extensive field of usefulness, and go from the city, if not from the country, that we may educate our children and hide them from that scorching,

[23]Ibid., August 12, 19, July 22, 1837; quotations in April 1, 22, 1837.

withering prejudice against their color, which is calculated to chain down their intellect, dry up the charity of heart, and make them haters of God and of man."[24]

In June 1838, therefore, Samuel Cornish, his wife, and their four children settled in Belleville. Here, Cornish reported ecstatically, he was accepted by his neighbors free from prejudice. He believed he was in an agrarian Eden where a man was a man, his color of no consequence.[25]

The idyll in Belleville was prelude to disappointment and denouement. Almost immediately, his younger son, Samuel, intrigued by a fish he was watching, slipped off a wharf and was drowned. Had he been so inclined, Cornish might have seen it as a sign. Within the year, he reported in the *Colored American,* he had been subjected to "*proscription* and *persecution,* and *assault*"; and that his older son, William, had been "denied the advantages of a common 'District School,' unless he [would] [s]ubmit to be degraded in the sight of all the [b]oys and of a professedly religious community, [o]n account of his color, in which he had no [a]gency."[26] Thus the pattern of prejudice, unnoticed or ignored when Cornish first settled in Belleville, quickly became evident, and the temporary Eden became the predictable Hell.

Hopes blasted, one son dead, and the other scorned, this was the time if any for Cornish to leave the country. Withdrawal, escape, expatriation were constant themes among antebellum blacks. The slave's only salvation lay in flight, and freemen in the North frequently felt the lure to flee to British territory or to Africa. But like most other free Negroes, Samuel Cornish rejected the notion and continued to seek ways to integrate the black man into a white society.

[24]Ibid., June 10, 1837, April 19, 1838, April 22, 1837.
[25]Ibid., June 2, 1838.
[26]Ibid., May 18, 1839.

It was not that he thought separation wholly unviable. In 1829, for example, he had supported a plan to buy land near Port Jervis and to establish a black settlement on it. In the same year, he had urged purchasing slaves and colonizing them in the self-reliant and self-dependent American West. None of this, however, was expatriation. To send slaves or free Negroes to Africa in numbers, as the American Colonization Society proposed, seemed to him the height of folly and little more than a trick to get rid of blacks. Involuntary exile, he asserted, was "unwished for on our part, uncalled for by circumstances, . . . injurious to our interests, and . . . unrighteous and meddlesome on the part of the society. . . ." To send forth missionaries was one thing; to disgorge 3 million blacks was quite another. Colonizationists, Cornish argued even more bitterly in 1837, were cheats and frauds intent upon clandestine profits from the slave trade. They talked of Christianizing Africa while they corrupted it with the most debased of American slaves; they mouthed the elevation of the colored man repatriated while in fact they "consign[ed] him to a wretched charnal house, to pine and die by inches. . . ." Driven by ambition, the American Colonization Society had been the "great despoiler of the colored man's interest and happiness in [America] for twenty years."[27]

Paradoxically, the very prejudice he had experienced only convinced him the more that the black man must fight his fight in America. "The few of us that have the qualifications for, and the means of leaving the country," he wrote in 1837, "should act the part of *base traitors* were we to do so, and leave behind the millions of our brethren, who are in bondage, and cannot go. . . ." As it turned out, even the escape to Belleville fell into the same category, and thereafter Cornish

[27]For the land schemes in New York State and the West, see *The Rights of All*, May 29, June 12, 1829; on the American Colonization Society, ibid., June 12, 1829, with quotation September 18, 1829; on statistics of colonization, ibid., May 29, 1829; the final quotations in the *Colored American*, December 8, January 27, 1838.

reestablished his identity in the black community to which his fate was linked. "We will never swerve from our purposes—universal emancipation, and universal enfranchisement—should we die in the pursuit, we will die *virtuous martyrs* in a holy cause."[28]

⛓️⛓️⛓️

Cornish never became a virtuous martyr, for he worked in less dramatic fashion. Rather, he turned his effort to the campaign for black participation in American politics, accepting, unlike the most militant black and most radical white abolitionists, the general governmental system as it was. As early as 1829, he had advised his fellow Negroes to use the vote as a weapon for social salvation. Add to the virtues of moderation, prudence, and modesty, he urged, the civic virtue which voting implied. He repeated the admonition time and time again. "If we would have our children accomplished and efficient citizens of our beloved country," he wrote in 1837, "we must set the example, by identifying ourselves and them, with all the interests of the government."[29]

Although as a black New Yorker, Cornish endured special property qualifications for franchise not required of whites, he was also in the heartland of political abolitionism. Thus, in the late 1830s when an antislavery third party was forming, Cornish gave eager support to political action. "Should abolitionists stay [away] from the polls and suffer the reign of political oppression," he wrote in August 1839, "they will not be less guilty of maintaining our unrighteous laws, than the tyrants themselves."[30]

Yet for all his political enthusiasm, Cornish was dubious about an antislavery third party. Essentially conservative, he hesitated to experiment. Moreover, he assessed the practical

[28]*Colored American*, April 15, 1837.
[29]*The Rights of All*, October 16, 1829; *Colored American*, July 15, 1837.
[30]*Colored American*, August 17, 1839.

futility of a small, specialized party at a time when the two major parties were solidifying. Finally, he recognized that party involvement had a style, a commitment, a standard of values incompatible with the idealism of the antislavery crusade. He feared that antislavery leaders thrust into politics would compromise their antislavery principles. "With all our confidence in our much beloved Birney, and Tappan, and Leavitt, and Weld, and Stanton and others, in political success," he cautioned in the summer of 1839, "we should not dare to trust them. They are but men and of like passions with other good men. Were they 'politically exalted' to the places and influence which govern our Republic and influence nations, we fear, like their predecessors, they might overlook and forget the colored man and the slave."[31] Thus, sympathetic though he was with the imperatives and potential of political action, Cornish isolated himself from New York antislavery politics after 1840 even though in 1844 he did support Birney.

As Cornish's response to politics was bifurcated, so also was his attitude to the antislavery religious debate. Like the Garrisonians, he had condemned the American church as the "STRONG HOLD of an unholy prejudice against color, more *oppressive* and *fatal* in its results, than any other sin." Yet Cornish was a cleric and a conservative. He was torn as Garrisonian condemnation of church fellowship with slaveholders became overt anticlericalism. Trying to avoid the acrimonious debate which the clerical issue engendered and which Cornish thought was carried on in "a spirit wholly unworthy the character of the brethren engaged in it," he was nonetheless thrust into it. Although he printed in the *Colored American* the pro-Garrison resolutions which Boston Negroes adopted, he was damned by them for failing to print Garrison's attacks on the clergy.[32]

Cornish's dilemma was acute. He could not damn the clergy

[31] Ibid., August 31, 1839.
[32] Ibid., March 11, October 7, 1837; *Liberator*, October 6, 1837.

outright; he shied away from the multireformism of Boston
abolitionists; and, unlike his Massachusetts brethren, he distinctly favored political action. When the antislavery movement split in 1840, Cornish was predestined for new organization. But there, too, his political views isolated him. His opposition to a third party was challenged in October 1839 by the
state antislavery society, which thereafter refused to support
the *Colored American* even though Cornish was no longer its
editor. Gerrit Smith launched the attack, which accused Cornish of temporizing with proslavery candidates in advocating
that abolitionists vote for the less offensive of the major party
candidates. In the eyes of William Goodell, a constant advocate
of independent political action, Cornish was only displaying
his Whig proclivities, which made a lie of his abolitionism
by leading him to oppose a truly antislavery third party. In
the end, even Cornish's former colleague and now sole editor
of the *Colored American,* Charles B. Ray, shifted ground to
oppose his old mentor. "He is," wrote Ray in a comment
as perceptive as any made about Cornish, "an old School man.
. . . He stands by the old paths, but does not enquire for the
new. . . . He is inclined to call every thing 'enthusiasm and
visionary or human measures' which divides [sic] in the least
from old tradition. . . ."[33]

❊❊❊

Thus Cornish, with a kind of perverse consistency, cut himself
off from the mainstream of antislavery activity. He was at
odds with both major antislavery factions in 1840. He had
given up his most effective antislavery medium in retiring
from the *Colored American.* After 1840, his career ceased almost
wholly to have meaning or significance. For a year, he served
a Negro church in Newark, where he had moved from Belleville. Then, in 1844, his wife died; and the following year

[33]The dispute is aired in the *Colored American,* October 5, 19, 1839; on
Ray, see the issue for November 9, 1839.

he returned to New York City where he ministered for a year to Emmanuel Church. But after 1846 what systematic effort he made for antislavery and religion he made through the American Missionary Association, which he served continuously for the next decade. In 1851, his daughter Jane fell ill and died insane four years later. Cornish himself, in ever poorer health, finally moved across the East River to the quiet of Brooklyn. There, three years later, in 1858, he died.

During the last eighteen years of his life, Cornish, it must be said, did stimulate public protest against both the 1793 and the 1850 fugitive slave laws. He served on the board of trustees of the New York Society for the Promotion of Education Among Coloured Children. He opposed publicly the rising tide of emigrationist sentiment, which, during the late 1850s, his associate Henry Highland Garnet and Pittsburgh physician Martin Delany supported so heartily.[34] But these were sporadic acts. Cornish had no forum for sustained effort; and, lacking the personal dynamism necessary for successful individual leadership outside a fixed structure or organization, he dropped away from significant antislavery work. Without an editor's chair, cut off from the Negro Convention movement, without a clear voice in the American and Foreign Anti-Slavery Society (almost nonexistent after the mid-1840s), never in the mainstream of political antislavery, unwilling or unable to devote more time to educational reform, Samuel Cornish quickly ceased to be of note in antislavery circles.

⛓⛓⛓

The career of Samuel Cornish presents a paradox. A leader among the antislavery host because he was considered a leader among free Negroes, Cornish's major work in both areas as an editor lasted little more than three years, ending at a

[34]*Frederick Douglass' Paper,* February 5, 1852.

moment of cresting both in the antislavery crusade and in the battle for black rights. Moreover Cornish was a man of many intellectual inconsistencies. While he chided Negroes for their lack of self-respect and self-reliance, he also praised them for conforming to white mores. Once mildly sympathetic to domestic colonization, he ultimately excoriated all colonization. Ardent in advocating a sense of black community and mutual responsibility, he fled to an illusory white haven in New Jersey when his own children's education seemed to demand it. Vigorous in affirming political antislavery action, Cornish discounted the utility of an antislavery political party in the critical period when the Liberty party was emerging. Finally, at the same time that, as editor, he denied the reality of color—as opposed to caste—prejudice, he recognized color prejudice when it impinged upon his own life, and he reacted to it as such.

If Cornish's life is frustratingly enigmatic, at least part of the reason must lie in the fragmentary evidence he left of his career and thought. Remove from the record *The Rights of All* and the *Colored American,* and Cornish becomes a passing reference, almost totally unidentified. His name is mentioned frequently, but only briefly, in the pages of the antislavery press. No one printed his sermons and lectures; none of the intensely epistolary white abolitionists preserved a significant number of his letters.

Perhaps this very paucity of evidence explains why he dropped out of the movement so completely after 1840. Yet his earlier career had portended continued activity during his prime productive years. Was he then a misfit in the antislavery movement, a man out of his element, out of his time, torn between modes of action and thus rendered ineffectual? Confronted with the need for action and decision, Cornish appeared weak and indecisive. He did not challenge the authority of Jim Crow seating on the railroads as Garnet did. He never effectively asserted his personal independence as Frederick Douglass did when he defied the Boston Clique by establishing the *North Star*. Nor did he ever decisively reject white society in favor of black settlements in Africa or Canada as Martin Delany and Henry Bibb did.

In short, Cornish was a follower, not a leader. He was a dynamic marshal neither of blacks nor of white abolitionists. Though his name appears fairly constantly on the rosters of executive committees and in the lists of officials of antislavery organizations, his role, in the context of the times, was that of the token Negro in a white society—a role Garnet refused and Douglass spurned. Essentially Cornish accepted white dominance in the antislavery movement and followed the leaders. Invited to join Arthur Tappan in the latter's pew at church, Cornish went. When Tappan needed a man to conduct investigations in Canada, Cornish went. When the American Anti-Slavery Society waxed paternalistic and instructed its agents to guide blacks along those lines upper-middle-class whites thought best for them, Cornish, on the society's executive committee, offered no known resistance.

It is quite possible that Cornish's failure to assert independent leadership was a function of his age. In 1839, he was already forty-five; twenty years Garnet's senior, twenty-two years older than Douglass. When these men, and others like them, shaped Negro militancy in the 1840s, Cornish was likely too old to adopt the new and radical stance. His background, in fact, made his obsolescence virtually inevitable. Conservative both by temperament and by Presbyterian training under John Gloucester, he lacked also the slave background that might have given him the drive and radical temper of the militant black leaders.

Cornish, in short, exerted power neither as a molder of predominantly white antislavery societies nor as a black leader. Yet he did serve as a bridge between white reformers and black protesters who together shaped the antislavery movement. Rather than illustrating its diversity, he suggests the means by which these elements could be held together.

8

The Black Militant:
Henry Highland Garnet

Jeremiah Myers, Negro, of Athol, Massachusetts, had been put into a Jim Crow car on the Stonington Railroad, and, in consequence, officials of that "aristocratic, purse-proud and over-bearing" line were treated to the spectacle of a protest meeting, held in Providence on the evening of April 3, 1848. Among the speakers at the meeting was a tall, distinguished-looking minister from upstate New York. Henry Highland Garnet had reason enough to volunteer his services while he was in Providence, for he knew through his own experience the principles and practices of Jim Crowism. He opened his address by calling the Stonington the most prejudiced railroad between Boston and Lake Erie, and then urged Negroes to resist the indignity of Jim Crow as a general policy. Garnet, however, was not all soberness as he described some useful techniques in terms to make his audience laugh at, and better endure, unpleasant realities. "He would not pretend to say how they should resist," reported one of the audience, *but they should resist.* "For his [own] part," Garnet continued, "he generally hugged the seats, and sometimes they would go

162

with him as a whole or in part." If, he added, his auditors would only "give their assailants affectionate embraces, after the mode of the grizzly bear, these upstarts would soon become weary of such manifestations of brotherly love. . . ."[1]

Two months later Garnet paid the symbolic price for his levity. Just before the train for Niagara Falls pulled out of the Buffalo station, he was ordered out of a rear car into one immediately behind the engine. He objected and returned to his original seat. Once again he was ordered out. Hobbling on his one leg and crutches, Garnet moved to comply until the conductor informed him that it was his color which had provoked the command. "Not being accustomed to yield up [his] rights without making at least a semblance of lawful resistance," Garnet again protested. This time he was physically attacked, choked, and beaten. His "eyes, temples, and bre[a]sts," he reported later were so "severely injured that he had to delay his journey and seek medical aid."[2]

What kind of man dared scoff at discrimination, laugh in its face, and suffer the consequences? Differentiated from white antislavery leaders by his color and from moderate black abolitionists by his insistence on action and his refusal to equivocate, his reform outlook was molded by his personal experience. Born in 1815 in Kent County, Maryland, Henry Highland Garnet was the son of slaves. Ill-used by their master, his entire family, nine-year-old Henry in tow, escaped to Pennsylvania in 1824 and a year later settled permanently in New York City. Young Henry knew firsthand what it meant to be a slave and he was soon to learn what it meant to be a fugitive in the antebellum North. Fortunate to have come north while still a young boy, his future ahead of him, he made the most of his opportunities. He attended the African

[1]The entire Stonington Railroad episode is described in Libertas to Frederick Douglass, April 4, 1848, in the *North Star*, April 14, 1848.
[2]The report of the Buffalo incident appeared first in the *North Star*, June 23, 1848. For the first quotation, see the *Anti-Slavery Bugle*, July 7, 1848; for the second, the *North Star*, July 7, 1848.

Free School on Mulberry Street and the high school on Canal Street where he received not only a good education but the stimulation of fellow students who, like him, were destined to become leaders of the race: Alexander Crummell, Samuel Ringgold Ward, George T. Downing, and James McCune Smith among them. Subsequently he attended briefly the Noyes Academy in New Hampshire and was trained in religion and reform at Beriah Green's Oneida Institute. Thus was Garnet prepared as a Presbyterian clergyman for the calling he pursued the rest of his life.[3]

Garnet's career was not, however, an unalloyed success story. First of all, he was black, of such "full, unmitigated, unalleviated and unpardonable blackness," Nathaniel P. Rogers observed bitterly, that it was, in American mores, "incompatible with freedom." Neither his father's success as a shoemaker nor his piety as a class leader and exhorter in the local African Methodist Church had freed him from the stigmas of slavery and racism. And the heritage of his father, only one generation removed from Africa, was visited upon the son. Moreover, Henry Garnet was a cripple for most of his life. Apprenticed in the late 1820s to a sea captain, he had injured his leg so severely that he was released from his contract. Yet the injury was fortunate because it opened the way to further education at the Canal Street school, Noyes, and Oneida. At the same time it condemned him to weakness and pain until his leg was amputated in 1840. That he never allowed his disability to impede his work is remarkable; that it made him more fierce and touchily proud is likely.[4]

Neither refugee status nor color nor the searing experience of his family's dispersal in 1829 to escape the scrutiny of

[3]Garnet completed his theological training under N. S. F. Beman in Troy, where he served as a schoolteacher and as secretary to the black congregation until he was licensed to preach in 1842. He was ordained in 1843.

[4]The quotation is from Nathaniel P. Rogers to William L. Garrison, July 8, 1835, in the *Liberator,* July 25, 1835. For a description of Garnet, aged forty-five, see the printed passport in the *National Anti-Slavery Standard,* October 26, 1861.

fugitive slave kidnappers made Garnet seek anonymity or
"learn his place." Rather they inspired him to devote his life
to ending slavery in the South and to improving the lot of
Negroes, free or fugitive, in the North. Moreover he became
the picture of health after his festering leg was amputated.
"Tall and commanding," with a "fighting chin" and "an eye
that looks through you," Henry Highland Garnet's physique
and carriage bespoke the measure of the man. If he had
the pragmatism to tack when tacking meant progress, he also
had the courage to face opposition and to speak his mind
whenever he would. Dragged from the train at Utica and
placed in an empty Jim Crow car, he addressed his oppressors
with steely wit: "Gentlemen, you are quite correct in supposing
that I have sufficient dignity to fill an entire car."[5]

A doer rather than a theorizer, Garnet organized Northern
blacks more actively than he preached antislavery to Northern
whites. In so doing, he both acted in harmony with the American Anti-Slavery Society's Declaration of Sentiments and recognized, as did most other antislavery crusaders, the enormous
difficulty of penetrating the South. Equally pragmatic was
his association with those abolitionists who pursued their aims
through existing political and religious institutions rather than
demanding a total restructuring of American society before
slavery could end. Thus he made political action the focus
for his most sustained antislavery work; and he used the
church as a means to elevate his fellows, shaping his religion

[5] The first and third quotations are from William Wells Brown, *The Black
Man, His Antecedents, His Genius, and His Achievements* (New York: Thomas
Hamilton, 1863), 150; the second one, Alexander Crummell, "Elogium on
Henry Highland Garnet, D. D., Before the Union Literary and Historical
Association, Washington, D.C., May 4, 1882," in his *Africa and America;
Addresses and Discourses* (Springfield, Mass.: Wiley and Co., 1891), 287; the
final one, from James McCune Smith's "Introduction" to Henry Highland
Garnet, *A Memorial Discourse . . . Delivered in the Hall of Representatives . . . Feb-
ruary 12, 1865* (Philadelphia: Joseph M. Wilson, 1865), 32n.

to sustain a practical social gospel rather than an intellectualized theology.

Similarly the child of an age of reform whose values he shared, Garnet strove to improve the secular lot of his parishioners. Whether in his church in Troy, Geneva, or New York City, he operated successful Sunday and day schools. Where possible, he encouraged integrated education; where necessary, he preferred segregation to no education at all. Enthusiastic for land reform, he believed that land ownership was the key to virtue, self-reliance, and worldly success. Consequently, he supported Gerrit Smith's project to distribute thousands of acres to the poor, especially to needy blacks. And, contemporary with the controversial Irish priest, Father Mathew, and Maine's teetotalling Neal Dow, Garnet preached against liquor, exploring the "terrible evils of alcohol" and trying to "allure the drunkard to the paths of soberness and peace."[6]

None of these reforms, however, indicative though they were of the enthusiasms of the period, enlisted Garnet's full energies. His vocation lay elsewhere. Unlike his fellow New Yorker, Samuel Cornish, whose commitment to parish work was sporadic, Garnet maintained an almost constant pastorate. Except for about three years, his adult life was spent ministering to a parish, which, in turn, provided him spiritual and practical strength. Even before his graduation from Oneida, he had accepted a pastorate among black Presbyterians in Troy, New York. Finding there an unorganized group of worshippers, he soon organized them into the Liberty Street Presbyterian Church, in which he was ordained in 1843. He stayed in Troy until 1848. Then, seeking a new field, he moved to Geneva, New York, where again he organized a Negro

[6]*Proceedings of the National Convention of Colored People and Their Friends Held in Troy, N.Y., on the 6th, 7th, 8th, and 9th October, 1847* (Troy: J. C. Kneeland & Co., 1847), 9; Garnet to George Whipple, July 10, 1850, AMA-FU; Garnet in the *National Watchman*, n.d., reported in the *Weekly Chronotype*, September 16, 1847. "W. D. Z." to the *Philadelphia Daily Republic*, n.d., as carried by the *Liberator*, November 10, 1848.

congregation and helped it build its own "Geneva Tabernacle."[7] Following an antislavery tour in England from 1850 to 1852, Garnet became missionary pastor of the Presbyterian church in Sterling, Westmoreland County, Jamaica, where he remained for three years. Returning then to New York City he undertook his final permanent parish, Shiloh Presbyterian, replacing his old mentor and pastor, Theodore S. Wright, and remained there until the end of his life in 1882.

Unlike Samuel Cornish, Garnet was a very successful minister. In Troy, he created a viable congregation and established a useful civic institution. His role in the Negro community there was attested to a decade after he left. "Although the Rev. H. H. Garnet has been so long absent from Troy," observed the *Weekly Anglo-African* in 1859, "his removal is always spoken of with great regret." As he had made the Liberty Street Church strong, so in New York Garnet undertook to revivify the Shiloh Church, which he found in 1856 in languishing condition. For this pastoral task, he had also been prepared by his sojourn in Geneva, "the most aristocratic, pro-slavery hole" the fugitive slave Henry Bibb ever encountered in the North. Indeed Garnet's efforts at church building were so respected that his application for aid from the American Missionary Association bore the ultimate seal of approval. "Mr. L[ewis] T[appan] thinks the Com[mittee] know H. H. Garnet well enough to decide without testimonials."[8]

Not confined to religious worship, Garnet's churches were establishments designed to achieve social, economic, and political uplift among their parishioners. Moreover, Garnet's sermons, as much as ancillary church functions, served social needs rather than developing theology. Indeed, his religious

[7]During part of the time he served the Geneva Church, he lived in Peterboro and also preached to a congregation there. Though it is not clear, it is very likely that he was substantially subsidized by Gerrit Smith at this time.

[8]*Weekly Anglo-African*, November 26, 1859; Henry Bibb to [Editor], January 29, 1849, in *North Star*, February 16, 1849; endorsement on Garnet to George Whipple, December 12, 1849, AMA-FU.

theory was largely a matter of social concern, starting with the child, then the family, and finally embracing the community as a whole. Good religion, he wrote to a friend in the early 1850s, was jointly the product of home environment and specific training: "Make home pleasant to your children. Make them love home more than any other place in the world. Encourage them in innocent amusements, and make the acquisition of wisdom and knowledge a pleasure." At the same time, "prepare them daily to fight the battles of freedom; help them to put on the Christian armor, for more than mere human fortitude is needed to prosecute our war. Teach them daily what they must do and suffer in years to come." "If slavery, prejudice and injustice are ever to be overthrown," he argued, "pure religion will be the principal instrumentality."[9] But pure religion was heavily overlaid with social awareness and responsibility, as church progress was largely the accomplishment of social welfare.

Thus Garnet found satisfaction in organizing a church in Troy, building one in Geneva, and reviving one in New York City.[10] He created weapons with which to prosecute his war against social injustice, nowhere more menacing than in New York. His concern for the evil and corruption that engulfed it was understandable enough. "Especially does there seem to be need of labour among our people in large towns, and cities," he wrote Simeon S. Jocelyn of the American Missionary Association in 1859. "New York, and the towns along the banks of the Hudson offer a field that is already ripe for the harvest." He wrote Jocelyn a year later:

> In taking my rounds, and walks among my people, I am constantly oppressed with the fact of the limited provission which is made for the spiritual wants, of the poor, the sick, and dying. Four years of experience, and observation convince me that many, very many annually pass away without Christian instruction, and the consolations of the gospel.

[9]Garnet to Brother B—, March 14, 1851, in *The Impartial Citizen*, May 10, 1851.
[10]See, for example, Garnet to Whipple, December 12, 1849, to Simeon S. Jocelyn, March 4, 1857, both in AMA-FU.

Our young people too need greatly more ample provision for their moral and intellectual culture—and any provission that even in a small degree meets these wants will be productive of a vast amount of good.[11]

His language was religious, but his spirit was social. Thus Garnet sought to strengthen both services for adults and Sunday school for the children at Shiloh. He went outside his parish to hold prayer meetings about the city wherever they were likely to do good, to operate a public reading room for the intellectual edification of the citizens, and to undertake "in any other way [to] do the work of a city Missionary...."[12] His use of the term "city missionary" was important, delineating as it did a mission for social as well as religious service to the citizens of the city.

Garnet's work for social betterment was aimed primarily at the black community. Just how firm the link between the church and black welfare was was indicated by the Evangelical Association of Presbyterian and Congregational Clergymen of Color, formed in 1859. Instrumental in organizing the group, Garnet helped shape its principal function of giving "the ministers of color throughout the Northern, Eastern and Western States an opportunity of interchanging views upon the best means to be employed for ameliorating the condition of their people, and of hearing reports of their progress in various parts of the country."[13] This was the ultimate hope: a nationwide church-based amelioration of the lot of the black man.

Garnet's dynamism was still more clearly demonstrated in politics. Unwilling to be submerged in the dispute over political action between old and new antislavery organizations, he

[11]For the quotations, see Garnet to Jocelyn, September 14, 1859, June 1, 1860, AMA-FU.
[12]Garnet to Jocelyn, November 29, 1859, AMA-FU.
[13]Specifically this function was tied by Garnet to the annual convocation of the association. See the *Weekly Anglo-African*, September 24, 1859.

turned his energies into channels better suited to black men's aims. First among them was equal suffrage. If, Garnet argued, manhood suffrage was essential for social well-being, it was as indispensible for the black community as for the white. His egalitarianism was typical of Jacksonian America; his application of it to race set him apart. In New York, all adult white men were automatically enfranchised while black men had to meet a stiff property qualification. Not surprisingly, then, even while he was still a student at Oneida, Garnet had joined with some twenty-five young Negroes to call a suffrage convention. When it met on August 21, 1837, in New York, Garnet offered a resolution asserting that "the laws which deprive free American citizens of the right to choose their rulers, are wholly unjust and anti-republican, and therefore ought to be immediately repealed."[14] Antirepublican, antidemocratic, unjust. What more could he say?

Clearly, a good deal more. For the next thirty years, Garnet continued his fight for full and equal suffrage in New York State. Thus in 1840 he joined other Negroes in calling a political convention of blacks. Blaming disfranchisement for their "depressed condition" in New York following the panic of 1837—their egalitarianism in this respect overshadowing economic logic—these black leaders argued specifically against the $250 New York State property qualification for Negro suffrage. The provision was onerous, they contended, because it "lower[ed] [them] in the scale of humanity, and reflect[ed] disparagingly upon [their] character." The convention, when it met in Albany on August 18, 1840, attracted a large audience, with sessions ranging from 40 to 140 delegates and supporters. Garnet, the *Colored American* noted, not only served as one of the three secretaries but spoke against prejudice, delivering "one of his happiest efforts."[15]

[14]*Colored American,* August 19, September 2, 1837.
[15]*National Anti-Slavery Standard,* June 18, 1840; *Colored American,* August 22, 29, 1840.

Garnet's agitation was not limited to conventions, debates, and pious resolutions. Activist that he was, he used the popular reform technique of sending petitions to local, state, and federal governments. On February 2, 1841, for example, he journeyed from Troy to Albany to deliver suffrage petitions to the legislators gathered there. The 1,300 signatures impressed at least some of the legislators, who agreed to present the petitions to their colleagues and to arrange special hearings.[16]

Pressing his advantage, Garnet returned two weeks later to testify at committee hearings on equalizing the franchise. Before the legislators, he extended his argument, insisting that Negroes, by right of birth and citizenship, ought to enjoy franchise privileges identical with those of whites. He said that the black man had vindicated his rights by his conduct at the polls on those few occasions when he had been permitted to vote. Asserting that the general public would readily accept universal manhood suffrage, he predicted a speedy success for black enfranchisement.[17]

But the battle was not to be easily won in 1841, if for no other reason than because the legislature was more interested in debating plans for a Hudson River bridge at Albany than in considering plans for universal manhood suffrage. Realist that he was, Garnet soon tempered his optimism. Once again he joined in calling a New York State Convention of Colored Citizens to assemble in Troy on August 25, 1841. Given its locale, he doubtless played a major role at the convention and probably drafted the convention's address to the state's electors. Injury to one group in the community, admonished the address, meant injury to all: "If you combine equals with unequals, the whole must be unequal; if you combine affranchised with disfranchised, free with slave labor, the result must be disastrous to the whole community." In New York, where Negroes were denied an equal franchise and

[16]*Colored American,* February 13, 1841.
[17]Ibid., March 13, 1841.

debased as citizens, they inevitably turned to crime. Here, the address went on, was the reason for a crime rate higher among black than among white citizens. The Negro was, the convention asserted, better fitted for the franchise than the immigrant who, despite his very recent exposure to democratic institutions and his long training under European despotism, was enfranchised. Look to Massachusetts, urged the address, where blacks did vote. There was no one to say that Massachusetts politics had suffered from the fact. Nor, the address argued in a final burst of indignation, could Negroes' exemption from fire duty, militia service, and some forms of taxation excuse denying them the vote. They had not sought such exemptions, and they regarded them as simply another form of discrimination.[18]

Thus Garnet and his colleagues argued, year in and year out. But no amount of talking and reasoning brought New York to alter its voting requirement for blacks. Indeed, on the very eve of the Civil War, the State [Equal] Suffrage Association was still pointing to black contributions to American life, Negro service in the American Revolution, and the principles of the Declaration of Independence in a vain attempt to achieve full franchise for blacks. But public opinion had not changed. The *Anglo-African* advised the association to "engage the services of Rev. H. H. Garnet" and others to tour the state and to lecture once more about equal suffrage. In 1864, Garnet addressed still another convention which, if it marked the futility of earlier efforts, did extend the suffrage campaign to include the entire nation.[19]

The overriding obstacle had been, and still was, white prejudice against blacks. In August 1845, Garnet had introduced a resolution at the Syracuse Colored Suffrage Convention

[18]*National Anti-Slavery Standard,* August 12, September 23, 1841.

[19]Smith, "Introduction," 52. *Weekly Anglo-African,* May 10, 1861. The quotation is from ibid., March 31, 1860. The Syracuse *Daily Standard,* October 6, 1864, reports the wartime convention at which Garnet and Douglass jousted for dominance.

that admonished naturalized citizens, who had "escaped the oppression of their own countries, . . . to remember *us,* when it goes well with them." It was a fine thought, nicely put, with all the piousness of the dedicated uplifter and all the naiveté of the committed reformer. In January 1846, in response to an "Address to the Voters of the State of New York, by the People of Color" an opponent, calling himself "Cartman," spelled out the nature of the hard-core opposition. In an indignant letter to the New York *Globe,* he called for defiance, urging his fellow citizens to select delegates to the forthcoming constitutional convention who were "opposed to taking the bread from the mouths of our wives and little ones, in order to give it to the negroes of the South, who . . . are invited hither." Continuing his argument, Cartman claimed that if Negroes were granted the suffrage they would next be granted cartmen's licenses. There was the rub. But it was not only economic competition. Negroes, he contended, constituted an inferior and servile class, and, if given the vote, would be the willing tools of merchants and others. "Thus, in a short time," predicted Cartman, "all white men, who are able, [will] be driven from the business, while those of us, too poor to get out of the way of the negroes, [will] inevitably be reduced to the same relative station in society that are the very poor men in our Southern cities—for it is negroism there, rather than Slavery, that causes their degradation."[20]

Those were the problems: color prejudice, economic competition, social degradation, political exploitation. Garnet, who had been more successful than most of his colleagues, was still black and a fugitive. He, as they, had to wait for civil war and national Reconstruction to bring equal suffrage. He and they smarted under the failure of their campaign.

[20]*National Anti-Slavery Standard,* September 11, 1845, January 29, March 19, 1846.

Garnet's political involvement did not stop with appeals for the franchise nor with the petitions and Negro conventions to press for them. Anxious to achieve full suffrage, he also sought a political party that would work for black goals. He was, therefore, impatient when the 1840 Albany convention refused to support the Liberty party because, it said, Negroes should not endorse a party which, lacking the franchise, they could not support at the polls. Garnet differed. No channel of action should go unexplored. As chairman of the Central [State] Committee on Petitions, he wrote to the county chairmen in October 1840 that "our political disabilities hinder as much as any human arrangements can, our moral elevation. . . . We are placed, just now, where we must assert ourselves, or we must perish. We have been thrown into a deep pit by our brethren, who have hated us, because we have politically dreamed away our nights of deep darkness."[21]

Himself wide awake, Garnet turned to consider a third party. Eager for governmental action to end slavery, unconvinced that preaching abolitionist truth in the North would change public sentiment in the South and bring emancipation, he saw in the Liberty party an organization through which antislavery men might gain legitimate control of governmental institutions. In his insistence on practical political action, he rejected confinement to moral suasion, which Garrisonian perfectionism enshrined. Fittingly, he outlined this conviction in Boston when, in February 1842, he addressed the Massachusetts Liberty party convention. Paying tribute to abolitionists and linking the rights of the free Negro and the hopes of the slave, he asserted that "those heaving fires that formerly burst forth like the lava of a burning volcano . . . when the colored man rose and asserted *his rights to humanity and liberty,* are kept in check, only by the abolitionists. They hold open," he continued forcefully, "the safety valve of the nation;—and these *enemies of the country,* as they are

[21]*Colored American,* August 29, October 17, 1840.

called, are the very men, sir, that prevent a general insurrection of the slaves from spreading carnage and devastation throughout the entire South. They confide in the assurances of the abolitionists," he continued, "that something is doing to hasten the day when they 'shall sit under their own vine and their own fig tree,' and their claims to liberty and happiness be asserted and ESTABLISHED BY LAW." Complimentary as his speech was to all the abolitionists of the Boston stronghold, Garnet went on to alienate the Garrisonians. Abolitionists, he charged, were not afraid of political action but were and must be constant and forceful in its use. Sanctified by religious and reform conviction, the new party must, he concluded, work for the slave; it must feel "as bound with them." The major parties were not to be trusted. The only logical choice was the Liberty party.[22]

Garnet made clear his political position in 1842 and clung to it. Nor did his placing before the Colored Convention at Buffalo in 1843 his "Address to the Slaves" alter his party loyalty though it did cast doubt on the value of restraining slave insurrection. As he wrote a friend in the spring of 1844, "I have put on my armour, joined the 'Neucleus of Liberty', and hoisted my banner with this motto inscribed upon it 'The Sword of the Lord and Gideon[.]' Pass around the Constitution it is short, and plain. Here it is, 'Enlisted during the war.' " As he had in 1844, so in 1848 he supported the Liberty party as the pure form of antislavery political activity against the merely antiextensionist though politically stronger Free Soil party.[23]

His advocacy of action through religious and political institutions necessarily lined Garnet up with the Tappan–Birney–Smith spectrum of antislavery, the new organization.

[22]*Emancipator and Free American*, March 3, 1842.

[23]*Minutes of the National Convention of Colored Citizens Held at Buffalo on the 15th, 16th, 17th, 18th, and 19th of August, 1843* ... (New York: Piercy and Reed, 1843), 15–16. Garnet to G. A. Thatcher, September 3, 1844, Box 17, MS-LC. *Weekly Chronotype*, June 24, 1848.

Almost as inevitably, he was caught in the cross-fire of old and new organization feuding. When Maria Chapman lashed out at his speech at the 1843 Colored Convention espousing slave insurrections, contending that he had been misled by bad advice from white men, Garnet replied perceptively that his real "crime" lay in spurning Boston's pure doctrine and espousing the Liberty party.[24]

As unhumbled by Chapman's chastisement as by her overbearing paternalism, Garnet continued firm in his path, willing to join with the old organization whenever it served his ends. Firm and iron-willed Abby Foster complained when in 1847 he arranged to hold a joint Liberty party and American Anti-Slavery Society celebration of West Indian Emancipation Day in Canandaigua. Resentful of having old organization talent exploited, she condemned Garnet and his colleague Samuel Ward as "bitter Liberty party priests, [who] had half the money tho' Douglas[s] drew the audience. Ward & Garnett [sic] could not have got out the people but made use of the old organizationists to get a hearing and fill their pockets."[25]

Undeterred, Garnet persisted. His antislavery doctrine harmonized with third-party politics. Supporting the Radical Abolitionists in the late 1850s as he had the Liberty party in 1848, he, like Stephen Foster, damned the new Republican party for its equivocation on slavery. In 1858, even the Radical Abolitionists merited his chastisement for their support of the Republican candidate, Edwin Morgan, for governor. Although he stood firm against temporizing and acceding to merely antiextension parties, Garnet found vindication for his faith in political action in the Civil War and the concomitant emancipation, which a Republican administration brought. Yet the gains needed guarantees, and to achieve them he turned again to Negro conventions. In 1864, he signed the call for a National Convention of Colored People to meet

[24]Garnet to Maria W. Chapman, November 17, 1843, in the *Liberator*, December 8, 1843.
[25]Abby Foster to Stephen Foster, August 24, 1847, F-AAS.

in the fall in Syracuse and there plan future consolidation and action. Subsequently he supported the Radical Republican program of reconstruction.[26]

❦❦❦

Whether he was presenting petitions, extolling the merits of a free and equal suffrage, or pressing political antislavery, Garnet was engaged in group action. Moreover, although personal independence characterized his style of involvement, his ideology reflected prevailing social norms. When he argued for property ownership, economic success, religious commitment, and virtuous living, Garnet reflected American Protestant values; when he urged suffrage and civil equality, he reflected the English political heritage of the American scene. Similarly, when he encouraged Negroes to be self-reliant, he accepted the American myth of the self-made man. In a major essay, "The Past and Present Condition and Destiny of the Colored Race," written and delivered in Troy in 1848, Garnet lamented that Negroes were divided into political, sectarian, and even racial factions. Their internal bickering vitiated their strength, just as their ostentatious idling and their frivolous consumption of baubles wasted their funds and energy. It was high time, he exhorted, that they mend their ways. Be good citizens, be patriotic, help build America, fight for right and equality.[27] He called them not to false humility, however, but to aggressive and active independence as individuals and as a race. These same goals had led Garnet to support the Negro convention movement as a distinctive technique, as well as a means to achieve a specific goal.

[26] For Garnet's later activity, see the *Radical Abolitionist,* December 1856, October 1857, October 1858; Garnet and J. W. Duffin to Gerrit Smith, September 10, 1858, S-SU; Garnet to Smith, October 23, 1865, S-SU; *Liberator,* September 9, October 14, December 23, 1864; *National Anti-Slavery Standard,* August 24, 1867, January 30, 1869.

[27] Henry Highland Garnet, *The Past and Present Condition, and the Destiny of the Colored Race . . .* (Troy: J. C. Kneeland and Co., 1848), passim.

In one of his earliest public appearances, Garnet had addressed the 1840 annual meeting of the American Anti-Slavery Society. There he introduced the theme he would later develop: although Negroes had contributed much to American culture, "no monumental piles distinguish their 'dreamless beds!' " and "scarcely an inch on the page of history has been appropriated to their memory."[28] Nor could blacks hope for spontaneous recognition of their accomplishments or their rights in a society that, at best, ignored them. So it was that Garnet seized upon black conventions as the vehicle for collective self-help.

Race conventions had been meeting since 1830 to deal with all manner of issues—education, temperance, suffrage, and civil liberties among them. Since his schooldays, Garnet had joined in their activities and had turned them to his equal-suffrage campaign. Yet the premise of racial separatism on which they rested led to antislavery debates about their efficacy and appropriateness. The *National Anti-Slavery Standard* blamed "wicked and damnable *prejudice*" for pushing Negroes into segregated conventions. Professing understanding that "the fetter galls and cuts deeply," it warned nonetheless that "we cannot unlock it instantly. In your desire to become freemen," it admonished black Americans, " . . . be careful that you do not tear down what you build up. You cannot be free until [the] community shall see and feel that you are men."[29] The logic of the *Standard's* position, resting as it did on the premise that only white decisions were important, irritated many blacks. But Negroes also challenged separatist conventions. William Whipper and Robert Purvis, both important and respected leaders from Pennsylvania, thought that the custom of "distinctive Conventions, (designed by complexional lines) for philanthropic purposes"—or, implicitly, for any other purposes—was to be deplored. If black men drew the color line, Whipper warned, then indeed "the white man

[28]*National Anti-Slavery Standard,* June 11, 1840.
[29]Ibid., June 18, 1840.

will be equally able to establish the dignity of his Anglo-Saxon blood, and the *virtue* of his complexion."[30]

Not to be discounted, such arguments emphasized the dangers to equality that the convention movement posed. The question they failed to answer, however, was how the black man was to further his aims. To wait for the white community might be to wait forever; to rely on white antislavery efforts was to accept freedom on white men's terms. If the individual must learn to be self-sufficient, its supporters argued, so must the distinctive community. Vehicle thus of black self-reliance, the convention movement served Garnet's purposes well. Its meaning for him was made clear in his "Address to the Slaves" of 1843 and in his support of the emigration movement in the 1850s.

On August 16, 1843, Garnet attended the National Colored Convention in Buffalo and urged that it support the Liberty party. Until he rose, the convention had been quiet—its conflicts only procedural, its resolutions innocuous.[31] But Garnet sought—and got—action. Perhaps his experience at Noyes Academy eight years earlier flashed through his mind. There his role, with several of his black schoolmates, in an antislavery-society-sponsored Fourth of July celebration, had inflamed the racial tension dividing the school from the community and had precipitated an attack on the school. The local bigots came in force, a week later, with oxen equipped to drag the school building from its very foundations. They succeeded, too, but not before a pitched battle had been fought and not before Garnet had led his fellow blacks, shotgun blazing, in defense of their school.[32] Now a man grown and a minister,

[30]William Whipper and Robert Purvis to David Ruggles, August 22, 1840, in ibid., September 10, 1840; Whipper to Charles B. Ray, January 17, 1841, in the *Colored American*, February 20, 1841.
[31]Resolutions included ones supporting religion, but condemning churches which did not condemn slavery, and calling for the establishment of a national Negro press.
[32]For the Noyes episode, see Nathaniel P. Rogers to William L. Garrison, July 8, 1835, in *Liberator,* July 25, 1835; also Crummell, "Elogium," 278–281.

Garnet presented the convention with a challenging and devastating address.

"In every man's mind," it read, "the good seeds of liberty are planted, and he who brings his fellow down so low, as to make him contented with a condition of slavery, commits the highest crime against God and man." The slaves, who have waited long and patiently for freedom, must wait no longer.

TO SUCH DEGRADATION IT IS SINFUL IN THE EXTREME FOR YOU TO MAKE VOLUNTARY SUBMISSION.... NEITHER GOD, NOR ANGELS, OR JUST MEN, COMMAND YOU TO SUFFER FOR A SINGLE MOMENT. THEREFORE IT IS YOUR SOLEMN AND IMPERATIVE DUTY TO USE EVERY MEANS, BOTH MORAL, INTELLECTUAL, AND PHYSICAL THAT PROMISE SUCCESS.... Brethren, arise, arise! Strike for your lives and liberties. Now is the day and the hour. Let every slave throughout the land do this, and the days of slavery are numbered. You cannot be more oppressed than you have been—You cannot suffer greater cruelties than you have already. *Rather die freemen than live to be slaves.*[33]

For an hour and a half Garnet defended his position, and, in so doing, he introduced new controversy into antislavery, rocked the convention to its depths, and made his mark on history. He appealed to the experience of Denmark Vesey and Nat Turner and urged the imperatives of vigorous action.[34] When he had finished and the convention turned to cast up its account, the delegates voted to expunge both speech and address from the official record. His fellow worker, the rising abolitionist Frederick Douglass, said the address might cause class violence. The Boston Clique, when it heard what had happened, were appalled at Garnet's brashness. Nothing he had said before, or would say after, could obliterate the reputation that the speech earned him: incendiary, black militant, slave-inciting revolutionary.[35]

Well might the North and South alike conjure up visions of Henry Highland Garnet, insurrectionist. Two years later,

[33]Garnet, "An Address to the Slaves of the United States of America," in his *Memorial Discourse,* 44–51.
[34]Ibid., passim.
[35]*National Convention at Buffalo,* 13.

he reinforced that image when he appealed to free Negroes to act for their own welfare in united fashion, "whatever for the present may betide them." And in 1847, at the Troy Colored Convention, he repeated the Buffalo challenge.[36] Yet the 1843 performance had been, for all practical purposes, an aberration. Fourteen years later, the chance to put the theory to the test presented itself. But when John Brown sought Garnet's support for insurrectionary action, the black militant turned him down. "The time has not yet come," he told Brown, "for the success of such a movement." Neither slaves in the South nor free blacks in the North were ready. "The break between the North and the South," he concluded, "has not yet become wide enough."[37] Clearly there was too much to be gained, reasoned Garnet pragmatically, to risk it all by ill-considered violence.

The Negro convention movement, which in 1843 had brought Garnet to a radical independence with violent overtones, brought him in the 1850s to a different independent action. His support for African emigration was both more pragmatic and more typical of the man than his "Address to the Slaves."

In the fall of 1850 Garnet went to England to lecture in support of free produce. Promising both significant and specific action, the idea appealed to Garnet. Readily accepting the British Free Labour Movement's invitation to lecture in England, he toured the British Isles for two years.[38] When his British tour was finished, however, he did not return to

[36]*National Anti-Slavery Standard,* September 11, 1845. *North Star,* December 3, 1847.

[37]The story and Garnet's remarks to Brown were reported by J. Sella Martin in an address in Boston's Tremont Temple on the day Brown was executed. See the *Liberator,* December 9, 1859.

[38]For Garnet's English tour see Smith, "Introduction," 53–54; *The Impartial Citizen,* October 11, 1850, and particularly "Extracts from the Minutes of the Belfast Anti-Slavery Society," in the May 17, 1851, issue; *Frederick Douglass' Paper,* March 11, 1852.

the United States. Fearful of his own and his family's enslavement under the 1850 Fugitive Slave Act, Garnet brought his
entire family to England.[39] When his work there was finished,
he sought an appointment from the United Presbyterian
Church of Scotland and under their auspices, in the fall of
1852, became a missionary pastor to the Presbyterian Church
at Sterling, Jamaica. Three years later, he sent his entire family, sick with the fever, back to the United States. The following
spring, 1856, he himself returned.[40] He settled again in New
York City, plunged into his new work at Shiloh Church and
became involved in his most important work for the race
since his suffrage campaigns of the early 1840s: the African
Civilization movement.[41]

Before his foreign sojourn, Garnet had had little sympathy
with African colonization. By the mid-1840s he had not only
denounced the American Colonization Society but had con-
curred with Thomas Folwell Buxton's contention that, while
colonization was good as an abstract idea, it had in practice
generated the very evils it was presumed to eliminate. Garnet
believed that the American Negroes' place was in America.

[39] There was some speculation that the primary reason for going to England
was because of the unsettled conditions over the then pending Fugitive Slave
Bill. This is doubtful, however, because there had been talk of his going to
England to lecture in 1849, and because when he first went he left
his family behind.

[40] The Jamaican episode may be traced in scattered correspondence in
AMA-FU, passim; also in S-SU, passim, for the years 1851–1856. See also
a report from the *New York Tribune,* n.d., on the Jamaican mission, in *Frederick
Douglass' Paper,* September 2, 1853. Garnet's return to the United States
may have been hastened also by growing defiance of the Fugitive Slave Law
at home.

[41] The movement was not without its antecedents in American antislavery
history. There had been numerous experiments with colonizing Negroes,
including Benjamin Lundy's abortive attempt in Mexico, the settlement of
refugee Negroes in Upper Canada, and Edward Coles' settlement of emancipated slaves in Illinois. Yet the focus of most colonization schemes rested
in the work of the American Colonization Society, originally planned to aid
free Negroes and slaves about to be emancipated.

"There are those," he wrote in 1848, "who either from good or evil motives, plead for the utopian plan of Colonization of a whole race to the shores of Africa." But, he continued, "We are now colonized. We are planted here, and we cannot as a whole people, be re-colonized back to our fatherland. It is too late," he stressed, "to make a successful attempt to separate the black and white people in the New World. . . . *This western world is destined to be filled with a mixed race.*" Garnet turned even discrimination to his argument that blacks were both destined for and suited to life in America. Constantly cheated by whites, Negroes were more honest than their exploiters. Barred by their color from military service, they avoided wartime deaths, which thinned the ranks of whites. Purified by their exclusion from white churches, they did not share the hypocrisy that marred Caucasian Christianity. In honor, religion, and sheer survival superior to whites, blacks could reject the doctrine on which the colonization rationale was based.[42]

Yet Garnet was well aware that prejudice and injustice limited the scope of talented blacks. For them, Africa might offer opportunity rather than forced exile. Furthermore, if cotton could be cultivated there, the supporters of free-labor produce would have a vast new source of raw material for English and American textile mills. To realize these goals, the African Civilization Society was organized. It offered a plan to develop Africa socially, economically, and politically, and at the same time to put to use the talents of black Americans denied exercise at home.

Even before his English trip to promote free produce, Garnet had been developing a rationale for limited African colonization. By 1848, he had decided that prejudice was based less on color than on condition and that the Negroes' condition

---

[42]Thomas Folwell Buxton to Richard R. Gurley, October 9, 1840, in *American and Foreign Anti-Slavery Reporter*, January 1841, 110–111. Garnet, *Past and Present Condition*, passim, the quotation is on 25–26.

in America was customarily dismal. He argued that in the
American West blacks as well as whites would improve their
condition. At the same time, however, he saw in Africa another
West for the black man and in colonization an exclusively
black frontier experience. As the West was the paradise of
opportunity for whites, so Liberia offered ambitious Negroes
similar freedom and opportunity. "I would rather see a man
free in Liberia, than a slave in the United States," he wrote
in 1849. More emphatically he wrote Samuel R. Ward, still
critical of any emigration that the success of newly independent Liberia opened up new possibilities "highly beneficial
to Africa in a commercial and a political point [of view]."
At the same time that American Negroes exploited these possibilities, they would assure Liberia's success, and Liberia's
success would, in turn, curtail the slave trade and raise the
condition and prestige of American Negroes. Without question, he concluded, Africa was a good place for black Americans who wished opportunities unavailable at home.[43]

Although in 1849 Garnet had no personal desire to be a
colonist, the events of the next decade made him reconsider
his position. He became an activist in the African Civilization
Society and yearned to see Africa. On the one hand, Liberia
intrigued him; on the other, a deepening discouragement
over American developments made him ever more receptive
to alternatives. The westward extension of slavery following
the Mexican War, the failure of the New York suffrage campaign, and the passage of the new Fugitive Slave Law of 1850
drove him to colonization as they had driven him to a West
Indian exile. Nor was his reaction unique. James G. Birney,
leader, hero, and presidential candidate of the Liberty Party,
had by 1852 turned bitterly to colonization, finding in it the
only remedy for an impossible condition. In Cleveland in

[43]Garnet, *Past and Present Condition,* passim. Garnet to Frederick Douglass,
January 21, 184[9], in *North Star,* January 26, 1849; Garnet to Samuel R.
Ward, February 10, 1849, in *North Star,* March 2, 1849.

1854, a National Emigration Convention of Colored Men assembled "to consider the expediency, and devise a practical plan of emigration to Central or South America, of the Colored People of the United States, there to establish an independent and free Republic of colored men, which could set an example to the world of civilization, progress and self-government, which would rejoice the hearts of all philanthropists, astonish the skeptical, and strike dumb the defamers and oppressors of the race."[44]

Their program was part of an emigration movement that sparked conventions throughout the decade in quest for a viable alternative to enduring prejudice in America. It was, however, Martin R. Delany's investigations that showed most clearly the potentials of the new colonization. Heading an exploratory group for colonization to the Niger River area of West Africa in 1859, he negotiated for land for future colonists. Supported substantially by American, Canadian, and English backers, Delany argued that Negroes were not Americans but Africans and that they should return to their homeland. He popularized a back-to-Africa movement and found ways and means to initiate it.[45]

By 1859, therefore, American Negro leaders were lining up for or against Delany and emigration. The ensuing battle strained the African Civilization Society, whose aims were not

[44]See James G. Birney, *Examination of the Decision of the Supreme Court of the United States, in the Case of Strader, Gorman and Armstrong vs. Christopher Graham . . . with an Address to the Free Colored People, Advising them to Remove to Liberia* (Cincinnati: Truman and Spofford, 1852). The Cleveland *Leader*, n.d., printed in the *Liberator*, September 29, 1854.

[45]See, for example, a speech by Delany reported in the *Weekly Anglo-African*, October 1, 1859. Also see the report of the Chatham, Upper Canada, *Planet* as noted in the *Liberator*, September 24, 1859; William King, autobiography ms., K-PAC, both on Canadian interest in neocolonization. For a study of the African civilization movement, see Richard K. McMaster, "Dr. Martin Delany, the Rev. Henry Highland Garnet and the African Civilization Society, 1856–1861" (Paper delivered to the Association for the Study of Negro Life and History, October 1966, Baltimore).

mass migration but individual emigration. Garnet, a staunch supporter of the society, was in the middle of the fight. In Boston's Melodeon Hall early in August 1859, the New England Colored Citizens Convention met to damn the African Civilization movement and to excoriate Garnet. The convention accused him of planning a virtual reservation for emigrant Negroes, of plotting a mass migration to Africa, of degrading the American Negro, of reviving the old Colonization Society and playing into its hands.[46]

To counter this onslaught, led by his old schoolmate and now Newport hotel keeper, George Downing, and the novelist William Wells Brown, a counterconvention assembled in J. Sella Martin's Joy Street Baptist Church later that month. There Garnet continued to distinguish between mass migration, which he opposed, and limited emigration to grow free-labor cotton, spread the gospel, and form a "grand centre of Negro nationality." Most American blacks, he said, would stay in the United States because conditions there would be improved by the African example. "He who tells me I shall leave my country," he threw out defiantly, "is an impudent man, and he who says I shall not go, is a fool. I will do as I please, either to go or stay. The *common-sense* of the world is in favor of this [African Civilization] movement."[47]

The debate continued into the spring of 1860. While Garnet, back in New York, encouraged a Cooper Union audience to form "a company of virtuous, intelligent and enterprising colored people, who are now ready to act as pioneers" in Africa with Delany, he insisted that equality should also be established at home. But for those who sought a new frontier, colonization promised much. As the West had bloomed under the hand of the pioneer so Africa would bloom, its agriculture prosper, its trade and commerce flourish, and the accouterments of western civilization—the school, the church, the arts

[46]*Liberator*, August 26, 1859.
[47]*Weekly Anglo-African*, September 17, 1859.

and sciences—would be American Negroes' gift to the land of their ancestry.[48]

Finally, however, the African Civilization Society's plans were shattered by African renunciation of Delany's land treaty, Yoruba warfare in the projected area of settlement, and endless bickering in the free black community. William C. Nell, closely identified with Garrison, charged that the African Civilization movement was simply a front for old-fashioned colonization. J. W. C. Pennington, formerly a Garnet supporter, complained that the Cooper Union meeting was ill-timed "because the leaders of the Republican party, with the Hon. F. P. Blair and Horace Greeley at their head, [were] joining in a crusade *with the African Civilization Society, to secure the expulsion of the free colored people from this country*." Another meeting at New York's Zion Church was so rowdy that the *Anglo-African* called it "one of the most unsatisfactory and unhappy demonstrations ever made in this city, . . . [which] fairly illustrated the truthfulness of the suggestion of one of our dailies, that there is much work here for a civilization society."[49]

Plagued by the desertion of former colleagues, attacked in the press by critics reluctant to debate him in person, Garnet continued to support the African Civilization movement until it collapsed in 1862; and Delany, converted to selective emigration, planned to lead a group from Canada to the Niger River region, until the Civil War drained its members back to the United States. Buoyed up by the optimism such activity generated, Garnet made a second trip to England to further the cause and, at the same time, accepted the American agency to encourage emigration to Haiti.[50]

[48] From the New York *Herald,* n.d., reprinted in *Weekly Anglo-African,* March 17, 1860.

[49] William C. Nell to Editor, September 10, 1859, in ibid., September 17, 1859. Also see ibid., April 21, 1860.

[50] The sources are scattered: see, for example, ibid., May 5, June 28, 1860; correspondence between King and Alfred Churchill and David Livingston

Those were, however, Garnet's last efforts on behalf of colonization. He had started to England just after the Civil War broke out. Soon he was drawn back to the United States to devote his efforts to the Union cause. Service as chaplain to Negro troops on Riker's Island, organization of a Ladies Committee for the Aid of Sick Soldiers, work with the Union League Club to end sutlers' exploitation of black troops, running a relief office for victims of the New York draft riots, and recruiting black troops occupied his time and mind fully. Amid the harsh reality of civil war, Africa became a dream.[51]

⛓⛓⛓

After the war, Garnet returned to his parish duties at Shiloh and also, for a time, served as president of Avery College near Pittsburgh. Finally, too, he fulfilled his long-time wish to see Africa. Backed by leading New York merchants, he was appointed minister to Liberia and sailed eastward in December 1881. In failing health since the mid-1870s, Garnet weathered the voyage and reached Africa only to die shortly thereafter.

The closing phases of Garnet's life—a thriving New York pastorate, a college presidency, and a diplomatic appointment—mark the successful man recognized by those of established position and power. Yet history has labeled him

---

(copy), March 9, 1861, and September 12, 1860, K-PAC; Chatham *Planet,* April 11, 1861; *Douglass Monthly,* January, November 1861 (including a copy of Garnet's passport and a letter to his wife, dated September 13, [1861]).

[51]See Smith, "Introduction," 57–61; Crummell, "Elogium," 297. James McPherson, *The Struggle for Equality, Abolitionists and the Negro in the Civil War and Reconstruction* (Princeton: Princeton University Press, 1964), 205, refers to Garnet's recruiting work. Maria Child praised his work during the draft riots in a letter to Henrietta [Sargeant], August 14, 1863, C-CoU. Toward the end of the war, Garnet offered to go to England again to explain the war and the Negro question to the English; see his letter to Henry W. Bellows, November 4, 1864, B-MHS.

a revolutionary. His insurrectionary appeal at Buffalo in 1843 has made Garnet's name live. Black and white historians alike have treated his "Address to the Slaves" as the beginning, end, and essence of Henry Highland Garnet. Similarly, his contemporary, Alexander Crummell, schoolmate in New York and New Hampshire and a life-long friend, emphasized the revolutionary and thought that had Garnet remained a slave, he would have led an insurrection.[52]

A study of his full career, however, suggests that Garnet was neither a conservative nor a revolutionary. Consistently an activist, he worked and struggled for rights and prosperity for free Negroes and freedom for slaves. As the occasion demanded, he urged slave revolt, supported emigration, worked for equal suffrage, extolled the Protestant ethic, and preached and practiced Christian brotherhood. Unquestionably Garnet unsettled the timid, baffled the unimaginative, incensed the orthodox, and angered the bigoted. Wendell Phillips reported the Garrisonian view to the English abolitionist, Elizabeth Pease: Garnet was "an *able* and *shrewd* man—& one of our most dangerous enemies."[53]

Garnet's ability to shift and maneuver, to fit the method to the time and problem, did not lead him to sacrifice ends to means. He was faithful to the dual goals of antislavery: freeing the slaves and elevating the free blacks. Thus it was that his diverse ideas and deeds fit a common pattern. "Give us our freedom," he admonished the American Anti-Slavery Society in 1840, "remunerate us for our labor, and protect

[52]See William Brewer's "Henry Highland Garnet," *Journal of Negro History* 13 (January 1928): 36–52; Carter Woodson's sketch of Garnet in the *Dictionary of American Biography*, eds. Allen Johnson and Dumas Malone (New York: Scribners, 1928*ff*), VII:154–155. See also the index references in Dwight Dumond, *Antislavery, The Crusade for Freedom in America* (Ann Arbor: University of Michigan Press, 1961); John Hope Franklin, *From Slavery to Freedom*, 3d ed. (New York: Alfred Knopf, 1967); Richard Bardolph, *The Negro Vanguard* (New York: Random House, 1959, 1961); Leon Litwack, *North of Slavery: The Negro in the Free States, 1770–1860* (Chicago: University of Chicago Press, 1961).

[53]Wendell Phillips to Elizabeth Pease, July 29, 1849, G-BPL.

our family altars, and, by the blessings of Heaven we will help make those fruitful fields to blossom and bloom as Eden." Though he dreamed of Africa, it was in America that he sought the ideal future. "Of all places in the world," he wrote Gerrit Smith in 1856 shortly after his return from Jamaica, "I think this land needs the labours of black men. . . . The Truth is, the free people of the North have been overlooked, and the world begins to see it."[54] America could be Eden when prejudice, discrimination, political disfranchisement, color barriers, and legal inequalities were eliminated.

The dramatic high point of Garnet's life, without doubt, was that day in Buffalo when he appealed to the slaves to rise and throw off their bondage. But more consonant with his long-term activities and goals was the sermon he preached on a February Sunday in 1865. Standing before the American Congress, he warned the lawmakers that emancipation and fast-approaching victory would not conclude the country's mission.

> The good work which God has assigned for the ages to come, will be finished, when our national literature shall be so purified as to reflect a faithful and a just light upon the character and social habits of our race, and the brush, and pencil, and chisel, and Lyre of Art, shall refuse to lend their aid to scoff at the afflictions of the poor, or to caricature, or ridicule a long-suffering people.[55]

Garnet's career embraces much of antebellum black militance. Superficially surprising, his willingness to shift allegiance from one proposed solution to another, his eagerness to use any means that promised success was the very stuff of this militance—to free and empower the American black by any possible means. In his failure to follow specific abolitionist credos and platforms, he offended many Garrisonians and sometimes frightened his non-Garrisonian co-workers. But neither he nor they monopolized the antislavery movement.

[54] From the *Emancipator,* n.d., copied by the *Liberator,* May 22, 1840; Garnet to Gerrit Smith, October 3, 1856, S-SU.
[55] Garnet, *Memorial Discourse,* 87.

9

The Perfectionist Radical:
Stephen Symonds Foster

🔗🔗🔗🔗🔗🔗🔗🔗🔗🔗

One Sunday morning in June 1842, the minister of South Church in Concord, New Hampshire, entered the pulpit to deliver his sermon. Hardly had he surveyed the congregation before a young man rose from the front bench and launched into a vehement warning against the evils of slavery. Undeterred by the startled disapproval of his auditors, undismayed by the hastily galvanized and lustily loud music of the choir, he was dissuaded from his harangue only when several parishioners, the secretary of state of New Hampshire among them, bodily removed him from the church. Undaunted by his expulsion, he returned for the afternoon service, but this time he was expected. With even less ceremony, he was seized, dragged down the aisle, literally thrown out of the church, and arrested by the Concord sheriff who carried him, limp, before the local court. The young man refused to recognize its jurisdiction, though he did finally pay the five-dollar fine it assessed.[1]

[1]Parker Pillsbury, *Acts of the Anti-slavery Apostles* (Concord, N.H.: Claque, Wegman, Schlick & Co., printers, 1883), 129–141.

Such drama was not new to Stephen Symonds Foster. For three years he had been preaching the antislavery doctrine in much the same way, defying convention, scorning decorum, and excoriating evil in vivid and bitter language. The urgency of his message pressed him to seize every opportunity to be heard. Slavery like fire created a crisis in which no man could sit quietly by.[2]

Foster had the zeal and grit the work demanded. Born in 1809, the ninth child of Asa Foster, he was trained in moral rigor and reform by his father, a Revolutionary War veteran who had refused his military land bounty because he had been convinced that all war was sinful. Following his heritage and reflecting his rugged youth, Stephen was completely a product of New England. "I should," he said at one point, "hate farming in the West; I should hate to put my spade into ground where it did not hit against a rock." Tall, thin, and "cadaverous-looking," he inspired comparison with Old Testament prophets.[3]

When he was twenty-two, Foster gave up the carpenter's trade in which he was trained to prepare for the ministry. After being graduated from Dartmouth in 1838, he matriculated at Union Theological Seminary in New York. There Stephen, who had been jailed at Hanover for refusing to do military duty, quickly ran afoul of the school authorities when they denied him the use of a room in which to conduct antiwar prayer meetings. Disillusioned, he left New York, abandoned the ministry, and decided to devote himself fully to reform. Here, in all likelihood, is the key to his reform career—the need to act out his commitments, to implement ideas which would be fruitless if they were only preached. So far did his enthusiasm and fiery techniques carry him that in

---

[2]Parker Pillsbury, "Stephen Symonds Foster," *Granite Monthly* 5 (1882): 369–375.

[3]The quotations are from Thomas Wentworth Higginson, "Anti-Slavery Days," *Outlook* 60 (September 3, 1898): 51; New York *Observer*, n.d., quoted in *Liberator*, June 27, 1845.

1842 the Hanover Congregational Church excommunicated him for having become a "disorganiser & a leveller," a fanatic, an infidel, and an agent of destruction.[4] Their action merely put the seal on his reform radicalism, for he had already dedicated his life to pacifism, anarchism, women's rights, egalitarianism, and abolitionism.

Like the French revolutionaries, Foster embraced liberty, equality, and fraternity, and he was convinced that the first of these was basic to the others. Thus his reform career was rooted in the steady assertion of free speech. While still a student at Dartmouth, he had helped organize the New Hampshire Young Men's Anti-Slavery Society and had invited Angelina Grimké to address his fellow students, thereby offending those who would deny the platform to women. Thereafter he insisted on a free platform until even his antislavery colleagues were unsure whether the liberty he demanded was actually license. Certainly his persistent interruptions of church services and political meetings to preach his antislavery message raised legitimate questions about the limits of a free platform.

How abrasive his tactics were he told his fellow radical, Nathaniel P. Rogers, early in 1843.

> Within the last fifteen months, four times have [my fellow countrymen] opened their dismal cells for my reception. Twenty-four times have they dragged me from their temples, and twice have they thrown me with great violence from the second story of the building, careless of consequences. Once, in a Baptist meeting house have they given me an evangelical kick in the side, which left me an invalid for weeks. Times out of memory have they broken up my meetings with violence, and hunted me with brick bats and rotten eggs. Once have they indicted me for assault and battery.... [And once,] *in the name of outraged law and justice, have they attempted to put me in irons!!*[5]

Foster constantly denied any authority that would curtail his freedom to speak. When, four years later in 1847, he

[4]Church Committee of Dartmouth College to Foster, October 4, 1841, F-AAS.
[5]Foster to Nathaniel P. Rogers, January 15, 1843, in *Herald of Freedom*, February 3, 1843.

attempted in Boston to lecture a Liberty party assembly after
it had adjourned, he was shouted down with threats. The
very same week, when he tried to address the Christian Anti-
Slavery Convention in the same city, he was thrown out of
the hall by police officers. Yet he clung to his principles and
demanded for his opponents the same freedom to speak which
he asserted. He denounced, therefore, Garrison's attempt to
deny clergymen the floor at the Boston Anti-Sabbath Convention in 1848. Similarly he rejected the authority of parliamentary procedure when, in his eyes, it curtailed free speech.
As a result, his course sometimes seemed one of uncontrolled
disruptiveness—as when he had stalked out of the New England Anti-Slavery Convention in 1843 damning the "despotic"
character of the chairman for insisting that speakers' remarks
be relevant to the subject at hand.[6]

Yet Foster was a moderate among the distinctive group
of New Hampshire anarchists. Only a year after he had
stormed out of the New England Convention, Abby Folsom
berated the subsequent convention for having any officers
at all and refused to stop speaking when she was called to
order. Thereupon Foster sided with the Chair. Folsom was,
all admitted, a special case. Famous for disrupting reform
meetings with her endless and aimless commentary, she was,
many thought, not quite right in the head. Foster therefore
joined two others and removed her bodily from the hall. Not
amused by Abby's raucous quip that Jesus had only one ass
to carry him while she had three, Foster defended his action
by observing that he did "not esteem it an act of philanthropy
to let an insane woman break up, or use up the time of a
meeting" in such a way.[7]

More indicative in separating Foster from the New Hamp-

[6]James N. Buffum to William L. Garrison, n.d., *Liberator,* January 29,
1847; for the Anti-Sabbath Convention, *Liberator,* March 31, 1848; Anne
W. Weston to Caroline and Deborah Weston, June 3, 1843, W-BPL; Edmund
Quincy to Richard D. Webb, June 27, 1843, Q-MHS.
[7]*Liberator,* June 7, 1844. For the quotation, see *National Anti-Slavery
Standard,* August 9, 1844.

shire radicals was his year long battle over the *Herald of Freedom*. Founded and edited by Rogers, the *Herald* was the official organ of the New Hampshire Anti-Slavery Society, even though the society paid neither its general expenses nor the editor's salary. Nonetheless, when Rogers refused to recognize the society's jurisdiction over the paper and sold it, the board of managers disclaimed the sale. The issue led quickly to vituperative infighting between the Rogers faction, which opposed all organizational structure, and Foster, backed by the Boston leaders, who represented institutional order. In the end, two *Heralds* emerged briefly, only to die from lack of support. More significant for Foster, however, were the limits which this episode defined for his radicalism, for he had deserted New Hampshire anarchism and was, at least in Rogers' eyes, no longer a "radical, ultra-fellow soldier."[8]

⛓⛓⛓

Rogers' view of Foster was scarcely a majority opinion. For most of his colleagues Foster remained an "ultra." To them, the style he developed during the 1840s not only offended by its vehemence but reinforced the radicalism of his message.

Central to his thought and action throughout the decade was "coming out"—a staple of antislavery radicalism. He developed it most fully in his major antislavery tract, *The Brotherhood of Thieves*, published in 1843. Concluding that the churches sustained slavery, *The Brotherhood* made it amply clear that those who fellowshipped with slaveholders were themselves guilty of slaveholding. Offensive to Northern Christians thus summarily labeled slaveholders, the tract accurately reflected Foster's customarily abusive language. The Methodist Episcopal Church, he wrote, without thereby excluding

[8]The *Herald of Freedom* dispute is covered in the *National Anti-Slavery Standard*, December 12, 1844, and June 12, 1845, particularly; and in *Liberator*, December 13, 1844, January 10, April 4, 1845. The quotation is from Nathaniel P. Rogers to William L. Garrison, February 1, 1845, in *Liberator*, February 21, 1845.

Bound with Them in Chains

other denominations, was "more corrupt and profligate than any house of ill fame in the city of New York. . . ." All churches tainted in any way with tolerating the peculiar institution, he charged elsewhere, were "man-stealing, woman-whipping, adulterous and murderous" institutions, "combinations of thieves, adulterers and pirates," "synagogue[s] of Satan." "Our Nation's Religion," he summed up in a letter to his fellow radical, Parker Pillsbury, "is a lie. . . ."[9]

As he attacked churches and clerics in writing and on the lecture platform, Foster also attacked political parties and politicians. Couched in terms of sexual depravity, his strictures spared neither Congressmen nor Presidents. Slaveholding politicians and their supporters had "consigned every sixth woman in the country to a life of hopeless concubinage and adultery." Included in that sweeping condemnation was even John Quincy Adams, who, in failing explicitly to demand the abolition of slavery and the slave trade in the District of Columbia, sustained there the debauchery of the Southern institution. And, after his March 7th speech in 1850, Daniel Webster led Foster's rogues gallery of Northern politicians who were even more guilty of slaveholding than individual Southern owners. His defense of Henry Clay's compromise made Webster a frightful combination of "bloody Nero" and "Judas Iscariot."[10]

If Foster's shocking imagery and vivid language were necessary to move the apathetic, as he claimed, they could also turn away support from the cause. Sarah Pugh, a quiet Quaker abolitionist from Philadelphia, discerningly remarked that

[9]Stephen Symonds Foster, *The Brotherhood of Thieves, or A True Picture of the American Church and Clergy* (New London: William Bolles, 1843), 7; Abby Kelley to William L. Garrison, August 31, 1841, in *Liberator,* September 10, 1841; *Liberator,* December 24, 1841; Thomas Hardy et al. to Ebenezer Adams, March 20, 1841, C-DC; Parker Pillsbury to Sydney H. Gay, September 2, 1848, in *Liberator,* September 15, 1848.

[10]Foster, *Brotherhood of Thieves,* 24; for Adams, see Foster's resolution to condemn him, offered at American Anti-Slavery Society meeting, May 1, 1842, in *Liberator,* May 27, 1842; *Anti-Slavery Bugle,* January 25, 1851.

"very many who are ready for *strong* meat would turn away in disgust if it were *first* set before them in its *raw state. . . .*"[11] The general public, which shared her distaste, were quick to turn to physical violence. Thus as he crossed the country from Maine to Michigan in the 1840s as an American Anti-Slavery Society agent, Foster was frequently the target for eggs and brickbats, and, on several occasions, firearms.

Even a conviction that he was an intended murder victim did not deter Foster, for he saw mob violence as instructive drama and willingly played the role of martyr-sufferer. On that occasion in Portland, Maine, when he thought himself closest to death, he had launched a severe attack upon the clergy and made a stirring plea for temperance. Although refused the use of the city hall until his final meeting, he had until then successfully defied hostile crowds. His last appearance, however, precipitated mayhem. His entrance into the hall was "received by the assembly with a fiendish grin that would have graced a conclave of New Zealand cannibals." The mob almost immediately began the evening's destruction, hurling eggs, destroying the furniture, and trying to set the building afire. The mayor, thoroughly frightened, ordered the hall cleared, and Foster, escorted by a flanking guard of ladies, was both clubbed and hit on the head by flying objects.[12]

Luckily the annals of hostility were not unrelieved. On a lecture tour in Massachusetts in 1841, he met Abby Kelley, the only woman lecturer in the field since the Grimké sisters had retired. Assertive and insistent, Abby personified the women's rights issue at the 1840 annual meeting of the American Anti-Slavery Society. Uninhibited by convention, Abby not only lectured before mixed audiences but appeared with men on the same lecture platform and traveled about the country from meeting to meeting with male antislavery cohorts. Such shocking and scandalous behavior made her

[11]Sarah Pugh to Maria W. Chapman, June 15, 1844, W-BPL.
[12]*Liberator*, February 17, 1843.

a perfect match for Stephen Foster. But despite their marriage in December 1845, they remained, to their antagonists, "low, degraded, licentious vagabonds."[13]

Abby was hurt by vicious tongues and frightened by angry mobs, and, by 1850, she had weaned Stephen from his persistent defiance of violence. After a decade of separate and joint campaigning, they announced that they would no longer lecture where their meetings would be "disturbed." They had, they asserted, established the principle of free speech. The time was propitious to concentrate on getting the widest possible hearing for their message. They consciously shifted from a style that provoked violence and disruption to one more likely to produce the emotionalism of a protracted revival meeting.[14]

Even so, the tone of Foster's lectures and the substance of his radicalism did not change greatly. That he met with more friendly audiences during the 1850s probably was due to greater Northern tolerance of antislavery rather than to a retreat from the vigorous tactics of earlier years. Indeed the shift in technique was overridden as the years went on by his increasingly radical religious views. If he expressed himself less violently about the churches, it was only because his anticlericalism had given way to the conviction that organized religion was inconsequential. He looked to men rather than to God for action to achieve "Right and Justice." He no longer relied on biblical arguments against slavery, for he had rejected its divinity.[15]

In abandoning orthodox theology, however, Foster did not

[13]"C" to the Editor, September, 1846, in *Anti-Slavery Bugle,* October 9, 1846.

[14]Abby Foster to Sydney H. Gay, February 7, 1850, in *National Anti-Slavery Standard,* February 14, 1850; Stephen Foster to William L. Garrison, March 31, 1851, G-BPL.

[15]For Foster's changing religious views, see, for example, E. Smith to *True Wesleyan,* April 15, 1846, copied in *National Anti-Slavery Standard,* May 7, 1846; also see *National Anti-Slavery Standard,* June 7, 1849, September 27, 1850, June 3, 1852, for Foster's views expressed at various New England Anti-Slavery conventions. Quotation from last item.

surrender the martyr role, which had enlivened his early
career and had carried him through its physical trials. He
still believed that, as a good Christian, he had no alternative
but to follow God's commands. "Tell me that God requires
me to go to the stake," he wrote in 1846, "and you could
not keep me from it, if I am a Christian."[16] Foster, however,
was more likely to glory in his trials than to ignore them.
Once, while addressing the New England Anti-Slavery Convention in 1844, he was interrupted by calls for the popular
Hutchinson Family Singers. Thoroughly annoyed, he stalked
off sulking, only to reappear at the next session with "his
coat that had one tail torn off in a mob, a stone that was
thrown at him and those chains & collar" which he had once
worn in jail. "Every time there was any noise or stamping,"
Deborah Weston wrote, "[he] shook his chains & put on the
collar."[17]

Ten years later, he was still "do[ing] the martyr," comparing
himself to St. Paul, playing, as Edmund Quincy said, "St.
Stephen, the connoisseur in martyrdom." The degree to which
he enjoyed the role Foster betrayed when he urged the much-
mobbed George Thompson to stay on at mob-threatened
meetings in Canastota, New York, in 1851 in order to "partake
the banquet." And, although he more and more internalized
the quest, he continued to congratulate himself for doing
right no matter what the cost. "A long & painful experience,"
he wrote Richard Webb in Dublin, "has taught me the folly
of looking for commendation from any quarter, & I have
at last learnt to be content with the inward consciousness of
an honest, earnest effort to discharge my whole duty, regardless of the opinions even of my most cherished friends...."[18]

[16]*Anti-Slavery Bugle*, April 10, 1846.
[17]Deborah Weston to Caroline Weston, n.d., W-BPL.
[18]*Detroit Democrat*, n.d., quoted in *Liberator*, November 18, 1853; Edmund
Quincy to Caroline Weston, June 2, [1843], W-BPL; George Thompson
to Anne W. Weston, March 7, 1851, W-BPL; Foster to [Richard D. Webb],
June 8, 1858, MS-UR.

Thus Foster retained the essence though he doubtless missed the drama.

If his fellow abolitionists were eventually to call him "saint, prophet, confessor & martyr," it was not always so, for Foster's manner brought disapproval from moderate and radical alike. Ellis Gray Loring admired his courage and his "disinterestedness" but questioned his "good sense & discernment." Samuel Coues, peace reformer of Portsmouth, New Hampshire, thought Foster so "rude" that he would likely alienate all who met him. Maria Child, eager always to avoid controversy, wrote that "*Stephen* Foster will be as good as an unleashed bulldog to keep *me* away from Anti Slavery meetings." The spokesmen for radicalism were equally upset. Garrison, always frightened by mobs and riots, wished that Foster would change his tactics. Wendell Phillips called him a "devoted, noble, single eyed, fate eloquent, John-the-Baptist character," often "wild & illogical." The best that Maria Chapman could say for him was that she was "always glad to have him at a convention . . . , as adding to the interest."[19]

Because of his controversial tactics, Foster remained on the periphery of the antislavery societies even though he spent almost twenty years as their agent. Too honest and awkward for internal maneuver, he was heedless of organizational loyalty and orthodoxy. Thus, as Phillips put it, "We in Massachusetts generally do not think [his] views and action correct." Or as Chapman told Abby Kelley in 1843, "You may always depend on him to blunder forward *for the destruction of the American Society. He has,*" she explained, "but little plan

[19]Theodore D. Weld to Abby Foster, October, 1881, F-WHS; Ellis G. Loring to Abby Kelley, September 27, 1841, F-AAS; Samuel E. Coues to Edmund Quincy, January 13, 1841, Q-MHS; Maria Child to Maria W. Chapman, July 26, [1859], C-BPL; William L. Garrison to Helen E. Garrison, November 27, 1842, G-BPL; Wendell Phillips to Elizabeth Pease, June 29, 1842, G-BPL; Maria W. Chapman to Abby Kelley, July 25, 1843, F-AAS.

or consistency, or stability, but what little he has, con-centres upon that." Unfair as the charges of malevolence were, fifteen more years of observing him left Chapman still deploring his inconsistency and instability. "Forethought enough to put the square pin in the square hole," she wrote Samuel May in Leicester, "does not enter Foster's mind."[20]

Indeed Foster was as impatient of organizational nicety within the cause as of apathy outside it. All gave way before his burning compulsion to end slavery; and, while his goal remained steady, his strategy for its accomplishment changed constantly. A radical extremist, he was ready to adopt those means that best suited the needs of the moment whether or not they were internally consistent or jibed with the current policy of any society.

During the 1850s, his need for action and his impatience with the limited results so far achieved became almost frenetic. Agitated by the failure of antislavery societies to prosper or proliferate and frustrated by slavocracy's triumph in the Fugitive Slave Law, the Kansas-Nebraska Act, and the Dred Scott decision, Foster urgently sought new methods for a more vigorous attack on slavery. The time for argument was past; the time for action had come. "We do not want men of intellect," he told Western abolitionists early in the decade, "we want *heart*, zeal, confidence and truth and humanity." "I wish I could get you all to praying for the slave . . . by taking right hold and *doing* the work that is to be done."[21]

By 1856, his impatience had become so intense that he verged on violence. "There is no necessity," he exhorted Massachusetts abolitionists in January, "for waiting a century or half a century for the liberation of the slaves. We may just as well break this accursed government in pieces in five years

[20]Wendell Phillips to Elizabeth Pease, August 12, 1842, G-BPL; Maria W. Chapman to Abby Kelley, September 9, 1843, F-WHS; Maria W. Chapman to Samuel May, Jr., March 17, [1857?], M-BPL.
[21]Foster's speech to the Western Anti-Slavery Society, August 27, 1853, in *Anti-Slavery Bugle*, September 3, 1853.

as in twenty-five. I am not willing to 'wait and hope on' as men tell us to." The old tactics were no longer adequate. "Let us," he had urged a year earlier, "have less profession, and more deed."[22]

Yet it was the means for accomplishing the deed that perplexed Foster. From its inception, the American Anti-Slavery Society had relied only on moral suasion. It was presumably from those who would contaminate such purity by political action that Garrison had saved the society in 1840. By the 1850s, however, Foster was convinced that simple conversion was inadequate. At the same time, he rejected political antislavery. Like Garrison, he averred that the major parties and the Constitution were proslavery. The Free Soilers lacked principle, and the Republican party was ready to compromise and thus "strengthen the chains of the slave." Nor could Foster accept the Liberty party's successor, the Radical Abolitionists, because their platform rested on an antislavery interpretation of the Constitution. The fallacy of that view was demonstrated by Gerrit Smith's single session in the House in 1853–1854 when, by his participation in congressional work, he cooperated with slaveholders. To Foster, Smith and his supporters were little better than their colleagues in the major political parties. Indeed it would seem that no political activity could meet Foster's approval since he was a charter member of the Non-Resistant Society and was committed thereby to the proposition that office-holding and voting were sinful.[23]

[22]*Liberator*, February 8, 1856, January 19, 1855. The remarks were made in speeches to the Massachusetts Anti-Slavery Society meeting, January 26, 1856, and to the Rhode Island State Anti-Slavery Convention, January 11, 1855.

[23]For illustrations of Foster's view, see generally his *Brotherhood of Thieves*, 3–28. On the Free Soil party, see his remarks to the New England Anti-Slavery Convention, May 31, 1854; and on the Republican party, his resolution to the Worcester County South Division Anti-Slavery Society, September 17, 1854, both in *Liberator*, June 9 and September 29, 1854, respectively. On Radical Abolitionists, see Foster to Emmett Densmore, March 4, 1860, in *Liberator*, March 9, 1860. For Gerrit Smith, see Foster's comments to Western Anti-Slavery Society, August 25, 1855, in *Anti-Slavery Bugle*, Sep-

It was not, however, that simple. Principle led in one direction; practicality in another. Most white American males prized the ballot. Very few were ready to use nonresistance. Should not the majority have an opportunity to oppose slavery at the ballot box? Despite his principles, then, Foster in 1843 and 1844 gave half-hearted support to the Liberty party, commending it as the best party for those antislavery people who were also "human government" men. He hoped that Liberty party might move closer to thorough-going abolitionism, and to this end he attended its Buffalo convention in the summer of 1843 and later suggested that the party become an auxiliary of the American Anti-Slavery Society.[24]

Disillusioned by the reaction on both sides, Foster soon retracted, but he never wholly abandoned political action. In 1845, he turned to disunion ballots, which he tried to develop into a systematic method to "demonstrate through the ballot box" the "moral power" of abolitionists.[25] The method was simple. In an era when political parties distributed their own ballots, abolitionists would print and cast ballots for men whose opposition to the proslavery Constitution precluded them from assuming office even if they were elected. Disunion balloting would, in short, preserve principle and yet allow the politically inclined to use the ballot in support of antislavery goals.

Although disunion balloting never achieved significant support, it reflected Garrisonian commitment to subvert the Con-

---

tember 8, 1855. The quotation is from Foster's address at the American Anti-Slavery Society meeting, May 7, 1856, in *Liberator,* May 16, 1856.

[24]Abby Kelley to Gerrit Smith, August 7, 1843, S-SU; *National Anti-Slavery Standard,* January 25, 1844; Foster to William L. Garrison, n.d., in *Liberator,* November 3, 1843.

[25]From Foster's speech to the Massachusetts Anti-Slavery Society, January 28, 1847, in *Liberator,* February 19, 1847.

stitution. For antislavery disunionists, the sooner the Constitution was overthrown and the Union dissolved, the sooner would slavery be ended. In urging political disruption, Foster took the lead in 1844 by welcoming the annexation of Texas. Because annexation was so clearly unconstitutional, it would, if carried out, "annihilate the Constitution."[26] Similarly he applauded the Fugitive Slave Law of 1850, whose content he disapproved even more than annexation. He had, in fact, long flaunted the old 1793 law by offering aid to fugitives. In 1842, he had been jailed for attempting to interfere in the arrest of the fugitive slave George Latimer, and, after 1847, his farm in Worcester offered shelter and aid to fugitives passing through central Massachusetts.

His very defiance of the old law made Foster see the use to which the new one might be put. By devising extralegal action to thwart its enforcement, he stretched his commitment to nonresistance to embrace hearty approval of physical opposition to the law by those not similarly committed. Vowing that he would never surrender a fugitive, he urged those who believed it right to use physical force on any occasion to "use it now." "When the wills of the people are decided that a system shall fall, no matter who is in power, it will fall before the voice of the people," he prophesied in the fall of 1850.[27] Vox populi was no longer expressed in the franchise and legislation but in open defiance of unjust laws.

When, in 1854, Anthony Burns was arrested in Boston as a fugitive, Foster urged the New England Anti-Slavery Convention to join the Massachusetts Free Soil Convention in establishing a vigilance committee to forestall similar arrests in the future. He had also, a few days earlier, publicly called on the men of Worcester to do their duty, to "combine and

[26]On dissolving the Union, see the "Protest" presented to the Twelfth Annual Meeting of the Massachusetts Anti-Slavery Society, in *Liberator*, February 2, 1844. For the quotation, Foster's speech to American Anti-Slavery Society annual meeting, May 8, 1844, in *Liberator*, May 24, 1844.

[27]Foster's speech at the Anti-Slavery Convention, Valley Falls, Rhode Island, September 27, 1850, in *Liberator*, October 11, 1850.

organize against kidnapping" and hurry to Boston to aid Burns.[28] That such aid was not confined to moral suasion, Foster's approval of Thomas Wentworth Higginson's and Martin Stowell's attempt to storm the Boston Court House and rescue Burns attested.

Defiance of human law was, in Foster's eyes, adherence to the higher law. Recently popularized in William Seward's speech opposing the Compromise of 1850, the principle he expressed had long been familiar to Foster. From those days in New Hampshire when he had been arrested for disturbing church services, he had refused to recognize the authority either of the constables or the courts. His response to arrest was to go limp; his response to the trial was to refuse to participate in the proceedings except when he could use the courtroom as a forum for his message. Thus when Passmore Williamson, the Quaker Philadelphian, relied on a lawyer to defend him in 1855 against charges of breaking the Fugitive Slave Law, Foster disapproved. "He should have trusted to his own tongue before that guilty Court," he lamented. "I would give the wealth of a life time for such an opportunity."[29] The law must not only be broken; it must be publicly defied.

The ideas which underlay his course during the 1850s Foster presented most pithily in his 1855 pamphlet, *Revolution the Only Remedy*.[30] When he had started preaching disunion in the mid-1840s, he had conceived of it as only another form of coming out. As honest men should leave proslavery churches and parties, so too they should come out from a proslavery government. By 1855, however, Foster had considerably sharpened this rather common antislavery theory into a revolutionary challenge for individuals to dissociate themselves entirely from government. He told a Western Anti-

[28]*Worcester Daily Spy,* May 29, 1854; quotation in *Liberator,* June 9, 1854.
[29]Foster's speech to Western Anti-Slavery Society Annual Meeting, August 26, 1855, in *Anti-Slavery Bugle,* September 15, 1855.
[30]Stephen Symonds Foster, *Revolution the Only Remedy for Slavery,* Anti-Slavery Tract No. 7, (New York: American Anti-Slavery Society, 1855).

Slavery Society meeting held in Ohio's Western Reserve, bailiwick of antislavery Congressman Joshua Giddings, that the time for action within political parties and government had passed, that it rested with each individual to place himself with the slaves outside of law, and that earnest opponents of slavery must free themselves from government-imposed restraints on their actions in behalf of fugitive slaves and slaves still in bondage.[31]

Foster had come to embrace a dual disunionism. He appealed to Northern states to withdraw from the Union and leave the South helpless in the face of servile insurrections she could not suppress by herself. In this spirit, he urged Massachusetts to take the lead in restoring the entire Union to freedom. But, as his frustration with inaction grew, Foster demanded ever more clearly a disunion that would completely restructure the government of North and South alike. Tempering his appeals for disunion and revolution in 1855 with professed loyalty to antislavery as a reform movement, by 1860 he insisted stridently that dissolution of the Union had always meant thoroughgoing revolution, not merely a separation of North from South but a direct confrontation between all the friends of freedom and all the supporters of slavery.[32]

Basic to Foster's argument were two assumptions. First, all men had a natural right to get and keep their freedom by whatever means necessary. Second, slaves would strike for their freedom at the slightest opportunity. These ideas he had clearly explored in *Revolution the Only Remedy*, and they became guiding themes at the Cleveland Disunion Convention of 1857. Boycotted by Garrison and his immediate associates ostensibly because its timing was not propitious, the conven-

[31] *Anti-Slavery Bugle*, September 8, 1855.

[32] Foster's speech to the Western Anti-Slavery Society annual meeting, August 26, 1855, in *Anti-Slavery Bugle*, September 15, 1855; his remarks to Cleveland Disunion Convention, October 28, 1857, in ibid., November 14, 1857; Foster to [Benjamin] Jones, February 25, 1860, in ibid., March 10, 1860.

tion was in the hands of the Fosters and their adherents.
From their deliberations emerged Foster's resolution that "it
[was] the duty of the Slaves to strike down their tyrants by
force and arms whenever the blow, however bloody, [could]
be made effective to that end, unless Washington was a murderer and the American Revolution a sin and crime against
God and man."[33]

Foster, an admirer of Nat Turner, was ready to lay aside
the moral suasion, which had been the essence of the antislavery movement, and to support slave rebellion. This was the
force disunion would loose, this the compulsion of abolitionists
to stand outside of government and against it on behalf of
the black man. Speaking to the Free Convention in Rutland,
Vermont, in 1858, he asked the delegates to "put their heel"
on a government that "rob[bed] four millions of human beings
of every day's work they perform[ed]" and of everything else
as well. "Some will say," he concluded, " 'This will result in
blood.' Very likely it will. What of it? I ask you, is not every
one ready to spill oceans of blood, if necessary, to secure
his own freedom?" Foster, the pacifist, smiled on bloody rebellion and servile insurrection. But the contradiction between
his nonresistance and his acceptance of violence had long
been present. He had from the beginning always left a
loophole for resort to force if God commanded it, and thereby
he justified both his own refusal to wield the sword and his
encouragement to others to follow their consciences to armed
violence.[34]

In any case, actual revolution seemed so distant and unlikely
that Foster turned to other tactics at the same time he espoused
the new philosophy. Casting aside his disavowal of political
action, he encouraged a state-level disunion party to achieve

[33]*Anti-Slavery Bugle,* November 7, 1857.
[34]Foster, *Revolution the Only Remedy,* 8, 15–16, 19; quotation is from *National Anti-Slavery Standard,* August 21, 1858. For nonresistance, see *Non-Resistant,* October 19, 1839; also Foster's remarks at Non-Resistance Society meeting, March 24, 1855, in *Liberator,* March 30, 1855.

his revolutionary goals. Hoping that the ballot might "revolutionize the world," he sought candidates who would take over his own state's government but refuse to support the federal government. By this unlikely device, he undertook to make the states "free and independent sovereignties," which would achieve secession and disunion and, ultimately, revolutionize the government.[35]

Visionary in concept and inconsequential in fulfillment, Foster's disunion party activity more and more isolated him and his small following from the mainstream of Garrisonianism. His repeated assertions after 1855 that the antislavery societies were diminishing in membership and effectiveness made their mutual antagonism more acute. The more accurate his assessment, the more it inflamed the Boston stalwarts whose reform loyalty was vested in those societies. In addition, his independence and outspokenness led him into severe clashes with those who dominated the organizations.

Nonetheless the principal rub came over the disunion party. Samuel May, Jr., won wide support for his view that it was "a most incongruous, self-contradictory, & absurd idea."[36] And, if the Boston leaders were annoyed with Foster's political conceptions, they were infuriated by his charges that they compromised their principles by supporting the Republican party and emasculated abolition by their enthusiasm for the free-state party in Kansas and Charles Sumner's martyrdom under Preston Brooks' cane. As a result, by the end of the decade, Foster and Garrison regularly aired their differences at public meetings, mutually impugning each other's motives and integrity.

The stage had long since been set for the explosion which

[35]The quotations appear in Foster's remarks to the American Anti-Slavery Society annual meeting, May 8–10, 1849, in *Liberator,* May 18, 1849; and in a resolution offered by him to the Western Anti-Slavery Society annual meeting, September 6, 1857, in *Anti-Slavery Bugle,* September 12, 1857; see also on separate political party, Foster to Samuel May, Jr., n.d., in *Liberator,* March 5, 1858.
[36]Samuel May, Jr., to Richard D. Webb, August 7, 1859, M-BPL.

occurred at the 1859 New England Anti-Slavery Convention. Garrison, riled by Foster's resolutions against the Republican party, whose ticket he had mildly and somewhat ambiguously endorsed in 1856, launched a personal and vituperative attack not against Stephen, but against Abby, who supported the resolutions. Both, however, bridled and withdrew almost completely from the American and the Massachusetts Anti-Slavery societies, which they had long served as agents. Wendell Phillips tried to mend the rift, but the Bostonians generally agreed with Maria Chapman. Stephen was, she said, too "Jonah & Jeremiah-like," too "weepingly prophetic," too generally in bad taste and likely to offend.[37]

Disenchanted with Boston and read out of the inner circle, Foster temporized briefly with Gerrit Smith's Radical Abolitionists, but he was ill at ease even in this highly impractical political action group. At last, linked to no antislavery organization and dissatisfied with each one's plan of action, Foster, now past fifty, might well have retired from the field. But he was too tenacious of his goals to give up until the slave was freed and the freedman given his full rights. Until then, he would fight on.

⬥⬥⬥

The year of Foster's final break with the Boston Clique, 1859, marked another jog in his antislavery thought. Until John Brown's raid, Foster had maintained that the Constitution was proslavery. Now, moved by Harpers Ferry and the "strict logical and moral consistency of John Brown's life and example," he further shocked the antislavery establishment by a public confession that thorough study of the Constitution had led him to the contrary conclusion.[38]

No doubt he was honest enough in his assertion that Brown's

[37]For the rift, see particularly the *National Anti-Slavery Standard*, June 4, 11, 1859; Wendell Phillips to Editor, July 21, 1859, in ibid., July 30, 1859; Maria W. Chapman to J. Miller McKim, September [1859], G-BPL.

[38]Foster's speech to the Massachusetts Anti-Slavery Society annual meeting, January 27, 1860, in *Liberator*, February 3, 1860.

action had triggered his conversion, but it was less by its "logical consistency" than by its vigor. Four years earlier he had already eyed the use to which an antislavery interpretation of the Constitution might be put. Though he still argued to the contrary, he had told the 1855 New England Anti-Slavery Convention that "if the Constitution is an anti-slavery document, then the slave-holders are usurpers, and it is the duty of the North to march into the States of Carolina and Mississippi, and *compel* the slave-holders to emancipate their slaves under the Constitution."[39]

The same logic underlay his decision in January 1859 to translate his plans for a disunion party from the state to the national level. "I can accomplish more," he wrote the antislavery interpreter of the Constitution, Lysander Spooner, "by laboring to gather a great national party whose avowed aim shall be the overthrow of the government . . . & whose will shall be expressed through the ballot box." Such a party would be useful and "would infuse new life into our movements." It would provide action. If it was at odds with his previous proposals, it mattered little, for the ends justified the means. Similarly he justified his new interpretation of the Constitution. It was useful, he wrote Benjamin Jones of Ohio. It opened the door for federal action against slavery, he told the Political Anti-Slavery Convention in Boston in May 1860, by making it "the imperative duty of the national government to protect all the inhabitants of the country in the full enjoyment of all their natural rights." If the niggling minds of lawyers and judges read the Constitution differently, they must be overridden, for the constitution of a democracy was neither a covenant nor a compact, but the people's instructions to their government. Constitutional interpretation lay not with the courts, but with all the people.[40]

---

[39]*Liberator,* June 8, 1855.

[40]Foster to Lysander Spooner, January 8, 1859, S-BPL; Foster to Benjamin Jones, February 25, 1860, in *Anti-Slavery Bugle,* March 10, 1860; *National Anti-Slavery Standard,* June 9, 1860.

The argument made sense to the Political Anti-Slavery Convention, which Foster had organized, but did not impel them to organize a party to implement it. It took another meeting in Worcester in mid-September to attempt that. Foster's supporters, however, were still few in number, and they were mostly local. Only eight people of any national antislavery stature attended the meeting, and four of them opposed the new departure. Of the gathering, Joseph Howland of Worcester wrote that "when the mountain labors, and brings forth only a mouse, it is still a farce, however honest and sincere the mountain may be."[41]

Feeble and farcical as it was for the organizing principle for an antislavery party in 1860, Foster's new constitutional argument provided him a methodological rationale for revolutionary change during the Civil War and Reconstruction. Moreover, it served as the foundation for the unionism he preached during the secession crisis. "If the North," he wrote on the eve of South Carolina's withdrawal from the Union, "were to secede, she would, by that act, voluntarily relinquish all her political connections with the institution of slavery, and would, consequently, lose all her power for good or evil over it." Nor did the fact that disunion originated in the South change his argument, for he told a Worcester County antislavery meeting in February 1861 that no state should be allowed to secede and that the North was "bound in duty & by the Constitution . . . to liberate the Slaves."[42]

Thereafter he maintained a constant tirade against the government's inadequate action to meet the issue. At the first major antislavery meeting after the war began, the customary Fourth of July antislavery picnic at Framingham, Foster

[41]*Liberator,* June 15, 1860; *National Anti-Slavery Standard,* October 6, 1860; J. A. H. to William L. Garrison, September 22, 1860, *Liberator,* September 28, 1860.

[42]Foster to Editor, [November ?] 1860, in *National Anti-Slavery Standard,* December 1, 1860; and, reporting Foster's remarks to the Worcester County meeting, Samuel May, Jr., to William L. Garrison, February 17, 1861, G-BPL.

announced that "he could see no reason for supporting the
government now that did not exist twelve months ago."[43]
Nothing could exonerate it short of full emancipation. Until
that was accomplished, war or no, abolitionists should give
it no support.

Although the Framingham group responded weakly to his
appeal, Foster was undeterred. He kept up his campaign
against the Washington administration. A year later, for example, he called Lincoln's failure to act against slavery evidence
that he was "as truly a slaveholder as Jefferson Davis." Then,
perhaps foreseeing the circumstances under which it finally
came, he announced that "when emancipation is used as a
dernier ressort, there will be no virtue in it."[44]

Once again, however, the moralist gave way to the pragma-
tist. Foster was ready to prolong "atrocities rarely equalled
in modern warfare" until "the last fetter [should] be broken,
and the government established upon the broad and com-
prehensive principles of impartial justice." When, after two
years of atrocities, the President finally issued the Emancipation Proclamation, Foster remained dissatisfied, for the proclamation left slavery intact in the border states and the Fugitive
Slave Law in force elsewhere. Frustrated beyond endurance,
he then made one of the most perplexing appeals of his career.
In December 1863, he addressed the third decade celebration
of the American Anti-Slavery Society in Philadelphia. "Proclaim emancipation to the slaves, to the men whom God
appoints as the true soldiers of this land; then, if they fail
to do the work, I will volunteer, non-resistant as I am; and
I will go down to Carolina and face the rebel armies; with
the sword of the spirit, however, and not with the sword
of steel. I will lead your armies if you want them led, unarmed.
I will not shrink from my share of the danger. Place me

[43]*Liberator,* July 12, 1861.
[44]Foster's speech to the New England Anti-Slavery Convention, May 28,
1862, in *Liberator,* June 6, 1862.

between you and the enemy. Only let me have an army of Liberators, and that is all I ask."[45] It was a quixotic appeal and demonstrated once more Foster's internal inconsistencies: militant in spirit, nonresistant in method. Foster would transform a vision of the apocalypse into a quest for the Holy Grail.

⊙⊙⊙

The radicalism with which he had attacked the government for its conduct of the war led Foster to more conflict with the antislavery societies. The majority on the governing boards of the Massachusetts and American societies supported Lincoln during the 1864 presidential campaign but met determined opposition from the radicals, led by Foster and joined by Wendell Phillips, who cast their lot with John Frémont. The political difference reflected a much deeper division about the future of the antislavery societies. The old guard, Garrison, Chapman, Samuel May of Leicester, and Edmund Quincy among them, argued that general emancipation and the war's end would complete the societies' work. The Foster-Phillips group, supported by those black abolitionists who remained active in the societies, demanded its continuation until the freedmen had achieved full civil rights and the means to protect them.[46]

The radicals won; and at the 1865 annual meeting, the Garrison-led faction withdrew. The significance of the victory J. Miller McKim had foreseen in 1864 when he described Frémont's supporters to Caroline Weston. In their Cleveland convention, he saw "elements . . . of fanaticism, ambition, and

---

[45]Foster's resolution at New England Anti-Slavery Convention, May 28, 1862, in *National Anti-Slavery Standard,* June 7, 1862; and Foster's speech to the American Anti-Slavery Society, Third Decade Anniversary Celebration, December 4, 1863, in *Liberator,* January 8, 1864.

[46]*Liberator,* May 20, 1864; *National Anti-Slavery Standard,* February 11, May 20, 1865.

mischief, which in the course of the next four years will be sure to make themselves felt. Such men as Jean Baptiste Pillsbury, & Jean Paul Foster... are not to be got rid of, in a time like this, with a guffaw of derision.... When a non-resistant turns politician, in time of revolution—taking his stand for God & the public—," he warned, "look out: *ça ira!*"[47]

Foster was indeed determined to pursue the revolution McKim so feared. His demands for the freedmen and his vision of Reconstruction marked even in the newly purged society a vibrant egalitarianism. His role was still that of a radical. Having criticized the Lincoln administration for its failure to evince a "genuine regard for [Negroes'] rights as citizens," and having opposed a peace settlement which failed "to recognize the manhood of the negro, or [which] would leave him an alien to the government which is to dispose of his destinies," Foster demanded for him "an equal share with the white race in the management of the political institutions for which he is required to fight and bleed...."[48]

In the 1860s as in the 1850s, Foster's enthusiasm for black insurrection was more frightening to conservatives than his egalitarianism. In the immediate postwar period, he predicted that the only alternative to a just reconstruction was "another war..., for the negro will never surrender the bayonet to resume the chain." He reiterated the theme he had struck in 1860: "The day is not distant when passive submission will cease to be a virtue, and duty and honor will alike require [Negroes], in imitation of our Revolutionary Fathers, to assume the defense of their own rights, and appeal for their

[47]*Liberator,* June 16, 1865; J. Miller McKim to Caroline Weston, June 2, [1864], W-BPL.

[48]Foster resolution at the American Anti-Slavery Society annual meeting, May 8, 1862, in *National Anti-Slavery Standard,* May 17, 1862; Foster's resolution at Massachusetts Anti-Slavery Society annual meeting, January 28, 1864, in ibid., February 6, 1864.

justification to the intelligence and humanity of the civilized world."[49]

Inevitably Foster was dissatisfied with Reconstruction. Sure that "the old system—the old Union—[was] gone forever, and [could] never be restored," he sought a new republic based "upon principles, fundamental and far-reaching." Even before war's end, however, the shadow of reality darkened his dream. He scored the Lincoln-Banks plan of reconstruction for Louisiana, which failed to give blacks the vote, as a "despicable fraud" that left freedmen unprotected against "the secession madness of their rebel masters." He believed Andrew Johnson was worse yet. He had, Foster charged, "no particle of care for the black man." Even such Radical Reconstruction measures as the Freedmen's Bureau bill and the Civil Rights bill Foster rejected, since none of them protected the Negro; all were aimed at preserving the dominance of the white man. Once again, therefore, in 1868, he called for a third party, this time to support universal suffrage for Indians as well as for Negroes, for women as well as for men.[50]

But he did not stop with political demands. As far back as 1843 he had concluded that slavery was an economic issue, ranging labor—slave and free—against "capital, learning, and gentility . . . the former contending for equality, the latter for supremacy and prerogative."[51] Familiar with poverty, debt, and hard physical work from childhood, hard put to support his family on his marginal Massachusetts farm, Foster clearly identified with the poor man and the laborer. He distrusted the gentlemen of town and country, backers of mobs and

[49] Foster's speech at Framingham Anti-Slavery celebration, July 4, 1865, in ibid., July 15, 1865; his speech to the New England Anti-Slavery Convention, May 30, 1866, in ibid., June 9, 1866.

[50] The quotations are from a Foster speech and resolution to the Massachusetts Anti-Slavery Society annual meetings for 1864 and 1865, respectively, in ibid., February 6, 1864, February 11, 1865; see also ibid., July 15, 1865, June 13, 1868.

[51] Ibid., April 20, 1843.

traducers of the poor, whom in their "cupidity, lust and oppression" he saw arrayed against him.[52] Therefore he pressed for land distribution to the freedmen, for only in economic self-sufficiency could they be politically independent. "God made the earth," he wrote, "not for the rich man, not for the man who had a rich father, but for you and for me; as much for me, the son of a pauper as for you, the son of a millionaire; . . . I can recognize no law," he concluded, "which secures to you a farm, and makes me dependent on you for a place to lay my head at night."[53]

That position was too extreme for Foster's antislavery colleagues, and at the 1869 annual meeting of the American Society, they watered down to ineffectiveness his resolutions supporting Southern land redistribution.[54] But Foster would not be dissuaded, and up to its final meeting he opposed dissolving the American Society until the Southern aristocracy was broken and the freedmen were given homesteads. Like most of his other battles, this, too, he lost. The land was never redistributed.

❀❀❀

When the American Anti-Slavery Society disbanded in 1870, Foster was an old man, less in actual age than in bodily weariness. Ailing, his health shaken by more than thirty years of lecturing and traveling, he retired to his farm in Worcester, where he engaged on a small scale in local temperance and feminist campaigns. Then, in 1881, after several years of invalidism, he died.

Modern critics have called Stephen Foster a neurotic, a chronic disruptionist, a gadfly, a monomaniac. His harsh language and prickly independence have provoked conclusions

[52]Ibid.; *Anti-Slavery Bugle,* August 17, 1850.
[53]Foster's speech at American Anti-Slavery Society annual meeting, May 11, 1869, in *National Anti-Slavery Standard,* May 22, 1869.
[54]Ibid., June 5, 1869.

that he was unpleasant as a person and as a reformer.[55] Without question, he was driven to achieve and accomplish, for he drew no satisfaction from the abstract ideology of a Maria Chapman. But at the same time he refused to temporize, to be expedient, to compromise; and he insisted on acting, for only by acting could Foster give meaning to his convictions. Though he sought mass support, his strict adherence to principle drove away all but the few who could adopt each of his constantly changing plans in succession. The major critic of the antislavery societies' failure to grow during the 1850s, he went on to create an even smaller and more isolated faction within the movement. His abrasiveness and his inconsistencies so isolated him that he was rendered almost impotent as an antislavery leader. Those not alienated by his radical message were often turned aside by his changing and provoking methods.

To be on the radical fringe of a movement generally acknowledged as itself radical is to be seen as an irresponsible fanatic. So Stephen Foster was viewed. His egalitarianism affronted the patricians of the movement; his impracticality, the organizers; his changing enthusiasms, the pragmatists; his inconsistencies, the doctrinaires. He was constantly characterized as a harsh and lonely prophet—an Isaiah, a Jeremiah, a John the Baptist. No branch of the antislavery movement was long comfortable with this dramatic loner in whose hands even "the olive branch became a war-club."[56]

[55]See, for example, Irving Bartlett, *Wendell Phillips: Brahmin Radical* (Boston: Beacon Press, 1961), 277–278; Martin Duberman, "The Northern Response," in *The Anti-Slavery Vanguard; New Essays on the Abolitionists*, ed. Martin Duberman (Princeton: Princeton University Press, 1965), 408; James M. McPherson, *The Struggle for Equality: Abolitionists and the Negro in the Civil War and Reconstruction* (Princeton: Princeton University Press, 1964), 103–104; John L. Thomas, *The Liberator: William Lloyd Garrison: A Biography* (Boston: Little Brown, 1963), 321.

[56]Thomas W. Higginson, "Obituary," *The Woman's Journal*, September 17, 1881.

10

The Political Gadfly:
Elizur Wright

After his graduation from Yale in 1826, Elizur Wright had gone off to Groton, Massachusetts, to teach school. There, nurtured in old-fashioned methods, Wright flogged learning into his pupils and, it appears, won their respect and esteem. He had less luck with the adults. A product of a dour New England heritage, Wright frowned on their balls, refused to dance, and was duly shocked by the locally prominent Unitarians, whose conduct and faith departed grievously from the standards set by his orthodox Calvinism. The townspeople, he dutifully wrote his mother, "would no doubt be pleased if I would attend balls and parties instead of religious meetings, ... if I would talk about liberality and candour and good feelings instead of the necessity of being born again, if I would not pray in my school, or at least, say nothing about sin in my prayers." Their religion smacked of self-satisfaction. On Sundays, after the week's revels, they went to church to thank God "that they [were] not bigoted, superstitious, illiberal fanatics," and to anticipate a hereafter of "perfect bliss."[1]

[1]Wright to Mr. and Mrs. Elizur Wright, Sr., November 16, 1826, October 19, 1826, both in W-LC.

Elizur Wright, who had attended Yale to prepare for the Congregational ministry, had been nourished there on an orthodoxy still reverberating against the heresies of Henry Ware and his associates at Harvard. Although Wright absorbed a good deal more from his school days in New Haven, his regret as he left was his failure "to serve [his] Redeemer in College," and his neglect of "the present moment, with perhaps high intentions for the future."[2] His lament was that he was still poorly prepared for a clerical career.

Born in South Canaan, Connecticut, in 1804, Wright was one of at least ten children of Elizur Wright. The elder Elizur, who combined farming with teaching mathematics, had moved his family to Ohio's Western Reserve when his namesake was only six, and taught there in the Tallmadge Academy. There, young Elizur, growing up amid the revivals that swept the West, underwent a conversion and decided, at sixteen, to become a Christian minister.

Well prepared by his father's teaching and Tallmadge Academy, he was less well endowed in pocket for a college education. Nonetheless, after two years of teaching in a local school and studying at home, he set out for New Haven with assets of six dollars in cash, one horse (which he sold), and 150 acres of land (which he mortgaged). At Yale, his religious orthodoxy was strengthened, although slightly modified, by his studies with Nathaniel Taylor, who enlarged the area of free will beyond the customary confines of Calvinist predestination.

Wright was unable to complete his study for the ministry because he lacked the funds to finance it. Consequently, he took the job in Groton, regarding teaching as a way station. Two years later, after turning down a teaching post at the newly founded Western Reserve College in Hudson, Ohio, he returned to Ohio to work as state agent for the American Tract Society. Six months in that capacity markedly

[2]Wright to William Hanford, May 29, 1826, W-LC.

diminished Wright's enthusiasm for a clerical career. This disappointment and his wish to marry his former Groton student Susan Clark determined his acceptance of a post as professor of mathematics at Western Reserve, after declining an instructorship at Yale.[3]

In later years, he doubted that he had ever felt "naturally qualified" to be a minister. The same was doubtless true of teaching, for after two years at Groton and four at Hudson, he left the field. That decision was not wholly negative, however, for Wright was already responding to the reform enthusiasm of his era. His father's dedication to education, his own advocacy of temperance, the religious and secular enthusiasms of the Western Reserve had all prepared him to respond when antislavery came to the West.[4]

❦❦❦

Already a colonizationist in 1829, Wright was invited that year to deliver a Fourth of July address in Franklin, near Hudson. He used the occasion to rally support for Liberian settlement, although the audience, he admitted to Susan, was not much interested in "the poor Africans." It was, however, Garrison's *Thoughts on African Colonization* rather than local apathy which, three years later, turned him from colonization to immediatism.[5]

[3]Wright to Rufus Griswold, August 8, 1842, RFG-BPL; for the Groton years, see scattered correspondence, 1826–1828, W-LC; William Hanford to Wright, April 24, 1827, W-LC; Wright to Rev. J. Day, March 19, 1829, MS-YU; Wright to Susan Clark, March 28, 1829, W-LC. See also Philip G. Wright and Elizabeth Q. Wright, *Elizur Wright: The Father of Life Insurance* (Chicago: University of Chicago Press, 1937), 50–55.

[4]Wright to Rufus Griswold, August 8, 1842, RWG-BPL. For Wright's temperance interests, see his unlabeled reminiscences, 1884, in W-LC; also Wright to Mr. and Mrs. Wright, December 25, 1827, W-LC; *Massachusetts Abolitionist*, February 13, 1840. He also failed to get a preaching license in Ohio; see Wright & Wright, *Wright,* 38–39.

[5]Wright to Susan Clark, July 15, 1829, W-LC; Wright to William L. Garrison, December 11, 1832, in *Liberator,* January 5, 1833.

The change signaled a move from a safe and ineffective nudge at the status quo to radicalism. Yet Wright made the shift with the college president, Charles Storrs, and its chaplain, Beriah Green. Apparently secure in their positions at Western Reserve, this trio inaugurated a strong abolitionist movement locally. Among their earliest converts was Theodore Weld, commonly regarded as the tyro of the Western movement.[6]

Wright was soon disillusioned if he thought that academic respectability would shelter him and his colleagues from the wrath of the community. In July 1832, he published a series of abolitionist articles in the Hudson *Observer and Telegraph.* He couched his arguments carefully. Reflecting the democratic premises he espoused, Wright urged that emancipation was a necessary result of the equality of persons. Since immediate emancipation was only a recognition of natural right, it was both safe and efficient. Colonization was not efficient but rather perpetuated the institution it presumed to eliminate. It removed slaves, not slavery; it rested on prejudice; it recognized the legitimacy and legality of slavery; and it made slavery more profitable to the South and thus increased its power. In addition to his *Observer* articles, Wright initiated a wide correspondence to press this message, publicly debated Colonization Society agents, and helped organize the Western Reserve College Anti-Slavery Society. It was, he said, "the duty of every man to speak out on this subject, and [to] give slavery its true character." One must take a stand, he added in a hortatory letter to the *Genius of Temperance,* regardless of the consequences.[7]

[6]*Letters of Theodore Dwight Weld, Angelina Grimké Weld and Sarah Grimké, 1822–1844,* eds. Gilbert H. Barnes and Dwight L. Dumond (New York: D. Appleton-Century Co., 1934), 96–97, for Wright to Weld, December 7, 1832; Benjamin Thomas, *Theodore Weld, Crusader for Freedom* (New Brunswick: Rutgers University Press, 1950), 35–36.

[7]One of the Hudson, Ohio, *Observer and Telegraph* articles appeared in *Liberator,* December 1, 1832; *Liberator,* October 12, 1833; letter to *Genius of Temperance,* January 23, 1833, copied in *Liberator,* February 23, 1833.

Consequences there were. Three of the college trustees publicly protested the abolitionists' activities because they were
"adverse to the feelings of a large majority of the Trustees"
and had created "expressions of dissatisfaction from the parents of students in College," as well as "from the friends of
the Institution in every part of the Reserve." Already a sick
man and near death, President Storrs made little or no reply.
Beriah Green let forth an indignant blast challenging the
authority of trustees, speaking as individuals, to control the
actions of the college or its members. "Do they imagine,"
he asked angrily, "that I can *know them* as legislators, when
the board is not in session?"[8]

Wright too was angry. In a letter, which Garrison published
in the *Liberator,* Wright etched a wittily cutting caricature of
colonization and the position of the three trustees. He suggested that a new society should colonize in Europe those
of European descent in America who rejected the idea of
equality for all. In Europe, "by the two-fold agency of king
and pope, the people are kindly relieved of all care, not only
for the body politic, but for their own souls." America, he
continued, would profit by removing those whose principles
conflicted with republican government and whose moral standards made their elevation or assimilation impossible. At the
same time, he said, Europe would benefit by receiving these
men, made into apostles of liberty by the same magic by which
an ocean voyage, according to colonizationist logic, miracu-
lously transformed Negro "nuisances" into Christian missionaries to Africa.[9]

After putting the trustees in their place, Wright headed
east with Susan, who was ill. When they arrived in Boston,
after stopping at numerous health spas, Wright met the Gar-

[8]David Hudson, Caleb Pitkin, and Harvey Coe, Trustees of Western
Reserve College, to *Observer and Telegraph,* February 4, 1833, Beriah Green
to *Observer and Telegraph,* February 8, 1833, both in *Liberator,* March 16,
1833.

[9]Wright to William L. Garrison, February 27, 1833, in *Liberator,* March
23, 1833.

risonians. There too he debated Colonization Society spokes-men—Robert Finley, in Boston's Park Street Church, and later Noah Webster in New Haven, though in New York he twice missed a chance at R. R. Gurley, a third colonizationist stal-wart.[10] The trip was satisfying. Susan's health improved. Wright met many abolitionist leaders and spread his antislav-ery reputation eastward. He had not improved his image in Hudson by so doing.

When he had left Ohio, he had cohorts. When he returned, he was alone. President Storrs had gone to Braintree, Mas-sachusetts, to die; Beriah Green had resigned to become president of the Oneida Institute in upstate New York. Wright was left to face the trustees, among whom was his brother-in-law, John Seward, whose patronizing advice was a constant irritant. He wrote Wright apologizing rather disingenuously for having slandered him in the past and sought his assessment on how the good of the college might best be served. In so doing, he made two points clear—that opposition to slavery was acceptable only in the guise of colonization and that the board was split with only President Storrs and Wright's father supporting the faculty's abolitionist stand.[11]

That the student body had been abolitionized and sponsored an active antislavery society only made Wright's position more offensive to the board. Finally, when the trustees seemed about to restrict student freedom of discussion, Wright, disgusted with the *"patch-work morality"* which dictated their decisions, resigned in protest and set out with his family for New York where a job with Arthur Tappan awaited him.[12]

⚭⚭⚭

[10]The trip east in scattered Wright letters, April–May 1833, W-LC; Wright to Theodore Weld, September 5, 1833, in *Weld-Grimké Letters,* 115; *Liberator,* June 1, 29, 1833.

[11]Wright to Amos A. Phelps, typed copy [1833], W-LC; John Seward to Wright, July 24, 1833, W-LC.

[12]Wright to Theodore Weld, September 5, 1833, in *Weld-Grimké Letters,* 116–117.

While the $500 salary Tappan offered Wright to be his anti-slavery secretary was no large sum, the opportunity to be close to the center of antislavery activity made up for it. Wright arrived just in time to participate in the formation of the New York City Anti-Slavery Society and to be elected its first corresponding secretary. He witnessed the mob turmoil which those meetings and Garrison's return from England touched off. And, although he shared Tappan's reluctance to pre-cipitate more violence, he joined in organizing the Phil-adelphia meeting, which formed the American Anti-Slavery Society. He attended its sessions in December 1833 and was elected secretary for domestic correspondence.[13]

Thus Wright was projected into the heart of antislavery work. Acting for the national society, he not only published antislavery pieces in the commercial press but also edited vari-ous antislavery publications, among them the *Anti-Slavery Reporter,* a monthly series of antislavery tracts published in 1834; *Human Rights,* a monthly propaganda publication which ran from 1835 to 1839; the *Emancipator,* the society's official organ, which he edited occasionally; and the *Quarterly Anti-Slavery Magazine,* which was his principal editing interest from 1835 to 1838 and which he modeled on the *North American Review.* He had such difficulty finding contributors for the *Quarterly* that he had to write many of its long articles. Though it never became the lively journal he had hoped for, it was a major forum for antislavery thought and the major vehicle for Wright's own ideas.[14] As secretary of the national society, Wright also administered its national headquarters. He was responsible for raising funds, and for finding, employing,

[13]*The Abolitionist,* October 1833; Wright, editorial in *Anti-Slavery Reporter* [Fall 1833], editorial, typed copy, W-LC; Wright to Elizur Wright, Sr., November 2, 1833, W-LC; *Liberator,* December 21, 1833.
[14]Scattered correspondence, 1834–1839, W-LC. On his commercial press articles, see Lewis Tappan, Journal for August 31, 1838–June 10, 1840, entry preceding November 7, 1838, T-LC.

and directing the varied activities of the society's agents. He was expected to attend local, regional, and national antislavery meetings. In short, he was responsible for the daily operation of the organization.

In the midst of all these activities, Wright refined his antislavery views. Most of his essays merely repeated the standard abolitionist arguments of the day, condemning colonization, espousing immediatism, and arguing the sin and guilt of slavery. He believed that the abolitionists' prime task was to create a public opinion, which, in turn, would lead to the practical work of emancipating and elevating the slaves. Familiar too were his *Quarterly* essays developing the standard biblical arguments against slavery, analyzing the system's demoralizing effects on slaveholders, and depicting the ways in which it dehumanized the slave.[15]

Far more original was his treatment of political rights and economic conditions. The peculiar institution, Wright argued, bred a class of men whose concern for "wealth and power and place" overshadowed their concern for civil liberties. "They do not freely accord to their fellow-men the right of thinking as they please on any subject. They are deeply jealous of free thought, and [they] depend less upon reason and truth to combat what they consider error of opinion, than upon management and gagging."[16] Wright's early attack on vested interest prefigured an ever more antipathetic reform view of the masters of capital, those lords of the loom whose interests united them with the lords of the lash. His Western egalitarianism set him apart from the ex-Federalists and Whigs

[15]For various Wright arguments see *Does the Bible Sanction Slavery?* ([title page missing, 1837? copy, Cornell University]); *The Sin of Slavery, and Its Remedy* . . . (New York: Printed for the author, 1833); articles in the *Quarterly Anti-Slavery Magazine:* "Influence of Slavery on Slaveholders" 1 (July 1836): 315–333, and "Pro-Slavery Testimony Examined" 1 (October 1835): 92–99, and 1 (January 1836): 117–132.

[16]American Anti-Slavery Society, *Fourth Annual Report* (New York: The Society, 1837), 60.

who dominated antislavery leadership in the early days and
served as a basis for his economic attack on slavery.

At the core of Northern capital's support for slavery lay
the banking and credit structure. Greed for wealth, Wright
argued, had led to an overextension of credit, which mortgaged the future to the bloated desires of the present and
joined the interests of Northern capital with Southern cotton.
"Since the genius of Arkwright . . . ," he wrote, "capitalists
have had the means of clothing the whole world. The cheapest
material is cotton, and unfortunately, the most available
resource for that has been our slave-cursed Southern country. . . ." Thus capitalists, with profitable investment in cotton
mills, extended credit southward to assure a steady supply
of raw materials and, accordingly, the continuation of slavery.
The panic of 1837 only illustrated Wright's major point. The
economics of slavery, which bound the various Northern cotton markets to the Southern luxuries markets, had produced
in this alliance national catastrophe. "Northern merchants,"
he wrote viciously, "anxious to partake the rich plunder . . .
have furnished their capital for the extension of slave labor. . . .
Madly hastening to be richer, they have outbid each other
in long credits, to secure Southern custom, till the South . . .
has squandered her own means and theirs, and they are left
in the lurch."[17]

Convinced that moral suasion alone would never shake such
an empire, Wright looked beyond the techniques current
among abolitionists in 1837 in search of more practical and
effective action. As his religious faith was increasingly
informed with reason, so he sought to inform antislavery
dogma with hard analysis and develop thereby a new, hard-
hitting program of action.

⛓⛓⛓

[17]Ibid., 50–51.

Wright's whole antislavery experience propelled him toward practicality and efficiency. As secretary of the American Anti-Slavery Society he had dealt with everyday management and detail. His efforts to keep peace among antislavery factions had also taught him the value of compromise and tact. No part of his work was more trying than his efforts to reconcile the radical and sometimes peevish demands of William Lloyd Garrison with the financial conservatism of Arthur Tappan.

Wright's early admiration for Garrison had led him to praise the editor in 1833 as "a noble spirited devoted servant of the Saviour." As soon as he became society secretary, Wright learned the difficulties inherent in Garrison's messianism, his pride, and his extreme abrasiveness. Only six months after his initial praise, Wright dared to give Garrison some brotherly advice. Do not take public satisfaction in the financial straits of the American Colonization Society, he warned, for such smugness will only create sympathy for it. The following year he admonished Garrison against pleading his own sufferings rather than those of the slave when he sought funds for the *Liberator*.[18]

At the same time Wright had constantly to reassure Arthur Tappan, whose business sense often seemed to obstruct the reform to which he was the most generous financial contributor. It did not, for instance, matter to Tappan that the *Anti-Slavery Reporter* urgently needed funds. He would not commit his money until he knew that needed funds would be forthcoming from others, too. Even more frustrating to the impetuous than this early version of the matching funds concept was Tappan's strict and dry businessman's regard for the imperatives of double entry bookkeeping and its like. "Our friend A. T[appan]," Wright wrote in exasperation to Theodore Weld in 1836, "should be disabused of the idea that if he and G. Smith and two or three others should fail

[18]Wright to Beriah Green, June 7, 1833, W-LC; Wright to William L. Garrison, January 30, November 12, 1834, G-BPL.

to pay their notes at *three o'clock* some day, the cause of God's oppressed would fall through!" Although Wright well understood the necessity for sound business practices, he shared a general impatience with Arthur Tappan's priorities, which his critics alleged placed prudence and business caution before human welfare. Frequently Wright mediated between the two views—a task made still more trying by his own precarious financial position. Even when Arthur Tappan failed in the panic of 1837, Wright, whose family had been struck by smallpox, whose children suffered a variety of illnesses, and whose wife nearly died in childbirth, calmly continued without his salary, unwilling "to take a dollar from [the] Society till necessity compel[led]" him to.[19]

Although Tappan's foibles hit him personally, they were far less disruptive to the movement than the clerical issue. Editing the *Emancipator,* in the fall of 1837, Wright only thought to keep it neutral when he refused to print the massive effusions sent from Boston on the treason of the clergy. "Suffice it to say," he wrote Amos Phelps, still a loyal Garrisonian, "that it is absurd in itself for the American Anti-Slavery Society to take sides in any *personal* controversy. . . ."[20] Wright's efforts to localize the issue, however, directed the anticlericals' ire at him.

His private assessment was that Garrison had overreacted to clerical charges that his radical style and message were subverting both antislavery and Christianity. Surely, Wright wrote Maria Chapman, Garrison needed no aid from New York, "for he seems to have left all his enemies thrice dead behind him, even if he has not killed some of his friends."

[19]Wright to Amos A. Phelps, August 8, 1834, P-BPL; Wright to Theodore Weld, August 14, 1834, in *Weld-Grimké Letters,* 166; on Wright's family troubles, see Wright to Beriah Green, February 7, 1837, and other scattered correspondence, 1837–1838, all in W-LC. Quotations are in Wright to Theodore Weld, November 4, 1836, *Weld-Grimké Letters,* 346–347; Wright to Elizur Wright, Sr., October 21, 1837, W-LC.
[20]Wright to Amos A. Phelps, September 5, 1837, P-BPL.

The clerics' accusations should have been "calmly met with the appropriate facts, and then left to be carried down to oblivion in the wheel barrow of contempt. We gain nothing," he admonished Chapman, "by stopping to punish 'traitors' much less vacillating and cowardly friends." Trying to keep the society running in the face of economic disaster, he sought cooperation, not rancor. In this vein, he warned Garrison that "the deceitful spirit of *sect* has stolen upon you unawares, and that you are unconsciously becoming . . . a *close-communion anti-sectarianist!*"[21]

Wright found Garrison more difficult even than Tappan. He disapproved Garrison's linking other reforms to the already unpopular antislavery movement because he thought it "downright nonsense to suppose that the Anti Slavery cause [could] be carried forward with forty incongruous things tacked on to it. You can't drive a three tined fork through a hay mow," he observed, "though turn it t'other end to, and you can drive in the handle." If multireformism offended his pragmatism, Garrison's newly espoused perfectionism offended his religious beliefs. "Perfect holiness" accorded ill with the sinfulness inherent in man. "I can not receive a revelation," he told Garrison, "which asserts that which my senses pronounce to be false, nor one which visibly fails to accomplish its object." Moreover, from a practical point of view, Garrison's course was sucking him "into a vortex of spiritual Quixotism" and absorbing "energies that might have shaken down the mountain of oppression." "At any rate," he had sighed wearily, Garrison's "plan of rescuing the slave by the destruction of human laws is fatally conflictive with ours."[22]

[21]Wright to Maria W. Chapman, September 15, 1837, W-BPL; Wright to William L. Garrison, October 10, 1837, G-BPL.
[22]Wright to Amos A. Phelps, September 5, 1837, P-BPL; Wright to William

As the clerical issue broadened into a full-scale struggle between New York- and Boston-led factions, Wright abandoned his neutral stance and his peacemaker's role to stand with Garrison's critics. As a result, in 1839 when the anti-Garrisonians in Massachusetts sought an editor for their new newspaper and a business manager, corresponding secretary, and general director for their independent antislavery society, they chose Elizur Wright.

It was a sound choice; Wright was both talented and experienced. Moreover, he had not formally joined in the clerical debate and seemed more likely than any other to reestablish links between the two sides. At the same time, his opposition to Garrison's course was firm. Wright had written Beriah Green in 1837 that he thought "the wind of *perfectionism* [had] blown off the roof of [Garrison's] judgment." He then added, "I have no more hope from him in the future, than I have for the inmates of Bedlam in general. His guns are all turned inward, and he is thundering away with his grape shot to the muzzle, at the *mice & chipmunks*." In line with this assessment of their leader, Wright conducted war on the followers. He had fired the extreme anarchist and perfectionist Henry C. Wright from his American Society agency. He had virtually instructed Amos Phelps, by 1838 a critic of Garrison, to organize a countermovement in the Massachusetts Society, of which he was an officer, or chance having the national society "take up the whole controversy from the first and clear themselves from countenancing the errors of either side."[23]

This impatience with quixotism and bickering won the confidence of the antiperfectionists without altogether alienating the perfectionists. Thus Phelps, long torn between clericals

---

L. Garrison, November 6, 1837, G-BPL; *Massachusetts Abolitionist*, December 5, 1839; Wright to Phelps, October 27, 1837, P-BPL.

[23]Wright to Beriah Green, October 17, 1837, W-LC; Wright to Amos A. Phelps, September 12, October 20, 1837, P-BPL.

and Garrisonians and seeing the merits of each, backed Wright for his new post. As Phelps endorsed Wright's solidity on the clerical issue, Henry B. Stanton approved Wright's political stance, and Lewis Tappan attested his soundness on the woman question. Burdensome as these endorsements were to Wright's repute among the Boston inner circle, he yet survived them. Even Maria Chapman, when she heard rumors of his impending appointment, wrote that under ordinary circumstances she would be delighted to see him in her city but that it was his coming to edit the *Abolitionist,* that "stench in the nostrils of every true Abolitionist in Massachusetts," which made her hesitate. Even then she still hoped that Wright might do something worthwhile with it. No better evidence was needed to buttress Chapman's later statement that he was still "well known and loved" in 1839 or, as Garrisonian Oliver Johnson put it fifty years later, that he had the "confidence and admiration" of the faithful.[24]

Wright tried to demonstrate to the two factions that the harmonious way was the practical way. As soon as he took over the *Abolitionist,* he tried to change its anti-Garrison image by making it a broad-based paper supporting immediatist theory and political action. In marking the issues that divided the movement, he hoped to reunite it around those of fundamental significance and to cast out the rest.[25]

Of those ancillary and distracting remainders, the woman question would not be buried, and on that issue the antislavery movement was thoroughly rent. Abby Kelley's appointment to the business committee of the American Society's 1840 annual meeting seemed to many to link women's rights with abolition, and the clerical–New York faction bolted the meet-

[24]Henry B. Stanton to Wright, typed copy, February 4, 1839, W-LC. Bertram Wyatt-Brown, *Lewis Tappan and the Evangelical War Against Slavery* (Cleveland: Press of Case Western Reserve University, 1969), 173; Maria W. Chapman to Wright, February 3, 1839, W-LC; [Maria Weston Chapman], *Right and Wrong in Massachusetts* (Boston: Dow & Jackson, 1839), 144; Oliver Johnson to Wright, copy, April 19, 1881, J-VHS.
[25]*Massachusetts Abolitionist,* May 23, 1839.

ing to found its own association, the American and Foreign Anti-Slavery Society. But that was only the final step in a prolonged and acrimonious debate. Wright would have played it down. He had moved in the last decade from the belief that meekness and submission comprised women's lot to approving women's participation in local voluntary societies. Yet his increasingly irrepressible humor made him view the battle of the sexes with some amusement. So he wrote to Phelps, whose arguments were burdened with St. Paul, that he would rather let the tom-turkeys gobble than hear hens crowing. The whole uproar, he quipped with a cheek that infuriated Abby Kelley, was brought on by having women led by a "clique of woman's rights men."[26]

Neither side shared Wright's wry view of the issue and consequently both disproved his assessment in a 1839 statement to the Massachusetts Abolition Society that the woman question was of secondary importance. To it he allotted two columns of his long document, ranking it more important than perfectionism, sectarianism, and clericalism, but much less important than political action, to which he gave five columns of fine print.[27] Nonetheless, when the moderates walked out of the national society the following year over Kelley's appointment, Elizur Wright was one of them. He had joined new organization.

Wright had protested to Chapman in 1839 that his sole interest was in freeing the slaves and that he did not care for "the credit that is to be got by one course or another." The assurance was misleading because he was already convinced that abolition could not be achieved without political action. To make

---

[26]Wright to Susan Clark, February 13, 1828, W-LC; Wright to Amos A. Phelps, August 17, July 11, 1838, P-BPL; Abby Kelley to Wright, August 28, 1839, in *Liberator,* September 6, 1839.

[27]*Massachusetts Abolitionist Extra,* July 18, 1839.

political action possible, Wright gave the Constitution an anti-slavery interpretation. He firmly believed that only truly republican government could long endure and overcome tyranny. Slavery was unrepublican and tyrannous. Therefore the federal government had a right to abolish slavery in the states. This simple syllogism could be realized because the people in a republic had the right to make laws coincident with public sentiment. Such laws would be valid in the courts because they had no power to overrule popular will in interpreting the Constitution. Only the rule of right, the higher moral law, stood above the popular will as it also stood above statute law and judicial review. But since it too was clearly antislavery, Wright concluded, and governed all man-made laws, the federal Constitution must also be antislavery.[28]

The argument was that of an earnest man sharing Jacksonian suspicion of the courts and enthusiasm for popular rule. Wright's enthusiasm for political action followed from it and shared the same premises. Optimistic that the moral crusade was creating an antislavery public opinion, he looked to democratic politics embodied in a new party to effect major social change. To this position he had come very slowly. In 1836, he had looked at the major parties and, distrusting them, had feared a "tendency in some parts to build hope too much on political measures." By 1837, he was more assertive: "What needs to be done is, to excite a sympathy for the oppressed which shall make itself felt through the law-making, and the law-executing powers.... Political action there must be. Law must be brought back from its unnatural alliance with despotism, before freedom can be established." In 1838, with Texas annexation threatening, he joined Birney and Stanton in urging citizens to elect antislavery legislators

[28]Wright to Maria W. Chapman, draft, February 18, 1839, W-LC. For Wright's developing ideas about the Constitution and its relation to slavery, see American Anti-Slavery Society, *Second Annual Report* (New York: The Society, 1835), 66–67; Wright to Editor, *New York Observer,* n.d. [1838?], W-LC; Wright, "Can an Abolitionist Take an Oath to Support the Constitution of the United States?" fragment, W-LC.

who would oppose annexation, support abolition of slavery in the District of Columbia, and vote for repeal of the Fugitive Slave Law.[29]

The difficulty in ensuring that either major party would run acceptable candidates led Wright to doubt the efficacy of working through them. The time had come, he urged Stanton in 1839, when the American Society should take "a decided step towards *Presidential Candidates.*" Antislavery people, he thought, should establish a nucleus for action which could, in time, free national politics from the vise in which the South held it. Such action by the society would have a number of advantages. It would give every man something practical "to *do*"; it would help clean up politics generally; and it would leave "non-resistance abolitionism *hors du combat.*" Third-party action was necessary, he added elsewhere, because the major parties had promised much but delivered little. "It is well to try the parties thoroughly," he advised. "But when this trial shall have fully satisfied reasonable men that nothing is to be gained through them, then is the time to hoist the standard of a true HUMAN RIGHTS PARTY."[30]

Wright's support for such action came less from any constitutional interpretation than from his quest for practical action. The antipolitical Garrisonians attacked him on the same grounds. Political action, they claimed with a pragmatism of their own, would encourage office seeking, corruption, and the loss of moral purity, which gave the antislavery crusade force. Wright countered that he doubted a new party would be any more corrupt than the old parties, and that a third party was a temporary expedient in any case and need not be feared as a permanent threat. Then he added caustically that abolitionists should not worry so much about their "moral

[29]Wright to Theodore Weld, April 21, 1836, in *Weld-Grimké Letters,* 292; American Anti-Slavery Society, *Fourth Annual Report,* 113–114; Wright et al. to Dear Sir, [July 11?, 1838], a circular letter, W-LC.

[30]Wright to Henry B. Stanton, October 12, 1839, W-LC, the so-called Streak Letter; *Massachusetts Abolitionist,* October 24, 1839.

sublimity. Indeed, what is that sublimity good for, if it cannot sacrifice its reputation for sanctity, and incur the odium of the tyrannical and the inhuman, in order to seize the best means of accomplishing its object.... We suspect," he concluded bitingly, that "there is a little self-righteousness to be sacrificed. Have we not set a rather high value on our own *purity?*"[31]

If Wright was attacked by the apolitical Garrisonians, he was also criticized by the politically traditional abolitionists. New organization leader Lewis Tappan complained that a third party violated the intent of the American Anti-Slavery Society. Wright, unmoved by appeals to a seven-year precedent, retorted to Tappan much as he did to Garrison. "A fig for *'sublimity'* which is opposed to efficiency."[32]

By 1840, then, Wright had not only left the ministry behind, but had largely given up the evangelical temper in favor of a more hard-hitting, secular political stance. Consequently he backed the Liberty party. The church-oriented Torrey–Phelps–Tappan group, who had led the exodus into new organization on the clerical and women questions, were appalled. Wright ignored them and concentrated his efforts on finding an effective means of antislavery action. Perhaps Whig enthusiasts in both factions—Lewis Tappan, David Child, and Francis Jackson, among others—let their dreams of partisan victory in 1840 divert them. Perhaps Wright's Democratic politics had been more disillusioning because his party had long been in power. In any case, Wright was among the most zealous about the new party. Throughout the 1840s, he attended local and national conventions, served on committees, helped organize campaigns, and, in 1847, ran on its ticket for the state senate in Massachusetts. But it was his initial role in 1840 in organizing the party and attending the Albany Liberty party convention, which nominated James G.

<hr />

[31]*Massachusetts Abolitionist,* October 31, 1839.
[32]Ibid., November 7, 1839.

Birney and Thomas Earle, that cost him the editorship of the *Massachusetts Abolitionist* in 1841 because it had lost him the support of its backers.[33]

For the rest of the decade, Wright worked independently. On occasion he helped edit other antislavery papers, the *Emancipator* and the *Free American* among them, until in 1846 he established his own paper. The *Chronotype* promoted "good nature, good neighborhood, and good government" and incidentally antislavery politics. It reflected Wright's views free of ties "to the creed or cause of any clique, association, party, sect or set of men."[34] The paper survived for four years, was revived briefly during 1850, and was then absorbed by the Free Soil *Commonwealth,* for which Wright worked a short time.

The *Chronotype* espoused a number of causes from Fourierism to temperance, from women's rights to tolerance of Mormons. Wright also used it to conduct a running opposition to the Mexican War as he made it a firm support of the Liberty party. The combination threatened his Garrisonian opponents, who feared that he would turn broad-based Mexican War opposition to serve Liberty party purposes. So, despite his increasing reform radicalism and his contributions to the antiwar cause, the Boston Clique never ceased their carping.

Once out of the Garrisonians' graces, Wright never again could please them. Living in Boston, sharing their immediatist doctrine, fighting with them against the Texas annexation and the Mexican War, he could not purge his record of heresy or of continued support of third party political action. The Garrisonians seemingly misjudged Wright's efforts to work with them and to reunite the movement. Certainly he, more than Phelps, Torrey, or Stanton, was suited to the task. But

[33]For Wright's activity in 1840 especially, see *Massachusetts Abolitionist,* 1840 passim; Wright to Gerrit Smith, March 20, 1840, S-SU; Wright to Beriah Green, August 10, 1840, W-LC.

[34]*Chronotype,* February 11, May 28, 1846.

years of personal recriminations on both sides made the task impossible.

The attacks on Wright were insistent almost from the time he arrived in Boston in 1839. In 1843, Edmund Quincy, who scorned the plebian Wright, was incensed when, as one of a broad antislavery committee seeking to address President Tyler on his Boston visit, Wright suggested adding Boston's most famous fugitive slave, George Latimer, to the group. Quincy, sure that Latimer's name would give Tyler grounds to reject the entire group, yet aware that once proposed his name could not honorably be stricken, lashed out at Wright. He was an "impudent varlet" who had once again made "mischief to the best of his small abilities." When Wright attended the meetings of the New England Anti-Slavery Convention, he was, so Nathaniel Rogers reported, snubbed.[35] Nor did those shapers of antislavery inner-circle attitudes, Maria Chapman and her sisters, ever cease their denigration of Wright.

The failure of the Liberty party and Wright's inability to find in Boston any group with which he could work comfortably gradually defeated him. The result was that when the time was ripe for the political antislavery he had long sought, his antislavery career was fast running out. Abolition, though still a compelling interest, was, after 1850, no longer the focus of his life. The exhaustion, despair, and pain that marked his private life in the 1840s took their toll of his energy, optimism, and reform zeal.

⛓⛓⛓

Although Wright had remained engaged throughout the 1840s and had even broadened the scope of his antislavery activity, he had become increasingly less effective as a leader and increasingly more pessimistic about achieving meaningful

[35]Edmund Quincy to Richard D. Webb, June 27, 1843, Q-MHS; *Herald of Freedom*, n.d., in *Liberator*, June 13, 1845.

results. He was constantly attacked by both the Garrisonians and orthodox clericals within new organization. As his political commitments irritated the former, so his increasing religious liberalism offended the latter. They were already suspicious of his views in 1839 but had backed his editorship of the *Massachusetts Abolitionist* to gain for it the benefit of his reputation. Over the years, Wright's orthodoxy had succumbed to the erosion which had started when he studied with Nathaniel Taylor at Yale. By 1838, he was writing Beriah Green that he found church services a "fog-land" in which he nearly lost "sight of the most precious beacons of the faith." He did not, he wrote his parents not long after, belong any more to any church. They were mere husks to the kernels of God's truth. He might have said, as he did to his brother James a decade later, that he rejected the "wretched, impious and even blasphemous cant which has been taught us by an interested and professional priesthood."[36]

Wright no more publicized his views than the clericals did their suspicions. Nonetheless the reason for his being dropped from his short tenure as editor of the *Free American* in 1841 seems to have been his religious heterodoxy. The rumor was widespread and the Boston Clique asserted it as fact. Wendell Phillips defined Wright's dilemma and his fall from orthodox grace in his report to Elizabeth Pease: Wright's "honesty on the church question obliged [the clericals] to turn him out of the editorship of the Free American & put in someone who would pander to sectarianism."[37]

His involvement in factional infighting was, however, only part of the strain which wore Wright down. Father of a huge and growing family, he was constantly trying to augment his unsure and sporadic antislavery income. His efforts, among them invention of a mechanical knitting machine and an

---

[36]Henry B. Stanton to Amos A. Phelps, September 2, 1839, P-BPL; Wright to Beriah Green, December 15, 1838; Wright to Mr. and Mrs. Wright, December 5, 1839; Wright to James Wright, August 26, 1850: all in W-LC.

[37]Wendell Phillips to Elizabeth Pease, October, 1844, G-BPL.

improved water closet, brought no rewards. In early 1841, he was reduced to peddling from house to house his translation of La Fontaine's *Fables* in an effort to recoup a heavy investment in its printing and illustration.

A small man, balding, looking, he once wrote, like a "singed cat," wholly unprepossessing, he inspired bemused sympathy or condescending pity. Daily enervated by greeting unfriendly strangers and frustrated by their unwillingness to buy, he was even more depressed at visiting friends, colleagues, and enemies in this role. But driven by his family's need, he made the calls. None was more painful than his attempt to solicit Quincy's patronage. It was unwise of Wright, for he had only recently attacked the sharp-tongued nabob of Dedham in the *Standard*. Quincy took his revenge when he found Wright, carpetbag in hand, knocking on his door. The author, as Quincy told it, thereupon pulled out "his murderous translation of Lafontaine," and thrust it at Quincy, bidding him "stand & deliver." His host, thinking he looked "like an Irish servant carrying a bag of duelling pistols in a novel by Gilbert Gurney," greeted him coldly. But Wright would not be put off and went into the parlor where he stayed and stayed, talking far too long, doubtless expecting the offer of a night's lodging customarily offered antislavery friends. Quincy, anticipating Wright's ultimate humiliation, let him ramble on, while his end of the conversation dragged. He quite deliberately never offered the lodging.[38]

Nothing, it seems, went well. By mid-1843 he wrote his wife that he could not "feel a particle of trust in God, as it is called. . . ." All his plans had failed. "The world does not seem to have much need of my services any way." Then, while he was in England trying to sell his books and doing "tolerably well," another of his children died and his house burned down. "E. W. Jr. & his family are poor & miserably

[38]Wright describes his selling trips in letters to his wife and Beriah Green, January 1841, W-LC; the portrait is Wright's own, *Chronotype*, January 7, 1848; Edmund Quincy to Richard D. Webb, September 22, 1844, Q-MHS.

off," Lewis Tappan told Weld. "They have thrown themselves out of all their social relations & the children are growing up non-descripts. What can we do for him when he returns?" the philanthropist asked. "He has almost all kinds of sense but one."[39]

Alienated from his antislavery fellows and made desperate by his personal and financial catastrophes, Wright found himself lashing out at his detractors and tormentors, who belittled the *Chronotype* as a mere "cockle shell" trying to "ride upon the crest" of other issues. He caricatured Quincy, "the noble and gentle, the well descended and the wealthy," the "silk-gloved anti-slavery highness," as "the man who writes anti-slavery articles in a New England palace and lives on the interest of money earned by his ancestors!" Chapman he cut down indirectly but pointedly for her damnation of Frederick Douglass' uppity independence. "Can you find a man in the editorial field who can bear the palm from Frederick Douglass?" he asked rhetorically, referring to the *North Star*. "Call him saucy, impudent, out of place. There he is, a whole man —though black and a runaway slave." And, when Garrison attacked Irish temperance crusader Father Mathew for not being sufficiently antislavery, Wright fired back that he doubted whether Garrison "care[d] the value of a copper cent for the cause of Freedom or Temperance except so far as it will build up his own fame." "If all," he added later, "were to adopt the principle of Garrison, to see no good in an enemy and no fault in a friend, there could not be, to take for granted the popular division of the Universe, any heaven or earth, but only three hells."[40]

⛓⛓⛓

[39]Wright to Susan Wright, August 21, 1843, W-LC; Lewis Tappan to Theodore Weld, letterpress, July 17, 1844, T-LC.
[40]Maria W. Chapman to Sydney H. Gay, n.d., G-CU; *Weekly Chronotype,* August 19, 1847; *Chronotype,* December 11, 1847, August 5, October 8, 1849.

The passage of the Fugitive Slave Law of 1850 was symbolic of the disillusionment which Wright felt. Depressed at the persisting dominance of the slavocracy in Congress, he despaired of a clearcut antislavery political victory and gave up his career as a professional reformer. Thereafter he worked willingly with any party that promised some improvement, no matter how slight, over the old parties.

In 1848 he had abandoned his loyalty to the Liberty party. The impetus for the shift lay in the party's nomination of John Hale, who believed that the Constitution guaranteed slavery. Sure that Hale's position made the party useless, Wright joined a rump convention, which nominated Gerrit Smith, and he placed Smith's name on the *Chronotype* masthead. But Wright, who had turned to politics for practical action, could not long deceive himself or support a splinter of an exhausted splinter party. As the election drew near, he shifted his support to the new Free Soil party and Martin Van Buren. Although he still yearned for the straightforward antislavery of "the real Liberty" party, Wright argued that the Free Soil party represented "the interests of all in all parts of the country, those who are free and those who ought to be."[41]

Having deserted the Liberty party standard, Wright ran for state representative from Boston on the Free Soil ticket in 1849 and 1850. He did not, of course, win, nor had he expected to. The suspicion bore in on him that his efforts were an exercise in futility. That mood dominated his life in the 1850s, when he directed his reform efforts at the insurance business, which he served as a consulting actuary after a term as state insurance commissioner. He did, however, rouse himself in 1856 to support the new Republican party, though not with the enthusiasm of his early years. Looking back on the Liberty party in 1860, he confessed to his good friend, Beriah Green, that it was an exercise in "shamming,"

[41]*Chronotype*, June 1, 26, September 20, 23, 1848.

and added that he had "ceased to expect or look for any
outward representative of [his] sense of justice in church,
party, or government. I have begun to learn," he said wearily,
"that such a thing is not possible & never will be."[42]

By the eve of Lincoln's election, Wright had concluded that
one should choose simply the lesser evil among candidates
of the major parties. To vote for a right principled man if
he had no chance of winning was to waste one's vote. With
a cynicism matured by age and adversity, he thought that
it would have been better in 1844 to have voted for Clay
rather than for Birney. All that Birney had achieved was the
ill-fated victory of Polk.[43] Such was the final, sad commentary
of a man who twenty years earlier had been eager to sacrifice
his livelihood, his friends, and his reputation in search of
a viable political solution to slavery.

Though Wright followed the course of antislavery events during the Civil War and concerned himself with the fate of
the freedmen after emancipation, his attention was lusterless,
his interest cursory. When the War broke out, he wrote Secretary Chase that the Union would benefit from the use of
black troops as it would benefit from emancipation. Increasingly insistent on the point, he wrote letters to the press and
issued pamphlets, among them *Lessons of St. Domingo* and *What
of the War*. He served on the executive committee of Boston's
Emancipation League and mournfully denounced, in company with many of his old comrades, President Lincoln's disavowal of General David Hunter's 1862 emancipation proclamation. In his pamphlet, *Programme for Peace*, he argued that
slaveholders' land should be confiscated by taxation and redistributed to poor whites and freed slaves. Before the war was

[42]Wright to Editor, n.d., in *Liberator*, August 15, 1856; Wright to [Beriah
Green?], October 8, 1860, W-LC.
[43]Wright to [Beriah Green?], October 8, 1860, W-LC.

over, he pressed for full Negro suffrage; once it had ended, he wholeheartedly endorsed Radical Reconstruction and condemned President Johnson's program.[44]

His involvement in the continuing battles of old-time abolitionists was minimal, and his attention turned to other matters. He broke with the Radicals in 1872 over the issue of corruption to support the Liberal Republicans, and, in one last token, ran in 1875 for the Massachusetts state senate on a reform ticket. The next year, sharing Henry Adams' contempt for corrupt American politics, he sat the election out.

Wright's career as a political abolitionist and his disenchantment with its inefficacy leaves the question whether a man who was a reformer first and politician second could make of politics an effective reform weapon. The theoretical basis of Wright's position would argue that it could. His antislavery interpretation of the Constitution made it an eminently usable political weapon and opened a way around Southern resistance by establishing conditions for federal intervention in the states.

On this platform Wright was ready to stand; on it he ran for office, and as editor and party regular he supported other candidates who shared his beliefs. But neither he nor they ever really learned the art of politics. He ran for office as though it were an unpleasant duty. Like most other third-party candidates, his efforts were more directed at registering protests than winning office. The failure to win, the failure to compromise and be expedient, the failure to do all those things which their purist critics were sure they would do made Liberty party politics ineffectual. They never even took the first step toward using the federal government to end slavery, for they

---

[44]Wright to Salmon P. Chase, draft, May 4, 1861, November 13, 1862, W-LC and C-LC respectively. See also Wright's *The Programme of Peace . . .* (Boston: Ticknor and Fields, 1862), 3–22. On suffrage, Wright to Gerrit Smith, August 19, 1864, March 6, 1865, S-SU. On Johnson, Wright to Gerrit Smith, June 12, 1867, S-SU.

never won a major office except for Gerrit Smith's election to Congress in 1852. If they were to use government for reform purposes, did they not have first to build a political base from which to win elections and attain office? The reformer who enters politics but scorns the art of politics seems little more practical than the reformer who scorns politics altogether. Wright put reform ahead of political astuteness. Compared to Joshua Giddings, a politician with a strong antislavery commitment, who for twenty years made the House of Representatives his forum for a reform message, Wright seems as wildly apolitical, even as antipolitical, as Garrison or Foster.

For all his enthusiasm for political action, then, Wright remained primarily a reformer. He shared the radical ideals of his era—immediatism, egalitarianism, and, later, religious liberalism. At the same time, his methods were those of a moderate. His radical ideals alienated him from the new organization, which he had joined for its methods; his practicality in action offended the official custodians of antislavery radicalism. About him was no touch of the saint or martyr or even the fanatic. Never as a mature man absolutely sure that he possessed the truth, he altered his position as experience and further thought dictated. He retained, however, the reformer's vantage point and vision of a better society. As a maverick or an independent, Wright was shunned by the organizations he had helped found and by the associates with whom he had early worked. No more than he could be a politician's politician could he be the reformer's reformer. His conscience, pledged as it was to libertarian and egalitarian principles, kept him consistently an opponent of slavery. Yet, his personal sense of irony and his growing inability to embrace any absolutism increasingly separated him from the earnest reformers whose political and social goals alike he shared.

11

The Political Regular:
Joshua Reed Giddings

"Mr. Giddings is a rough, plain, unpolished man . . . [with] the appearance of a plain and unpretending farmer, accustomed to get his living by the labor of his hands in the field." Standing over six feet tall in his moccasins or "capacious cowhide boots," large of frame, his long, narrow face topped by prematurely gray hair, Ohio's Joshua Reed Giddings was a stereotype of the raw frontiersman. Uncomfortable in eastern garb and with eastern ways, painfully shy in the Washington world, which he entered in 1838 as Congressman from the Western Reserve, he was nonetheless tough, flexible, and determinedly independent. Pragmatic politician by choice and social reformer by principle, he worked within government for antislavery. Ironically, although he was more closely identified with politics than Elizur Wright, Gerrit Smith, or James G. Birney, Joshua Giddings became a kind of folk-hero to even the most fastidious Garrisonians. They regretted his political temporizing, sure that it tarnished his character; but they admired the man who so vigorously supported their cause in Congress.[1]

[1] For the quotations, see *National Anti-Slavery Standard*, April 7, 1842; *Cleve-*

Like Wright, Giddings was a product of Ohio's Western Reserve. His family, however, had started the migration from Connecticut earlier than Wright's, and Joshua was born in the western Pennsylvania village of Tioga Point in 1795. Within months, the family moved north to Canandaigua, New York, where the boy spent his early youth. Not until 1806 did the Giddings family make its last move to Wayne Township in northeastern Ohio's Ashtabula County.

Giddings' father was a farmer–frontiersman of the poorest order, unable even to secure legal title to his land until 1817, by which time Joshua was already an independent farmer. With no formal education except nine months of Latin and mathematics studied under a local minister, "Young Gid" became a schoolteacher when he was only nineteen and was already a veteran of five months' Indian fighting during the War of 1812. By the time he was twenty-six, he had read law with a local lawyer and established his own practice. His rise in society marked the success of a poor but ambitious man on the frontier—though even the local bar nearly denied him admission because of his poor preparation and lack of social standing.

After a short period in Williamsfield, he moved his office to Jefferson, the county seat of Ashtabula County, and there built a practice and reputation less on genius or brilliance than on hard work and reliable competence. Investing his fees in land speculation in true Western style, Giddings quickly amassed a fortune so comfortable that he retired from the law when he was forty-one. Then, almost within the year, he lost all in the panic of 1837.

In 1838, eager for a new career and source of income,

land *Times,* n.d., quoted in *Anti-Slavery Bugle,* February 25, 1848. For other contemporary descriptions, see that of Giddings' son-in-law, George W. Julian, *The Life of Joshua Reed Giddings* (Chicago: A. C. McClurg & Co., 1892), 29, and Giddings' own comments about his shyness in Washington in his letter to his wife, May 3, 1842, G-OHS.

he was elected as a Whig to fill out the unfinished term of his old law teacher, Elisha Whittelsey, in the House of Representatives. Giddings was distinguishable from other freshman congressmen only by his antislavery enthusiasm. His susceptibility to the radicalism of the day may have lain in his coincidental failing health and loss of fortune and may have provided him an emotional compensation. That he came from the Western Reserve, heart of Western antislavery, made possible his combining a political career with his new commitment to antislavery, which was reinforced, if not hatched, by the forceful oratory and personal influence of Theodore Weld. Giddings went to Washington as a new kind of congressman.[2]

Almost as soon as he had arrived in the capital, Giddings was caught up in its excitement. He was awed by the political luminaries, but he was disillusioned by the slothful habits and manners of his fellow congressmen. Determined to do his duty, he had already dressed, walked three miles, and started his writing and studying for the day before most others had gotten up. Worse still, they avoided debate, voted the party line, and let principle take the hindmost. He found the Northerners to be "diffident, taciturn, and *forbearing*," and the Southerners, "confident," "bold," "self assertive," and "over-bearing."[3]

[2]Benjamin Thomas, *Theodore Weld, Crusader for Freedom* (New Brunswick: Rutgers University Press, 1950), 102; Robert T. Ludlum, "Joshua R. Giddings, Radical," *Mississippi Valley Historical Review* 23 (1936): 50. James B. Stewart, *Joshua R. Giddings and the Tactics of Radical Politics* (Cleveland: Case Western Reserve University Press, 1970), published and read by the authors since this chapter was written, is now the principal work on Giddings and is in substantial agreement with the interpretation here presented.

[3]Giddings to Laura Waters Giddings, December 16, 1838, G-OHS. Because Giddings had also a daughter, Laura, to whom he frequently wrote, subsequent citations will be to wife or to Laura (daughter). The quotations are

The situation made Giddings abandon his initial resolution
to remain quiet and merely observe from the sidelines
throughout his first session, and he was soon in the fray.
He was immediately caught up in the annual debates on the
Gag Rule when the crusty and irascible elder statesman, John
Quincy Adams, defended again the right of petitioners to
be heard by their legislature. Troubled by the resolutions
to table antislavery petitions without comment and full of
admiration for Adams, Giddings decided to speak. "Not that
I think my feeble efforts could affect the subject," he wrote
a constituent back home, "but to let the world know my abhor-
ance of every attempt to Curtail the right of petition or of
discussion."[4] He was right. The Gag Rule passed despite his
opposition. His attempt two months later, in February 1839,
to end it was futile, but his position was clear: he had begun
a twenty-year congressional struggle against the slavocracy.
With Adams, he fought the Gag Rule until it was overturned
six years later.

Indeed the influence of Adams in shaping Giddings' con-
gressional career was crucial. At first sight, nothing could
be more incongruous than the stiff and sophisticated little
old Yankee with his massive frontier partner. Adams' appearance and diffidence had at first constituted part of Giddings'
Washington disillusionment, but that reaction quickly passed.
For him, the elder statesman seemed a living link with the
Revolution and a keeper of its meaning. "Father Adams,"
Giddings thought, was "the most extraordinary man living."[5]
Both personal attachment and political alliance led the younger congressman to draw heavily on his mentor's legal and
parliamentary expertise. Under his influence, Giddings con-
cluded that the Constitution was an antislavery document and

in Joshua R. Giddings, "Diary of a Member of Congress," ms. December
14, 1838, G-OHS.
  [4]Giddings to Ephraim Brown, November 31, 1838, MS-WRHS.
  [5]Giddings to Wife, February 6, 1842, G-OHS.

provided a platform from which to tackle problems touching on slavery. At the same time, like Adams a practicing politician, he stayed in the Whig party, convinced that it best served his political philosophy.

❧❧❧

In a series of public letters written under the pseudonym "Pacificus" and published in 1842 as *The Rights and Privileges of the Several States . . .*, Giddings outlined his constitutional interpretation. The federal Constitution left slavery within the sole purview of the states. Prior to its adoption, "each State had acted, in regard to slavery, according to the dictates of its own will" and had exercised "supreme, indisputable, and uncontrolled jurisdiction over that institution within its own limits." The situation was unchanged after 1789 because the Tenth Amendment reserved to the states and the people thereof, powers not specifically delegated to the federal government. The Constitution's silence on slavery placed that institution in this category. The federal government could neither abolish nor sustain slavery in the states. "The people of the free States . . . delegated to the Federal Government," Giddings averred, "no more power to involve them in slavery, than the south did to involve *them* in its *abolition*."[6]

Thus the Ohioan utilized states' rights in a long campaign to end all federal support of slavery whether in the District of Columbia, in the territories, or on the seas. Only municipal, not federal, law governed slavery. Therefore, Giddings told the House at the end of the Mexican War: "I have nothing to do with the southern States. . . . If they see fit to make one-half of their people the property of the other half, we cannot interfere with their laws. If, with the inhabitants of

---

[6] Joshua Reed Giddings (pseud. "Pacificus"), *The Rights and Privileges of the Several States in Regard to Slavery; Being a Series of Essays, Published in the Western Reserve Chronicle, (Ohio), After the Election of 1842 . . .* (n.p.: n.p., [1842]), 1–2.

the Fejee Islands, they become cannibals and eat each other, we have not the power to prohibit such revolting practice by our legislation. All we can do," he concluded, "is to see that they shall not disgrace nor degrade this Government, nor the people of the free States, either by their slavery or their cannibalism."[7]

Giddings did not confine his battle to constitutional theorizing but linked it with efforts to guard the public purse. Shocked by any squandering of public moneys, he fiercely condemned federal expenditures on behalf of the peculiar institution. With considerable deftness, he combined states' rights theory with the economic interests of his Ohio constituency. By defending his own constituents from taxation to support slavery, he popularized his antislavery position at home and retained his seat. Similarly, he turned the argument to Whig politics, charging that the slave states denied funds to the West for internal improvements while demanding that their peculiar interests be served. In Congress, from the vantage point he had gained as a member of the House Claims Committee, he battled claims on the government for slaves lost in the public service. Insisting that both precedent and principle barred such payments, for no man had the right to make property of his fellow men, he pursued his agitation so persistently that after a year as chairman of the committee, he was stripped of his position in December 1843.[8]

More dramatic was his campaign against the second Seminole war. Complicated by the interrelated issues of escaped slaves, Indian intratribal rivalries, federal Indian

[7]See, for example, Giddings' speech in the House, February 13, 1844, in *National Anti-Slavery Standard,* March 14, 1844; the quotation is from his speech of May 13, 1848, in *Congressional Globe,* 30th Cong., 1st sess., Appendix, 542.

[8]Julian, *Giddings,* 58–60; Edward C. Reilley, "Politico-economic Considerations in the Western Reserve's Early Slavery Controversy," *Ohio State Archeological and Historical Quarterly* 52 (1943): 141–157; Giddings ["Pacificus"], *Rights and Privileges,* 8–9; Julian, *Giddings,* 102–103; Giddings to John Addison Giddings (hereafter Addison), January 15, 1843, G-OHS; *National Anti-Slavery Standard,* February 2, 1843; Julian, *Giddings,* 148.

removal policy, and Georgia's westward expansion, the war provided Giddings another forum for antislavery propaganda. Secure because his Ohio constituents were no longer subject to Indian attack, he opposed appropriations for the war and the peace settlement which followed it. And he found also in the Seminole war an opportunity to circumvent the House ban on discussion of slavery.[9]

Giddings' careful turning of other issues to serve his antislavery politics was the mark of a competent political maneuverer. More and more, too, he succeeded in dealing directly with slavery through this technique. Troubled like other abolitionists by the flamboyant display of slavery and the slave trade in the District of Columbia, Giddings felt its impact daily when he was in Washington. Indeed it was this exposure, during his first term, that emphasized to him the brutality of the whole system, as a similar exposure had done for Lundy. On one occasion, hearing a "thrilling cry of distress which continued for some minutes," he had left his boardinghouse to investigate. He saw a slave, who had broken away from a whipping, seized, knocked down, beaten, and dragged through the streets to the stable like "a dead hog." Similarly he saw a slave coffle driven through the city, its lagging members hustled by a bull whip in the hand of the driver. He attended a slave auction, where he watched the sale of a man reputedly free who had been seized as a fugitive and then sold to cover jail costs. Giddings left the auction rooms, he noted in his diary, with "no very exalted views of [his] Countrys honor."[10]

In consequence, he seized upon an 1839 House debate on a bridge across the Potomac to speak on slavery in the District. Noting that Ohioans had no voice in District affairs since

[9]Joshua Reed Giddings, *Speeches in Congress* (Boston: John P. Jewett & Co., 1853), for two speeches relating to the Seminole war issue, February 9, 1841, February 18, 1846, see 4–5 and 164–172, respectively.
[10]Giddings, "Diary," February 14, 16, 1839, for the quotations, January 29–30, 1839, for the slave coffle description, G-OHS.

their petitions for abolishing slavery there were automatically laid on the table, he asked why they should tax themselves for the District's benefit. He then charged that the bridge would benefit the slave trade by facilitating the movement of slaves and would, therefore, be unconstitutional as well. If, he added in implied threat, the bill passed, it would encourage the *"probable* removal of the seat of Government to some free state."[11]

Giddings' patience was soon exhausted with such indirect attacks, and in 1843 he turned his attention directly to eliminating slavery in the District. It was protected there only by federal reenactment of the Maryland law code when that state ceded the territory to the new government. Since, however, according to his constitutional view, slavery had ceased to exist there as soon as it became federal property, the Congress had acted improperly and should repeal the slave law, which it had had no right to pass in the first place. After five years of pressing this rather mild solution, he turned in 1848 to suggesting a plebescite in the District on the abolition of slavery. The shock of his proposal lay in the provision that all male residents over twenty-one, black as well as white, slave as well as free, should vote on the issue. Not surprisingly it was quickly laid on the table.[12]

Though his moves on behalf of Washington's slaves were marked by constant defeat, Giddings' course frightened and antagonized his fellow congressmen. And as they silenced antislavery petitioners, so they sought to silence him. The

[11]Ibid., February 12, 1839; the speech on the Potomac Bridge was delivered February 13, 1839, and is reported in *Liberator,* February 22, March 22, 1839, quotation from the latter issue.
[12]Giddings ("Pacificus"), *Rights and Privileges,* 10; *Congressional Globe,* 30th Cong., 2d sess., 55; Giddings, "Diary," December [18 and 26] 1848, G-OHS.

opportunity arose from his resolutions on the *Creole* case. On October 27, 1841, the brig *Creole* had sailed from Hampton Roads for New Orleans with a cargo of slaves. They mutinied at sea and ordered the captain to take them to Liberia. Convinced that there were inadequate supplies for such a long journey, they then agreed to put in at Nassau, where a British court set them free. The dealers who claimed to own these slaves then pressed the Tyler administration to seek compensation from Great Britain.

Giddings, in response to Secretary of State Daniel Webster's report of the negotiations to Congress early in 1842, presented a series of resolutions to the House restating his constitutional argument that slavery was exclusively a state matter. Slaves on the high seas, he argued, were outside of state and municipal law and consequently free. Giddings concluded that the slaves had violated no laws and that efforts to reenslave them or to gain compensation for their owners violated American law, contravened American efforts to end the slave trade, and injured the rights of the free states.[13]

Giddings was fully aware that his resolutions stood no chance of adoption in the hostile House; therefore, having made his point by introducing them, he sought to escape the political consequences by withdrawing them almost immediately. Nevertheless, his fellow Whig, John Minor Botts of Virginia, moved to censure him for subverting his country's position while she was involved in "delicate" negotiations with Great Britain, "the result of which [might] eventually involve . . . [both] nations, and perhaps the whole civilized world in war. . . ." Botts' resolutions, in sum, labeled Giddings a traitor to his country in time of grave national crisis and said he deserved "the severe condemnation of the people of this country, and of [the House of Representatives] in particular." Moreover his justification of "mutiny and murder" was

---

[13]*Congressional Globe*, 27th Cong., 2d sess., 342. The resolutions were published in *Liberator*, April 1, 1842.

"shocking to all sense of law, order, and humanity." He was, in short, a common scoundrel.[14]

Giddings was denied time to prepare a defense against these charges, and the censure resolutions passed easily the day after they were offered. When the vote was announced, he "gathered up his documents and papers, shook hands with Mr. Adams," left the House, and resigned his seat.[15] Then he went home to Ohio to campaign for reelection.

The relief with which Southerners had greeted Giddings' departure was surpassed by the enthusiasm with which his constituents greeted his arrival in the Western Reserve. Almost before he had unpacked, he laid his case before them in a pamphlet, *An Expose of the Circumstances which Led to the Resignation by the Hon. Joshua R. Giddings,* made up largely of excerpts from the *Globe.*[16] Not retreating from his position in Congress, he toured his district, spoke at rallies, and welcomed interminable resolutions supporting his stand. Just a month after he had been censured in the House, he was triumphantly reelected.

When he returned to Washington, Giddings wrote his son in May, he "was soon surrounded by friends who certainly appeared glad to see [him] back," among them, "Father Adams." But while "many looked up with smiling faces" as he was introduced to his colleagues in the House, "others looked down and appeared to be perfectly dum[b]founded."[17] Giddings had triumphed, and the dumbfounded had reason

[14]Botts' censure resolutions, March 21, 1842, appear in *Liberator,* April 1, 1842.

[15]Ibid.

[16]Joshua Reed Giddings, *An Expose of the Circumstances Which Led to the Resignation by the Hon. Joshua R. Giddings, of His Office of Representative in the Congress of the United States from the Sixteenth Congressional District of Ohio, on the 22d March, 1842* (Painesville, Ohio: J. Leonard & Co., Printers, 1842).

[17]Giddings to Addison Giddings, May 8, 1842, G-OHS.

for their distemper. He had proved that one district at least would sustain its antislavery Congressman in the face of persistent attack on him by the slavocracy. It signaled an antislavery politics which could not easily be silenced.

The censure fracas embodied the essence of Giddings' first eight years in Congress. From the time he took his seat in December 1838 until the outbreak of the Mexican War, he remained as loyal a Whig as he was a dedicated opponent of slavery. Thus, he combined party politics with abolition, tempering the reformer's purity with the politician's maneuver. Ignorant of antislavery's doctrinal fine points and unconscious of the factional struggle within the movement, Giddings played no role in the antislavery societies. Although he occasionally attended abolition meetings, he found his forum in Congress where, as he put it, he did in one speech on the Oregon question "more for the promotion of humanity than Garrison and all that portion of the abolitionists have done for a whole year."[18]

As a politician, however, Giddings was bound by party commitments. A Whig into whose following third-party antislavery cut, he struggled against Liberty party attractions. Overconfident from the special election which returned him after his censure, he almost lost the regular election of 1842 as the Liberty party drained off his support. To counter this trend he wrote his "Pacificus" pamphlet, hoping to woo ex-Whigs back from their Liberty party flirtations. Contending that the Liberty party held Whiggish political and constitutional principles, he argued that in turn Whigs held the same views on slavery as did Liberty party men. Admittedly Whigs had been negligent in pushing antislavery principles, but more ground would be lost than gained in dividing the vote between the two similar parties and giving victory to the Democrats. Only a reunion could save their ideals and that unity must be achieved in the Whig party, for the Liberty party with its

[18]Giddings to Laura (daughter), February 22, 1846, G-OHS.

single issue was ineffectual politically. Then, playing both ends against the middle, he wrote the democratically inclined Salmon P. Chase, "I think it would be a great misfortune if all antislavery men were to come out and unite in one political party. Thereby separating themselves from the others and cutting themselves off from that influence which they now are exerting upon their political friends."[19]

Giddings tried to exert such influence on his political friends, but he was constantly embarrassed by their association with slavery. His support of Clay in the 1844 election readily demonstrated the awkwardness of his position. He argued that Henry Clay's slaveholding did not disqualify him as a presidential candidate, for he lived in a state in which slaveholding was legal. He extolled Clay's Raleigh speech in the spring of 1844, which upheld a strictly states' rights view of slavery and lamented that the printed version omitted much of the argument. He persisted in the efforts to fuse Whigs, North and South, on the basis of states' rights much as he had sought to do in 1842 when he had queried John Calhoun on the relationship of federal power to slavery. Although his efforts failed, he still remained in the Whig party for purely practical political reasons. As he told Salmon Chase, he needed political office to implement his program, and a shift in party allegiance would lose him his constituency.[20]

By picking his way carefully and judiciously through the political maze, Giddings seemed to have the best of both worlds. As a Whig, he could be politically effective; as an abolitionist, he could turn politics to the cause. But the seeming equilibrium was an unstable mixture as each side demanded a more exclusive loyalty. "The abolitionists," he wrote concern-

[19]Giddings ("Pacificus"), *Rights and Privileges*, 1, 13–16; Giddings to Salmon P. Chase, February 19, 1843, C-HSP.
[20]Joshua Reed Giddings, *A Letter from Hon. J. R. Giddings upon the Duty of Anti-Slavery Men in the Present Crisis* (Ravenna, Ohio: W. Wadsworth, 1844), 7–12; Giddings to Wife, April 28, 1844, Giddings to Henry Clay, draft, July 6, 1844, G-OHS; Giddings to John C. Calhoun, draft, December 1842, G-OHS; Giddings to Salmon P. Chase, February 19, 1843, C-HSP.

edly in 1843, "have constantly been urging me to action against slavery, and by letters and conversation manifesting their distrust of my sincerity." And, from the other side, he felt pressure from "some of [his] Whig friends exhorting [him] to be *prudent,* to consult [his] own reputation and say *nothing. . . ."*[21]

He was puzzled particularly by the abolitionists' criticism. They were, to be sure, pleased that he, like Adams, presented their antislavery petitions. They rallied to his support when in 1842 he was censured for his *Creole* resolutions. They praised his "zealous and unflinching course" in Congress to sustain free speech and the right of petition.[22] Not all their comments, however, were so laudatory. Lewis Tappan chastised Giddings in 1840 for supporting a proslavery Whig rather than an antislavery Democrat for Speaker of the House. Joshua Leavitt, Liberty party polemicist, accused him the following year of putting economic interests before antislavery concerns. If the moderates found him wanting, so too did the Garrisonians. The *Liberator* scolded him for failing to reintroduce his *Creole* resolutions on his return to Congress. Stephen and Abby Foster opposed an 1846 American Anti-Slavery Society resolution commending him and added to it an unflattering amendment that he was only "as faithful as his false position will permit him to be to his duty." Their complaints paled, however, in the light of the use that could be made of him. Maria Chapman lauded Giddings for his "good anti-slavery speeches" and letters and applauded his efforts "to vote for abolition in the District of Columbia, and for the removal of every taint of slavery from our Constitution and country."[23] Giddings had a public and an impact not to be scorned.

[21]Giddings to J. A. Briggs, September 12, 1843, MS-WRHS.
[22]A resolution of the American Anti-Slavery Society annual meeting, reported in *Liberator,* May 27, 1842.
[23]Lewis Tappan to Giddings, letterpress, February 7, 1840, T-LC; Joshua Leavitt to [Giddings], October 29, 1841, G-OHS; *Liberator,* July 22, 1842, May 22, 1846, August 25, 1843.

Among these contrary currents, Giddings was perplexed
indeed. His efforts to unite the Whigs had failed. His attack
on slavery brought praise but also scorn from abolitionists.
His efforts to curtail the slave power through constitutional
arguments had had practically no effect. By 1846, therefore,
as the crisis of Texas annexation deepened and the likelihood
of war with Mexico became reality, Giddings began to change
the character of his antislavery fight.

Early in his congressional career, Giddings had argued that
the annexation of Texas would give slave states power to
dominate Congress, nationalize slavery, defeat a protective
tariff and internal improvements, increase military expenditures, and saddle free labor with the costs of the venture
while it would return vast new profits to the South in expanding the slave market. His assessments had not mellowed when,
in 1845 on the eve of annexation, he foresaw that adding
Texas, a sovereign foreign power, to the Union would mean
the dissolution of the old Union and the creation of a new.
So basic a change in the form of government without consulting the people violated the constitutional guarantee that powers not delegated to the federal government remained with
the people. When the joint resolution for annexation passed,
therefore, Giddings saw his entire antislavery argument collapse. Appeals to the Constitution and the Union were mean-
ingless. Slave-power representation was disproportionately
increased in the extension of the three-fifths ratio to Texas.
Congressional legality was threatened by an influx of representatives who lacked the citizenship qualifications requisite for
Congressmen. The federal government had acted positively
to extend slavery and shattered thereby the states' rights of
the free states.[24]

[24]Giddings to Dear Sir, in Cleveland *Declaration of Independence*, n.d.,
reprinted in *National Anti-Slavery Standard*, September 15, 1842; Giddings

It portended disaster. When, in the spring of 1844, President Tyler had ordered troops to the Texas border and the navy to the Mexican coast, Giddings had assessed the move as "an act of hostility which carried out will constitute *actual war*." The following January, when annexation was accomplished, he became desperately pessimistic about the country's future. It was "the great crisis which was to determine the fate of the slave during [his] life and the life of [his] children . . . the act which is to consign [the slave] for generations to chains and bondage and a premature death, or to set him free at no distant day."[25]

Congress had joined the chief executive in open violation of the Constitution. Angrily Giddings sought to apply the same illegality of action to the Oregon question and thereby revenge the North upon the South. On January 5, 1846, he rose from his seat in the House to demand that the United States hold to its claim on Oregon to the 54° 40′ parallel. Doubtless it would mean war with Great Britain, but even that would be beneficial for it would permit American annexation of Canada, thereby adding five new free states to the Union. In addition, such a war would precipitate a slave insurrection. Rather disingenuously insisting that he personally did not seek such an uprising, he told his Southern colleagues that he "doubt[ed] not that hundreds of thousands of honest and patriotic hearts will 'laugh at your calamity, and mock when your fear cometh.' "[26]

It was a startling performance, which won universal attention and almost universal condemnation. If it accomplished

---

to Addison Giddings, April 13, 1844, G-OHS; Giddings, *Speeches,* 97–118; Giddings to Editor, *Republican and Whig,* August 28, 1845, partially copied in *Anti-Slavery Bugle,* October 10, 1845; Giddings to Addison Giddings, January 25, 1845, G-OHS; *Congressional Globe,* 29th Cong., 1st sess., Appendix, 828.

[25]Giddings to [Laura (daughter)], May 17, 1844, G-OHS; Giddings to Addison Giddings, January 25, 1845, G-OHS.

[26]*Congressional Globe,* 29th Cong., 1st sess., 139–140.

nothing, it did mark a critical turning point in Giddings'
career. Thereafter his constitutional arguments rang hollow,
his ties to the Whig party dissolved, and his attack on slavery
became more direct.

The war with Mexico, which he had predicted two years
earlier, isolated Giddings almost wholly from the Whig party.
When the war came in May 1846, he wrote his wife that
it created "an important crisis to our country and to our
Whigs." "I greatly fear the cowardise of the Whigs," he continued. "It is the curse of our country and of our party that
northern men are too craven hearted to maintain their own
rights. I expect a portion of the Whigs will desert us and
go over to the support of the outrageous war waged by the
Executive, upon an unoffending people who merely oppose
the robbery which we [are] attempting to perpetrate upon
them." So Giddings defied his colleagues by refusing consistently to vote supplies for the war and he constantly asserted
that the war was a revolutionary move designed to destroy
both Constitution and Union.[27]

His support of Democrat David Wilmot's proviso demonstrated clearly Giddings' willingness to sacrifice Whig party
loyalty to a new antislavery political alignment. Wilmot's proposal, first made in the summer of 1846, which would prohibit
slavery in any territory acquired in the Mexican War, caught
Giddings' imagination. Almost immediately he wrote to Salmon Chase proposing that Whig and Liberty party leaders
meet in Ohio and draft a joint statement in its support. By
November, he was urging Chase that it was now "time to
form a Union" among Whig and Liberty party abolitionists.[28]
Party distinctions had become largely irrelevant. The imperative was to defend freedom for a free people.

No longer a party regular, Giddings, in the session which
began in December 1847, launched an open attack on Whig

[27]Giddings to Wife, May 10, 1846, G-OHS; the speech on revolution, May
12, 1846, is in Giddings, *Speeches*, 191*ff.*
[28]Giddings to Salmon P. Chase, August 3, November 23, 1846, C-HSP.

leadership. He had long supported the young Massachusetts Conscience Whigs against the older Cotton Whigs who dominated the state party. Now, when Robert C. Winthrop, a cotton conservative, sought the House speakership, Giddings refused even to attend the Whig caucus, lest he be bound by its decision to support Winthrop for Speaker. His opposition went well beyond this silent abstention when he published his remembrance of the Whig caucus on the Mexican War Bill at which Winthrop had supported a war vote by warning Whigs of the Federalists' decline when they had opposed the War of 1812. But Winthrop was elected Speaker, and he pushed Giddings further out of the party by excluding him from official parties and gatherings which he held and, more personally cutting, by omitting his name from the House committee that arranged the funeral of Giddings' friend and hero, John Quincy Adams.[29]

If Winthrop, the Cotton Whig, won his opposition, Zachary Taylor, slave-owning hero of the Mexican War, won his enmity in his campaign for the Whig presidential nomination. Giddings would support no one who would not subscribe to the Wilmot Proviso, least of all the general who, by his disposition of troops along the border, bore heavy responsibility for the war. After the June convention when Taylor was nominated, Giddings finally ended his remaining loyalty to the Whig party. "This is the time," he concluded, "for party ties to sit loosely upon us. The parties have abandoned their principles, and we must choose between our principles and them."[30] With that aim in view, he attended in August the Buffalo Free Soil convention. There, convinced that he was still advocating Whig principle, Giddings pledged himself to the Democracy's old leader, Martin Van Buren, who had led New York State's

[29]Giddings to Seth M. Gates, December 4, 1847, S-SU; Charles Sumner to Giddings, February 3, 1848, G-OHS; Giddings to Robert C. Winthrop, February 7, 1848, Wn-MHS. On the Adams' funeral, Giddings to Wife, February 27, 1848, G-OHS.

[30]Giddings' remarks to Free Soil convention in Worcester in late June 1848, reported in *National Anti-Slavery Standard,* July 6, 1848.

Barnburner faction into the Free Soil party with more enmity
to the Hunkers than to slavery.

When the lame-duck session of the Thirtieth Congress
assembled in December 1848, therefore, Giddings put his
experience and mastery of congressional procedure at the
disposal of his Free Soil colleagues. Shunned for a while even
by antislavery Whigs and hurt by the coolness of old friends,
he stuck with his new party and won for it a measure of
success. For the first time, the Committee on the District
reported out a bill to end the slave trade in the capital. More
important was his leadership in the new Congress, which met
in December 1849, with the Free Soil contingent holding the
balance of power between Whigs and Democrats on straight
party issues. Giddings made the most of it. Holding their
small group in line, they defeated, after a three-week fight
and sixty-three ballots, Winthrop's bid for the speakership,
electing thereby the Georgia slaveholder, Howell Cobb.
Although little of principle was gained by this device,
Winthrop's defeat foretold the imminent death of the old
Whig party.

For Giddings himself, the change of party was less evident
in any new course of action than in his rationale and orientation. His votes on substantive issues during the Thirty-first
Congress did not vary much from customary antislavery Whig
positions. What was important was that his responses were
now those of a spokesman for a small splinter party. He coped
in the Free Soil party with the same difficulties and criticisms
which he had earlier attributed to the Liberty party. On matters of slavery, the Free Soil party and the antislavery Whigs
were not far apart, nor were they consistently at odds on
other issues. But now Giddings justified the third party as
a refuge from association and cooperation with slavery. He
had, by 1850, ceased fellowshipping with a slaveholding party.
His antislavery campaign was freed from the restraints which
his Whig affiliation had always implied. And his attack was
more radical because, by viewing Texas annexation and the

Mexican War as a revolution, he had freed himself from a narrow constitutionalism.

⬤⬤⬤

For Joshua Giddings as for many other abolitionists, passage of the Fugitive Slave Law in the fall of 1850 marked a new phase in the antislavery movement. With them, he turned to more direct and less legal ways to effect abolition. Before, Giddings had always worked within the framework of established law. He had construed the 1793 Fugitive Slave Law so narrowly that it meant only that the master of a fugitive was free to claim him and to return him to slavery from the Northern state to which he had fled. Aside from that one exception, a fugitive slave had all the rights of other residents of free states, and his fellow citizens were in no way constrained from helping him.[31]

So Giddings as a Congressman, in 1845, had lauded the slaves who escaped and the Underground Railroad, which helped them. Ohioans, he told the House, treated the fugitive properly: "We feed, clothe, and lodge him, knowing him to be a slave. We teach him his rights, show him the road to Canada, and furnish him with the means to get there. We furnish him with the means of defending himself, in the same manner that we furnish others with weapons. In short, we treat him in all respects as we do other persons, except defending him against his master, or secreting him."[32]

Safe enough in Ohio, such behavior would provoke mobs in Washington. Yet Giddings gambled his own safety if occasion required. When, in 1848, the schooner *Pearl* was becalmed near the mouth of the Potomac and was seized with eighty fugitives aboard, Giddings immediately went to the Washington jail to assure Captain Daniel Drayton and mate Edward Sayres that their legal rights would be defended. In doing

[31]Giddings ("Pacificus), *Rights and Privileges,* 2–4.
[32]*Anti-Slavery Bugle,* February 27, 1846. Giddings, *Speeches,* 175.

so, he encountered a lynch-prone proslavery mob, which surrounded the jail and which, once he was inside, swarmed in after him. Though his escape was narrow, Giddings was angered rather than intimidated. When he addressed the House on the incident, he condemned the government for failing to control the mob assembled, as he charged, by the District's slave dealers. Still more disgraceful, members of the Congress had not only justified the mob but had acted with it. Flaunting his defiance, he then asserted that if he could, he would inform all slaves of their natural right to freedom and would encourage them to achieve it.[33]

Though this defiance went beyond customary political action, it still fell within the bounds of Giddings' constitutional interpretation. When, however, the new Fugitive Slave Law was enacted, he absolutely and openly defied it. In response to President Fillmore's promise to veto its repeal, Giddings charged that, in passing it, the Congress had "overstepped the limits of civil government, and attempted to usurp powers which belong[ed] only to God." Ohioans, he swore, would

> never turn out to chase the panting fugitive; . . . never be metamorphosed into bloodhounds, to track him to his hiding-place, and seize and drag him out, and deliver him to his tormentors. They may be shot down; the cannon and bayonet and sword may do their work upon them; they may drown the fugitives in the blood of freemen; but never will freemen stoop to the degradation of catching slaves.[34]

The issue had moved from constitutional to moral law.

Under its propulsion, Giddings soon scorned to argue in terms of statute law and abandoned his central reliance on the constitutional argument, basing his appeal on a higher ethic. "Let no man," he said, "tell me there is no higher law than this fugitive bill. We feel there is a law of right, a law of justice, of freedom, implanted in the breast of every intelligent human being, that bids him look with scorn upon this miscalled law." Giddings advised his constituents that it was

[33]Julian, *Giddings*, 242–244; Giddings, *Speeches*, 227–228, 230, 237.
[34]Giddings, *Speeches*, 427, 435.

better to "commit common murder, or ordinary piracy" than to "give chase to the flying bondman as he hastens to a land of freedom—to seize him and rivet the cold iron upon his trembling limbs, to drag him back and deliver him over to bondage, to chains, to the scourge, to a barbarous death by torture under the lash of an inhuman overseer...."[35]

As he now encouraged whites to resort to arms, so Giddings praised blacks for their defiance of the law. When William Parker and his fellow Negroes killed the Maryland planter Edward Gorsuch in Christiana, Pennsylvania, to save three fugitives from a return to bondage, Giddings approved their action. Similarly he applauded the "just and holy manifestation of the popular mind at Syracuse" where blacks and whites together rescued the fugitive Jerry McHenry from the law; the blacks' rescue of Shadrach from a Boston courtroom, also in 1851, he labeled consonant with the higher law. The failure of other would-be rescuers in 1854 to save the fugitive Anthony Burns from the same courthouse saddened him immensely.[36]

Quite obviously the pacifism Giddings had adopted during the Mexican War was highly selective. Well aware from his own experience that Southerners would use cane, pistol, and bowie knife to defend their institutions from attack on the House floor, Giddings was sure they relied on force elsewhere to suppress all challenge to slavery. An 1845 incident in which Edward Black of Georgia had threatened to cane him while Black's associate, John Dawson of Louisiana, drew a pistol and offered to shoot him was only the most dramatic of these occurrences. Together they convinced him that a close link existed between the development of slavery and the progressive denial of the right of self-defense to the slave. The

---

[35]Ibid., 435–436; Giddings to [the Citizens of Palmyra, Ohio, n.d.], Ravenna, Ohio *Star,* n.d., quoted in *Anti-Slavery Bugle,* December 28, 1850.

[36]Giddings, "Address to the Pennsylvania Anti-Slavery Society Convention," December 17, 1851, in *National Anti-Slavery Standard,* January 8, 1852; Giddings, *Speeches,* 484; Giddings to Grotius R. Giddings, May 21, 1854, G-OHS.

slaveholder held title to his property not from natural law but "entirely from statute law–from the laws that authorize the master to whip and shoot his slave, and which take from the slave his natural rights of self-defence and locomotion."[37] On them slavery depended. To them slaves owed no obedience.

As a result, Giddings insisted that the fugitive had full right to arm himself and "to use [arms] in defence of his person and his liberty." In like manner, he justified slave insurrection. Having argued during the *Creole* case that slaves had no "moral obligation to obey their oppressors, or the laws which held them in degradation," he had added the corollary that "if they had at any moment possessed the power of releasing themselves from bondage, it would have been just and right and proper for them to do so, at any expense of life and treasure to those who oppressed their freedom." Speaking later of the *Amistad* case, in which Africans who had seized a slaving vessel were freed by the federal courts, Giddings contended that "slavery itself, in its most legal form, [was] nothing less than a state of war between masters and servants . . . [that] it [was] guided by no law of nature or of nature's God."[38]

By the early 1840s—for his comments on the *Creole* and *Amistad* cases date to 1842 and 1844—Giddings had accepted the use of extralegal force by slaves, whose status placed them beyond law and the Constitution. The passage of a decade only made him more explicit. Of one of the Drayton-Sayres fugitives who was sold South, Giddings warned Congress that if he was not yet dead he was surely "preparing the minds of southern slaves for that work which [lay] before them;

[37]Giddings, *Speeches*, 66; the Black episode is described in Julian, *Giddings*, 172–174. The antislavery press, G-OHS, GJ-LC contain numerous references to violence in the Congress against Giddings.

[38]Giddings to Isaac Pierce, August 16, 1854, in *Anti-Slavery Bugle*, September 9, 1854; Giddings, *Speeches*, 24, 90.

a work which, if not accomplished by the voice of truth and justice, [would] be perfected in blood."[39] Slaves were learning the truths of the Declaration of Independence and preparing to defend them as did the revolutionaries of 1776.

Throughout the 1850s, Giddings played on this revolutionary theme. While most Northerners denounced filibustering expeditions to Cuba, Giddings explored their insurrectionary potential. The conquest of Cuba would open the profitable Caribbean market to the American slave trade, and the slaves transported from the American South would infect the whole area with their revolutionary ideas. In time, they would organize a slave revolt, which would soon spread to Florida, Alabama, and the rest of the South. "Fire and sword," he dramatically and frighteningly depicted, "will be called into service; devastation, rapine, and slaughter will be carried by infuriated slaves over the plantations and villages. Two hundred thousand colored men rendered desperate by barbarous oppression will constitute no mean force when fighting for life and liberty." Two years later, in 1854, he charged that President Pierce's response to Spanish seizure of the American merchantman *Black Warrior* for false manifests was designed to produce a *casus belli*. The United States would then be free to seize Cuba and, incidentally, precipitate slave insurrection at home. Again he welcomed the event for it would enable the North to restore peace on the basis of universal emancipation. "I do not say 'we will laugh at your calamity, and mock when your fear cometh,' " he intoned, again using one of his favorite biblical verses, "but I do say, when that time shall come, the lovers of our race shall stand forth, and exert the legitimate powers of this Government for freedom. We shall then have constitutional power to act for the good of our country, and do justice to the slave." That time was fast coming and he hailed it as "the approaching dawn of

[39] Giddings, *Speeches,* 485.

that political and moral millennium which I am well assured
will come upon the world."[40] Giddings, the erstwhile political
realist, had been driven by events to use the language of
the apocalypse.

Despite his radical rhetoric, Giddings did not share Stephen
Foster's enthusiasm for revolution and disunion. As he understood it, the revolution for freedom, which had been achieved
in 1776, was threatened by counterrevolution in the 1850s.
"The two great [political] parties are striving to convert this
free government into a slave-holding, a slave-breeding republic." Therefore revolutionary change was to be resisted
whether it was presidential policy in Kansas, judicial decision
in the Dred Scott case, or extragovernmental adventure like
filibustering. His whole position was as internally inconsistent
as his condemnation of filibustering while he happily anticipated its insurrectionary results. He continued to argue as
he had since Texas annexation that the old Union of 1775
was dead, but he dedicated himself to perpetuating "the
doctrines on which it was based."[41] It was Union as principle,
not Union as fact, that was central to Giddings' position.

Still, he failed to press the distinction because he thought
the Southern threats of disunion mere bluff. And if they
were in earnest, the Union as fact would better be destroyed
than saved by more concessions from the Union of principle.
Thus he was relatively indifferent when South Carolina and
her sister states seceded in 1860–1861. Nor could he be led
to embrace disunion for he argued, as he had earlier vis-à-vis
the Whig party, that it was better to stay in the Union and

[40]*Congressional Globe,* 32d Cong., 2d sess., Appendix, 40, 33d Cong., 1st
sess., 647–648 (quotation on 648).

[41]For Giddings' equivocation on slave revolt, see ibid., 34th Cong., 1st
sess., 47, and 3d sess., 79–80. On Kansas and Dred Scott, see Giddings'
article in *Anti-Slavery Bugle,* October 3, 1857; Giddings to Roger Taney, n.d.,
in Cleveland *Leader,* n.d., copied by the *Bugle,* April 25, 1857. The quotations
are in Giddings, *Speeches,* 510; Giddings to Editor, *Ohio Statesman,* n.d.,
reprinted from Ashtabula *Sentinal,* n.d., copied by *National Anti-Slavery
Standard,* December 12, 1857.

struggle there for liberty and equality. "Speak of dissolution with utter contempt," he therefore advised his editor son, Addison, in 1850. "It can have no effect upon our duties, we are not to surrender our rights in order to bring in the South to the Union." In 1857, he told the Worcester Disunion Convention that the real job was to return the Union to its original purpose, not to destroy it. His program was to "increase the number of free States, until the slave power shall be dwarfed to an insignificant portion of our federal Union" and to elect no man to office "who hesitates to exert his political and moral influence to carry out the designs of those who established our government." Once the national conscience was convinced, it would confront the Southern states with the alternatives either to *"unbind the heavy burdens and let the oppressed go free;* or, if you prefer to maintain that institution, *'perish with it.' "*[42] This was both his unionism and his disunionism.

Increasingly willing in the 1850s to substitute radical and humanitarian arguments for constitutionalism, Giddings' actual political stance did not change significantly. He did, to be sure, speak to the natural rights of Negroes. By 1859, he challenged the government directly when, in his impatience with attempts to enforce the Fugitive Slave Law, he concluded that if legal appeals did not free men who broke that law then "finding this government to have become *'destructive of the lives, the liberties and the happiness of its citizens,* [the people would] ALTER OR ABOLISH IT; and *organize its powers in such form as to them shall seem most likely to effect their* SAFETY AND HAPPINESS.' "[43] He even went so far as to organize a Sons

---

[42]Giddings to Addison Giddings, February 3, 1850, G-OHS; Giddings to Thomas W. Higginson, January 7, 1857, in State Disunion Convention Held at Worcester, Massachusetts, January 15, 1857, *Proceedings* (Boston: Printed for the Committee, 1857), 9.

[43]Giddings to Ralph Plumb, May 4, 1859, in *Anti-Slavery Bugle,* May 14, 1859.

of Liberty Vigilance Committee in his own Ashtabula County to defy the Fugitive Slave Law, just as the original Sons of Liberty had defied the unjust incursions of Great Britain.

Yet in the House he continued to play by the rules. He used the prestige of his extended tenure and his mastery of procedure to support in 1855 an antislavery program virtually identical to action he had proposed in 1839–1840, adding only the repeal of the Fugitive Slave Law. Thus he recognized the limits under which Congressmen acted. "While speaking or acting on the subject of legislation," he wrote to Marius Robinson of the Ohio *Anti-Slavery Bugle,* "we speak and act under the limits, and restrictions of the Constitution. Were we to attempt legislation beyond its boundaries such legislation would not only be void but would render Congress contemptible."[44]

So too he helped organize the Republican party and stumped extensively for its candidates. In Congress, his course was little different from that of most other Republicans. He joined his fellow antislavery Congressmen in seeking a repeal of the Kansas–Nebraska Act and a return to the policy of the Northwest Ordinance. He joined his fellow Republicans in condemning Justice Roger Taney's decision in the Dred Scott case, charging that the court had violated its constitutional power. He joined the coalition of Republicans and Douglas Democrats in opposing the admission of Kansas under the proslavery Lecompton constitution. Thus from his first session, when he and Adams had stood almost alone in opposing the slave power, Giddings, maintaining the same platform, found himself now in the mainstream of Northern politics. His role as a congressional protester had, as events moved his way, been rendered largely nugatory.

[44]*Congressional Globe,* 33rd Cong., 2d sess., 318–319; Giddings to Marius Robinson, March 20, 1855, in *Anti-Slavery Bugle,* March 31, 1855.

Finally what censure had failed to accomplish in 1842 and what partisan redistricting in the Western Reserve had failed to accomplish in 1852, ill health, advancing age, and Republican politics finally achieved in 1858 when Giddings was defeated for renomination to the House seat which he had held for twenty years. But unlike Cassius Clay, Giddings had come to the end of his political ambitions. He had hoped to be sent to the Senate in 1848 and 1850, and in 1856 had eyed the House Speakership, but he had been denied all these. Now his constituents had denied him renomination, and even that he accepted graciously, perhaps because at each election during the 1850s he had considered retiring. In all likelihood he had chosen otherwise largely because he needed the income his post provided and because in Congress he could still do most good for the antislavery cause.

But at last the congressional career was over, and, in March 1859, Giddings returned to his home in Jefferson as a private man still fascinated by the national scene. Like abolitionists generally he was thrilled, in the fall of 1859, by John Brown's raid. Speaking in Philadelphia a few days after the Harpers Ferry incident, he attested his sympathy by repeating a comment he had once made in Congress. "Were I a slave, I would escape, if in my power, though compelled to walk upon the dead bodies of slaveholders from Mississippi to Malden." Denying complicity in the venture and regretting the shedding of blood, he did wish that Brown had escaped with some slaves. Had he done so, without shedding blood, "he would have deserved the character of a hero." As it was, he wrote Oliver Johnson, the event "should be sufficient to satisfy all that we cannot be long held in subjection[.]"[45]

Exhilarated by Brown's exploit, Giddings tried to hold the Republican party up to some measure of antislavery truth. At the nominating convention in 1860, he walked out when

[45]*Liberator*, November 4, 1859. On the complicity charge, see *National Anti-Slavery Standard*, October 29, 1859. Giddings to Gerrit Smith, October 20, 1859, S-SU; Giddings to Oliver Johnson, November 6, 1859, GJ-LC.

the platform committee rejected his motion to insert "the declaration of human rights and the assertion that human gov[ernmen]ts are based upon them" into the platform. "I took my hat," he wrote to Gerrit Smith, describing the flourish which he had created, "and in the presence of the vast multitude walked out of the hall."[46] This gesture by the old warrior worked; the phrases were put into the document, and Giddings returned to the convention floor. For all that, however, he was still willing to temporize with the realities of politics and within the month wrote to his old Whig messmate Abraham Lincoln advising him to dodge all questions about applying the Chicago platform. After the election, again combining politics and principle, he pressured Lincoln to appoint to cabinet posts at least three radical Republicans, that is, men who denied the constitutionality of the Fugitive Slave Law.[47]

His voice, however, was that of the past, respected but little heeded. Giddings was simply too sick, too tired, and too old to keep up a sustained fight. He made little comment on the events of the crisis winter, the new administration, or the coming of the Civil War. From his patronage post as Consul General in Montreal, he watched events, trying in a small way to further the interests of freedom through diplomacy. Even that strained his endurance, and, having already suffered three heart attacks, he died of a fourth at the billiard table of the St. Lawrence Hotel in 1864.

❄❄❄

As his congressional colleague and son-in-law George Julian attested in his filial biography, Joshua Giddings had served the abolitionist crusade as both politician and propagandist. Both facets were part of that "agitation" which eventually

---

[46]Giddings to Gerrit Smith, May 24, 1860, S-SU.
[47]Giddings to Abraham Lincoln, June 19, 1860, Ln-LC; Giddings to Gerrit Smith, December 24, 1860, S-SU.

ended slavery in the United States. That he was no orator, that he was mild and retiring made no difference. Giddings had been a great antislavery agitator.

He was, nonetheless, constantly under attack from those more conscious of the role of agitation, for they could not accept his dual approach. The Garrisonian *Anti-Slavery Bugle*, published in his home state, praised Giddings' opposition to Texas annexation and the Mexican War, but condemned his remaining in the Congress whose legal basis, by his own argument, had been destroyed. Elizur Wright, more politically attuned, could extend only partial praise. "Up to a certain point," Wright wrote, "Giddings is true blue in his feelings," though, he added, "rather weak in his judgment." Or, as the Liberty party spokesman Henry Stanton put it, Giddings' stand on emancipation was like that of a temperance clergyman "who apologiz[ed] for rumselling or the deacon who [kept] a respectable rumselling hotel."[48]

Even his more radical stance after the Mexican War did not garner unstinted praise. When Garrison at the 1848 New England Anti-Slavery Convention praised him "for his fearless and unsparing rebuke of the slave power on the floor of Congress" and for his "frank co-operation with the most unpopular measures of the anti slavery movement in Ohio," he added that Giddings' support of the federal Constitution "greatly impair[ed] the force of his moral testimony." Samuel May of Leicester and Wendell Phillips both linked Giddings with Charles Sumner in his earnest and noble political opposition to slavery; yet both of them criticized him for having made "concessions to the Slaveholder" and given his "immensely powerful aid in supporting that government, which is the great Engine of the Slave Power for accomplishing all its ends." Like all other antislavery congressmen, Giddings was, the Foster faction claimed, "shorn of [his] moral strength, and . . . rendered comparatively powerless in the presence of

[48]*Anti-Slavery Bugle*, September 18, 1846, April 9, 1847; *Chronotype*, July 9, 1847; Henry B. Stanton to Giddings, November 15, 1847, G-OHS.

slaveholders, while [he] solemnly [swore] to respect the alleged pro-slavery compromises of the Constitution."[49]

Somewhat perplexed and sometimes annoyed at the abolitionist carping, Giddings persisted in his course. He did not have a brilliant mind. He lacked training in formal logic. He was inconsistent. But, confronting reality as he saw it, he responded with an independence of mind, a forthrightness of character, and a steadiness of principle, which fitted well with the image he portrayed of the frontiersman. In 1855 he wrote Marius Robinson that his views of the Constitution might be wrong, but that he had come to them after much reflection and that he would continue to fight for liberty according to his own ideals. "Were I to lay aside my own judgment in order to carry out your views my identity would cease," he declared. "I should become a collatteral [sic] appendage to yourself. I should no longer be a man."[50]

Giddings was not a purist. He was too much of a realist to try to solve all problems with abstract idealism. He knowingly relied on and worked within imperfect institutions. Aware that purging his soul of the sin and guilt of slavery was necessary, he knew also that it was insufficient to end the reality of bondage, so he used political parties and the Congress as vehicles for his message and sought to convert them so as to achieve the action he sought. He grasped what Elizur Wright glimpsed, Stephen Foster flailed for, and Maria Chapman understood best of all, that efficient organization was the requisite of accomplishment. Giddings took the steps and made the compromises that enabled him to bring politics to the service of antislavery, and it was this which separated him from his fellow crusaders. By so doing, he met frustration

[49]*Liberator,* June 9, 1848; Samuel May, Jr., to Richard D. Webb, February 8, 1856, M-BPL; Wendell Phillips to Samuel J. May, n.d., M-CU; Irving Bartlett, *Wendell Phillips, Brahmin Rebel* (Boston: Beacon Press, 1961), 167–168; resolution presented to the Western New York Anti-Slavery Society Convention, January 16, 1851, in *North Star,* January 23, 1851.
[50]Giddings to Marius Robinson, March 20, 1855, in *Anti-Slavery Bugle,* March 31, 1855.

and defeat. But that his choice of method was less efficacious than that of the evangel in creating a moral consensus remains still to be proved.

12

The Gentle Humanitarian: Samuel Joseph May

Of all the American abolitionists, no one better than Samuel Joseph May embodied the spirit of the Peaceable Kingdom. Active in a movement torn by ideological dispute, organizational factionalism, and personal rancor, he was loved and respected by all and universally regarded as "the angel of Anti-slavery," "whose temper [had] not been poisoned" by bitterness.[1]

May, an intimate of Maria Chapman's antislavery salon in the middle 1830s, had dropped out without garnering the customary public denunciation for heresy, but only a light and private chiding for "Shilly-Shally" during the clerical controversy.[2] Concurrently he retained his good standing in the clerical faction despite his heretical Unitarianism. Refusing to join in organizational feuding, he also refused to retreat into

[1] John Jay Chapman, *William Lloyd Garrison* (New York: Moffat, Yard, & Co., 1913), 78; Theodore Weld to Gerrit Smith, October 23, [1839], in *Letters of Theodore Dwight Weld, Angelina Grimké Weld and Sarah Grimké, 1822–1844*, eds. Gilbert H. Barnes and Dwight L. Dumond (New York: D. Appleton-Century Co., 1934), 811.

[2] Maria W. Chapman to Deborah Weston, March 14, 1839, W-BPL.

privacy. Totally apolitical, he was a close associate of Gerrit Smith and eagerly watched the Liberty party and its successors throughout the 1840s and 1850s. At the same time, he supported practical politicians like John Quincy Adams and Joshua Giddings.

Early in their careers, May warned Garrison that doctrinal rigidity and extremism would turn away potential followers. Yet for forty years he remained the Boston leader's friend, subject to occasional scoldings but never to ideological denunciation. No matter that his peacemaking efforts in the movement failed, as they did in 1850 when, at a meeting he sponsored in Syracuse to reunite the American Society and the Liberty party, difference exploded in controversy between Stephen Foster, Parker Pillsbury, and Charles Remond on the one hand and Gerrit Smith and Frederick Douglass on the other. May continued to work serenely with both factions.

Samuel J. May was born in Boston in 1797, son of Joseph May, a prominent member of King's Chapel and a molder of early American Unitarianism. A patrician, Joseph May was also a man of conscience, concerned for the common weal. May's mother was Dorothy Sewall, a descendant of Judge Sewall, famous a century earlier for condemning the Salem witches and then publicly repenting his action, as well as for writing one of the first American antislavery tracts. Their home was near that of William Ellery Channing on whom young Samuel frequently called, developing a friendship, which lasted until the elder's death in 1842. His continuing dialogue with Channing was only part of May's superlative education. After attending private schools in Boston, he took his bachelor's degree from Harvard and received his theological training at the Divinity School in Cambridge. Diligent and thoughtful, he was not a brilliant student, though he acquitted himself creditably enough. He had taught school while still a student and after his final year at Harvard. Then, when he had completed his theological training, he practice-preached for a year, ranging as far afield as Richmond, Virginia. Finally, in 1822, he accepted the pastorate of the Brooklyn Unitarian church, the only Unitarian parish in Connecticut.

Moving from Boston to Brooklyn, May left the stronghold of religious liberalism to enter a bastion of Calvinist orthodoxy where Unitarians were regarded as anti-Christian heretics. It made him neither a dogmatic Unitarian nor a convert to orthodoxy, but strengthened his liberal convictions as it trained him to meet opposition generously though firmly. Developing his faith in the transcendental brotherhood of man, he inevitably offended the orthodox. He refused to wear the customary black gown and preacher's bands because to him they symbolized a religion removed from everyday life. He offered communion to all, whether or not they were church members. He baptized indifferently by immersion or sprinkling, according to the preference of the recipient. He preached that Sunday should be a pleasant and refreshing day of rest.[3]

May's Unitarianism emphasized the unity of God and the manhood of Christ. Jesus, particularly in the Sermon on the Mount, showed men the way to salvation, which they must act on their own to achieve. Not "wholly prone to evil," but "made in the image of God," man was "a partaker of the Divine nature." The human condition rather than the fine points of theology, therefore, was the focus of May's religion. Doctrinal questions took second place to "the *great moral principles,* on which [was] based the Kingdom of Christ–the Kingdom

[3]George B. Emerson, Samuel May, and Theodore J. Mumford, *Memoir of Samuel Joseph May* (Boston: Roberts Press, 1873; Reissued Boston: American Unitarian Association, 1882), 88–90. The first 128 pages constitute May's autobiography, written about 1864 and covering the years to 1829.

of righteousness." The whole meaning of religious liberalism was to make religion serviceable to men. When May said that he did "not feel so much united to a Unitarian, who [was] not an Abolitionist, as [he did] to one of any other sect, who [was] an Abolitionist," he had clearly established his order of priorities.[4]

Like Channing, May sought full realization of men's Christlike character in the world. His career was an unsparing delineation of society's failings. Challenging without fear or favor those institutions and practices which kept men from transcending their mortality, he singled out as most pervasive that "lust for wealth, which has plunged many of our citizens into reckless if not unprincipled speculations, and the arts of dishonest traffic."[5]

May did not, however, seek to reform the American economy but rather the social ills, which the drive for riches bred. Dismayed by intemperance, "political discord," land speculation, and slavery, he sought "the complete and harmonious developement [sic] of all the intellectual and moral powers" that man possessed. Education, so essential to wideranging reform, must not teach "the multitude of learners to think alike, and speak alike, and move alike," but rather help them to "become what God has made [them] capable of being."[6]

[4]Samuel J. May, Dedication Sermon for Church of the Messiah, Syracuse, New York, April 14, 1853, from an unidentified clipping, Book of Church Records, Syracuse Unitarian Church (May Memorial Church). May to William L. Garrison, February 21, 1837, in *Liberator,* March 4, 1837.

[5]Samuel J. May, *A Discourse on Slavery in the United States, Delivered in Brooklyn, July 3, 1831* (Boston: Garrison and Knapp, 1832), 4. Similar concern about wealth can be found throughout May's writing and his life; see, for example, his letter to Samuel May, Jr., June 14, 1842, M-CU; May to Henry W. Bellows, May 4, 1858, B-MHS.

[6]Samuel J. May, "Errors in Common Education: An Address Delivered at the Lyceum in Brooklyn, Conn., Oct. 22, 1828," *American Journal of Education* 4 (1829): 214; and Samuel J. May (pseud. Derby), "Individual Development," *American Annals of Education and Instruction* 4 (1834): 370.

In an era when educational innovation emphasized social control and rote learning, May's pedagogical ideas placed him among the vanguard of imaginative reformers. Reflecting the educational theories of his brother-in-law Bronson Alcott, May urged the Essex County Teachers Convention in 1844 to "love the unlovely [and to be] especially mindful of the neglected, ill-looking, ill-dressed, ill-tempered, not wishing them away, but rejoicing to have an opportunity to do for them in school what is not done for them at home. Let this class of children," he continued, "be at once made to feel that they are really cared for; that they are not shunned, but sought after; not despised, but valued; not doubted but trusted; not despaired of, but hoped for . . . ," and they will "put their unloveliness away."[7]

May's theory of general reform was like his theory of education. If the favored classes would love the unlovely then both groups would combine to cast out the evils besetting American society. The reformer's role was to waken this love, not to plan the change. As May observed in 1832 while explaining antislavery immediatism, "None of the great moral changes that have taken place in our world, were effected precisely in the way pointed out by those, who first cried out, 'They must be made!' The first step, in all public (as well as individual) improvement," he averred, "is to make the public feel there is need of improvement." The effort embraced May's three vocations: preacher, teacher, and reformer. Consequently there was little distinction among them. The office of all was to lead men to transcendental self-fulfillment. "For all our penny wisdom, for all our soul-destroying slavery to habit," he once said, quoting Emerson, "it is not to be doubted that all men have sublime thoughts; that all men value the few real hours of life; they love to be heard; they love to be caught up into the vision of principles. . . . Discharge to men the priestly

[7]Emerson et al., *Memoir of S. J. May,* 181, quoting May to Horace Mann, October 20, 1844.

office,and, present or absent, you shall be followed with their love as by an angel."[8]

❦

No sooner had he assumed the priestly office in Brooklyn than May plunged into reform. Already a peace enthusiast, he joined one of his parishioners, George Benson, a retired, well-to-do merchant from Providence, in forming the Windham County Peace Society in 1826. As pastor of the First Parish, serving ex officio, therefore, on the school committee, he initiated a series of state education conventions. He also helped found a Sunday School, a social library, and a lyceum in the village. And, to set a good example, he foreswore all alcoholic beverages, joined the American Total Abstinence Society, and converted much of the village to teetotalism.

May also promoted antislavery. In 1819, while still a student, he had heard the rising New England political leader, Daniel Webster, denounce the Missouri Compromise and the African slave trade. Impressed by Webster's logic and further influenced by reading the antislavery *Letters* of John Rankin, May soon joined the American Colonization Society and, in 1829, formed a local branch in Brooklyn. Yet he was not wholly satisfied with African colonization. He had met and talked with Benjamin Lundy the year before and had invited him to lecture from his Brooklyn pulpit. But, in 1830, when he heard Garrison launch his vigorous attack against slavery, he was wholly won, in a way that Cassius Clay was not, to the abolitionism which shaped his life for the next forty years.

May accepted the young journalist's contention that

[8]*Liberator*, March 10, 1832; *Services in Honor of Samuel Joseph May Held in the May Memorial Church, Syracuse, N.Y., on Unveiling a Monument to His Memory Upon the Anniversary of His Birth, Sunday, Sept. 12, 1886* (Boston: George H. Ellis, 1886), 29. The quotation is from Ralph Waldo Emerson's "Divinity School Address."

"holding human beings as property" was "a sin of the deepest dye" and that expiation lay in individual repentance. Still, his position was less absolute than Garrison's. One might not, he thought, "insist that *all* slaveholders [were] sinners of the deepest dye," for their guilt must be measured by their awareness of sin.[9] His Unitarianism thus led May to differ substantially from the Calvinist orthodoxy in which Samuel Cornish and Elizur Wright were trained. May's interest was not in sin but in man's relationship to other men. Guided in reform as in religion by the brotherhood of all men, he responded most sharply to the prejudice that, in his eyes, underlay slavery, rather than the sin that slaveholding involved. This sensitivity molded his antislavery career and led him to honest, if not sophisticated, explorations of prejudice and its effect on the condition and aspirations of black Americans.

May's first antislavery sermon was derived from a sermon on prejudice which he had prepared in June 1830, at the height of the anti-Masonic hysteria, for a Masonic convention in Brooklyn. Asked to preach in one of Boston's churches shortly after he first heard Garrison, May penciled appropriate illustrations in the margin to turn that sermon into an antislavery discourse. The response it provoked prefigured the rejection abolitionists were long to encounter. "The minister of the church . . . spoke to [May] in terms of stern reproof, and said [he] should never enter his pulpit again."[10] Thus began May's systematic exclusion from most Boston pulpits.

Still, there was no objection to the sermon except as it touched on slavery, for the American Unitarian Association later published it as a tract with the references to Negroes excised. May soon regretted having permitted this censored version to be published and later revised it to deal expressly

[9]May to William L. Garrison, November 24, 1834, G-BPL.
[10]Samuel May, Jr., "Journal," June 24, 1830, M-MHS; the quotation is from S. J. May's recounting of the affair to the 30th Anniversary Celebration of the American Anti-Slavery Society in 1863, in *Liberator,* December 25, 1863.

with color prejudice, publishing it anew as an antislavery essay.[11]

Northerners, he contended, tolerated slavery because of their prejudice. "It is this prejudice," he said, speaking from Ralph Waldo Emerson's pulpit, "which checks our rising sympathies, and reconciles us to the conclusion, that slavery and degradation are their irrevocable lot." The enslavement of twenty white Americans would bring loud protest, but the bondage of two million black Americans was justified on grounds of presumed racial inferiority, an inferiority to which whites reduced blacks by denying them education and the protection of the law. "We are," May concluded, "prejudiced against the blacks; and our prejudices are indurated . . . by the secret, vague consciousness of the wrong we are doing them. Men are apt," he added pointedly, "to dislike those most, whom they have injured most."[12]

Even his antislavery colleagues had to give up their false notions of racial inferiority, so May continued to argue the matter. Racial differences, which he did acknowledge, inhered not in blackness of skin but in environmental factors like climate, food, and occupation. He begged white Americans therefore to admit blacks to a full "enjoyment of the same privileges, and the exercise of the same prerogatives as others." That he did not allow the sentimentality into which his compassion sometimes ran to cloud the rigor of his argument, he demonstrated in an admonition to a friend in 1834. "We Abolitionists are not so foolish as to require or wish that ignorant negroes should be considered wise men, or that vicious negroes should be considered virtuous men, or poor negroes to be considered rich men. All we demand for them," he continued, "is that negroes shall be permitted, encouraged, assisted to become as wise, as virtuous, and as rich as they can, and be acknowledged to be just what they have become,

---

[11]Samuel J. May, *On Prejudice* (Printed for the American Unitarian Association, Boston: Gray and Bowen, 1830); May, *Discourse on Slavery.*
[12]May's sermon, May 29, 1831, reported in *Liberator,* July 23, 1831.

and be treated accordingly." If equal treatment and opportunity resulted in racial intermarriage, May answered those who played on irrational fear of "amalgamation," so be it. "Such connections would be incomparably more honorable to the whites, as well as more consistent with the laws of God, and the virtue of our nation, than that illicit intercourse which is now so common especially at the south."[13]

For May, the Negro was a man and a brother. "I wish to stand on the broad platform of a common brotherhood, on the summit level of humanity," he said in 1846. "On that platform every man should be allowed to stand, if he can. Nay, more, if he falter, he should be holden up. If he fall, he should be raised again. And never until he has degraded himself below the reach of recovery, should we abandon him, and give up the hope of his becoming a true man."[14] On these propositions May rested his antislavery career.

"Though I have written but little on the subject of slavery," May observed in 1832, "I have talked much about it in the Lyceum, in stage coaches, in social circles—and in my public prayers, in the house of God, his oppressed children are never forgotten." As teacher and preacher, but not yet as professional reformer, he pressed the antislavery case. Less precipitate than Garrison, May remained a member of the American Colonization Society despite his new allegiance to immediatism. In March 1831, he found Garrison's attack on the society "too severe" and "too indiscriminate." He was pre-

[13]May, *Discourse on Slavery*, 23. Providence Anti-Slavery Society, *The Report and Proceedings of the First Annual Meeting . . . With a Brief Exposition of the Principles and Purposes of the Abolitionists* (Providence: H. H. Brown, 1833), 7; May's own copy bears the notation that he wrote the *Report*. Samuel J. May, *Some Recollections of Our Anti-Slavery Conflict* (Boston: Fields, Osgood & Co., 1869), 29. Samuel J. May, *The Right of Colored People to Education, Vindicated . . .* (Brooklyn, Conn.: Advertiser Press, 1833), 23–24.

[14]*National Anti-Slavery Standard*, December 10, 1846, quoting a May sermon, November 1, 1846.

pared to stay in the society until something better replaced it, and he did not resign from it until the spring of 1833. He was equally reluctant to damn compensated emancipation summarily, for not only was it better than war but it was just in itself, making the entire nation bear the burden of the abolition of slavery as collectively it bore the guilt.[15]

Although May already thus deviated from the Garrisonian path, his antislavery enthusiasm was never in doubt. Hesitant about the efficacy of forming a New England Anti-Slavery Society in November 1831,[16] in January 1833 he was elected a vice-president of the new organization at its first annual meeting. He held that post in the New England Society and its successor, the Massachusetts Anti-Slavery Society, until he moved to Syracuse in 1845. He also joined in founding not only the Plainfield, Connecticut, antislavery society but also the American Anti-Slavery Society.

By the end of 1833, therefore, unwilling as he was to play the extremist, May had become a central figure in the organized antislavery movement. Indeed he was on his way as a professional reformer from the time he was caught up in the fight over Prudence Crandall's school in Canterbury, Connecticut. Young Miss Crandall had opened a school for girls in the village in 1832. Shortly thereafter, at the request of a local Negro, Crandall admitted his daughter. At once incensed villagers, led by Crandall's neighbor, Andrew Judson, demanded that the child be dismissed. When Crandall refused and the demands continued, she decided to turn her school wholly into one for "young ladies and little misses of color." The decision infuriated lawyer Judson and his following.[17]

[15]The quotations are from May to William L. Garrison, December 17, [1832], in *Abolitionist*, February 18, 1833; May to William L. Garrison, March 26, 1831, G-BPL. See also May, *Discourse on Slavery*, 20.

[16]May to [William L. Garrison], January 1, 1857, in *Anti-Slavery Bugle*, January 17, 1857.

[17]Resolutions offered by Rufus Adams to anti-Crandall public meeting, March 9, 1833, quoted in May, *Right of Colored People to Education*, 8.

May, alert to good causes and quick to detect prejudice, soon learned what was happening in the neighboring village. In February 1833, he offered Crandall his help, warning her simultaneously, however, that his dubious reputation as a Unitarian might do her more harm than good. The young schoolteacher, devoid of local support, readily accepted May's help and that of young George Benson, son of May's Peace Society cohort. So on March 9, 1833, May and Benson went over to Canterbury to defend the young woman at a public meeting called by Judson. There they found, too, to their delight, Arnold Buffum, Rhode Island antislavery enthusiast and agent of the New England Anti-Slavery Society.

The meeting was called to order, and Judson quickly ruled that only town residents could speak. Since neither Benson, Buffum, nor May qualified, all were denied the floor. Charges against Crandall were made, and she was advised to close her school, but she and her supporters went unheard. Only when the meeting adjourned did May and Buffum have a chance to address those of Crandall's fellow-townsmen who chose to listen—out of doors on the village·green. There May condemned Judson for playing upon prejudice and resorting to alarmism. He contended that the meeting had denied due process to Crandall and had refused her representation. The issue in Canterbury involved not only the town but the larger community, he said; therefore, he and his associates had a right, even an obligation, to speak. In denying them this right, Judson had violated the principles of free speech and fair play, debauched justice, and encouraged prejudice. "You twanged every chord that could stir the coarser passions of the human heart," he told the lawyer. "You relied upon the prejudices of the people; and having excited them to the utmost, hurried on a decision which you plainly foresaw would gratify your wishes."[18]

But it was Judson, not May, who had the public's ear and

[18]A summary of the events at the Canterbury public meeting is contained in ibid., 4–14. Quotations on 9 and 11. See also May, *Recollections,* 45.

sympathy. He and his townsmen persuaded the Connecticut legislature to prohibit the establishment within the state of any school for nonresident Negroes and to forbid anyone's teaching them without the consent of the citizens of the town in which they were to be taught. Crandall, on May's advice, ignored the new statute, and May posted bond for the good behavior of her students. Determined to test the law, he encouraged her to challenge it directly. But court battles and public defense cost more than either Brooklyn or Canterbury could afford. Opportunely, however, Arthur Tappan, a long-time friend of the May family and now a resident of New Haven, provided money for lawyers and a subsidy for a pro-Crandall paper, the *Unionist*. After a first trial, which resulted in a hung jury, a second, in October 1833, convicted Crandall of breaking the new law. Her counsel then appealed the case and the constitutionality of the law to the Connecticut Court of Errors. A full decision was never rendered, however, because the court refused to hear the case on the grounds that the state's attorney had presented a faulty brief. There the matter died.[19]

Even so, the antislavery forces could claim some measure of victory at Canterbury. They had used the case skillfully to win wider support. May had arranged, for instance, that when Crandall, a highly respectable young woman, was arrested, she would spend one night in jail, occupying—by special arrangement and after a thorough cleaning—the cell of a recently incarcerated murderer. It was excellent propaganda, but it was hard on Crandall and her students and fatal to her school. Her well was polluted, rocks were thrown

[19]Samuel J. May, "A Tribute to Arthur Tappan," in Lewis Tappan, *The Life of Arthur Tappan* (New York: Hurd & Houghton, 1870), 154–158, originally published in the New York *Independent*. The arguments presented in the second Crandall trial, October 1833, are contained in *Abolitionist* (November 1833), 161–164. For the summary of the entire court proceeding, see *Report of the Arguments of Counsel, in the Case of Prudence Crandall, Plff. in Error, vs. State of Connecticut, before the Supreme Court of Errors, at Their Session at Brooklyn, July Term, 1834*... (Boston: Garrison & Knapp, 1834).

through the school windows, and arson was attempted against the building. In the end, even May, who had from the begining counseled defiance, advised Crandall to close the school. It was he who, "mortified and indignant," went to Canterbury to tell the students. He had understood racial prejudice before; now he had shared in the humiliations and defeats it imposed.[20]

Scarcely anything better could have been devised to make May change his mind about an antislavery agency. He had refused numerous requests to act for the Massachusetts and American AntiSlavery societies in order to continue his Unitarian missionary work in hostile Connecticut. Yet, by the time the Canterbury fight was over, his parishioners were complaining that antislavery occupied too much of his time and brought disrepute upon their church. They were undoubtedly right, at least in part, for even his wife gently scolded him for spending too much time away from home on antislavery business, and their complaints made May uneasy about his choice of priorities. But he was now ready, in January 1835, to accept an agency from the New England Anti-Slavery Society. Still-orthodox Elizur Wright thought May's Unitarianism and lack of business sense disqualified him. Mrs. May was sure that the poorly paid peripatetic life of an agent ill-suited a married man. Even May realized that the clamor of the city and the harassments of constant travel were not for him. Still, for fifteen months he canvassed New England, exhorting the people to abolition, lecturing, writing, and collecting funds.[21]

His job was exciting, too, for it came at the very peak of

[20]May's reminiscences to the 30th Anniversary Celebration of the American Anti-Slavery Society, in *Liberator*, December 25, 1863; Almira Crandall to George Benson, July 9, 1833, G-BPL; the quotation is in William L. Garrison to May, September 29, 1834, G-BPL.

[21]For May's antislavery activities and his wife's complaints, see her letters to him, 1833–1834, M-CU. See also May to Amos A. Phelps, March 18, 1834, P-BPL; May to Samuel E. Sewall, January 14, 1835, G-BPL; Elizur Wright to Amos A. Phelps, January 13, 1835, P-BPL; Phelps to Charlotte Phelps, March 6, 1835, P-BPL; May to Lucretia May, May 13, 1835, M-CU.

antiabolitionist mob activity. There were rumors in New York that every prominent abolitionist had been assigned an assassin. Elizur Wright barred and bolted his house against riot. In Boston, Henry Benson wrote his father, neither Garrison nor May would be safe should they attend an antiabolition meeting in Faneuil Hall. It was not just idle gossip or paranoid delusion. In New York the year before, a mob had burned Lewis Tappan's house, and in Boston in 1835 another mob threatened Garrison with lynching. The dangers only convinced May that he must continue his work, homesick and guilty at leaving his family though he was.

His first personal encounter with mob violence came on a late summer tour in Massachusetts with the controversial George Thompson. They arrived in Haverill on August 29. The following day, May's meeting was interrupted by a mob of men and boys who had mounted a cannon outside the hall. Fearing for the safety of his audience, May dismissed them before the artillery piece was discharged. Routed, he went on to Bradford, Amesbury, West Newbury (where he had a successful meeting), then to Boston on September 5, and back to Haverill the next day to recapture the ground lost a week earlier. This time the audience was "one of the largest [he] ever addressed," he wrote his wife, and he expected a good meeting. But some Haverill residents were still determined to the contrary. "I had not spoken more than 15 or 20 minutes," he continued to his wife, "—when a parcel of rude men and boys assembled around the house and commenced throwing stones or brickbats through the windows." Even though no one brought up the cannon, May was still "obliged to dismiss the congregation," which "dispersed without molestation."[22]

The second Haverill encounter convinced May that it was unwise "to tempt the community any where to commit outrage upon us—for it will be all the more difficult afterwards to

[22]*Liberator,* September 12, 1835; May to Lucretia May, September 7, 1835, M-CU.

get a hearing from them." Yet though he perceived the long-range ill-effects of mobs and though he took no joy in such dangers, he persisted in his lecturing. "When the principalities and powers are combined against us, it behoves us to be stead-fast, immoveable." Thus for the rest of the tour and through-out his antislavery career, May endured mobs, not with the enthusiasm of a Stephen Foster, but with a slogging determina-tion to ride out the storm until "the right to discuss the subject of Slavery will be accorded to us. . . ."[23]

That right was also threatened in 1836 by government. Governor Edward Everett of Massachusetts, sensitive to the economic ties between North and South and therefore respon-sive to Southern complaints, sought new laws to curb abolition-ist propaganda. At once, Massachusetts antislavery leaders requested a legislative hearing, carefully planning their appearance before the appropriate committee. May would discuss the purposes, course, and progress of the antislavery cause. Garrison would answer charges that their propaganda incited slave rebellion. Then lawyers Ellis Gray Loring and Samuel E. Sewell, May's cousin, would present the legal argu-ment against restrictive legislation. It was a careful plan, to be executed without histrionics by men of assured competence.

At the state house the plan went awry. The committee was openly antagonistic. Other abolitionists were insistent on add-ing their testimony, occasionally in a manner openly offensive to the legislators. When Representative Lucas called the hear-ings improperly timed, May responded that the governor's speech with its apparent predisposition against the reformers had made them act at once in order to save their freedom to act at all. To this, Lucas retorted that the state would never infringe upon civil rights. May became involved in sharp exchange with Lucas over the pictorial illustrations common in antislavery propaganda, which the latter charged were designed to incite servile revolt. Finally Charles Follen, a politi-

[23]The first quotation is in May to William L. Garrison, September 2, 1835, G-BPL; the others in May to Lucretia May, September 7, 1835, M-CU.

cal refugee and avowed German revolutionary, stirred committee ire when he charged that the tone of its hearings would spark mob violence. Chairman George Lunt immediately ruled that Follen had shown disrespect to the committee. May jumped to Follen's defense and was put down by the Chair. "Whatever you, Sir—and your associates may think of the remarks of Dr. Follen," replied Lunt, "it is for the committee to decide whether they are proper or improper. You are not to dictate to us in what manner we shall regulate the proceedings of this examination. You have no right to claim from us a hearing on this subject. It is a matter of special favor on our part, that you are admitted to this interview at all. . . ." May was not silenced. "We are not here, Sir, as culprits. We do not feel like culprits, nor do we mean to act as such. . . . We have come [before this committee] in the hope that we may do something to induce the State of Massachusetts to take a stand, worthy of herself—yes—to stand up as a bulwark that shall stay, and turn back, the proud waves of oppression, that are rolling over the land." Unmoved, the committee held to its ruling, and the session ended.[24]

A second hearing, which May requested to establish their right to be heard, ended equally disastrously. The implications were discouraging: "The Union is practically dissolved," May told the New England Anti-Slavery Convention a few weeks later; "the Constitution is no longer the supreme law of the land. The Constitution secures to us the freedom of speech, but we cannot enjoy the immunities of the Constitution as citizens, unless we shut our mouths!"[25]

[24]Plans for presentation at the committee hearings are in William L. Garrison to Helen E. Garrison, March 5, 1836, G-BPL. For the hearings themselves, see Massachusetts Anti-Slavery Society, *An Account of the Interviews Which Took Place on the Fourth and Eighth of March between a Committee of the Massachusetts Anti-Slavery Society, and the Committee of the Legislature* (Boston: Massachusetts Anti-Slavery Society, 1836); the quotations appear on 10.

[25]New England Anti-Slavery Convention, *Proceedings . . . Held in Boston, May 24, 25, 26, 1836* (Boston: Isaac Knapp, 1836), 52.

Shortly after the state house fracas, May resigned his antislavery agency, returned briefly to his Brooklyn parish, and then moved to the Unitarian church in South Scituate near Boston. There he stayed for six years, combining with his pastoral duties a good measure of antislavery activity. He largely ran the Old Colony Anti-Slavery Society, worked on the business committees of various American, New England, and Massachusetts antislavery conventions, and served as a vice-president of both the American and the Massachusetts Anti-Slavery societies. Even in his church he engaged in antislavery action, for when he resigned in 1842, it was partly because he had challenged the church's segregation of black parishioners in special pews.

When he left South Scituate, May became principal of the State Normal School at Lexington, and there the issue of prejudice arose again. He insisted that qualified black students be admitted to the school. Although only one student was involved directly, May firmly upheld the right of Mary Miles to a normal school education against state board of education secretary Horace Mann, who argued that practical considerations forbade him to "alienate those whose support he desperately needed to keep his public-school mission alive." May had anticipated the trouble and had even offered to resign only months after he took the post, foreseeing "the difficulty, that might arise, between the Board of Education and [himself], if a coloured girl should happen to apply for admission."[26] Yet once the occasion presented itself, May stayed to fight.

As he had earlier told Mann, he reminded him in February 1843 that he would not drop his antislavery work "for the sake of the school" but would, on the contrary, "without neglecting [his] duty to the school" continue that work. The immediate issue that had produced May's note was his having

[26]Carleton Mabee, "A Negro Boycott to Integrate Boston Schools," *New England Quarterly* 41 (1968): 347; May to Horace Mann, September 29, 1842, Ma-MHS.

taken a group of pupils to a Waltham antislavery meeting on a Saturday evening. "It happened to be fine sleighing—and several of the young ladies expressed a longing desire to take a ride. I told them where I was going.—They all at once were eager to accompany me. . . ." And off they had gone.[27] May could see no grounds for complaint. Having made his point, he continued to run the school until 1844, maintaining, unabated, his antislavery activities. If his two years at Lexington had done much for the school, they had also educated May further in the lessons of prejudice and the hazards of reform.

A peacemaker by nature, May was always disturbed and upset by controversy, and the years around 1840 were full of it. Not only did the South Scituate congregation and the school at Lexington produce hassles that immediately involved him, but the whole antislavery movement also engaged in internal wrangling, which constantly touched him. He had never accepted the vehemence with which Garrison presented his message and the violence with which he attacked his opponents. Although loyal to his friend, May rejected his language and his techniques, declined to tell atrocity stories, refused to retort to the heckler's jibe. Moreover he was baffled and appalled by his colleagues' exclusion of those with whom they did not agree. All people, he thought, should be welcome at antislavery meetings and invited to join antislavery societies. If the goal was universal brotherhood, no other course was open.[28]

May, therefore, was repelled by the bitterness and ill-will engendered by the clerical dispute and the clashes between Massachusetts and New York over society funds, leadership control, the woman question, political action, and new organization. Sometimes he avoided meetings where floor fights were

[27]May to Horace Mann, February 7, 1843, Ma-MHS.
[28]See, for example, May to William L. Garrison, March 26, 1831, G-BPL; May, *Discourse on Slavery*, 22–23; [Maria W. Chapman], *Right and Wrong in Massachusetts* (Boston: Dow & Jackson, 1839), 19.

promised; sometimes he attended them and tried to reconcile the parties. Though the various factions honored him for his position, they ignored his peacemaking until he began to question the utility of the societies. He had in 1835 praised his old friend Channing's *Essay on Slavery* but had also defended abolitionist tactics and organizations against his mentor's disapproving commentary. By 1839, however, he was less sure that Channing was wrong. Though May never abandoned organizational activity, he increasingly came to rely on individual action. Explaining why he had avoided the acrimonious 1839 annual meeting of the American Society, he wrote the eager controversialist, Henry C. Wright, "I joined the Society not with any thought of making it the keeper of my conscience, or the guide of my actions—but in the belief that those of us who thought alike on this momentous subject [of slavery] might effect more by our joint, than by individual effort." If the society claimed more than that, May continued, then he would withdraw. "I find," he told the Non-Resistance Society the same year, "that I place every year less value on organization, as I more clearly discern the power that rests in the individual." His years as a lonely Unitarian minister in the Congregational confines of Connecticut, he told Edmund Quincy, had led him to rely on individual judgment. "It has appeared to me," he explained about the factional fighting, "that you were getting to be uncharitable and sectarian—that you have felt unkindly and spoken harshly of some because they could not see their way clear to follow certain great principles as far as you have done."[29] May no longer was at ease with the Boston stalwarts.

As intellectual conviction had separated May from his Boston

---

[29]Massachusetts Anti-Slavery Society, *Annual Report...* [1835] (Boston: Isaac Knapp, 1836), 30, 35; May to Henry C. Wright, May 2, 1839, G-BPL; *Liberator,* October 11, 1839; May to Edmund Quincy, June 18, [1840], Q-MHS.

friends, so his acceptance of the Unitarian pulpit in Syracuse separated him from the hub of old organization. He arrived in upstate New York in the spring of 1845 at the peak of abolitionist dismay over Texas annexation and was caught up at once in antislavery affairs there. As annexation led to war, May held firm to his opposition. Shortly before he had left Massachusetts, he had served with Elizur Wright in the antiannexationist Middlesex County Convention that had caused no great disturbance. But sentiments tolerated in peacetime were not so placidly received in wartime. When, on June 18, 1846, a peace meeting assembled in Syracuse's Empire House, it was invaded and taken over by a prowar faction, which forced the peace majority to leave the hall. When they reassembled in the Congregational church, they accepted the resolutions that May presented. War "except, perhaps, in an extreme case of self-defence" was "utterly repugnant to the distinctive principles of the Gospel." War with Mexico would cost America its "opportunity of giving to the other nations of this continent an illustrious example of national forbearance and magnanimity—of showing how a nation may overcome evil with good." No sooner had the resolutions been seconded than the prowar group, which had by then set up a cannon at the rear of the church, fired it twice. Although only a couple of windows were smashed, the meeting, fearing more violence, speedily adopted the resolutions and adjourned. May's good friend, Wendell Phillips, remembering the similar Haverill meeting, wrote him in jest, "I smile . . . to think how successful you are in getting up mobs! Stephen's occupation's gone—the proof is clear. You act in Connecticut. A Judson mobs. You come to Boston [—] the mobs of Oct 1835. You go into exile at Syracuse[.] lo! war mobs. Is it not clear that, summer-calm as you seem, it is but *seeming*, & underneath lies the veritable mob-compeller S.J.M?"[30]

[30]William A. White to William L. Garrison, January 27, 1845, in *Liberator*, January 31, 1845; William H. Willicott to Editor, June 21, 1846, in *National*

Luckily for May these tensions soon gave way, and life in the young city became less exciting if no less interesting to the active reformer. There were canal boys to be assisted, women's rights to be gained, and Onondaga Indians to be schooled. But inevitably the pressing national issue of slavery soon drew May back into the antislavery orbit. For him, as for Foster and Giddings, enactment of the Fugitive Slave Law marked a shift from moral protest and general political action to explicit defiance and open breaking of the law. While the Senate was still debating the bill, May attended a Fugitive Slave Convention in the Finger Lakes village of Cazenovia and pledged with his colleagues to aid fugitives and, if not to offer them arms, to encourage and advise them to use arms rather than to surrender their freedom. Just two weeks after the bill had passed, he wrote that he was expecting three or four fugitives at any moment. "We must trample this infamous law under foot," he added as he explained what he was doing, "be the consequences what they may. Fines, imprisonment shall not deter me from doing what I can for the fugitive, and the sooner and the oftener we have trials of this law, the better. It will agitate the country, as it has never been agitated before, and if *we* do right, it will hasten rather than retard the consummation, of the anti-slavery reform. I rather covet than dread the conflict."[31]

Strong language for a pacifist, May's words announced as well a new politics; to defy the law and the government, which passed and enforced it, was not a withdrawal from human government but a direct challenge to its very being. Human brotherhood forbade the requirement of the law that private citizens assist in its administration. It was, May told his parishioners, their moral duty not to obey the law as it was

---

Anti-Slavery Standard, July 2, 1846, describes the Syracuse meeting and gives the resolutions; Wendell Phillips to May, July 6, 1846, M-CU.

[31] For the Cazenovia meeting, see particularly *National Anti-Slavery Standard,* August 29, 1850; May to [?], October 2, 1850, in *North Star,* n.d., as reprinted by *Liberator,* October 25, 1850.

their moral duty "not to lie, steal, or commit murder." They were "not at liberty," he assured them, "to inflict wrong upon others, to oppress; . . . directly or indirectly to assist to make any fellow-man a slave, or consent to his being enslaved. The command of God is upon you," he exhorted them, "to refuse to do anything, that this fugitive slave law requires at your hand."[32]

An activist since the Crandall affair, May both preached and practiced his message of defiance. Early in March 1851 he appeared at a local antislavery convention with five fugitive slaves. Surrounded by the black men, he led his audience to express public defiance of the law. "Shall these fugitives be taken from Syracuse?" he asked. The audience answered "No." "Will you defend [them] with your lives . . .?" The answer was "Yes."[33] That their responses were not simply to showmanship and crowd psychology, his townsmen demonstrated that fall.

There had been speculation that the Fillmore administration was determined to apply the law in Syracuse, citadel of upstate antislavery. Whether or not this lay behind the arrest of Jerry McHenry, the federal government was directly challenged. The city was full of visitors on October 1, 1851; the Agricultural Fair was in session and the Liberty party was holding a local convention. About noontime the federal marshal seized McHenry and took him before the special commissioner appointed to enforce the law. Soon the news was out, and the courtroom was packed as the hearing proceeded. The district attorney, the slaveholder's agent, the marshal, the attorney for the claimant, and a "bevy of city constables," all made a show for law and order. From their midst McHenry leaped suddenly into the crowd and darted out of the building. A few blocks away, he was captured and returned to the city jail. Then, about nine o'clock that evening, the crowd, which

[32]Sermon of November 3, 1850, in *Anti-Slavery Bugle*, April 5, 1851.
[33]*Liberator*, March 21, 1851; also George Thompson to Anne W. Weston, March 7, 1851, W-BPL. Quotation in the former.

had been milling about, stormed the jail, released the prisoner, and carried him in triumph on their shoulders down Genessee Street. "No sneaking man-thief, or filthy policeman, or crafty demagogue, dare[d] show his head, in the vast concourse of humanity who sent up their joyous roar to the clouds in response to the joys of Heaven," John Thomas reported to *Frederick Douglass' Paper.* Jerry McHenry was safe. Placed in a wagon, he drove off and was gone.[34] Some days later he was spirited from his hiding place to Canada.

May's exact role in the "Jerry Rescue" is unclear. Probably he had nothing to do with the fugitive's first break for freedom, but he had helped plan the evening foray. Although he was not present at the rescue itself, he was conveniently near and could rush to the scene. Later, when the rescuers were indicted, May hoped to be among them and was disappointed when he was not indicted. Readily admitting that "he did what he *could*" toward the rescue operation, he had wanted to appear in court "to admit at once his participation in the rescue, and to base his defence upon the unconstitutionality of the slave-catching act; and ... upon its monstrous and inherent unrighteousness."[35]

Although May missed the dramatic confrontation he had planned in court, he continued his open opposition to the law. He was a chief organizer of the annual Jerry Rescue celebrations, held in Syracuse until the Civil War. He raised funds to operate the active Syracuse branch of the Underground Railroad. In mid-decade, he helped organize a Fugitive Aid Society to coordinate the Underground efforts between New York City and the Niagara frontier. He lobbied for a

[34] The account of the Jerry Rescue is from *Frederick Douglass' Paper,* October 9, 1851, based on published accounts from the Syracuse *Journal* and on a long letter, John Thomas to Frederick Douglass, October 3, 1851. See also *Liberator,* October 10, 1851.

[35] May to William H. Seward, September 7, 1853, S-UR; May to Charlotte Coffin, October 15, 1851, G-BPL; the quotations are in D. S. Whitney to William L. Garrison, November 1, 1851, in *Liberator,* November 14, 1851. See also, on May's role, his *Recollections,* 373–384.

New York personal liberty law. And through his hands passed a stream of bewildered fugitives, whom he sheltered, fed, clothed, and sent on to Canada.

❧❧❧

May's conception of the nature of law and of his relationship to it was as distinctive as the rest of his antislavery career. Unlike Foster and Garrison, who sought to destroy government and Constitution, and unlike Giddings and Clay, who sought to use them to end slavery, May was indifferent to them and largely ignored politics and government. He did not so much wish to remake society and its institutions as to lead the individual to self-realization and fulfillment.

So, because he took it less seriously, May easily changed his interpretation of the Constitution, finding it—in almost random fashion—antislavery, proslavery, or neutral on the issue of slavery as time and circumstance dictated. His 1831 *Discourse on Slavery* argued that the Constitution was an antislavery document; his 1836 "Slavery and the Constitution" found it only partially so. By 1850, May was sure that it had been explicitly framed to uphold slavery and that the courts had so interpreted it. Yet a year later, in complete reversal, he told a Toronto audience that "the fathers of our Republic never meant to perpetuate slavery," that "the language of the Constitution [did] not require such an interpretation," although as he confessed "with shame [that] it [had] generally received that interpretation." Finally, in 1854, he admitted that the various constitutional arguments he heard "kept [his] mind vacillating, until [he] was satisfied that [he] could come to no settled decision." But no matter, he added, "the question is really one of little, if any, practical importance . . . the Constitution of the United States will present no barrier to the entire abolition of slavery, whenever the people of the land are ready for that consummation of our wishes."[36]

[36]May, *Discourse on Slavery*, 10; see also on antislavery interpretation, his

May pursued the same latitudinarian course about voting. Generally an adherent of no-voting principles, he did occasionally go to the polls. He probably did not vote in 1848, because he distrusted Van Buren, although he was in favor of the Free Soil party. But if he lived in the right congressional district, he remarked in 1853, he would vote for Gerrit Smith on the Liberty party ticket. Three years later he actively supported the Republican presidential candidate, John C. Frémont, only to regret it a year later when he confessed to be appalled at "what had been said in the late campaign by the Republican leaders." Distrustful of Republican integrity and strength, he apparently did not vote at all in 1860, although he liked Lincoln and might have swallowed the party to get the man, had he thought his vote was critical.[37]

Similarly May vacillated on the question of disunion. Willing as early as 1831 to sunder the Union if that would end slavery, he wished a decade later that the subject of disunion had never been broached. After another decade he was back where he started, calling disunion "the only standard under which the friends of freedom can either consistently or successfully rally." In 1852, he saw it as the only alternative to living with the Fugitive Slave Law; yet in 1857 he argued that disunion was not necessary for abolition and that slavery could be ended under the Constitution. The next year, he again favored disunion, while in 1860 he feared that "the dissolution

---

speech, May 8, 1834, to American Anti-Slavery Society Annual Meeting, in *Liberator,* May 24, 1834. Samuel J. May, "Slavery and the Constitution," *Quarterly Anti-Slavery Magazine* 2 (1836–1837): 73–90, 226–237. May to Editor, n.d., *National Anti-Slavery Standard,* July 11, 1850. Quotations are in *North Star,* April 17, 1851; May to William L. Garrison, January 13, 1854, in *Liberator,* January 27, 1854.

[37] May to Francis Jackson, July 25, 1839, G-BPL; May to [Joshua Giddings?], August 2, 1848, M-CU; May to Samuel May, Jr., August 12, 1848, in *Liberator,* August 25, 1848; Speech at Second Annual Meeting of the Garrison Association, December 19, 1853, in *Liberator,* January 6, 1854; Remarks at Rochester Anti-Slavery Convention, February 10, 1857, in *Liberator,* February 27, 1857; May to Samuel May, Jr., November 18, 1860, G-BPL.

of our Union would indeed be a great calamity" and would
not resolve the slavery issue.[38] If there was an underlying
consistency, it was that he preferred disunion to slavery, but
Union to disunion.

About the use of violence May was clearer in his thought.
Having from his early days in antislavery predicted that the
alternative to peaceful abolition was the direct violence of
Toussaint L'Ouverture or Nat Turner, he pressed the harder
for peaceful change to avoid war. His only direct encounter
with war and battle, prior to the Civil War, was the Italian
war against Austria, which he encountered during a year of
European travel for his health in 1859. It brought home to
him the abstractions he had long preached in the cause of
peace. The soldier, committed to blind obedience and taught
to kill unknown people for unknown reasons, was degraded,
debauched, and dehumanized. "The subjection of slaves," he
concluded, "is not more entire."[39]

When, a year after his return, John Brown descended on
Harpers Ferry, May's initial responses were clearcut. "I have
not confidence in a resort to violence even for Liberty &
Humanity," he wrote shortly afterward. "Violence never leads
to unmixed good," although it might well precipitate slave
revolt or civil war. Six months later, the tremendous impact
of Brown's trial and execution made him call the fanatical
captain a *"martyr of impartial liberty,"* whose "death [was] working, and [would] work in [the slaves'] behalf, a far mightier,
happier, holier result, than would have been accomplished,

[38]May, *Discourse on Slavery,* 25; Maria Child, letter fragment, [1841?], C-BPL;
Resolution presented to American Anti-Slavery Society annual meeting, May
7, 1851, in *National Anti-Slavery Standard,* May 22, 1851; a discourse on Daniel
Webster in *Liberator,* December 31, 1852; Speech to Anti-Slavery Convention
in Rochester, February 13, 1857, in *Radical Abolitionist,* May, 1857; Remarks
to Anti-Slavery Convention in Albany, March 8, 1858, in *National Anti-Slavery
Standard,* March 20, 1858; Thanksgiving Day sermon, in *Liberator,* December
21, 1860.
[39]May, *Discourse on Slavery,* 15–16; *National Anti-Slavery Standard,* July 9,
1859, quoting a May letter written from Vienna, May 22, 1859.

if he had slain hundreds of slaveholders, and given deliverance
to thousands of their bondmen."[40] Brown's failure was his
redemption in May's eyes.

Indeed May could not join in the revolutionary rhetoric
so common to his fellows and increasingly used by them to
justify a servile insurrection, for he had never been able to
justify the violence of the American Revolution. He granted,
as early as 1835, that the slaves had as much right to throw
off their bondage as had the colonists of 1776 to seize their
freedom. But he could not encourage such action when he
was certain that "to the vast majority of that [revolutionary]
generation, which fought the battles, endured the hardships,
incurred the losses, moral and pecuniary, incident to that
conflict, . . . it was a calamity, which they never cease[d] to
deplore."[41] War did not promise a way out any more than
politics or disunion did.

The crisis of 1861 made May's dilemma no simpler. Unable
to overcome the repugnance for individual human misery
which war brought—even a war to end slavery—he was less
ready than his colleagues to visualize it as a contest for emancipation, less insistent that black troops be used, and less optimistic about its long-range benefits.

In a special sermon delivered in May 1861, he tried to
reconcile the imperatives of war with his peace principles.
The war, he said, was insane and criminal. But since it had
begun, it must be fought to its end and to the end of slavery.
Reviving the theology of an earlier day, he argued that the
war was a violent purging of sin, needless except that the
nation had not repented and cleansed itself earlier. "The loss

[40]May to [?], [December 1859], G-BPL; Samuel J. May, *An Address Delivered
Before the American Peace Society . . . May 28, 1860* (Boston: American Peace
Society, 1860), 19.

[41]May's remarks in a public debate, April 4, 1835, in *Liberator*, April 11,
1835; May, *Address Before the American Peace Society*, 13.

of tens of thousands of lives; the maimed bodies, ruined health, depraved morals of hundreds of thousands more, and the destruction of an inestimable amount of property," he said, "are now inevitable." Since the only melioration lay in quick victory, he urged the wide use of black troops. But the horror of war and his pessimism about its results never left him. Its defiance of the brotherhood of man, its denial of each individual's spark of divine goodness, its rejection of individual conscience made May's tepid support ring hollow. And he knew it. Scarcely a year after he delivered his war sermon, he wrote Garrison, "I now see more clearly than ever that war is not a means appointed or approved of God for the redress of wrongs, or the maintenance of civil or religious freedom. It is a coarse, clumsy, cruel, complicated contrivance to attempt what can only be done by moral, religious, spiritual instrumentalities."[42]

Notwithstanding his abhorrence of war, his humanitarianism made May act and be involved. He organized Syracusans to send food to the local regiment and to provide delicacies and hospital facilities for the wounded. As agent of the city's Soldiers Relief Committee, he went to Washington, visited the military hospitals, and saw the wounded brought in from the Battle of the Seven Pines. "I did not know," he wrote in horror, "that the human body could endure such mutilations—or such intrusions of lead and steel, without giving up its life."[43] Later, recalling the scene in a public address, he was overcome by emotional stress and collapsed on the stage.

Still he persisted. He worked for the Sanitary Commission, which provided medical supplies and care to soldiers at the front and behind the lines. He helped in 1863 to organize the Syracuse Freedmen's Relief Association, in which he continued active long after the war, seeing in its charitable and

[42]May's National Fast Day sermon, May 5, 1861, in *Liberator,* December 13, 1861; May to William L. Garrison, October 16, 1862, G-BPL.
[43]May to R. F. Wallcut, June 17, 1862, G-BPL.

educational activities more hope for the freedmen than he detected in the politics of Reconstruction. Yet he also recognized its inadequacy. The freedmen, long degraded by bondage, needed economic as well as personal freedom, legal equality and the franchise as well as training. Ever the preacher and teacher, however, May assigned greatest importance to providing religious and secular instruction that the freedmen might, as men and brothers, fulfill their individual potential.[44]

Twenty years earlier May had written, "We would rather strike off their chains, lay aside every weight that encumbers them, remove every impediment from their path, lend them an helping hand, if they need it, raise them up when they fall, and in every way encourage them to run the race, which is set before them, as well as us, and to stretch forward that they may attain, if they can, nearer than ourselves to the mark of our high calling—the stature of perfect men." It was paternalistic to be sure, and it reflected May's admiration of British emancipation, in which the "favoured classes of society [acted] in behalf of the most unfortunate." It reflected as well the humane benevolence and responsibility that permeated reform of this era. With it May brought to Reconstruction an understanding as sensitive as any held by the white abolitionists. He respected the integrity which the endurance of prejudice had bred in blacks. When his former Lexington student, Mary Miles, was accused by the Boston school board of insubordinate and rude behavior toward it, May had come to her defense with a response born less of theoretical brotherhood than human observation. "It may be difficult for you, Gentlemen," he had written the board, "to imagine yourselves in the position of colored persons in our community. If you would do so, I think you would not wonder, that their manners are sometimes cold and repulsive. They are apt to be so, unless they are servile and cringing." He

[44]On the "paramount importance" of education for freedmen, see May's comment in Syracuse *Daily Standard,* August 17, 1868. On economic needs, see, for example, May to William L. Garrison, April 16, 1863, G-BPL.

understood too the loss of self-respect which slavery and prejudice exacted. "Coloured men," he explained, "have not confidence enough in each other, or they do not like to be led or directed by one of their own complexion . . . [because] they have been so taught and accustomed to defer to white people, to adopt their opinions, and submit to their dictation, that they do so almost instinctively. But those of their own complexion, they have always seen depressed, treated as if they were inferiors, incapable of wise, independent action; and they have come, perhaps unconsciously, so to regard one another."[45]

Those sympathetic observations were in part the results of May's long working association with Negro leaders like Frederick Douglass in Rochester and J. W. Loguen, his Syracuse collaborator in the Underground Railroad. With them, when the war was over, May fought to end segregation in New York schools—much as twenty years earlier he had joined Garnet's struggle for equal suffrage in the state. And while he profited from association with such proud and talented men, he knew also the humble men and women who had with tremendous resolution escaped Southern bondage, and he understood from them the better the needs of those who remained in the land of oppression.[46] The dual exposure shaped May's activity for freedmen as it had always informed his quest for human brotherhood.

❦❦❦

When May died on July 1, 1871, he had been fifty years a minister and almost as long an active reformer. In death as in life he was widely marked as one of the party of hope: "genial and gentle," "morally heroic," ready to uphold his beliefs, not in search of martyrdom but in the assurance that

[45]*Anti-Slavery Bugle,* December 3, 1847; *National Anti-Slavery Standard,* August 12, 1854; May to the Primary School Committee of District No. [?], May 24, 1844, G-BPL; May to Editor, August 3, 1852, in *National Anti-Slavery Standard,* August 19, 1852.
[46]May, *Recollections,* 271–272.

by so doing he would effect change. A tall and handsome man with a voice "made to pronounce the Beatitudes," he was the epitome of the transcendental reformer, the man Theodore Parker once called "a philanthropist without cant, and a Christian without bigotry." Solid, not brilliant, May was neither philosopher, theologian, nor litterateur, but an activist "trusting always in God, and believing always in man."[47] But through this optimism ran the dark Sewall heritage of Salem—a fear of violence, an awareness of the evil which degrades man, and a knowledge that such evil, unpurged and unrepented, leads to violence.

Never quite reconciled and most frequently brushed over and hidden, these contradictory drives made May sympathetic to all factions and certainly the most universally beloved of the abolitionists. But that very position weakened the drive and impact of his reform. From his years as an outcast Unitarian amid Connecticut orthodoxy, May was always a marginal man, seeing both sides of issues, belonging wholeheartedly to neither. His very lack of unquestioning ideological loyalty made him a thoroughly unsystematic reformer.

Although he had been on virtually all sides of all antislavery issues during the course of his career, he showed a peculiar, almost childlike consistency. All men shared a transcendental divinity, which might lead them to perfection. All men were brothers. But the prejudice of the imperfect world had degraded the black man, barring his progress toward perfection and his realization of human brotherhood. Only when prejudice was conquered could all men achieve fulfillment in the perfect society.

[47]The quotations are from Aaron M. Powell, *Personal Reminiscences of the Anti-Slavery and Other Reforms and Reformers* (New York: Canton Press for Anna Rice Powell, 1899), 67; *Services in Honor of Samuel Joseph May*, 9, the quotation is attributed to Theodore Parker; the second Parker quotation is from his sermon in Syracuse in 1852, reported in *Liberator*, March 12, 1852; James Freeman Clarke, "Samuel Joseph May," in *Memorial and Biographical Sketches* (Boston: Houghton, Osgood & Co., 1878), 210.

May lived by the love and brotherhood he taught. He brought to antislavery a simplicity and naiveté refreshing in their directness and honesty. It was his tragedy, as well as his country's, that civil war, emancipation, and reconstruction moved whites and blacks so little closer to his vision. May shared this failure with his more worldly and more abrasive fellow abolitionists.

13

Some Reflections

Maria Chapman once quipped with a perception born equally of talent and snobbery, *"God* makes use of instruments that *I* would n't touch with a pair of tongs." Widely diverse instruments they were, as she well knew. Some antislavery workers, she had written back in 1837, tried to free the slaves, others to secure them "their inalienable rights"; some were concerned with their temporal welfare, others with their spiritual sustenance; some labored to raise the blacks' economic status, others to ensure their political freedom. Whatever differences there were, however, in persons or in methods, she concluded, "Our hopes and our hearts are one."[1]

The differences and divergencies that characterized individual antislavery workers were soon mirrored in the differences and divergencies of antislavery associations. By the early 1840s, therefore, Chapman's judgment had changed. There was no longer unity, as national and state organizations

[1]Maria Child to Samuel J. May, January 11, 1866, M-CoU in which Child quotes Chapman. Boston Female Anti-Slavery Society, *Fourth Annual Report* ... (Boston: Isaac Knapp, 1837), 80–81.

split and the importance of both major national associations declined. Yet the blurring of structural unity did not destroy the role that organized antislavery had played and would continue to play. Without the national and state societies, there would have been few paid lecturers and a much weaker antislavery press. Though their initial mission of rallying abolitionists and coordinating their activities soon passed, their meetings remained an arena for lively and frequently bitter exchanges of views. In communicating to the general public and in generating broad participation, they were largely replaced after 1840 by political parties and sectarian societies, but that did less to detract from their role than to broaden the alternatives available to those opposed to slavery. In their societies, abolitionists struggled to achieve one set of methods and attitudes or another. Frequently and vigorously, they debated organizational structure, participation, and procedure. But through it all, they held to their collective vision and their ultimate goal: evolving the various plans for emancipation, which they and their societies offered to the public.

In the continuing and exhausting struggle to find means appropriate to the dual goal of universal liberty and equality, exclusively antislavery associations failed, however, to develop modern function-oriented structures or techniques. Consequently, since no such design informed institutional action, the leadership of individuals remained critically determining. These leaders reflected the same diversity that marked the various antislavery organizations. They came, for example, from different social and economic classes. Best represented were the professions—ministers, lawyers, doctors, and teachers in diminishing numbers. The clerics represented less a coherent social class than a group bound by the common moral and religious imperatives of the antislavery appeal. They were men like Hiram Wilson, Amos Phelps, Samuel Cornish, both Samuel Mays, Theodore Weld, and Henry Highland Garnet. Fewer, though still significant in number, were the lawyers—Ellis G. Loring, David Child, Joshua Giddings, and Wendell Phillips among them. Less numerous were physicians and teachers. Prominent, perhaps because their economic independence allowed them greater time and energy, were rentiers like Edmund Quincy, Maria Chapman, and Phillips; merchants like Arthur and Lewis Tappan, Francis Jackson, and James Mott; and large landowners like Cassius Clay and Gerrit Smith. These patrician and upper middle-class crusaders did not, however, wield sole control. Artisans, too, there were, though they were more frequently activists in the field than powers at society headquarters. Stephen Foster started adult life as a carpenter, Henry C. Wright as a hat maker, James Forten as a sailmaker, and Benjamin Lundy as a saddler. If any one craft contributed more than its share of prominent abolitionists, it was probably printing, from which came Oliver Johnson, Isaac Knapp, and William Lloyd Garrison.

The artisans were fewer in number than the professionals, but those still more closely bound to prolonged daily labor were even less active. Few dirt farmers or common laborers assumed important roles, though from the ranks of the latter and out of slavery came Frederick Douglass. And, though for different reasons, almost no actively engaged industrial entrepreneurs joined the movement until the Civil War drew to it men like railroader John Murray Forbes and financier Edward Atkinson.

These assorted crusaders shared almost no common economic attitudes. Clay sought emancipation to serve his economic self-interest, while its economic consequences were quite irrelevant to Quincy, Smith, and Chapman. Garnet and Cornish, personally touched by the economic impact of discrimination, fought against it. For Foster, slaves were, like himself, part of an oppressed laboring class, warring against capital. Lundy, Garnet, and David Child were committed to the concept of free produce. From a different vantage point, both Chapman and Tappan viewed other abolitionists with the employer's eye, suspecting that at least some of them put income before service. Though men like Wilson and Phelps could probably have done little better in other work, the minimal salaries the societies paid provided little basis for such suspicions. Nonetheless, both Maria Child at the *Standard* and Giddings in Congress explicitly acknowledged that financial need spurred them to action. In Syracuse, Samuel May seldom thought either of economics or of economies.

On one economic point alone was there almost universal agreement. Abolitionists of whatever cast scorned the slothful greed of slaveholders and the energetic greed of the Northern industrialists and financiers who backed them, although they did not inveigh against money or comfort as such. Even Stephen Foster took no vow of poverty; Elizur Wright welcomed the business potential of actuarial science; and the wealthy abolitionists like Gerrit Smith, Maria Chapman, Lewis Tappan, or Edmund Quincy quite unmonkishly reserved sufficient to satisfy their personal and business needs.

Abolitionists not only represented a variety of social and economic backgrounds; they also spanned the spectrum of American Protestantism. They were Congregationalists, Presbyterians, Quakers, Unitarians, Methodists, Baptists, and even Episcopalians. Secular antislavery societies were disproportionately Congregational and Presbyterian because of their New England origins in the 1830s and because Theodore Weld drew so heavily from Lane Seminary and Oberlin College for the evangelical "Seventy" who proselytized both East and West in 1837. The sectarian societies, prominent in the 1840s, were largely Methodist and Baptist.

For one group of abolitionists there was a significant denominational correlation. Women who were active in other than local and exclusively female societies were almost all Unitarians and Quakers: Maria Chapman, Maria Child, Sallie Holley, and Eliza Follen among the former; among the latter Abby Kelley, Lucretia Mott, and Angelina and Sarah Grimké. There was also a particular correlation between religious liberalism and antislavery radicalism. Very few religious liberals joined or long remained in the conservative new organization, which the clerical issue had tied to religious orthodoxy. Those, like Garrison, Foster, Parker Pillsbury, and Henry C. Wright, who rejected the old orthodoxy were most likely to be radical in their abolitionism. The correlation, however, was not complete, for the radical Wendell Phillips remained a Calvinist, and such religious liberals as Samuel J. May, Elizur Wright, and Lucretia Mott were antislavery moderates.

Even less correlative is a single psychological explanation for antislavery motivation. Response to physical danger differed. Foster pursued it avidly. But May endured it, and Chapman mainly talked about it. Some, like Chapman and Lewis Tappan, who mutually despised each other, found in reform an outlet for their authoritarian natures. But others, like Wilson and Cornish, found in the close comradeship of the small outgroup a bulwark against personal inadequacy.

Although no psychological theme was common to all participants, one was widely prevalent: nearly all who were important leaders in the antislavery cause were men or women of two minds. Torn by conflicting commitments and personal aspirations, they teetered between two sets of ideals or two social structures. Clay never reconciled his desire for the political preferment characteristic of a Kentucky gentleman with his desire to free Kentucky of slavery. Wright was tugged back and forth by the demands of reform and his family's necessities, which led him ultimately to business success. Giddings, even in the 1850s, eyed political prestige as he continued to carry the banner of an unastute political idealism. Chapman wanted both ladylike prestige in the world of society and masculine authority in the world of reform. Cornish was shattered by the incompatibility of his desire for respectability in the white community and his demand for black self-respect. And Garnet progressively tempered his radicalism in order to achieve personal fulfillment within the established system.

Perhaps reformers must be on the fringes of two incompati-

ble systems. Were they totally at home in the dominant structure there would be no compulsion to change it. Were they
wholeheartedly alienated from it, they would become total
revolutionaries or would totally withdraw. But the abolitionists
did neither. They turned rather to the variegated patterns
of Middle Period reform. As reformers in general or as
abolitionists in particular, they were dissatisfied with things
as they were and sought to change them. Like most disturbers
of the status quo, their enthusiasm was in large measure a
function of their age. They were young, unsure of their own
identities, in search of an ideal world. If Giddings was a notable
exception—he was forty-two when he came to antislavery—yet
even he was propelled to reform by the collapse of his world
in the panic of 1837 and by the urgings of Theodore Weld's
evangel. But most of the other leaders were still in their
twenties. Foster was twenty-five when he decided upon a
reform career; Lundy was twenty-seven when he founded
the Union Humane Society; May a mere nineteen when he
espoused the peace crusade. And when they turned explicitly
to antislavery, Wilson was old at thirty, Wright and Clay were
but twenty-five, and Garnet was only twenty. Youth was a
significant catalyst.

That antislavery in one way or another did feed the psyches
of those who worked in its behalf does not override the fact
that they sought universal emancipation when American slavery was a flourishing and powerful institution subverting their
personal, religious, political, and economic ideals. That they
derived personal satisfaction from their work does not detract
from the genuineness of their idealism. Had they not believed
in the justness of their course, they could not have obtained
from it either martyrdom, sublimation, or romantic identification.

As varied as their motivations were the abolitionists' degrees
of radicalism. They ranged from the essential conservatism
of Samuel Cornish to the revolutionary egalitarianism of
Stephen Foster, but efforts to construct a neat progression

stumble on the shifting nature of that radicalism itself. Garrisonianism was an abstract theory positing fundamental change. It gave little attention to ameliorative functions like schooling for blacks, communal experimentation, or assistance to fugitives. Where its adherents did aid fugitives, oppose Jim Crow facilities, fight antimiscegenation laws, and seek to enfranchise blacks, they thought of them as activities peripheral to their real purpose. Theirs was the responsibility to change public opinion to eliminate slavery, not to tinker with symptoms. Chapman was logically consistent when she rejected all practical action and said that the only way to end slavery was to join the American Anti-Slavery Society.

In contrast to Garrisonian abstractionism, which supported only immediate and uncompensated emancipation, was an antislavery eagerness for positive, if only meliorative, action. That militant blacks like Henry Garnet and Samuel Ward affiliated with new organization and that after 1850 Frederick Douglass joined political abolitionists does not necessarily conflict with the fact that, by Garrisonian standards, these groups were conservative. Black abolitionists, who felt the actuality of slavery more than whites, sought results more immediate than coming-out and disunionism were likely to achieve. Thus Garnet, who in 1843 called for slave revolts, was unwelcome among Garrisonian radicals, for at the time they rejected all use of force and would postpone emancipation until human government had been replaced by more divine arrangements.

Nor was this the only divergence. In the 1850s, antislavery radicalism was neither the coming-out of the 1840s nor even the disunionism that Garrison's public burning of the American Constitution in 1854 had expressed. It was closer to the violence sanctioned by Garnet's 1843 address. Old moderates like Giddings and May were strangely allied with extreme radicals like Foster and Parker Pillsbury, all mutually determined to challenge government directly, to disobey its laws, to defy its courts, and to refuse it any support. Kindled by the 1850 Fugitive Slave Law, the new radicalism was more than simple rejection; it was direct, deliberate, and head-on confrontation with the entire government. Foster's explicit and open rebelliousness was rare indeed. But when May and Gerrit Smith sought arrest and trial for their role in the Jerry McHenry rescue, they came close to Foster's customary stance. Both Thomas Higginson's and Martin Stowell's armed assault on the Boston courthouse and Smith's and Theodore Parker's support for John Brown's raid made Garrison's disunionism seem pallid and Garnet's exile in Jamaica timorous.

In essence, though not necessarily in rhetoric, antislavery radicalism thus shifted from one primarily of means in the 1840s to one of both means and goals in the 1850s. Although perfectionists of the 1840s had looked to millennial change, their antislavery means were usually simple and total disfellowship from slaveholders. In the 1850s, radicals attacked government directly and espoused more revolutionary reconstruction of society as the requisite of emancipation.

From all the diversities of the antislavery crusade one final question, perhaps unanswerable, emerges vexatiously. Why did the reformers here studied choose to become abolitionists? Possibly, in the biblical motto which defined the movement, "Remember them that are in bonds, as bound with them," they provided the essential clue themselves. Born into a post-revolutionary world in which freedom was no longer a privilege but a general expectation, and confronted with the distressing fact of its denial in American slavery at the very moment England was abolishing it, every abolitionist felt himself in some way bound, restricted, unfree, as the slave was bound, restricted, unfree. The manner of that bondage differed from reformer to reformer, but for each of them it was very real. Their perceptions of unfreedom turned them to antislavery.[2]

[2]Aileen S. Kraditor, *Means and Ends in American Abolitionism: Garrison and his Critics on Strategy and Tactics, 1834–1850* (New York: Pantheon Books,

For Henry Garnet, a fugitive slave, bondage was, of course, reality itself. For Samuel Cornish, who had never been a slave, the possibility of slavery was ever present. And for all blacks, the reality of racial discrimination was bondage too. White abolitionists, however, understood bondage somewhat differently. Benjamin Lundy reflected the quiet piety of his Quaker faith, while Hiram Wilson expectantly strove for personal salvation through his evangelical Christianity. Both of them, however, knew that the slave could not follow his own conscience, and, so long as he could not, they too were unfree in theirs. Touched, each in his own way, by the personal suffering that slavery entailed, these four reformers defined the antislavery crusade by the human misery which befell their brothers.

Others responded less to the plight of the individual slave than to the consequences of the institution upon all society, themselves included. For Elizur Wright, early in his career uneasy in conscience like Wilson, to be bound later meant the loss of civil liberties as his experience at Western Reserve College first demonstrated. Similarly, but much more clearly, both Cassius Clay and Joshua Giddings understood that not only they but also Clay's Kentucky and Giddings' Ohio were enthralled by the peculiar institution, which threatened the economies of their states and set against them a slave-power conspiracy.

Samuel J. May and Maria Chapman felt bound in yet other ways. The latter, restricted by society and convention because she was a woman, turned to antislavery as a way to break those bonds and, at the same time, to confront the threat to civil liberty, which the early attacks upon George Thompson had clearly defined for her. For May, on the other hand, the peculiar institution and the human suffering it entailed

---

1969), 237–239, construes the bonds referred to in abolitionist usage of the biblical injunction as empathy and thus misses the broader cohesiveness it brought the antislavery movement.

restricted the betterment of individual men. To purge one's self of the sin and guilt of slavery meant, for him, to restore the promise and potential of human progress.

Finally there was Stephen Foster. Of all the abolitionists, none, surely, except the blacks themselves, felt more strongly the sense of bondage. His was a thralldom imposed by any restrictions upon his own personal expression. The anarchist, the revolutionary of the group, Foster, in any place at any time, would have responded the same, for if he could not be his own man he felt trapped, unfree. That was his own peculiar kind of slavery.

Bondage for the abolitionists was no mere motto, no convenient device to put upon the antislavery banner. It had meaning, real and personal. Because it was a bondage of unfreedom, of restraint, antislavery enthusiasts clearly and fully identified themselves with the institution or with the black man, slave or nominally free.

Thus through nearly forty years of antislavery struggle, from the halcyon days in Philadelphia in December 1833 to the tired and acrimonious days of Reconstruction, in the midst of which the American Anti-Slavery Society finally disbanded the movement to end slavery and to fulfill the dream of equality for all had engaged the attention of Americans. Through its organizations, it had sought the strength of associational action, yet its leaders individually had been the decisive molders of events. Through the credo of immediatism it had, through most of the era, found purpose and aim; but the urgencies of events made individual abolitionists redefine those goals in less than harmonious ways. Through the common methods of reform, purpose was to be given direction and focus; yet the dream of action was played out by crusaders in a variety of ways. In emancipation, all were to find the climax of a course well run; but in the event, each participant chose his own evaluation of the deed, which made of jubilee a moment of acrimony.

It is tempting to conclude, as some have done, that no phenomenon so disparate as the antislavery crusade can rightly be called a coherent movement. Yet the diversity which characterized the antislavery host masked an underlying unity of purpose which gave it an identity clear to those who supported it as well as to those who opposed it, to those who observed it then and to those who study it a century or more later.[3]

That there was an antislavery movement is not to be doubted. That it succeeded is attested by emancipation. That it failed is the testimony of incomplete freedom. To understand its complexity and its paradox is first to understand the diverse individuals who made it.

---

[3] Peter G. Filene, "An Obituary for 'The Progressive Movement,' " *American Quarterly* 22 (Spring 1970): 20–34 applies the sociological definition of a conscious and cohesive movement to the Progressives and finds they did not constitute a movement in this sense.

Bibliography

General Studies

Every study of the antislavery movement must still start with the classic Garrisonian interpretation of the movement, Wendell Phillips Garrison and Francis Jackson Garrison, *William Lloyd Garrison, 1805–1879; The Story of His Life as Told by His Children* (New York: The Century Co., 1885–1889), 4 vols. Studies emphasizing Western antislavery and the New York political axis include Gilbert H. Barnes, *The Antislavery Impulse, 1830–1844* (New York: D. Appleton-Century Co., 1933); and two books by Dwight L. Dumond, *Antislavery Origins of the Civil War in the United States* (1939. Reprint. Ann Arbor: University of Michigan Press, 1959), and *Antislavery: The Crusade for Freedom in America* (Ann Arbor: University of Michigan Press, 1961). Among the more recent studies, which reemphasize the importance of the Garrisonians and stress their radical nature, are Louis Filler, *The Crusade Against Slavery, 1830–1850,* The New American Nation Series (New York: Harper & Brothers, 1960); Aileen S. Kraditor, *Means and*

Ends in American Abolitionism: Garrison and His Critics on Strategy and Tactics, 1834–1850 (New York: Pantheon Books, 1969); James M. McPherson, *The Struggle for Equality: Abolitionists and the Negro in the Civil War and Reconstruction* (Princeton: Princeton University Press, 1964), which emphasizes the continuing role of abolitionists, and which is partly questioned by Richard O. Curry, "The Abolitionists and Reconstruction: A Critical Appraisal," *Journal of Southern History* 34 (November 1968): 527–545; and two articles by Bertram Wyatt-Brown, "William Lloyd Garrison and Antislavery Unity: A Reappraisal," *Civil War History* 13 (March 1967): 5–24, and "Abolitionism: Its Meaning for Contemporary American Reform," *Midwest Quarterly* 8 (October 1966): 41–55.

In addition, numerous other works treat the movement from a variety of points of view. Moderate in its tone and focusing on the complexity involved in the whole reform effort is Russel B. Nye, *William Lloyd Garrison and the Humanitarian Reformers* (Boston: Little, Brown and Co., 1955). In "The Antislavery Myth," *The American Scholar* 31 (Spring 1962): 312–328, C. Vann Woodward deplores the "total hero" approach to and oversimplification of the antislavery crusade. His viewpoint is reinforced by such books as Leon F. Litwack, *North of Slavery: The Negro in the Free States, 1790–1860* (Chicago: University of Chicago Press, 1961); Lorman Ratner, *Powder Keg: Northern Opposition to the Antislavery Movement, 1831–1840* (New York: Basic Books, 1968); and Larry Gara, *The Liberty Line: The Legend of the Underground Railroad* (Lexington: University of Kentucky Press, 1961). David Donald, in "Toward a Reconsideration of Abolitionists," in his *Lincoln Reconsidered: Essays in the Civil War Era* (New York: Alfred Knopf, 1956), 19–36, argues the class origins of antislavery crusaders. Robert A. Skotheim challenged Donald's view in "A Note on Historical Method: David Donald's 'Toward a Reconsideration of Abolitionists,' " *Journal of Southern History* 25 (August 1959): 356–365. Abolitionists' failure to achieve the goal of racial equality is discussed in Merton L. Dillon, "The Failure of the American Abolitionists," *Journal of Southern History* 25 (May 1959): 159–177; and Martin Duberman emphasizes the individuality of abolitionists in "The Abolitionists and Psychology," *Journal of Negro History* 47 (July 1962): 183–191. The question of prejudice is treated in Leon F. Litwack, "The Abolitionist Dilemma: The Antislavery Movement and the Northern Negro," *New England Quarterly* 34 (March 1961): 50–73; and in William H. Pease and Jane H. Pease, "Antislavery Ambivalence: Immediatism, Expediency, Race," *American Quarterly* 17 (Winter 1965): 682–695. Internal tensions within the movement over leadership and race are treated in Benjamin Quarles, "The Breach Between Douglass and Garrison," *Journal of Negro History* 23 (April 1938): 144–154; and in William H. Pease and Jane H. Pease, "Boston Garrisonians and the Problem of Frederick Douglass," *Canadian Journal of History* 2 (September 1967): 29–48. In addition, three collections of essays provide a rich source of interpretations: Richard O. Curry, ed., *The Abolitionists: Reformers or Fanatics?*, American Problem Studies (New York: Holt, Rinehart and Winston, 1965); Martin Duberman, ed., *The Antislavery Vanguard: New Essays on the Abolitionists* (Princeton: Princeton University Press, 1965); and Hugh Hawkins, ed., *The Abolitionists: Immediatism and the Question of Means*, Problems in American Civilization (Boston: D. C. Heath and Company, 1964).

Special topics are covered in a variety of books and articles. Louis Ruchames, "Race, Marriage and Abolition in Massachusetts," *Journal of Negro History* 40 (July 1955): 250–273, and "William Lloyd Garrison and the Negro Franchise," *Journal of Negro History* 50 (January 1965): 37–49; Lewis Perry, "Versions of Anarchism in the Antislavery Movement," *American Quarterly* 20 (Winter 1968): 768–782; Hazel C. Wolf, *On Freedom's Altar: The Martyr Complex in the Abolition Movement* (Madison: University of Wisconsin Press, 1952); and James

B. Stewart, "The Aims and Impact of Garrisonian Abolitionism, 1840–1860," *Civil War History* 15 (September 1969): 197–209, which discusses the political awareness of the Garrisonians, also his "Peaceful Hopes and Violent Experiences: The Evolution of Reforming and Radical Abolitionism, 1831–1837," *Civil War History* 17 (December 1971): 293–309. For the early movement, see Thomas E. Drake, *Quakers and Slavery in America* (1950. Reprint. Gloucester, Mass.: Peter Smith, 1965); Alice D. Adams, *The Neglected Period of Anti-Slavery in America (1808–1831)*, Radcliffe College Monographs (orig. ed. 1908. Reprint. Gloucester, Mass.: Peter Smith, 1964); and Arthur Zilversmit, *The First Emancipation. The Abolition of Slavery in the North* (Chicago: University of Chicago Press, 1967). Other studies include David B. Davis, "The Emergence of Immediatism in British and American Antislavery Thought," *Mississippi Valley Historical Review* 49 (September 1962): 209–230; Alma Lutz, *Crusade for Freedom: Women of the Antislavery Movement* (Boston: Beacon Press, 1968); Jane H. Pease and William H. Pease, "Confrontation and Abolition in the 1850s," *Journal of American History* 58 (March 1972): 923–937; Philip J. Staudenraus, *The African Colonization Movement, 1816–1865* (New York: Columbia University Press, 1961); Kenneth Stampp, "The Fate of Southern AntiSlavery," *Journal of Negro History* 28 (January 1943): 10–22; Norman L. Rosenberg, "Personal Liberty Laws and Sectional Crisis: 1850–1861," *Civil War History* 17 (March 1971): 25–44; and Howard H. Bell's studies on black abolitionists, which include "The American Moral Reform Society, 1836–1841," *Journal of Negro Education* 27 (Winter 1958): 34–40, "National Negro Conventions of the Middle 1840's: Moral Suasion vs. Political Action," *Journal of Negro History* 42 (October 1957): 247–260, "The Negro Emigration Movement, 1849–1854: A Phase of Negro Nationalism," *Phylon* 20 (Summer 1959): 132–142, and *A Survey of the Negro Convention Movement* (Ph.D. dissertation, 1953; New York: Arno Press, 1970).

Biographies

There are still many antislavery leaders who do not have good biographies. Of those that are available, some of the more useful include Betty Fladeland, *James Gillespie Birney: Slaveholder to Abolitionist* (Ithaca: Cornell University Press, 1955); Helene G. Baer, *The Heart is Like Heaven: The Life of Lydia Maria Child* (Philadelphia: University of Pennsylvania Press, 1964); Milton Meltzer, *Tongue of Flame: The Life of Lydia Maria Child* (New York: Thomas Y. Crowell, 1965); Lowell H. Harrison, "The Anti-Slavery Career of Cassius M. Clay," *Register of the Kentucky Historical Society* 59 (October 1961): 295–317; David L. Smiley, *Lion of White Hall: The Life of Cassius M. Clay* (Madison: University of Wisconsin Press, 1962); Philip S. Foner, ed., *The Life and Writings of Frederick Douglass* (New York: International Publishers, 1950–1955), 4 vols.; Benjamin Quarles, *Frederick Douglass* (Washington: The Associated Publishers, 1948); William M. Brewer, "Henry H. Garnet," *Journal of Negro History* 13 (January 1928): 36–52; Walter M. Merrill, *Against Wind and Tide; A Biography of William Lloyd Garrison* (Cambridge: Harvard University Press, 1963); John L. Thomas, *The Liberator: William Lloyd Garrison: A Biography* (Boston: Little, Brown and Company, 1963); James B. Stewart, *Joshua R. Giddings and the Tactics of Radical Politics* (Cleveland: The Press of Case Western Reserve University, 1970); Gerda Lerner, *The Grimké Sisters from South Carolina: Rebels Against Slavery* (Boston: Houghton Mifflin Company, 1967); Richard H. Sewell, *John P. Hale and the Politics of Abolition* (Cambridge: Harvard University Press, 1965); Tilden G. Edelstein, *Strange Enthusiasm: A Life of Thomas Wentworth Higginson* (New Haven: Yale University Press, 1968); Merton L. Dillon, *Elijah P. Lovejoy. Abolitionist Editor* (Urbana: University of Illinois Press, 1961), and *Benjamin Lundy and the Struggle for Negro Freedom* (Urbana: University of Illinois Press, 1966); George B. Emerson, Samuel May, and Thomas Mumford, *Memoir of Samuel Joseph May* (Boston: Roberts Brothers, 1873); Irving H. Bartlett, *Wendell Phillips: Brahmin Radical* (Boston: Beacon Press, 1961); Otelia Cromwell, *Lucretia Mott* (Cambridge: Harvard University Press, 1958); Frank Otto Gatell, *John Gorham Palfrey and the New England Conscience* (Cambridge: Harvard University Press, 1963); Ralph V. Harlow, *Gerrit Smith: Philanthropist and Reformer* (New York: Henry Holt and Company, 1939); Bertram Wyatt-Brown, *Lewis Tappan and the Evangelical War Against Slavery* (Cleveland: The Press of Case Western Reserve University, 1969); Benjamin P. Thomas, *Theodore Weld, Crusader for Freedom* (New Brunswick: Rutgers University Press, 1950); and Philip G. Wright and Elizabeth Q. Wright, *Elizur Wright, the Father of Life Insurance* (Chicago: University of Chicago Press, 1937).

Primary Sources

Research in the antislavery movement sooner or later takes one to the major collections, printed and manuscript. Because of their size and scope, three libraries stand out as indispensible repositories for researchers. The Antislavery Collection of the Boston Public Library is an almost inexhaustible source of manuscripts particularly strong in the Garrisonian phase of the movement. The Antislavery Collection at Oberlin College is a treasure trove of printed antislavery material, which is currently being made available on microcards by the Lost Cause Press. At Cornell, the antislavery collection is a rich source of materials, both manuscript and printed, built on the original collection of Samuel J. May. The location of all of the major and most of the minor manuscript collections is indicated in the key to manuscripts at the beginning of this volume. There are in addition several printed collections of primary material. Two collections of letters are *Letters of Theodore Dwight Weld, Angelina Grimké Weld and Sarah Grimké, 1822–1844,* eds. Gilbert H. Barnes and Dwight L. Dumond (1934. Gloucester, Mass.: Peter Smith, 1965), 2 vols.,

and *Letters of James Gillespie Birney, 1831–1857*, ed. Dwight
L. Dumond. (New York: D. Appleton-Century Company,
1938), 2 vols. Other primary material is contained in William
H. Pease and Jane H. Pease, eds., *The Antislavery Argument,*
The American Heritage Series (Indianapolis: The Bobbs-
Merrill Company, 1965); Louis Ruchames, ed., *The Abolition-
ists. A Collection of Their Writings* (New York: G. P. Putnam's
Sons, 1963); and Howard H. Bell, ed., *Minutes of the Proceedings
of the National Negro Conventions, 1830–1864* (New York: Arno
Press, 1970). Among the more useful antislavery newspapers
are the *Anti-Slavery Bugle* (New Lisbon and Salem, Ohio,
1845–1861), *Colored American* (New York, 1837–1841),
Emancipator (New York, 1833–1841), *Free American* (New
York, 1839–1841), *Genius of Universal Emancipation* (Mt.
Pleasant, Ohio, Greenville, Tennessee, Baltimore, 1821–
1837), *Herald of Freedom* (Concord, New Hampshire, 1835–
1846), *Liberator* (Boston, 1831–1865), *National Anti-Slavery
Standard* (New York, 1840–1865), *North Star* (continued as
Frederick Douglass' Paper and then *Douglass' Monthly*
(Rochester, 1847–1863), and *Pennsylvania Freeman*
(Philadelphia, 1836–1854; 1836–38 styled *National Enquirer
and Constitutional Advocate of Universal Liberty).*

Bibliographies

The best single source for primary printed material is Dwight
L. Dumond, *A Bibliography of Antislavery in America*
(Ann Arbor: University of Michigan Press, 1961). For the
essential literature on the movement as a whole see Louis
Filler, *The Crusade Against Slavery,* above. For an excellent
survey of the most recent literature see Merton L. Dillon,
"The Abolitionists: A Decade of Historiography, 1959–
1969," *Journal of Southern History,* 35 (November 1969),
500–522.

Index

Abolitionists
  Age grouping, 313
  Psychological characteristics, 312-313
  Social and economic class origins, 3, 21, 309-310
Academic freedom, 221-223, 292-293
Adams, John Quincy, 110-111, 196, 248-249, 254, 261, 277
African Civilization Society, 182-188
African Free Schools, 144, 147, 163-164
American and Foreign Anti-Slavery Society, 6, 14, 51, 142, 151, 232
American Anti-Slavery Society, 10-14, 19, 34, 36, 39, 41, 49, 54, 117-118, 121, 139, 142, 148, 189, 197, 202, 212, 213, 224-225, 227, 230-232, 285, 288

American Colonization Society, 9-10, 74, 101, 155, 182, 186, 227, 281, 284-285
American Convention for Promoting the Abolition of Slavery, 93-94, 96, 99, 102
American Convention of the Free People of Color, 103
American Missionary Association, 133-134, 142, 159
American Moral Reform Society, 146-148
Anarchism, 194-195
Anglo-African, see Weekly Anglo-African
Antiabolition riots, *see* Violence
Anticlericalism, *see* Clerical issue, Come-outerism
Antislavery
  Economic arguments, 61, 63-65, 80, 98-100, 215, 225-226, 250, 310-311

327

Antislavery (*cont.*)
  Evolution of early sentiment, 8-11
  Financing, 44-47, 117-118, 121-122, 130-131, 133-135, 227-228
  Historical interpretations, 3, 19-22
  Ideology, 11-14, 27, 35-39, 95-99, 114, 205-207, 225, 266-269, 281-284, 313-317
  Petition campaigns, 33, 95, 171
  Political action, 15-17, 25, 50-52, 65-68, 78-84, 94-95, 137, 156-158, 169-177, 202-203, 207-211, 213, 232-237, 241-242, 243-244, 247-275, 299-300; *see also* Free Soil party; Liberty party; Republican party
  Practical action to aid free blacks, 17-18, 91, 115-116, 118-132, 139, 142-143, 145-147, 149, 166, 168-169
  Press, *see names of individual newspapers*
  Religious forces, 9, 12-13, 23-25, 32, 40, 91-92, 123, 138, 141-142, 166-169, 238, 311-312
Antislavery bazaar, *see* Antislavery fair
Anti-Slavery Bugle, 39, 71-72, 75, 273
Anti-Slavery Convention of American Women, 33, 50, 112
Antislavery fair, 44-46, 58
Anti-Slavery Reporter, 224, 227
Assimilation, 149-150, 183
Associationism, 24, 294
Atkinson, Edward, 310
Austin, Moses, 104

Ball, Lucy, 38
Barnes, Gilbert, 20
Beecher, Henry Ward, 5
Bell, Howard, 22
Bell, Philip, 148
Benson, George (father), 281
Benson, George (son), 286
Benson, Henry, 289
Bibb, Henry, 161, 167
Birney, James G., 25, 51, 60, 157, 184, 242
Blackaller, J., 105, 107
Black nationalism, *see* Emigration
Black suffrage, *see* Civil rights for free blacks
Black troops, 188, 242, 303
Black Warrior incident, 267
Boston Anti-Sabbath Convention (1848), 194
Boston Clique, 39-40, 237-240
Boston Emancipation League, 242
Boston Female Anti-Slavery Society, 32, 33, 38, 42-44, 58
Botts, John Minor, 253
Bourne, George, 4
Bradburn, George, 51
British American Institute of Science and Industry, 124-125, 130, 138
Brown, John, 4, 181, 209, 271, 301
Brown, William Wells, 186
Buffum, Arnold, 51, 286
Burleigh, Charles C., 26
Burns, Anthony, 204-205
Buxton, Thomas Folwell, 182

Canada Mission, 121, 125, 138

Canadian Anti-Slavery Society, 139

Channing, William Ellery, 5, 24, 32, 277, 294

Chapman, Henry G., 24, 28-30, 32, 34, 48-50

Chapman, John Jay, 58

Chapman, Maria Weston, 22-23, 24, 25, 26, 27, 28-59, 72-73, 137, 200-201, 209, 213, 231, 237, 240, 257, 276, 308, 310, 311, 312, 314, 316

Child, David Lee, 4, 38, 49, 109, 235, 310

Child, Lydia Maria, 4, 25, 44, 49, 109, 200, 311

Christian Anti-Slavery Convention, 194

Chronotype, 236, 241

Civil liberties, 32, 35, 50, 55, 77-78, 82-85, 98, 193, 198, 225, 290-291

Civil rights for free blacks, 98, 111-112, 170-173, 214, 304

Civil War, 53-58, 86-87, 188, 211-214, 242, 272, 301-302

Clay, Brutus J., 72

Clay, Cassius Marcellus, 23, 24, 37, 60-89, 310, 312, 313, 316

Clay, Green, 61-62

Clay, Henry, 63, 67, 78-79, 101, 242, 256

Clerical issue, 40-42, 157, 228-230

Cleveland Disunion Convention, 206

Cobb, Howell, 262

Coles, Edward, 9

Colonization, 9-10, 100-109, 113-114, 220-223; *see also* Emigration

in Africa, 182-188; *see also* African Civilization Society; American Colonization Society

in Canada, 103

in Haiti, 101-102

in Mexico, 103-109

in Tamaulipas, 107-109

in Texas, 104-107

Colored American, 136, 143, 148, 153, 157

Colver, Nathaniel, 56

Come-outerism, 25, 35, 195-196

Commonwealth, 236

Confrontation, 201-202, 206, 265

Conservatism, 26, 41, 156-157, 161, 189, 313-315

Constitutional interpretations, 81-84, 97, 203-204, 209-211, 233, 249-250, 264, 299

Cornish, Samuel Eli, 23, 25, 26, 140-161, 309, 310, 312, 316

Coues, Samuel, 200

Crandall, Prudence, 285-288

Creole, 252-254, 257

Crummell, Alexander, 145, 164, 189

Cuba, 267

Dall, Caroline H., 48

Dawn Mills, 122-131

Delany, Martin R., 4, 161, 185-188

Dillon, Merton, 113n

Disunion, 52-53, 83-84, 203, 206, 208, 268-269, 300-301

Donald, David, 3, 21

Donelson, Andrew, 108

Douglass, Frederick, 6, 49, 75, 161-162, 176, 240, 277, 310, 314

Downing, George T., 164, 186

Drayton-Sayres Case, 263-264

Dred Scott decision, 201, 270

Drouet, Nicholas, 107

Drummondsville Convention of Canadian and American Negroes, 127

Duberman, Martin, 21

Dumond, Dwight, 20

Education for free blacks, 119-120, 122, 124-126, 131, 133, 138, 144-147, 150-151, 166

Educational reform, 280-281, 296

Emancipation proclamation, 54, 212

Emancipator, 224, 236

Emigration, 154-156, 181-188

Evangelical Association of Presbyterian and Congregational Clergymen of Color, 169

Everett, Edward, 290

Fee, John G., 68-69, 84

Feminism, 46-49; *see also* Women's rights

Filibustering, 267

Finley, Robert, 223

Fladeland, Betty, 21, 22

Follen, Charles T. C., 4, 290-291

Follen, Eliza L. Cabot, 73, 311

Folsom, Abby, 194

Forbes, John Murray, 38, 310

Forten, James, 4, 310

Foster, Abby Kelley, 4, 6, 25, 26, 27, 56, 176, 197-198, 209, 231-232, 257, 311

Foster, Stephen Symonds, 6, 13, 23, 25, 26, 191-217, 257, 277, 310, 311, 312, 313, 314, 317

Fourierism, 236

Free American, 236, 238

Free labor, 65, 76-77

Free labor produce, 100-101, 103-104, 181-184

Free Soil party, 16, 25, 52, 79-80, 202, 241, 261-263

Free speech, *see* Civil liberties

Freedom's Journal, 143-144

Frémont, John C., 213

French, Mansfield, 4

Friends, *see* Quakers

Fugitive Slave Law of 1793, 234, 263

Fugitive Slave Law of 1850, 82-83, 132, 184, 201, 241, 263-266, 270, 272, 296-299

Fugitive slaves, assistance to, 18, 204-205, 263-265, 296-299

Fuller, James Cannings, 121, 123, 131

Gag rule, 248

Gallego, Peter, 135

Gannett, William C., 4

Gara, Larry, 22

Garnet, Henry Highland, 6, 23, 27, 49, 145, 161, 162-190, 309, 310, 312, 313, 314, 316

Garrison, Francis Jackson, 20

Garrison, Wendell Phillips, 20

Garrison, William Lloyd, 6, 7, 11, 25, 27, 54, 56, 74, 91, 206, 213, 220, 227-232, 240, 244, 273, 277, 281, 290, 310, 312

Garrisonianism, 4, 13-14, 31, 35-40, 157, 234-235, 314

Gay, Sydney H., 57
Geneva Tabernacle, 167
Genius of Universal Emancipation, 11, 92-94, 112-113
Giddings, Joshua Reed, 23, 52, 244, 245-275, 277, 310, 311, 312, 313, 314, 316
Goodell, William, 4, 20, 121, 140
Gradual emancipation (gradualism), 78, 97
Graham, R. R., 108
Green, Beriah, 51, 221, 223
Grimké, Angelina, *see* Angelina Grimké Weld
Grimké, Sarah, 311
Gurley, R. R., 223

Hale, John P., 241
Harper, Robert G., 9
Harpers Ferry raid, *see* John Brown
Henson, Josiah, 122, 125-126, 128
Herald of Freedom, 195
Heyrick, Elizabeth, 98
Higginson, Thomas Wentworth, 31, 205, 315
Higher law, 205, 264, 266
Holley, Myron, 15
Holley, Sallie, 6, 311
Human Rights, 224

Immediatism, 11, 37, 98, 220

Jackson, Francis, 235, 310
Jay, William, 5
Jefferson, Thomas, 9
Jerry Rescue, 297-298
Johnson, Andrew, 87, 215, 243
Johnson, Oliver, 20, 54, 57, 231, 310

Judson, Andrew, 285-287

Kansas-Nebraska Act, 201
Kelley, Abby, *see* Abby Kelley Foster
King, William, 139
Knapp, Isaac, 310
Kraditor, Aileen, 21, 315n
Ku Klux Klan, 87

Latimer, George, 204, 237
Leavitt, Joshua, 51, 126, 157, 257
Lecompton constitution, 270
Liberal religion, *see* Religious liberalism
Liberator, 11, 34, 71-72, 137, 257
Liberty Bell, 34-35
Liberty party, 6, 15-16, 25, 51-52, 60, 67, 137, 140, 157-158, 174-176, 194, 202, 234-236, 241, 243, 255-256, 277
Liberty Street Presbyterian Church, 166
Lincoln, Abraham, 212, 214, 242, 272
Loring, Ellis Gray, 39, 200, 290, 310
Lovejoy, Owen, 4
Loveland, Anne C., 21
Lowell, James Russell, 39
Lundy, Benjamin, 6, 10, 23, 24, 27, 90-114, 281, 310, 313, 316
Lunt, George, 291

McHenry, Jerry, 297-298
McKim, James Miller, 213-214
McPherson, James, 21
Madison, James, 9
Martin, J. Sella, 186
Martineau, Harriet, 29
Martyr complex, 30, 197, 199

Maryland Anti-Slavery Society, 94

Massachusetts Abolition Society, 232

Massachusetts Abolitionist, 137, 231, 236

Massachusetts Anti-Slavery Society, 33, 39, 139, 213, 230, 285

May, Lucretia, 288

May, Samuel Joseph, 6, 24, 25, 26, 276-307, 309, 311, 312, 313, 314, 315, 316

May, Samuel, Jr. (of Leicester), 39, 45-47, 56, 213, 273, 309

Mercer, Charles, 101

Merrill, Walter, 20

Methodology, 5-7

Mexican War, 16, 30, 72-74, 184, 236, 260-261, 295

Mob violence, *see* Violence

Mott, James, 4, 310

Mott, Lucretia, 4, 311, 312

Myers, Jeremiah, 162

Nashoba, 103

National Anti-Slavery Standard, 34, 45, 54, 71-72, 75, 137, 178

National Anti-Slavery Tract Society of Maryland, 94

National Emigration Convention of Colored Men, 185

National Enquirer, 110-112

Negro conventions, 145, 146, 170, 178-179

Nell, William C., 187

New England Anti-Slavery Convention, 34, 41, 139, 194, 199, 204, 209, 237, 291

New England Anti-Slavery Society, 285, 288

New Jersey Freeman, 71-72, 73

New York Anti-Slavery Society, 142, 224

New York Society for the Promotion of Education among Colored Children, 159

Newman, William, 127

Nonresistance, 12, 50-52, 62, 202, 302-303

Nonviolent disruption, 191, 205

North Star, 240

Nye, Russel, 3

Pacificus, 249

Parker, Lorena, 130

Parker, Mary, 42-43

Parker, Theodore, 306, 315

Peace reform, 281

Pennington, James W. C., 187

Pennsylvania Anti-Slavery Society, 110

Pennsylvania Freeman, 39

Pennsylvania Hall, 33, 50, 112

Pennsylvania Society for Promoting the Abolition of Slavery, 93-94

Perfectionism, 229-230

Phelps, Amos A., 4, 24, 26, 41, 51, 75, 230, 235, 309, 311

Philanthropist (Mount Pleasant, Ohio), 92

Philbrick, Edward L., 4

Phillips, Wendell, 6, 25, 39, 49, 54, 200, 209, 238, 273, 295, 310, 312

Phoenix Society, 146

Pillsbury, Parker, 13, 54, 214, 277, 312, 314

Political Anti-Slavery Convention, 210-211

Porter, Samuel, 121
Prejudice, *see* Racial prejudice
Protestant ethic, 143-144, 149-150, 177
Provincial Freeman, 136
Pugh, Sarah, 196
Purvis, Robert, 178

Quakers, 91-92
Quarles, Benjamin, 22
Quarterly Anti-Slavery Magazine, 224-225
Quincy, Edmund, 29, 34, 39, 62, 199, 213, 237, 239, 310, 311

Racial prejudice, 101, 151-154, 183-184, 282-284, 292, 306
Racism, 66-67, 76, 136, 173
Radical Abolitionists, 85, 176, 202, 209
Radicalism, 7, 26, 41, 74, 189, 201, 213-216, 313-315
Ray, Charles B., 136, 158
Reconstruction, 19, 87-88, 173, 177, 215-216, 243, 304
Reform ideology, 280
Religious liberalism, 198, 238, 278-279
Remond, Charles L., 277
Republican party, 17, 52, 79-80, 176, 202, 208, 241, 270-272
Revolution, 205-208, 268-270
Rice, Isaac, 126
Rights of All, 143-144
Rogers, Nathaniel P., 164, 195, 237
Ruggles, David, 4, 146-147
Russwurm, John, 143
Rutland Free Convention, 207

St. Clair, Alanson, 41
Segregation, 162-163, 165, 305
Seminole War, 250-251
The Seventy, 118, 121
Sewall, Samuel E., 290
Seward, John, 223
Seward, William H., 4
Shadd, Mary A., 136
Shiloh Presbyterian Church, 167
Slave insurrection, 66-67, 69-70, 81, 93, 97-98, 180-181, 189, 207, 214-215, 259, 266-268, 302
Slave trade, 66, 67
Slave trade in the District of Columbia, 251-252, 262
Slavery in the District of Columbia, 96, 251-252, 257
Slavery in territories, 97
Smiley, David L., 62n
Smith, Gerrit, 51, 121, 144, 227, 241, 277, 310, 311, 315
Smith, James McCune, 164
Spaulding, Lyman, 108
Stanton, Henry B., 41, 51, 157, 231, 273
Stewart, James, 22, 247n
Storrs, Charles, 221, 223
Stowell, Martin, 205, 315
Subscription Anniversary, 45-47, 54

Tappan, Arthur, 7, 13, 51, 148, 161, 223-224, 227-228, 287, 310
Tappan, Lewis, 4, 7, 13, 26, 29, 51, 75, 126, 129, 133-134, 157, 167, 231, 235, 240, 257, 310, 311
Tappanites, 13-14, 137, 175
Taylor, Nathaniel, 219, 238
Taylor, Zachary, 68, 261

Temperance, 62, 166, 197, 236, 240, 281
Tennessee Manumission Society, 94, 102
Texas annexation, 72, 110-111, 113, 204, 233-234, 258-259, 268, 295
Thomas, John, 298
Thomas, John L., 20
Thompson, George, 32, 199, 289
Torrey, Charles T., 41, 42, 137, 235
Towne, Laura, 4
True American, 69-73, 75
True Wesleyan Connexion of Canada, 127
Turpin, William, 108

Underground railroad, 135, 298-299
Union, *see* Disunion
Union Evangelical Anti-Slavery Society, 142
Union Humane Society, 92
Union Missionary Society, 142

Valle, Santiago del, 105
Van Buren, Martin, 241
Vaughn, John C., 72
Vigilance committees, 146, 269-270
Violence, 32, 35, 50, 69-71, 85, 179, 193, 197, 199, 265-266, 289-290, 295, 301-302

Ward, Samuel Ringgold, 4, 164, 176, 314
Washington, Bushrod, 9, 101
Wattles, Augustus, 4
Webb, Richard D., 29, 56-57
Webster, Daniel, 64, 196

Webster, Noah, 223
Weekly Anglo-African, 167, 172
Weld, Angelina Grimké, 193, 311
Weld, Theodore, 60, 117, 157, 247, 309, 311
Western Reserve, 247
Western Reserve College, 219-223
Western Reserve College Anti-Slavery Society, 221
Weston, Anne, 39, 45
Weston, Caroline, 39, 75
Weston, Deborah, 39, 199
Whig party, 67-68, 255-258, 260-262
Whipper, William, 178
Whittelsey, Elisha, 247
Wigham, Eliza, 46
Wilberforce community, 103
Williamson, Passmore, 205
Wilmot Proviso, 260
Wilson, Hiram, 23, 27, 115-139, 309, 311, 312, 316
Winthrop, Robert C., 261
Wolf, Hazel, 3
Women's rights, 12, 25-26, 41, 62, 197, 231-232, 236, 296; *see also* Feminism
Worcester Disunion Convention, 269
Wright, Elizur, 23, 25, 26, 117, 218-244, 273, 288, 289, 295, 311, 312, 313, 316
Wright, Frances, 10, 103
Wright, Henry C., 75-76, 230, 312
Wright, Susan Clark, 220, 222-223, 228
Wyatt-Brown, Bertram, 21, 22

Zinn, Howard, 21